THE EVOLUTION OF THE VICTORIA CROSS

Frontispiece
Queen Victoria making the first presentation of the Victoria Cross in Hyde Park on 26th June 1857. This was also the first time The Queen had ever ridden on horse-back at a Review; she rode between the Prince Consort and her future son-in-law, Crown Prince Frederick of Prussia. By George H. Thomas (1824-68)
(By permission of The Army Benevolent Fund)

THE EVOLUTION OF THE VICTORIA CROSS

A Study in Administrative History

M.J. Crook

MIDAS BOOKS · Tunbridge Wells, Kent.

in association with

THE OGILBY TRUSTS · London

ISBN 0 85936 041 5

First published 1975 by
MIDAS BOOKS
12 Dene Way, Speldhurst, Tunbridge Wells, Kent TN3 0NX
in association with
THE OGILBY TRUSTS
85 Whitehall, London SW1A 2NP

Produced by PJH Graphic Services, Tunbridge Wells,
Printed in Great Britain by
Lewis Reprints Ltd.,
member of Brown Knight & Truscott Group,
London and Tonbridge.

CONTENTS

LIST OF ILLUSTRATIONS

Plates 1 - 4 are located between pages 52 and 53,
Plates 5 - 8 are located between pages 68 and 69.

Plate 1
(a) Henry Pelham, Fifth Duke of Newcastle, Secretary of State for War and Colonies, 1852-1855.
(By permission of the National Portrait Gallery)
(b) Fox Maule, Lord Panmure and later Earl of Dalhousie, Secretary of State for War, 1855-1858.
(By permission of the National Portrait Gallery)

Plate 2
(a) A forerunner of the final design of the Victoria Cross. From the Royal Collection, Windsor.
(Reproduced by Gracious Permission of Her Majesty The Queen)
(b) The original specimen of the Victoria Cross approved by Queen Victoria 3 March 1856.
(By permission of the Curator of the Royal Fusiliers Museum)
(c) Specimen Victoria Cross and bar from the Royal Collection, Windsor Castle.
(Reproduced by Gracious Permission of Her Majesty The Queen)

Plate 3
(a) H.R.H. the Duke of Cambridge, Commander in Chief of the British Army, 1856-1895.
(By permission of the National Army Museum)
(b) Sir Colin Campbell, later Lord Clyde, Commander in Chief in India, 1857-1860.
(By permission of the National Army Museum)

Plate 4
H.M. King George V decorating Sergt Oliver Brooks, 3rd Batt. Coldstream Guards, with the V.C. in the Hospital train at Aire, France, Nov. 1st, 1915.
(Reproduced by Gracious Permission of Her Majesty The Queen)

Plate 5
Record of votes cast to select recipients of the Victoria Cross under Rule 13 of the 1856 Warrant by the 4th Royal Marine Bn for the Zeebrugge Raid 23 April 1918.
(By permission of the Commandant General, Royal Marines)

Plate 6
King George V presenting the Victoria Cross to the Revd T.B. Hardy at a field investiture in France, 1918.
(By permission of the Imperial War Museum)

Plate 7
Bronze ingot which supplies all the metal used for the casting of Victoria Crosses. Now held at the Central Ordnance Depot, Donnington, this was formerly stored at Woolwich Arsenal.
(By permission of the Central Ordnance Depot, Donnington)

Plate 8

(a) Field Marshal Lord Roberts VC, Field Commander in Afghanistan 1879-1880, Commander in Chief South Africa 1899-1901, Commander in Chief of the British Army 1901-1904.
(By permission of the National Army Museum)

(b) Sir Redvers Buller VC, Quarter-Master-General to the Forces 1887-1890, Adjutant-General to the Forces 1890-1897, Commander in Chief in South Africa 1899, Field Commander in South Africa 1900.
(By permission of the National Army Museum)

BUCKINGHAM PALACE

FOREWORD BY

HIS ROYAL HIGHNESS
THE PRINCE PHILIP DUKE OF EDINBURGH, K.G., K.T.

Stories of gallantry in war have always stirred the emotions and throughout history heroic acts have been recognised and recorded in one way or another. For over a hundred years the Victoria Cross has been the supreme decoration for gallantry in the British and Commonwealth armed services.

A great deal has been written about the men who have been awarded the Victoria Cross, but in this work the author traces the events which led up to the institution of the decoration and follows its evolution down to the time of writing.

Mr Crook has made excellent use of all the available sources and from them has traced a fascinating record of the personalities, opinions and discussions involved in the creation of this unique award, and revealed the changing outlook of succeeding generations. He has performed a most valuable piece of historical research and the Ogilby Trusts are to be congratulated on making it available to historians and the general public alike.

THE OGILBY TRUSTS

The Army Museums Ogilby Trust was founded by the late Colonel R.J.L. Ogilby, DSO, DL, in 1954, with the principal object of encouraging, equipping, caring for and maintaining existing Army and Regimental Museums. Since its formation the Trust has helped Regimental and other military Museums in a number of ways. As well as providing finance to enable them to purchase historical items of particular Regimental interest for the improvement of Regimental Collections, the Trust has itself purchased items of military and historical importance, and it has provided an advisory service which is available to Museum Trustees and Curators.

The Trust has also endeavoured to foster interest in regimental and military tradition by sponsoring the publication of certain printed works and catalogues. A number of copies of each book sponsored in this way have been distributed free of charge by the Trust to existing Army and Regimental Museums so as to provide them with authoritative works of reference. In addition, by making such books available to the general public, the Trust has endeavoured to stimulate and encourage interest in regimental and military tradition.

The Robert Ogilby Trust was founded in 1964 with aims similar to the Army Museums Ogilby Trust, but with wider powers of publication. This book has been produced by collaboration between the two Trusts.

The Trusts have their offices in the Ministry of Defence at 85 Whitehall, London SW1.

PUBLISHER'S NOTE

In order to compress the author's monumental work of research into a length both economically and physically practical, it was apparent from the outset that some degree of editing would be required.

So fascinating and interdependent are the facts and episodes, however, that the removal of any one of them could have had an adverse effect on the book as a whole.

It was thus decided, with natural reluctance, to use abbreviations widely and to simplify punctuation. Every effort has been made to assist the reader, to avoid confusion, and to ensure that the first mentions in each chapter of ranks, titles and offices are recorded in full.

Moreover, a complete list of all abbreviations used, with explanations, appears at the end of the book.

It is hoped that the reader will quickly become accustomed to the style and, appreciating its need, find the greater enjoyment in Mr Crook's invaluable contribution to the records of military history.

Introduction

As with the Common Law, my interest in the Victoria Cross dates from an age 'when the memory of man runneth not to the contrary'. Certainly I can trace my serious study back to the age of ten when a school contemporary, whose interests ran along similar lines to my own, brought to my attention the book he had unearthed on the shelves of our local library, Rupert Stewart's *The Victoria Cross*, and my studies took a major step forward when some eight years later I acquired my own copies of this work and its compeer, Creagh and Humphris' *The VC and DSO* (for the princely sums, I recollect, of 7s.6d. and 45 shillings respectively!).

It was natural that my subsequent training in historical research should lead me to pursue my interest in war medals in general among the documents at the Public Record Office and it was here that the idea grew upon me that among its resources must lie material that would be germane to my interest in the Victoria Cross. But a question immediately presented itself. Like most students of the Victoria Cross I had started by the compilation of biographical information on recipients, but this is already a well-tilled field, so the chances of making any significant contribution to my subject in that aspect seemed small. So with what purpose in mind would I be seeking documentary evidence on the Victoria Cross?

It needed very little reflection to answer this question. When one considers all the books that have been written on the Victoria Cross, it is at once apparent that, if described as histories, they have been histories of how the decoration has been *won*, and that the question the historian would wish to ask, namely, how does it come about that we have a decoration called the Victoria Cross at all, taking the form it does and awarded in the way that it has been? — remained not merely unanswered but unposed. To fill this gap in knowledge was, therefore, the task I set myself and, since I regarded myself as following the traditions of historical scholarship, my hope was that the answer could be provided from primary sources.

Suitable material proved, on investigation, to be available in several sources but my greatest windfall in this connection was undoubtedly to discover some dozen boxes at the Public Record Office, each containing some fifteen to twenty files from the War Office 012 series, constituting the great bulk of all War Office papers on the Victoria Cross from its institution up to the end of the South African War. At the time I unearthed these they were not shelf-listed in the PRO search rooms and I am inclined to believe that until then they were virgin territory so far as researchers were concerned. With these I was faced with *embarras de richesse* and one of my problems in compiling this book has been to strike a balance between details of those individual cases which are of interest in themselves and those which serve to illustrate the broader themes of the development of the Victoria Cross. Certainly those who are interested in a specific VC exploit may find it worth consulting these files for themselves since my quotations by no means exhaust their contents.

Having nailed my colours to the masthead of documentary evidence, certain problems arose for, although much War Office material has survived, not all has and certain gaps are left. In some instances I have attempted to fill these by surmise, but I would not attempt to disguise the fact that absolute certainty is not established in these cases – the award of the Victoria Cross to Lieutenant the Hon. F.H.S. Roberts is one such – and in some instances, for example the very puzzling award of the Victoria Cross to Captain Scott in Quetta in 1877, lack of any documentary evidence allows a mystery to remain. It is always possible that further papers may come to light which would provide the answers, but it is difficult to imagine from what source these could come and I am inclined to believe that a residue of mysteries is always going to remain.

Certain oft-repeated legends find no place in this work either, for the same reason, that they have left no trace in any primary source. This does not invariably indicate scepticism on my part but, as a general rule it may be assumed that this is so.

The enquiries which I had to undertake in the course of compiling this work were many and far-flung – if not the proverbial 'from China to Peru' their geographical range did in fact extend from Tokyo to New York – and those to whom I am indebted for aid in my quest are numerous. First of all I have to record the gracious permission of Her Majesty the Queen for the inclusion of material from the Royal Archives at Windsor Castle and for the reproduction of specimens from the Royal Collection. In this connection I must also acknowledge a very special debt of gratitude to Miss Jane Langton, MVO, Registrar of the Royal Archives, to whose labours I owe the unearthing of all this material for me. I would also express my thanks for assistance received from Mr N.E. Evans and Mr T.J. Donovan of the staff of the Public Record Office, Lieutenant-Colonel C.D. Thornton and the staff of MS3 at the Ministry of Defence, Stanmore, Mrs M.A. Welch and Miss H.D. Brewster of the Department of Manuscripts, Nottingham University, Miss Shirley Bury of the Victoria and Albert Museum, Colonel C.A.L. Shipley, DSO, Regimental Secretary of the Royal Fusiliers, to whom I am indebted for permission to reproduce the specimen Victoria Cross from their Regimental Museum, Colonel W. Skelsey, Regimental Secretary of the Duke of Wellington's Regiment, Mr G.L. Hancock Dore of Hancocks the Jewellers, to whom I am indebted for information from his firm's records, to the late Colonel Peter Fleming and Mr Erik Watts for information regarding an episode in the Boxer Rising, and Miss Barbara Cartland, one of whose ancestors, Captain G.T. Scobell, figures prominently in this book.

Numerous of my fellow members of the Orders and Medals Research Society have made their contribution. Among these I would mention here Mr G.W. Harris, who has been most helpful in checking references in works that were on his shelves but not on mine, and Mr Alec Purves, for a number of helpful comments. Others form a considerable proportion of those to whom I have indicated particular indebtedness in footnotes at the appropriate point. But beyond this I must acknowledge a collective indebtedness to those numerous colleagues who have made the odd suggestion or the appropriate comment which now bears fruit here.

I am also indebted to Messrs Hodder and Stoughton Ltd, publishers of *The Panmure Papers* for permission to make the extensive quotations from that work which appear here, to the National Portrait Gallery, the National Army Museum, the Imperial War Museum and the Commandant General, Royal Marines for supplying and permitting reproduction of pictures of various items from their collections which figure among my illustrations.

I am also deeply indebted to my very old friend Mr David Bonner, who is, in fact, the school contemporary referred to at the beginning of this note, who by reading the chapters of this work in draft was able to give me much help in deciding the most effective deployment of my material in its published form.

Despite all the help I have received from other quarters this work could never have reached the world at large without the sponsorship it has been given by the Trustees of the Robert Ogilby Trust and the Army Museums Ogilby Trust. I would like, therefore, to place on record my gratitude to the Trustees for extending this to me, and at the same time express my thanks to the Secretary of the Trusts, Colonel P.S. Newton, MBE, for his efforts in gaining the support of his Trustees and for all his work in bringing this book to its final form; to his assistant, Major J.M.A. Tamplin, TD, to whom I owe the preparation of the index and to both of them and Mrs E.M. Newton for completing the arduous task of proof-reading.

The present work has been entirely a spare time occupation, fitted in with the demands of a normal nine-to-five working life. There is therefore one person to whom I am indebted above all for the fact that I have been afforded the time to accomplish the task of researching and writing that this had entailed, and this is my wife. Without her support and forbearance over all the years that it has occupied me this undertaking would have been completely impossible, and at the last it was by her care that my final draft was checked for errors and pruned of my more reprehensible preciousities of style. My thanks to her must therefore be my final word.

July 1974   M.J. CROOK

Chapter 1

The need for a new decoration

WITH THE OUTBREAK of the Crimean War, Britain found herself, for the first time since the battle of Waterloo almost 40 years previously, engaged in a struggle with a major European military power. That defects and deficiencies of Britain's military organisation were then revealed is well-known[1] but it is the particular deficiency of a lack of any appropriate award for gallant conduct in action, and how it was met, that provides the starting point of this work.

Attention was drawn to the deficiency in three ways. First, the actions of the military command demonstrated the ossification of the existing means of recognition of meritorious service. Secondly, there was a greater awareness at home than ever before of the deeds of the forces in the field. Thirdly, there was the comparison that was inevitably to be made with the very different situation of awards operating in the forces of France, the principal ally fighting alongside the British in the Crimea.

So far as the existing means of reward were concerned, at the commencement of the war there were three – the Order of the Bath, promotion by brevet, and mentioning of an individual in the field dispatch of the Commander-in-Chief. The limitations attached to the Order of the Bath are mentioned by Prince Albert in his memorandum of 22 Jan 1855 [see Appendix II]; it was only bestowed on officers above a certain rank, it was limited as to the numbers which could be bestowed and, due to the unwillingness of the CinCs to discriminate between individuals, it was tending to become a mere appendage of rank. In fact, the attitude of the military went even further than this, as is shown by the letters of the Duke of Newcastle, as Secretary of State for War, to the Queen on 5 and 29 Dec 1854. In the first he says that he 'cannot help feeling that the defect of Lord Raglan's dispatch of 11 Nov

---

1 These are well summarised in E.L. Woodward, *The Age of Reform*, Oxford 1938, pp254-264.

is that he recommends nearly every officer of a certain rank and class —
and he fears that if decorations are to be given to all who are named in
that dispatch some who have done little to deserve such reward will
receive them whilst many who have borne the burden and heat of the
day will feel slighted.

'The Duke of Newcastle will endeavour to consider these difficulties
carefully with Lord Hardinge [the CinC] before making any recommendations to Your Majesty'.[2]

The military attitude was, however, unhelpful, for in his second
letter he writes, 'Lord Hardinge entirely dissents from the view which
the Duke of Newcastle ventured to submit to Your Majesty and main-
tains that no principle can be properly adopted but that of giving to all
officers according to their rank the various degrees of the order without
distinction of whether they took part in the action or not...

'The Duke of Newcastle confesses that he is not convinced by Lord
Hardinge's argument... for he thinks that the Bath would then become
little more than an appendage to certain rank in the Army provided
only the officer served in the field... Lord Raglan... [has] great aversion
to making what he would consider invidious distinctions...'[3] [It is
obvious how much of the phraseology of this letter was borrowed by
Prince Albert when he drafted his memorandum of 22 Jan].

It is true that during the course of the war something had been done
for ranker gallantry by the institution of the Distinguished Conduct
Medal for the Army, and the Conspicuous Gallantry Medal for the Navy,
but it is evident how little this met the need for some signal recompense
from the fact that neither award appears ever to have been referred to
in the discussions which led to the eventual establishment of the
Victoria Cross.

Brevet promotion for distinguished services in the field could prove
a useful means of rewarding gallantry, and *The Times* of 15 Dec 1854
applauded a War Office announcement that one sergeant per regiment
should be eligible for a commission on such grounds, though it foresaw
some social difficulties for such officers, who would be without the
same financial means as their brother officers, as well as being a good
deal older. The real grievance here, however, was that virtually all the
brevet promotions were being conferred, not upon company officers
who were in the firing line, but upon those holding staff appointments.
As one correspondent pointed out in *The Times* of 18 Dec 1854 following

2   Nottingham University, Newcastle Collection, NeC 9786

3   *ibid*

the publication of a list of such brevets subsequent to the battle of Inkermann, no subaltern had been so honoured and in the 47th and 49th Regts, both of which had distinguished themselves in this engagement, the captains so honoured were those holding staff appointments and not those serving with their companies. To which another correspondent added on 20 Dec that of fifty-two captains promoted to major by brevet for distinguished services, forty held staff appointments.

The shortcomings of the mention in dispatches as a mark of merit partook of both the above. As in the case of the Bath, it was indiscriminate; as with brevet promotions, it was almost entirely confined to staff officers. *The Times* wrote, in a leader of 5 Dec 1854, 'After every battle appears a solemn document, according the meed of praise to those who have distinguished themselves in it. To be mentioned in the Gazette is an object of the most ardent ambition; and the ceremony is suggestive of the Fame that we see in our monuments, crowning her sons with undying bays. But here again, routine comes in with its usual crushing severity, and the whole affair has sunk to such a matter of form that very few readers think it worth while to go through the document, looking on it much as they would on a page of the Army List. In the Gazette we published on Monday, Lord Raglan named *all* the Generals of Division and Brigade, and *all* their staff. As a record of service, nothing could be less to the purpose. The battle of Inkerman was fought and won entirely by the battalion officers and soldiers. It is called in the camp "the Soldiers' Victory". In such a conflict we would think that the battalion officers and even the most prominent soldiers should be named – certainly not that they should be omitted, while officers on the staff, even not engaged, are duly enumerated...'

Each of the three existing means of conveying marks of approbation of military conduct were thus proving unsuited to their purpose, either because they had never been envisaged as meeting the precise need, or because of the way in which they were being administered. Moreover, this was occurring when, for the first time, the world at large was being given first-hand information as to the actual events which were taking place at the front. It is significant how much comment on the deficiency of the system of reward has already been quoted from the columns of *The Times*; but the criticisms were being made by, and in, that paper because it was giving its readers the information upon which such criticism could be based. Russell, in his dispatch from the Crimea of 20 Nov 1854, published in *The Times* of 14 Dec, spoke of the gentlemen of the press 'who accompany them (the Army) but to herald their deeds and to record their valour and their names to their fellow-countrymen...

assuredly all who are known to have done brave deeds are willingly celebrated, and are not sepultured in the dismal columns of the *London Gazette*'. Ian Bisset, indeed, says that the original idea for the Victoria Cross came from Russell.[4] The present writer has, however, found nothing in his dispatches to substantiate this. The suggestion of a correspondent in *The Times* of 8 Dec, following on the already-quoted leader of 6 Dec, is also significant. 'My proposition is that you, who have already shown the wrong, should also provide the remedy, by devoting a certain column of your almost ubiquitous journal to what you might term "The People's Gazette"! In this might be related, in brief but emphatic language, the various extraordinary deeds of our soldiers and sailors during this bloody campaign, particularly specifying names, regiments or ships. And I venture to express the opinion that, should you carry out this proposition, a place in that Gazette will be as great an object of ambition and as great a spur to exertion among both officers and men — aye, and as acceptable a reward — as any that could possibly be devised, I am also sure that no portion of your journal would be more eagerly devoured by your readers. Your able correspondent in the East could furnish you with plenty of cases, and you might throw it open to any well-authenticated anecdote from any quarter. As you well say, glory is still the great incentive and the best reward for the true soldier. He may be almost said to pine for it, but our cold system of routine forbids any reasonable hope of its attainment. It is the cheapest reward, though the most highly prized, and yet we resolutely refuse it to them...'.

The world at large was, then, in a position to know what did not get into the official dispatches. It was also, again probably for the first time, to learn of those who were too lowly to catch the eye of the CinC. *The Times* made the practice of printing in its columns many letters home, forwarded to it by the relatives who had received them. Many of these were from men in the ranks, and this acquaintance at first hand with the common soldier came as a revelation. 'It was once feared that men who enlisted were seldom good for much else', it commented in a leader of 4 Dec 1854, 'but the letters from the camp indicate qualities in the writers which would fit them creditably for any station in life... Everyone must be impressed with the evidence thus conceded of the character of the British soldier'. Here, then, were yet further grounds for regretting the deficiencies of the system; those too humble to come within its ken were not 'the scum of the earth' about whom no concern

4   Ian Bisset, *The George Cross*, London 1961, p18

need be felt, but worthy men who were entitled to have their merits recognised.

The third important factor in bringing about the creation of a new British award must have been that the British forces were fighting alongside the French, to whom the Legion of Honour was available. Here was an award which, in its junior grades, was open to all ranks, freely available for the recognition of acts of heroism. It was to be referred to on several occasions in the course of the discussions which led to the institution of the Victoria Cross, and the fact that the French soldiers were decorated with it in respect of their services at the battle of the Alma before the end of the year, whereas the British Government had conferred no awards on its soldiery must have caused some bitterness in the Crimea. It must be admitted, however, that the distribution of the Legion of Honour to the French forces passed unremarked by *The Times*.

Chapter 2

The Idea

IF ONE MAY equate public opinion at this period with *The Times,* then there was clearly a feeling of deficiency in the system of military honours. What was to be done about it, however, was another matter. 'Of all the topics embraced by the recent speeches,' wrote *The Times* in a leader of 15 Dec 1854, on the recent opening of Parliament, 'none was expressed with more genuine fervour or has commanded more universal approval than that drawn from the behaviour of the British soldier. The discipline, the patience and the courage of these admirable troops, their endurance under privation, and their daring in the field, supplied all statesmen of all parties with themes unfailingly successful, nor was there any point on which the Speech from the Throne found a more responsive echo in the hearts of the people than when Her Majesty paid her graceful and well-merited tribute of "admiration and gratitude" to the soldiers of her unconquerable army... Naturally, then, it may be asked what acknowledgement is to be made of these extraordinary services and in what way the country is to recompense its defenders? Undoubtedly we may say that the meed which is thought the dearest of all in a soldier's eyes — that which has been described as the breath of his nostrils — HONOUR — is there already for never were praises bestowed more abundantly than upon the army of the Crimea... Such conduct as our troops have displayed deserves some honourable recognition which may be felt by the men themselves, and there could obviously be none more consistent with military feeling than that which is conveyed by decorations and promotions... We are not without hope that the solution of the difficulty may be found in a variety of conditions resulting from the event of the war.'

The distinction of being the first person to gather all these arguments into a public demand for a new award for military merit must go to Capt G.T. Scobell, MP, who on 19 Dec 1854 moved in the House of Commons 'That an humble address be presented to Her Majesty praying that she would be graciously pleased to institute an "Order of Merit" to be bestowed upon persons serving in the Army or Navy for distinguished and prominent personal gallantry during the present war and to which every grade and individual, from the highest to the lowest, in the United Services, may be admissible'. [5]

George Treweeke Scobell, born in December 1785, entered the Navy as a midshipman in 1798, served for fourteen years, reaching the rank of Commander and seeing some action in the Napoleonic Wars. He was unable to secure employment after 1812 and accepted the rank of Capt on half pay in 1843. He married the daughter and co-heiress of Charles Savage, Esq, of Midsomer Norton, Somerset, in 1818, became a JP for Somerset and in 1823 invented and submitted to the Admiralty a 'dissecting paddle-wheel' which was worked by winches and used with some success on an Arctic expedition. [6] He lived at High Littleton, Somerset, and entered Parliament in June 1851 as Liberal member for Bath, on the succession of Lord Ashley to the Earldom of Shaftesbury.[7] He was again returned for Bath at the general election of July 1852[8] but did not sit after that Parliament rose in 1857. He seems to have been an active back-bencher taking a special interest in various service matters [9] and he died in 1869. [10]

In speaking to his proposition, Capt Scobell said that if he received any information from the Government that they would take the matter into favourable consideration he would be content to leave it in their hands. He was convinced that if some such an Order as that referred to in his Motion were immediately instituted it would be equivalent to reinforcing our Army of the Crimea, so great would be its effect on the spirits and temper of the troops. The real question before the House was whether the medals and orders at present available were sufficient for the purposes of the great war such as that in which the country was now involved. Now the Order of the Bath was entirely confined to the upper ranks of the Army and Navy, for no one under the rank of major in the Army, or Captain in the Navy, could partake of the distinction of that Order. That showed it must be vastly too exclusive and that its

5   *Hansard,* 3rd Series, cxxxvi cols 505 et seq
6   O'Byrne, *Naval Biography, sub nomen*
7   *Official Returns of Members of Parliament,* Part II p404, and *The Times,* 24/25 Jun 1851
8   *Official Returns of Members of Parliament,* Pt ii p420
9   *Hansard,* 3rd Series, cxxxvi, passim
10 Barbara Cartland, *Polly, My Wonderful Mother,* p12 (Polly was G.T.Scobell's great-niece)

regulations demanded immediate alteration. Then again, a custom prevailed of giving medals to the Army and Navy for certain battles, which applied as well to those actually in action as those out of it; but that custom had no reference to individual bravery, and many ships taking no part in an action would get the medal equally with those obliged to bear the brunt of the fight. He thought, therefore, since the grant of medals under existing rules did not sufficiently distinguish personal merit, some change was immediately required. At the present moment the country was engaged in a war which demanded the putting forth of all its strength but it was a question whether there were those incentives and inducements to the display of courage and endurance on the part of our soldiers and sailors which there ought to be. The soldiers of the Crimea were fighting side by side with the army of France, which possessed an Order which extended down to the meanest drummer-boy in the ranks. He thought, therefore, that the present was the most appropriate juncture for the institution in this country of an Order similar in character. If, however, he should receive the assurance of the Government that the matter would be taken up by them, and that the objects of his motion met with their assent, he was quite willing not to press the matter any further — but in no other circumstances would he consent to submitting the subject to their hands.

Lord John Russell thought that a proposition of this kind ought properly to come from the Crown. He could, however, assure the Hon and gallant Gentlemen that the whole question was under consideration; while he was at the same time quite willing to admit that the Order of the Bath did not appear to him to comprehend all the persons who ought to receive it.

Capt Scobell said that, although no distinct promise was given on the subject, he was content for the present to withdraw his Motion. But he would do so subject to the hope that HMG would not try to supply the want so universally felt by making a partial change in reference to the Order of the Bath; it was better to make no change at all than that it should be a partial one. The only way of dealing with the subject was to institute an Order that could comprehend every individual in both services, Navy and Army. [11]

Although Capt Scobell withdrew his motion he had succeeded in setting affairs going for, on 20 Jan 1855, the Duke of Newcastle followed up the subject with a crucial letter to Prince Albert.

11 *Hansard,* 3rd Series, cxxxvi, cols 505/7

'Your Royal Highness will recollect that some time ago I expressed an opinion that the circumstances of the present campaign and the alliance in which we have engaged in it seem to render either an extension of the Order of the Bath or the institution of some new Order of Merit, if not necessary, at any rate desirable.

'Subsequently to the conversation... the question was raised in the House of Commons, and no doubt will be raised again – more especially because no grant of the honours of the Bath has yet been made.

'Your Royal Highness mentioned several objections to the proposition of adding to the three classes of the Order of the Bath, and I hope I am not taking too great a liberty if I ask Your Royal Highness's opinion upon the other suggestion, the institution of a new decoration to be confined to the Army and Navy, but open to all ranks of either service.

'I confess it does not seem to me right or politic that such deeds of heroism as this war has produced should go unrewarded by any distinctive outward mark of honour because they are done by Privates or by Officers below the rank of Major, and it is impossible to believe that HM troops fighting side by side with those of France do not draw an invidious contrast between the rewards bestowed upon themselves and their allies.

'The value attached by soldiers to a little bit of ribbon is such as to render any danger insignificant and any privation light if it can be attained, and I believe that great indeed would be the stimulus and deeply prized the reward of a Cross of Military Merit.

'There are some Orders which even Crowned Heads cannot wear, and it would be a military reward of high estimation if this cross could be so bestowed as to be within the reach of every Private Soldier and yet to be coveted by any General at the head of an Army.

'Such a reward would have more effect in the Army than the grant of Commissions, and the sight of one of these crosses on the breast of a Soldier returned home invalided would bring more recruits than any of the measures we can now adopt.

'Of course, great care would be requisite to prevent abuse, but I am sure Your Royal Highness will not consider the danger of abuse a sufficient reason to reject this proposal if there appears sufficient good in it to justify its adoption.' [12]

12   Nottingham University, Newcastle Collection, NeC 9786, p33

This letter is printed by Martineau [13] who, not unreasonably, makes it the basis for attributing the origin of the Victoria Cross to the Duke of Newcastle. However, it is evident from this letter that, even though the Duke had raised the matter with Prince Albert previously, nothing had then come of it, and it was only as a direct result of Capt Scobell's speech in the Commons [which, though fully reported in *The Times* of 20 Dec 1854, drew no editorial comment] that he was now taking up the matter again. The letter also shows how little in fact lay behind Lord John Russell's assurance to Capt Scobell that the matter was under consideration.

However, the Duke's letter clearly indicates that he had been thinking along these lines prior to the debate of 19 Dec. No record of his discussion with Prince Albert appears to survive from either participant, but its general line is fairly clear. Obviously the Duke had suggested extending the Order of the Bath by a number of lower grades, to which those below the rank of Major could be admitted, so that it would closely have paralleled the structure of the Legion of Honour, but Prince Albert had seen objections to this. The Duke had evidently also mentioned the possibility of creating some entirely new order, as an alternative method of achieving the same end, but for some reason this idea had not been pursued. Equally there is no record of when the discussion took place, but there is one occasion which may be suggested with some plausibility. The Court Circular of 11 Nov 1854 records that the Duke of Newcastle arrived at Windsor Castle that afternoon and remained there until the following afternoon, as shown by the Court Circular of that day. [That seems to have been his only visit to Windsor between the commencement of hostilities in the Crimea and Christmas 1854.] He would undoubtedly have had the events of the war very much on his mind at that time; almost his last act before leaving London for Windsor must have been the issue of the dispatch from the Crimea which was printed in a *London Gazette Extraordinary* of 11 Nov, dated from the War Office at 11.55 am, and it must have been while he was at Windsor that the dispatch reached him, to be published in another Gazette of 12 Nov, at 4 pm, describing the battle of Balaclava. [14] Whilst, therefore, there can be no absolute certainty as to when this discussion with Prince Albert took place, 11 or 12 Nov would seem to have provided both an appropriate opportunity and an

13   John Martineau, *The Life of Henry Pelham, Fifth Duke of Newcastle*, London 1908, pp248/9

14   *The Times,* 13 Nov 1854

occasion when the subject of rewards for the forces in the Crimea might naturally have been raised. A two-month interval prior to the Duke's letter of 20 Jan 1855 would also seem to agree well with the use of the phrase 'some time ago'.

Prince Albert replied to the Duke with great promptitude, on 22 Jan 1855. 'The question regarding an Order of Merit has been considered by me with all attention and I now enclose a Memorandum which contains all I have been able to make out. Will you kindly consider it with those of your colleagues who would be desirable. Amongst others I would ask you to show it to Lord Clarendon, with whom I have often spoken on the subject and who looks to means of largely giving to the French Army'. [15]

The memorandum referred to is the document reproduced as Appendix II. It is through quoting this memorandum without realising that it was, in fact, a reply to the Duke of Newcastle, that leads Fulford to mis-attribute the proposal for the VC to the mind of the Prince.[16] Bolitho, also, describes the Prince as devising the Cross,[17] but the context makes it clear that he is simply following Fulford at this point.

With this memorandum in his possession, the Duke evidently felt that matters had reached a sufficiently advanced state of development for a public announcement to be made, and this he did in the House of Lords on 29 Jan. His occasion was the raising by Lord Vivian of the question of the sanctioning of a clasp to the Crimean Medal for those who had taken part in the battle of Balaclava.

'I think I have here,' he said, 'a not unfitting opportunity for making a communication to the House which I feel sure will be most agreeable to your Lordships as well as to our gallant army. After very careful consideration − a consideration which ought always to attend changes of such a description − Her Majesty has been advised to institute a Cross of Merit which will be open to all ranks of the army in future. It is not intended... that this new Order shall in any way affect the present Order of the Bath, but that a separate and distinct Cross of Military Merit shall be given, which shall be open to all ranks of the army and which, I hope, will be an object of ambition to every individual in the service, from the General who commands down to the privates in the ranks. My Lords, I cannot say that the rules for this new Cross are

15   Original in Nottingham University, Newcastle Collection, NeC 9701a, Copy
     in Royal Archives, Windsor Castle, RA E5/17
16   Roger Fulford, *The Prince Consort,* London 1949, p176
17   Hector Bolitho, *Albert, Prince Consort,* London 1964, p157

entirely matured, for the subject requires a great deal of consideration. It will be somewhat analogous to those existing in some countries of the Continent − I believe in Spain, Prussia and Austria ... generally... its distribution will be so arranged as to obviate the invidious task of selecting the individuals upon whom it is to be conferred from devolving upon officers; for in all cases the principle will be adopted of adjusting the distribution according to a verdict of a jury of the peers of the individual who is to be distinguished; that verdict, however, will have to be confirmed by the decision of the home authorities. I believe, my Lords, that the rule I have here stated is that which guides the distribution of rewards under those orders of Spain and Prussia to which I have just referred'. [18]

The impact of this announcement, significant as it was, seems to have been remarkably slight, for the next speaker in the debate, Lord Ellenborough, who had himself been much concerned with the institution of campaign medals as Governor-General of India twelve years previously, immediately turned the discussion back to the question of a Balaclava award.

Nor was the Duke of Newcastle to be allowed to pursue this project any further. For, on the same evening that he made his announcement in the Lords, the Commons was to carry Roebuck's motion for the appointment of a Select Committee 'to enquire into the condition of our army before Sevastopol, and into the conduct of those departments of the Government whose duty it has been to minister to the wants of the army', and the Government of which he was a member resigned in consequence the following day. It was the end, too, of the immediate influence of Prince Albert's memorandum, for the Duke clearly regarded it as a private paper, taking it with him when he relinquished office, as is shown by the fact that the original is to be found, not among the WO papers in the Public Record Office, but among the Newcastle papers at Nottingham.

This is, perhaps, a convenient point at which to consider the place in the story of the document reproduced as Appendix I. This document is neither signed nor dated but bears an apparently contemporary endorsement, 'The Original VC Warrant'. Plainly, from its contents, it represents an early stage in the thinking, but whose? There are two copies of it in the file and obviously, from the various emendations in the margin, they were copies circulated for comment. An obvious thought is that one copy might have been for the Admiralty and the other for the WO.

18   *Hansard,* 3rd Series, cxxxvi, cols 1064/5

By and large the marginalia do not represent points of any great substance, but they do rather suggest the departments trying to get the terminology into their preferred form. One of the more interesting amendments is to make the ribbon of the Cross blue and red — a suggestion later to be offered by Mayo in his *Medals of the British Army and Navy.*

However, these points are peripheral to the main task of dating the document itself. Reading the documents in Appendices I and II together it seems reasonable to conclude that the author of one had not seen the other but, since the Duke of Newcastle had retained Prince Albert's memorandum in his own possession, Lord Panmure would not be ruled out as the author simply on these grounds as it would not have been available for his inspection. There is one point, however, which seems to be decisive; there is no reference in the 'Original Warrant' to selection involving a jury of the peers of the recipient. This idea comes from the Prince's memorandum and, since the Duke of Newcastle had specifically mentioned this in his speech of 29 Jan, no one drawing up a warrant after this date could be unaware that this was a feature which had to be incorporated — it was, in fact, much modified in the final form of the Warrant, but the elective principle of Clause 13 is plainly its final embodiment. It seems reasonably certain, therefore, that the document in Appendix I represents the original thinking of the Duke of Newcastle on the subject of the new award, prior to the receipt of Prince Albert's memorandum. A further stylistic point can be adduced to support this authorship. It will be noticed that, in Newcastle's speech in the Lords, although speaking of an award for both services, he omits all mention of the Navy. It is the Army, generals and privates throughout. Exactly the same is true of the 'Original Warrant', where the lack of the appropriate naval terminology is particularly apparent in Clauses 7, 8 and 9 — indeed, a good deal of the marginal notes on the two copies represent various suggested insertions to remedy these omissions.

The likely time limits within which this document was drafted would seem to be subsequent to the debate of Scobell's motion on 19 Dec 1854 and prior to Newcastle's letter to Prince Albert on 20 Jan 1855. It seems unlikely that it would have been drafted after the letter had been sent, as the obvious thing would then have been to wait for the Prince's reply. The likely course of events would seem, rather, that the draft having been circulated within the departments, a letter should then be addressed to Prince Albert to see what additions his ideas would make to a subject upon which thinking was fairly well formed within the Government. So the probable date of the draft would be towards the beginning rather than the end of these four weeks.

Newcastle's new military distinction had still some way to evolve before it assumed the final form of the Victoria Cross as instituted a twelvemonth later, but many of its ultimate features are present in the document of Appendix I. These points from it which can be seen embodied in the final warrant can be listed as follows:

(i)   The new distinction was to bear the name of the Queen.

(ii)   There were to be no different grades within it.

(iii)   The insignia was to be a cross, possibly of bronze.

(iv)   The insignia should be worn on the breast, from a blue ribbon for the Navy and a red ribbon for the Army.

(v)   It was only to be won by a signal act of valour in the presence of the enemy.

(vi)   Conspicuous bravery was to be the only qualification for the award.

(vii)   The distinction might be conferred on the spot in respect of an act performed in the sight of a senior commander, or recommended by him when the act had been reported to him by a junior commander, and proved to his satisfaction.

(viii)   The distinction was to be publicly conferred in the presence of the force to which the recipient belonged, when it was conferred on the spot.

(ix)   The names of all recipients were to be published in General Orders, and a register of them was to be kept.

(x)   Cases falling outside the strict rules might be considered, so long as conspicuous bravery was established.

(xi)   The distinction should carry with it a pension for recipients who were not commissioned officers.

(xii)   Misconduct would cause forfeiture of the distinction.

(xiii)   The number of recipients should be unlimited.

(xiv)   Further acts of bravery would be recognised by the addition of a bar to the decoration and an additional pension.

In the event, the main points at which Newcastle's document departs from the 1856 Warrant are only where he is making the provisions appropriate to the setting up of an order, the motto, and the amount of the pension. On this last point, Prince Albert's memorandum [Appendix II] shows that he was thinking of a smaller sum, and it is from this same source that comes the one substantial addition to the Duke of Newcastle's scheme that was incorporated in the final warrant, namely the bestowal of a certain number of awards upon a body of men, with the choice of individuals being made by a jury of those concerned.

Where the ideas of the 'Original Warrant' were included in that of 1856, the actual wording was frequently followed almost exactly. The ordering of the clauses changes somewhat and the marginal notes on the copies of the 'Original Warrant' show this very process taking place. The following table shows just how closely the two can be matched, the clause in the 'Original' being followed by that in the 1856 Warrant, as and where applicable.

Clause in Original Warrant	Clause in 1856 Warrant	Clause in Original Warrant	Clause in 1856 Warrant
Preamble	Preamble	10	9
1	—	11	10
2	—	12	11
3	—	13	12
4	Part of 1,2	14	—
5	5	15	Part of 14
6	6	16 and 17	15
7	7.1	18	—
8	7.2	19	4 and part of 14
9	8		

Chapter 3

The Warrant

THE SITUATION which faced Lord Panmure when he succeeded Newcastle as Secretary for War was that a good deal of thinking had taken place on the subject of a new military distinction, but that all the practical work of putting its statutes into a form which could be submitted for royal approval, and designing the emblem, had still to be undertaken. He seems to have become aware fairly quickly that this was to be an item on his agenda, the first reference to it being made by him in a letter to Lord Raglan on 26 Feb 1855 when he had been in office for less than four weeks '... I am very busy with the Bath and the medals, both of which I find had made no progress. The new Order of Merit will take time, I fear.' [19]

Evidently Capt Scobell was not satisfied with the progress of the Government in his particular subject, or it may simply have been that he wished to sound out the views of the new Ministry, for on 19 Mar 1855 he asked in the Commons 'whether HMG had decided to recommend the institution of an Order of Merit; if so whether such Order was intended to be a new and distinct one restricted to the military and naval service and applicable to every grade therein, and whether it was determined to bring such Order of Merit into prompt action?' Palmerston himself replied to the question, as Prime Minister [Panmure was, of course, a member of the Lords]. 'It is the intention of HMG, as was stated on a former occasion in the other House, to establish an Order of that description. Of course it will apply to both services because we hope that merit will be equally prominent in both. The particular arrangements of that institution have not yet been settled. Information has been sought in other countries in which a similar institution exists and, until that information is obtained, the Government cannot frame the regulations under which the Order will be distributed'. [20]

19   *The Panmure Papers,* ed Douglas & Ramsay, London 1908, i p80
20   *Hansard,* 3rd Series, cxxxvii, col 774

Although Palmerston seems to have been taking some advantage of this excuse, there is at least one piece of evidence which supports his statement that the Government were making enquiries of other countries regarding the statutes of comparable orders. Bound up among the printed documents of the WO at the PRO is a translation of the statutes of the Spanish Orders of St Ferdinand and St Hermenegild. [21] The date of publication given on the document is 1855, and on it has been written in manuscript '2.55'. There is every reason to think, therefore, that this was the reply to such an enquiry. Although these particular statutes do not seem to have provided much of use — the Order of St Hermenegild being purely for long service — a few points may have been taken from those of St Ferdinand which carried an inscription 'For Military Merit'. The statutes did include the words. 'The King shall... confer crosses according to the deserts of individual soldiers', which was very much what was in mind for the new British award. It was stated to be the duty of junior ranks to solicit recompense for performance of appropriate acts [thus agreeing very much with the thinking of Prince Albert], pensions were provided, and both cross and pension could be forfeited for dishonourable conduct.

Despite the lack of any documentary evidence on the point, it seems highly probable that the examples of the Russian Order of St George and of the Austrian Order of Maria Theresa had a considerable influence on the framing of the rules for the new British award. At that time these two countries were regarded as amongst the most powerful nations in Europe, and their military institutions commanded respect accordingly. For these two countries the orders mentioned were the military awards commanding the highest esteem and, in the entire field of honours at that time, the Order of Maria Theresa stood second to none in prestige. Both were given only in wartime. The Russian order had been founded for rewarding military service exclusively, and was bestowed as a reward for bravery in action of a distinguished nature. The Knight's Cross of the Order of Maria Theresa was awarded to officers only for the greatest personal combat heroism, claims to it being ruthlessly examined by the Council of the Order. By statute neither rank, nor wounds, nor long or distinguished service could be taken into consideration, a sentiment which was to be closely echoed in the warrant of the new British award. The mere existence of these awards and the respect in which they were held means that it was impossible for those who were engaged in drawing up the conditions of the new British award to have acted in ignorance of them, and they must certainly have made their contribution to thinking on the subject. [22]

Apart from a passing reference by Panmure in a letter to Lord Raglan of 26 Mar 1856, in which, apparently forgetting his remark of a month previously, he says, 'You know, I presume, that an order of merit is under preparation which will pervade all ranks', [23] the developments of the next nine months have left no record. Obviously, this was the period within which the drafting of the warrant and the commissioning of the designs for the award were being discussed within the WO, but no trace of these events is to be found in the records now surviving. Evidently however, the question of drafting the terms of the warrant proved unexpectedly difficult for, when Lord Elcho [24] asked in the Commons on 27 Jul 1855 if the intention of instituting a new Order of Merit for distinguished service in the field, which had been publicly announced by the Duke of Newcastle in December [sic] had been abandoned, and if not, what was the cause of the delay, and when was it probable that it would be instituted and ready for distribution, Palmerston's reply was that it was the intention of HMG, as soon as possible, to issue the regulations of the new Order. The only cause of the delay that had taken place had been that when they came to make detailed arrangements as to the practical test to be applied to the claims of private soldiers, and other matters of this kind, there had been found more difficulties in making satisfactory arrangements than had been anticipated; but he hoped that very soon these difficulties would be overcome. [25]

Despite this hope, however, it was not until late in December of that year that the drafting of the Warrant reached a stage at which it could be submitted to the Queen for her preliminary approval. A copy of this document was taken [presumably by one of Prince Albert's clerks] and

---

22   I am indebted to Mr J.C. Risk of New York for drawing my attention to the significance of the Orders of St George and Maria Theresa

23   *Panmure Papers,* i p128

24   Born 4 Aug 1818, Cons MP East Glos 1841/6. Haddingtonshire 1853/83, when succeeded as 10th Scottish Earl and 3rd UK Baron Wemyss. Lt-Col, Scottish Volunteers (the London Scottish) 1859/79, his prominent part in the Volunteer movement included the founding of this regiment; its honorary colonel until 1900, first chairman National Rifle Association, Volunteer ADC to Queen Victoria, King Edward VII and King George V. Died 30 Jan 1914. (GEC *The Complete Peerage,* sub Wemyss).

25   *Hansard,* 3rd Series, cxxxix, col 1459

was retained in the Royal Archives; it is reproduced as Appendix III. To a very large extent this draft follows the text of what has been called the 'Original Warrant' [Appendix I], though the ordering of the clauses is somewhat different — not always with the happiest of results, since in the new version reference to the additional pension following from the award of a bar preceded any reference to the bar itself. A good many of the verbal alterations are devoted to amending the wording so that a document which had been drafted from too exclusively an Army point of view would meet the requirements of both services; thus, in fact, taking up many of the marginal amendments which had been inserted on the earlier document. Amendments representing changes of thought appear at four points; a new set of mottoes was suggested, both of the original Latin ones [including the singularly infelicitous *Mors aut Victoria*] being dropped, powers of conferring the award were no longer bestowed on commanders of detached corps, the pension was reduced from £20 to £15 and, most interestingly, the expulsion clauses in cases of misconduct disappear.

On 28 Dec 1855 Prince Albert wrote to Panmure, 'I return you the Draft of Warrant for the new decoration. Having gone through it carefully together with the Queen, I have marked in pencil upon it all that occurred to us. I should recommend, however, a reference to Lord Hardinge before the places of the Army and Navy are assigned in such a formal document, so that the Army should have been heard on the subject as well as the Navy', [26] from which it appears that, in revising the draft to incorporate the reference to naval terminology, Panmure's draft had gone to the other extreme and now gave the impression of being too Admiralty-orientated.

Prince Albert's pencil notes were incorporated into the copy of the draft Warrant which was preserved in the Royal Archives. [27] Of these the most fundamental change was suggested against the first clause, where the title 'The Military Order of Victoria' is struck out and the suggestion 'Victoria Cross?' written in the margin. With this are three alternative suggestions for a motto — 'The Reward of Valour?', 'The Reward of Bravery?' and 'For Bravery?'. Interestingly enough, the one permutation of terms used here that was not suggested was that finally adopted. A note explaining the thinking behind the suggestions reads, 'NB. The Motto should *explain the decoration* and exclude the possibility of its object being misunderstood'. Certainly, it could be objected that the exhortatory mottoes in the draft, as submitted to

26   *Panmure Papers*, ii pp37/8
27   Royal Archives, E6/69

Prince Albert, said nothing as to what the award was for, but it should be realised just how original was the thought involved in this comment; the mottoes of all British orders up to this time had been exhortatory and never explanatory. The thinking that conduct should be recognised by bestowal of a decoration and not by admission to an order was almost unprecedented; the nearest British parallel was in the Peninsular Gold Medals and Crosses, but even this was not very close, since these had been distinctions for one campaign only, and in any event confined to principal commanders.

This change of character is carried through the whole of the draft. Against the second clause, referring to the Queen as Sovereign of the Order, is noted 'It is questionable whether this being copied from the Statutes of most of our *Orders of Knighthood* which imply the existence of a fraternity, it would properly apply to a Cross given by the Sovereign, *as such,* to reward the gallantry of his Troops'. And against the next two clauses, which also refer to membership of an order, 'NB. I would throughout drop the designation Member of the Order &c and treat it, as it is, as a cross granted for distinguished service, which will make it simple and intelligible'. In most places where the word 'order' appears in the draft it has been struck out and the 'cross' substituted. The draft Clause 15, setting up the machinery of an Order with its Grand Master and officers naturally attracts a comment 'NB. As it is not properly an order implying a Fraternity of which the Sovereign is one, but a mark of distinction given by the Sovereign for special acts, this would appear unnecessary. A Secretary and Registrar in the War Dept would be all that is necessary'.

As has been seen, one of Prince Albert's favourite ideas for a new decoration had been that it should incorporate selection by election but the document in which he had advocated this had never come to Panmure's notice. [28] He now took the opportunity to bring it forward once more, as a long note at the end of the draft warrant he was returning: 'A most important case has been left unnoticed, viz, where a body of men, say a Brigade, a Regiment, a Company, &c may have performed a deed of valour superior to any an individual could perform and influencing the fate of a field or even campaign: in such a case it would not do to refuse the Cross on account of there being too many brave men, and yet to give it to all of them would not answer the purpose of the institution. In such a case the deed might be rewarded by a certain number of Crosses being given to the whole body

28   See Chapter II

participating in it, leaving to a "jury" of those engaged to select the proper representatives. I even hope that this will be the most common case. For instance, the maintenance of the Sandbag Battery at Inkermann, the charge of Balaclava, the storming party of the Quarries, 7 Jun, &c. These are deeds more valuable than the throwing of a shell out of a Battery, or carrying a wounded Officer off the Field'.

A few other points in the draft also occasioned comment. The reference in Clause 7 to those who might 'project and by personal bravery contribute to the success' of an operation drew the remark, 'A doubtful clause as it is not clear to what it is to extend'. Against Clauses 9 and 10, relating to acts performed under the eye of a superior commander, and those not so performed is noted, 'It is here not stated whether the subordinate commanders are to exercise their right without the concurrence of their superiors in command. It may be that a Brigadier or Commodore may consider an act as qualifying, which the General of Division or Admiral or CinC might *not* so consider; is the opinion of the superior to be set aside? There is great danger of this clause causing a kind of competition between Brigadiers, who would get the most Crosses for his Brigade, which in time must degrade the value of the Cross. Clause 10 seems all right and the proper model for Clause 9.'

The suggestion that the Cross might be of steel is also deleted in Clause 5.

Two points appear to have raised issues of Royal protocol. The words in Clause 14, 'Her Majesty being graciously pleased to bind Herself herein' are struck out, with the comment, 'The Queen must be *supposed* to adhere to the rules which She Herself promulgates', and against the words, 'appointed by the Queen on recommendation of S of S' in Clause 15 is written, 'To be appointed by the Crown (Queen) Her pleasure being taken by the S of S', which would seem to represent an enhancement of the Royal Prerogative.

The real force of the Royal amendments was clearly grasped by Lord Panmure who wrote, acknowledging the return of the draft with these comments, on 30 Dec, 'Her Majesty and Your Royal Highness have greatly improved this reward for military exploits by changing its character from an 'order' to a 'decoration'. I will have the warrant redrafted with the alterations proposed and will submit it to Lord Hardinge...' [29] It is from this point in time that it is justifiable to refer to the new award as the Victoria Cross and to lay the choice of name and style of the decoration to the credit of Prince Albert.

Albert had made no comment on the absence of any expulsion clauses, nor of the fact that the pension proposed was a good deal more than suggested in his memorandum to the Duke of Newcastle, even though the sum had been reduced, presumably as a result of consideration by the WO, from that named in the earliest draft of all. Both of these matters were to vary again in the warrant as finally issued, which restored an exclusion clause and reduced the pension yet again. Whether these amendments arose from reconsideration by the WO or by Albert is not clear, particularly since the redrafted warrant promised by Panmure on 30 Dec, and Albert's comments upon it, do not survive but, since Albert had made no comment on these points in December, it seems more likely that these revisions were the work of the WO. Presumably the revised draft was submitted by Panmure about 12 Jan 1856, and the Queen's approval, together with a letter from Prince Albert, recommending that it should be made clear whether the document in question was a draft of the Royal Warrant or of a recommendation to the Queen, sent to Panmure on 13 Dec, for on the following day he wrote to Prince Albert, 'I received Your Royal Highness's note yesterday, with HM's final approval of the decoration. I will attend immediately to the instrument by which the new order [sic] is to be instituted. It must declare throughout, the Royal Will and Pleasure of the Queen, and bear the stamp of her own prerogative. The Sovereign is the fountain of all honours, and commands their institution as well as their revocation. The drafts which I have hitherto sent for Your Royal Highness's perusal were for the object of ascertaining in what manner it would be most agreeable to the Queen to have her commands carried into effect'. [30]

The process of preparing this 'instrument' seems to have taken somewhat longer than expected, at least by Albert, for on 28 Jan he wrote to Panmure, 'Might I remind you of the Victoria Cross? Parliament meets on Thursday [31 Jan] and the subject will immediately be discussed in debate. It would be very desirable that the statutes should be signed by the Queen and published before.'[31]

Lord Panmure replied the same day. 'I have the honour to acknowledge the receipt of Your Royal Highness's note. I have placed the draft of the Statutes of the "VC" in the hands of Mr Woods [Garter King of Arms] to be put into proper shape for the confirmation and signature of The Queen and I have been carefully through them, with

30   *Panmure Papers,* ii p66
31   *ibid,* 81

him. I shall submit the Statutes to HM on Wednesday in such form as, I think, will be satisfactory. I have adopted most of Your Royal Highness's suggestions. The Statute No 13, which provides for selection in cases where the act has been distinguished but no individual has been eminently conspicuous, has given me and Sir C.Woods [First Lord of the Admiralty] considerable trouble, but I think I have reduced it to a clear shape.

'I agree with Your Royal Highness as to the pension beginning from the date of the act by which the decoration has been won in the cases of Warrant and Petty Officers, Seamen and Marines and of NCO and Soldiers, and I think it may be reduced from £15 to £10 in the first instance. I have added a statute for deprivation of the order in cases of unworthiness, preserving to The Sovereign the power of restitution. This statute is based upon a similar one in the statutes of the Bath'. [32]

Bearing in mind that a forfeiture provision existed in the earliest draft of statutes for a new military distinction, and that the idea of an elective element had been announced in Newcastle's statement to the Lords almost exactly a year previously, it is somewhat of a surprise that the final form of the relevant statutes was only arrived at so very late. That the elective Clause 13 had caused difficulty in drafting is, however, hardly surprising as it was again to do so when the warrant was the subject of general review in 1918. It also seems probable that there had been some prolonged difference of opinion over the amount of the pension, and that the figure now named was something of a compromise. As will be seen from Appendix IV, the final draft reproduced the original wording of Newcastle at many points. The view expressed in Albert's memorandum, that individuals should claim the distinction, can also be seen in the phraseology of Clause 8.

In fact, Panmure was better than his word, for the VC Warrant was actually laid before the Queen and signed by her on Tuesday, 29 Jan 1856, a day earlier than he had expected to present it. A minor curiosity is that it was signed at Buckingham Palace, since Queen Victoria mentions in a letter written to King Leopold from Windsor that morning, that she was going to attend a wedding in St George's Chapel that same morning, [33] and one wonders at the inconvenience of a trip to Buckingham Palace the same day, when there would seem to have been no special objection to the documents being sent to Windsor for signature.

---

32   Royal Archives, E6/90
33   Benson and Esher, *The Letters of Queen Victoria*, London 1907, iii p169

Prince Albert's expectations regarding discussion on the subject on the reassembly of Parliament were apparently not fulfilled, there being no record of any reference being made to the new decoration in its debates at this time. *The Times* made its comment a week later and was entirely approving. 'An order of merit has been established at last, and the principles which are to regulate the distribution of its distinction are laid down in so broad and satisfactory manner that nothing remains but to express our full satisfaction at the concession of this tardy measure of justice'. [34]   The last few words of this comment do suggest that Albert may well have been right in thinking that the subject would have been raised in Parliament had the Warrant not been signed by then.

No very active steps seem to have been taken to keep Parliament informed on the subject and a year was to pass before Capt Scobell on 24 Feb 1857 moved an address seeking information as to the regulations under which the VC was to be awarded, which secured the presentation to the Commons of the terms of this warrant. [35]   His demand was undoubtedly occasioned by the fact that the first list of awards had been published in the *London Gazette* that day. There is evidence that Panmure would have wished to involve Parliament more in the awards, for on 15 Feb 1857 he had written to the Queen, 'It is proposed to gazette the names as in the case of the Bath, and to lay the lists before Parliament, attaching to the name of each member of the Order the service by which he has gained the honour'.[36] Victoria took a very different view of the matter, as is shown in her reply of 17 Feb. 'The Queen would wish the first notice of these rewards to be in the *Gazette*, and to have the explanations of the grounds upon which they are granted appended to each case as is done in the list submitted to her. To make such a report to Parliament by laying it on the table of the House would look like an appeal to its decision in a matter which clearly belongs solely and entirely to the discretion of the Crown'.[37] Panmure did not resist the Queen's view, even though he evidently did not share it, for in his letter of 18 Feb he replied to the Queen, 'It was Lord Panmure's intention, after gazetting the names, to present the list to Parliament by Your Majesty's commands, but he will take the course indicated by Your Majesty'. [38]   The actual award of the VC was established, as it was to remain, as a matter for the Crown itself, and one in which Parliament was to have no share.

34   *The Times,* 7 Feb 1856
35   *Parliamentary Accounts and Papers 1857 (1st Session),* ii pp207/10
36   *Panmure Papers,* ii p352
37   *ibid,* p355
38   *ibid,* p357

Chapter 4

The Cross

IT SEEMS CLEAR THAT, coincidental with War Office discussions on drafting of the warrant, equal consideration was being given to the form which its insignia should take. As with the warrant, no records survive to throw light on the early proceedings, and the question of design had obviously reached an advanced stage when the first surviving record occurs, in Panmure's letter of 3 Jan 1856 to the Queen. 'Lord Panmure... submits... two drawings of the "Victoria Cross" and a piece of metal showing the size of it. The cross, however, will not be so thick or heavy. The revised rules are at present with Lord Hardinge and will in a few days be laid before Your Majesty in draft, before Your Majesty's pleasure is formally taken on the subject.' [39] As already stated, the draft rules were probably submitted to the Queen on 12 Jan.

The Queen replied, returning the drawings, on 5 Jan, '...she has marked the one she approves with an X; she thinks, however, it might be a trifle smaller. The motto would be better "For Valour" than "for *the* brave", as this would lead to the inference that only those are deemed brave who have got the Cross'. [40]

It will be noted that the suggested motto was not one of those on the original draft of Appendix I. One can only speculate as to its source and also on that of the drawings submitted by Panmure. It is commonly suggested [41] that the design of the Cross was the work of the Prince Consort, the origin of the suggestion being in *The Times* of 27 Jun 1857 reporting the first presentations which had taken place in Hyde Park the previous day. 'The merit of the design, we believe, is due to the same illustrious individual who once invented a hat.' This attribution, which was not intended as any sort of compliment, for *The Times* quite clearly

39   Royal Archives, G42/65
40   *Panmure Papers*, ii p50. Also printed in *Letters of Queen Victoria*, iii p203
41   in e.g. L.L. Gordon, *British Orders and Awards*, London 1959, p18, S.C. Johnson, *The Medal Collector*, London 1921, p201. Ian Bisset, *The George Cross*, London 1961, p18

did not think that there was any merit in the design of the cross, remains unsupported and it seems, in the light of the other documents, to be implausible. As Panmure's letter of 3 Jan shows, the design reached the Queen through him, from whatever source obtained, and then in two forms. Had Albert been the designer it is difficult to see how the S of S would have been involved in laying the drawing before the Queen or, indeed, why there should have been two designs to choose between or any question of the size of the decoration at this stage; all matters which one would expect to have been settled informally between the Queen and her husband,. were they his handiwork. The fact that Victoria, in her journal account of the first presentation of VCs, makes no reference to the cross as of Albert's design [42] also tends to confirm this, especially as the events of 1881 [43] show his responsibility for the warrant as clearly recognised. Plainly, whoever did prepare the designs was acquainted with the Peninsular Gold Cross but, as the designer of this in its turn is also obscure, this does not advance matters. Mayo suggests [44] that the Peninsular design was probably prepared by the London firm of jewellers, Messrs Rundell & Bridge. He also suggests that the collar given to the Duke of Wellington by the Prince Regent and based upon this was probably designed by the contemporary Garter King of Arms, but investigations at the College of Heralds has brought to light nothing bearing on the design of the VC. Nor, in view of the unheraldic shape of the Cross[45] can this be regarded as a very likely source for the design.

One further possibility remains. No documents survive, either among WO papers or the records of Messrs Hancocks, by whom the Cross has always been manufactured, regarding the actual manufacture of the first versions of the Cross, nor even as to how this firm came to be selected to undertake the task. Nevertheless the then recently established firm, [founded in 1848] was from its outset a manufacturing goldsmith and silversmith. What more probable, then, than that the firm which was to make the cross should also have supplied the design for it? For this supposition there does appear to be a little supporting evidence, for in its issue immediately preceding the Hyde Park presentation the *Illustrated London News* referred to 'Mr Hancock of Bruton Street, by whom the cross was *designed* and executed'. [46]   This reference

42   See Chapter VI
43   See Chapter XV
44   J.H. Mayo, *Medals and Decorations of the British Army and Navy*, London 1897, i pp190 and 209
45   See Appendix XIX
46   *Illustrated London News*, vol xxx, p632

commands respect because this publication was clearly well-informed on the subject of the VC. On 7 Mar 1857 it had printed the first list of names of VC recipients and accompanied this with what must have been the first picture of the Cross ever to appear, in a black and white engraving that seems quite accurate, though on this occasion Mr Hancock is only credited with the execution of the work. [47] The issue in which the design is credited to him also contains the remark, 'We have reason to believe that Her Majesty and the Prince took great interest in the design of this new Order of Valour, and the cross was adopted on their entire approval', the accuracy of which comment the evidence of this chapter confirms. Also worth noting is Parry's reference, in describing the scene of the first presentation, to '... the Crosses, designed and executed by Messrs Hancock of Bruton Street'. [48] Whilst he was writing forty-five years after the event, and may simply have been quoting the ILN of 1857, his support of this view commands respect, since he is one of the very few sources [and apparently unique in his day] correctly attributing the origin of the idea of the Cross to the Duke of Newcastle. [49]

If, then, the source of the design is to be looked for in the firm of Hancocks, the question arises as to whether the individual responsible can be identified. This does seem to be possible for although Hancocks possess no other records for this period they do preserve the bound volumes of photographs of trophies designed and manufactured by them, dating back to this time. From these it appears that all the major designs of this date were produced either by H.H. Armstead or by Raffaeli Monti. Whilst it is difficult to trace any direct resemblance between the VC and these trophies [which are, in any case, works of a very different type] the designs of Monti are much more florid and seem clearly to rule him out as their designer. On these grounds alone Armstead would be the preferred candidate, but it is possible to go a little further than this; generally there seems nothing inconsistent between the style of the Armstead designs and that of the VC, more specifically there is a common use of comparatively low relief and of compartments with double borders. On all these grounds, therefore, the design of the VC may be attributed to H. H. Armstead with reasonable assurance.

The fact that despite a lengthy article on Armstead in the *Dictionary of National Biography* this attribution has not been made before is not

47   *ibid*, p202
48   D.H. Parry, *The VC – Its Heroes and Their Valour,* London 1913, p97
49   *ibid*, p4

altogether surprising. Although he had been exhibiting at the Royal Academy since 1851[50] he was still at this time quite a young and obscure man, having been born in 1828 and with little formal schooling. The author of the article also lays far more stress on his employment at Hunt & Roskell's, where he eventually became chief designer. His other employment is simply dismissed as 'a brief engagement by Hancock's firm of like character', and several of the works appearing in the Hancock albums are listed in this article with no reference to the fact that they belonged to this period of his career. The article does, however, mention the significant facts that he was the son of a heraldic chaser, working in his father's workshop from the age of eleven, and that during his working life he did a great deal of designing, modelling and carving in gold, silver and bronze. He also carved two of the statues for the Albert Memorial. He subsequently became an ARA in 1875, a Royal Academician in 1879, and died in December 1905.[51]

From Jan 1856 onwards the evolution of the design of the VC is well-documented, with abundant proof of the meticulous care attributed to the Queen in connection with it. The transformation of the cross from a design on paper into a physical reality in metal seems to have taken almost exactly a month, for it was on 4 Feb 1856 that Panmure wrote again to the Queen, '... to forward... a proof of the Victoria Cross which [he] hopes will meet with Your Majesty's approval. The back being plain, the name of the recipient and the occasion on which it was conferred can readily be engraved upon it. It has been suggested... for consideration whether there might not be a little less metal in the cross'. [52]

There is in the Queen's collection of medals at Windsor Castle what is evidently a preliminary design of the VC, the reverse of which is quite plain, and instead of the V on the suspender bar connecting with the Cross there are small round links; the suspender bar is also plain without any laurel spray. [53] As Queen Victoria disapproved of the plain reverse on the specimen submitted to her on 4 Feb, it seems certain that this was the only occasion upon which the Cross was manufactured in this form and it follows, therefore, that this specimen is indeed that which was then submitted.

50   Groves, *Royal Academy Exhibitors, sub nomen*
51   *Dictionary of National Biography, Second Supplement, sub nomen*
52   Royal Archives, E6/93
53   See Plate 2a. This specimen was exhibited in 'The Royal Review of the British Soldier' at Buckingham Palace 1967/8, and again at the VC and GC Exhibition at the Imperial War Museum 1970/1, and is described in Arthur Jocelyn's *Awards of Honour*, London 1956, p140

The Queen's letter to Panmure of 5 Feb shows that she was by no means finally satisfied with the proof. 'The Cross looks very well in form, but the metal is ugly; it is copper and not bronze and will look very heavy on a red coat with the Crimean Ribbon. Bronze is, properly speaking, gun-metal; this has a rich colour and is very hard; copper would wear very ill and would soon look like an old penny. Lord Panmure should have one prepared in real bronze, and the Queen is inclined to think that it ought to have a greenish varnish to protect it; the raised parts would then burnish up bright and show the design and inscription. The reverse ought not to be quite flat, but should be finished as much as the front'. [54]

A further fortnight seems to have elapsed during which a new specimen was prepared to meet these criticisms, for the next surviving letter on the subject is from the Queen to Panmure on 21 Feb when she writes, 'The Queen likewise returns the VC, merely burnished up by rubbing, with a little green colour put on the sunken parts; something like this is what the Queen would wish to have prepared for inspection, but with bolder relief by sinking the die deeper'. [55] To which the following day Panmure made the courtierly reply, 'Your Majesty's commands in regard to the VC shall be forthwith attended to. The alterations made by Your Majesty are very great improvements upon its appearance'. [56]

The V-link of the suspender of the cross has been spoken of as a late afterthought of the Queen and, whilst there appears to be no documentary evidence on this point, that it should have been her suggestion is well in accord with the tone of this correspondence and it may be guessed that it was at this moment in time that the suggestion would most naturally have arisen.

No letter survives from Panmure submitting the VC to the Queen in what was to be its final form, but this must have taken place about a week later for on 3 Mar 1856 she returned the samples '... having chosen the one, into the case of which she has placed a paper. She wishes later to have one to keep, and wishes that one should also be kept as a pattern at the WO, as the Tradesmen invariably alter the original pattern agreed upon if they are not watched'. [57]

There is, however, no evidence in the WO papers that any pattern copy was deposited with them.

54 *Panmure Papers*, ii pp94/5
55 *ibid*, p117
56 *ibid*, p121
57 *ibid*, p138

In 1922 a specimen VC was presented by Col M.P. Hancock, grandson of the founder of the firm which has manufactured the VC from its inception, to the Royal United Services Institute Museum. This was stated to be the original VC struck for the inspection and approval of Queen Victoria, and that it had come into the possession of the donor through his grandfather. On the dissolution of this museum in 1963 the cross was allocated to the National Army Museum who, in turn, placed it on permanent loan in the museum of the Royal Fusiliers in the Tower of London, this being Col Hancock's old regiment. [58] On the supposition that the sample cross which had been designated as the Queen's choice must, of necessity, have been returned to its manufacturers as the pattern to be copied, there seems little reason to doubt that the cross in the museum of the Royal Fusiliers, illustrated in Plate 2b, is indeed the one she selected on 3 Mar 1856.

No time was lost by the WO in ordering the manufacture of the new crosses, Mr Hancock being instructed on 4 Mar to prepare 106 specimens. [59]   The Queen herself acknowledged the receipt of one of these from Panmure on 5 May of that year; [60]   this seems more likely to have been the specimen which was to be placed under the foundation-stone of Netley Hospital when she laid this on 19 May, [recovered when that building was demolished in 1966] than the one requested for her own collection. It was, no doubt, the receipt of this mass order which forced Mr Hancock to adopt the process of casting in manufacturing the VC, the metal employed being so tough that it broke the dies when striking was attempted. [61]

The first occasion upon which the new cross was to be seen by the general public was after the first presentation of the award in Hyde Park on 26 Jun 1857. If *The Times* report of the occasion is to be trusted, the reaction was unfavourable. 'The greatest anxiety was manifested on the part of the people to see the Cross of Valour men as they dispersed and left the ground; and the course of almost each could be traced by the little group that followed him, anxious to get a glimpse of the Cross, with which all found more or less fault at the very first. Than the Cross of Valour nothing could be more plain and homely, not to say coarse-looking. It is a very small Maltese Cross, formed from the gun-metal of ordnance captured at Sebastopol. In the centre is a small crown and lion, with which latter's natural proportions of mane and

58   See Col C.A.L. Shipley's letter in *The Times,* 9 Dec 1966
59   VCR, i p56
60   *Panmure Papers,* ii p217
61   See *The Times,* 27 Jun 1857

tail the cutting of the cross much interferes. Below these, is a small scroll (which shortens three arms of the cross and is utterly out of keeping with the upper portions) bearing the words "For Valour" ... But even with all the care and skill which distinguishes Mr Hancock, the whole cross is, after all, poor looking and mean in the extreme'. [62] As this report is also the source of the earliest allusion to the design being the work of Prince Albert there are some grounds for regarding the ascription as malicious in its intent, and the description equally biased. However that may be, it seems reasonable to claim that the virtues of the design of the VC — and the idea was, as has already been shown, from its earliest inception, that the insignia should be simple and unpretentious — have triumphed over such criticism. The rightness of this adoption of simplicity will readily be appreciated if the design of the VC is contrasted with that of the Congressional Medal of Honor of the United States Army adopted in 1904.

62   *ibid*

Chapter 5

The Selection

WITH THE conditions of award and the design of its insignia settled, the next item requiring attention was the selection of recipients — though two internal matters had first to be dealt with. Payment of a new pension was involved, and someone had to be made responsible for the departmental work. A letter was sent to Sir C. Trevelyan at the Treasury, on 5 Feb 1856, enclosing a copy of the warrant to be laid before the Lords Commissioners for their sanction of the expenditure involved in the provision of the pension under Clause 14. This was given the same day. [63] The matter of staff responsibility was raised simultaneously; a note with the papers, dated the following day, observes that '... a new business will thus devolve on this Department, and if war continues it will doubtless be considerable'. The writer goes on to suggest that the work should be performed under the Permanent Under Secretary by Mr Pennington '... who is conversant with the somewhat similar duties for the Bath', a suggestion approved by Panmure on 8 Feb. [54] Twelve months later these duties were in full operation with the approval of the first list of awards, and then a further piece of departmental organisation took place. The Admiralty had submitted their first list of names to be included among the recipients on 13 Feb 1857, but on 28 Feb asked for certain details of Christian names and spelling to be corrected. Mr Pennington submitted on 4 Mar that a reply should be sent that the S of S had given directions for these mistakes to be rectified 'in the Registry' and, evidently anticipating a question as to what registry he was talking about, added, 'A suitably bound book for a Registry has been ordered from the Stationery Office and will be ready, I am informed, in about a fortnight'.[65] This was to become Volume One of The Victoria Cross Register, which is still in use in the Ministry of Defence at Stanmore.

Lord Panmure had lost no time in bringing the existence of the new award to the notice of the Admiralty and Horse Guards. Indeed, the Service departments were quick to demand information as is shown by

63   PRO, WO32/7301
64   *ibid*
65   PRO, WO32/7302

the letter from Col Mundy at the WO, to the Admiralty, on 20 Feb 1856. 'Having laid before Lord Panmure your letter of 15th instant, I am directed to request you will state to the Lords Commissioners of the Admiralty that it is not intended that services rendered previous to the commencement of the present war shall be considered as coming within the limits of the new decoration which HM has been pleased to institute under the designation of the Victoria Cross'. [66] This is not a point explicitly stated in the Warrant and the responsibility for the ruling appears to have been Panmure's own. The necessity for the restriction is shown by the number of letters of which evidence survives, urging the claims of men who had served in many previous campaigns. One of the earliest concerned the service of the writer's son in the Kaffir War, and has been annotated 'The first drops of a shower of such applications which we shall have'. [67] Others related to service in New Zealand in 1847 [68] and, though this claim was not received until 1860, for the Peninsular War! [69] One other claim that was rejected related to service against the Combo rebels in the West Indies in Jul and Aug 1855. [70] This case is of particular interest, as the individual recommended was a *capitaine de fregate* in the French Navy, M Ducrest de Villeneuve, and produced the ruling from Panmure that 'the terms of the warrant constituting the VC do not include foreigners among those eligible for the decoration'.

The matter was spelled out more explicitly in a letter from Col Mundy to the Secretary of the Admiralty on 25 Feb 1856: 'relative to the period from which the decoration of the VC is to take effect. I am directed by Lord Panmure to request you will state to the Lords Commissioners of the Admiralty that his lordship proposes that the grant of the decoration, so far as the Navy is concerned, shall be made to all those officers of the lower grades in the Navy or Warrant and Petty Officers, seamen and marines, who by the performance of deeds of gallantry since the commencement of the present War may be enabled to substantiate their claim to it according to the conditions laid down in the Instrument under the Royal Sign Manual instituting the decoration, and I am to request that you will move the Lords Commissioners to favour Lord Panmure with their opinions on the subject'. [71]

66   PRO, WO6/130
67   PRO, WO32/7299
68   VCR i, p2
69   *ibid,* p265
70   *ibid,* p16
71   *ibid,* pp2/3

A letter in similar terms went to Lord Hardinge as CinC on the same day [72] and these may be regarded as the first moves in the quest for names of recipients. It will be noted, however, that this letter, in its reference to officers in the lower ranks, misconstrues the warrant which contains no such limitation. This is clearly a last survival of the original idea that the new decoration was being created to supplement the Order of the Bath, the award of which was confined to officers of the higher ranks. The error was put right on 20 Mar 1856 when Col Mundy wrote to Maj-Gen Sir Charles Yorke, the MS at the Horse Guards and the Secretary to the Admiralty. 'With reference to my letter of 25th ultimo I am directed by Lord Panmure to request you will state... that it is intended that the decoration of the VC may be bestowed on officers of all ranks, who have distinguished themselves by conspicuous bravery.' [73] Despite this, however, the notion long lingered that this was not to be a commanding or field officer's decoration, as is shown by the letter from Yorke to the WO on 21 Jul 1860 regarding the claims to the VC of Lt-Col Forbes, concerning whom a month previously the Duke of Cambridge had expressed doubts as to his coming within the terms of the warrant and who had, in fact, been given the Bath and promotion. He wrote that '... the only question is whether the VC should be awarded to a Commanding Officer who gallantly leads his Regt. in some very desperate service, which the attack of a Square of Infantry formed to receive the charge of Cavalry must be considered to be. Nothing could be more conspicuously gallant than the conduct of Lt-Col Forbes is shown by these papers to have been, and the only reason why HRH did not recommend him as well as the other officers for the VC was, I believe, that he thought the Order of the Bath was the proper distinction for the Commanding Officer, and that had been granted to Lt-Col Forbes. The only instance, I believe of the Comd. Officer of a Regt. having obtained the VC as well as the 3rd Class of the Bath is Lt-Col Maude of 3 Foot who as a Major commanded the Regt. in the attack on the Redan on 8 Sep 1855. He was promoted to Bt-Lt-Colonelcy and whether he was granted the Cross before or after he recd. the Bath I do not at the moment remember. There is, however, this precedent, and if the Secretary of State is generally considering the interpretation of the Warrant in a doubtful case, and the 6th Clause of the one in question perhaps bears out Mr Herbert's view of Forbes' case [presumably the Secretary of State was favourably inclined towards it], HRH may perhaps be

72   *ibid,* pp3/4
73   *ibid,* p8

indisposed to resist the grant of the honour to an officer who seems to have shown a notable example to his Regt. although it was certainly what his duty required of him, and it is not impossible that the conferring of the Distinction in this instance may give rise to claims on the part of other Comd. Officers'.

Nor did this letter stand alone, for on 24 Jul, Cambridge added his own views to Sidney Herbert. '... I concur with Yorke's opinion that Forbes' conduct... was admirable but I think that the Bath to a superior officer stands in place of the VC and I feel that if you depart from the rule, you will get into great difficulties. The fact is that the Bath can only be given to officers of a certain rank in the service, whereas the VC is open to all, even the private, and I have always understood that this was one of the objects for establishing this order of Merit. Of course, if you take another view I am quite ready to adopt your reading, but if you want my advice I am against conferring the VC to [sic] a Commanding Officer, who would be entitled to the Bath which in this case he has got'.

Sir Edward Lugard had previously commented, in putting forward the names which had accompanied that of Col Forbes, and whom Cambridge had recommended, that he could not see the distinction drawn by the Horse Guards in omitting him. 'He was the leader, and I should have thought equally entitled to the Cross.' The two letters of 21 and 24 Jul were, evidently, the explanation of the Horse Guards for drawing the distinction they did. Sidney Herbert's final ruling was, 'As Col Forbes recd. the Bath and a Bt-Lt-Colcy for this I think the Duke is right in objecting to giving him the VC too'. So Forbes' name was not submitted to the Queen for the award of the VC. [74]

Somewhat similarly, Parry relates that Lt-Col James Hagart was recommended for the Cross for his very gallant part in the same action in the Indian Mutiny as that in which Cornet Bankes won his Cross, but that, 'Sir Colin [Campbell] had no desire that officers of his rank should receive [this] decoration... and he refused to forward the recommendation'. [75] Many years later objection was still taken to the award of the Cross to officers of senior rank. On 7 Jul 1900 the then MS wrote to the CinC in South Africa, 'With regard to Col (local Maj Gen) Ian Hamilton, I am to observe that the act for which he was recommended was performed when he was commanding a Brigade, i.e. in the position of a General Officer. The VC has never been conferred upon an officer so high in rank. The CinC thinks this

74   PRO, WO32/7344 for all the above
75   *The VC – Its Heroes and Their Valour*, p193

limitation a wise one, and that it would not be desirable to establish a precedent opposed to it. He is unable, therefore, to submit Maj Gen Hamilton's name to the Queen.' [76] The precedent was not breached until 1917, when the VC was awarded to Clifford Coffin for his gallantry on 31 Jul of that year when holding the rank of Temporary Brig-Gen.

To return to the events of 1856, a further departmental query was to come from the Admiralty. On 12 Jun it wrote to enquire as to the course of action to be pursued with those who had received the medal and gratuity for conspicuous gallantry. Were they excluded from consideration for the VC, or might they receive this in lieu or in addition to their original award? Mr Pennington referred the matter to Panmure on 16 Jun and he replied on 29th, 'I don't think that any act of gallantry can be *twice* rewarded. If a medal and gratuity being the only reward of gallantry has been given to a man he may change the *medal* for the VC and receive the pension assigned to the possession of the Cross but he cannot wear both medal *and* Cross. The gratuity, of course, would not be recalled'. [77] This view was conveyed by Col Mundy to the Secretary of the Admiralty on 2 Jul. [78]

However, matters were not proceeding as fast as some would have wished and on 27 Jun 1856 Scobell asked in the Commons whether arrangements for the distribution of the 'Victoria Order of Valour' were completed, or nearly so, and whether it would be brought into operation at an early period. He referred to the profuse distribution of Baltic and Crimea medals to all who served there, worthy or unworthy, and hoped the excellent rules of the Order in question would be adhered to. The reply by Sir Charles Wood, First Lord of the Admiralty [appropriately in view of his department's interest] that he believed arrangements to be all but completed was an overstatement for no beginning had yet been made on selection of recipients. [79]

Nor was Scobell alone in his thinking. On 21 Jul the Queen wrote from Osborne to Panmure, 'Now that the Queen's Crimean Army has almost entirely arrived in this country, the Queen wishes to remind Lord Panmure of the "Victoria Cross"; these distinctions always have the most effect when they are given without delay, but the Queen feels that the selection will be dreadfully difficult, and possibly may give more heart-burnings than satisfaction. It can evidently not be given to all those men who received the Medal for distinguished conduct, for that

76   VCR, iii, p7
77   PRO, WO 32/7301
78   VCR, i, pp12/3
79   *Hansard*, 3rd Series, cxxxi col 2090

would be an immense number. Lord Panmure will be so good as to consider all this with the Duke of Cambridge, and then inform her what course it is intended to pursue'. [80]

The promptitude of Panmure's reply suggests that he must already have been discussing the matter, for on 22 Jul he wrote to the Queen that Cambridge and he concurred in advising that as soon as Sir William Codrington had reached home he, Sir J. Simpson, and some third officer of high rank to be recommended by HRH to the Queen, should consider claims, or rather the merits, of the officers and men and recommend them. [81] However, it was not necessary to wait for the board of officers to be set up before Commanders could be invited to submit names and, in fact, Panmure wrote to the Duke of Cambridge on 5 Sep. '... that as the Army has now returned from the Crimea and officers in command... are within easy reference, ...no time should be lost in ascertaining the names... whose conspicuous gallantry entitles them to be recommended to the Queen for the VC. I... request that you will call on the officers in command... to furnish the names of those... whom they may consider entitled to this order. It will be necessary to give a full detail of each claimant's service and the occasions upon which he has distinguished himself so that I may be able to form a judgment on each case previously to submitting it to Her Majesty.' [82]

Panmure so informed the Queen the following day and mentioned that he had seen Codrington on the subject. [83] One would have expected from his letter to the Queen of 22 Jul that the setting up of the board of officers that he then mentioned would have followed immediately, but such was not to be the case, and it was not until 19 Dec 1856 that a letter was sent by command of Cambridge to Gen Simpson, informing him that he was to preside over a board of officers 'to assemble at the Horse Guards for the purpose of considering the lists of those Officers and subordinate ranks who served in the Crimea and selecting from them the names of such individuals who the board may deem worthy of being recommended for the order of the Victoria Cross'.[84] There is no apparent reason for the delay nor for the fact that Codrington was not one of the board's members. These were: Gen Simpson [sent as Chief of Staff to Lord Raglan in the Crimea in Feb 1855 and his successor as Commander on Raglan's death though

80   *Panmure Papers,* ii p274
81   *ibid,* p275
82   VCR, i, pp13/4
83   *Panmure Papers,* ii p293
84   PRO, WO3/120

resigning this in Oct 1855 to be succeeded by Codrington];[85] Maj-Gen Lord Rokeby [who commanded the Guards Brigade from Dec 1854, and had mainly failed to get a division until the Sixth was largely created for him because it was felt that too many divisional commanders were Guardsmen; he was also one of those over whose head Codrington was preferred as Simpson's successor];[86] and Col the Hon W.L. Pakenham [later Fourth Earl of Longford; he had served as Assistant Quartermaster-General at Crimea HQ and succeeded Estcourt as Adjutant-General].[87]

Although there is no documentary evidence regarding the selection of the membership of the board, it appears that the advice originally tendered by Panmure was being followed and that the two individuals now joined with Gen Simpson were, respectively, the nominees of the Duke and Codrington; in view of the very close relationship between the Royal Family and the Household troops it would be natural for the Duke to select a Guards officer such as Lord Rokeby, whilst Pakenham, as one of his senior staff officers, would be an equally natural choice by Codrington as his representative.

Meanwhile, Cambridge had evidently sought clarification concerning selection, producing significant rulings from Panmure in a letter from Gen Peel to Yorke on 29 Sep 1856 that '... his Lordship does not think that this department is in a position to assign any limit at present to the number of recipients of... the VC. ... further ... it would be better that HRH [the Duke of Cambridge] in giving the warrant instituting the decoration in question a retrospective effect as regards the late War would be very strict in requiring a rigid compliance with its directions. His Lordship considers that there should be a personal act of valour in each case so signal as to make evident the propriety of awarding a decoration'. [88]

As already mentioned, instructions went from the Horse Guards to COs of regiments that had served in the Crimea ordering them to submit the names of those deserving consideration for the new decoration. The replies of many, with lists of names on the form which had been supplied, headed '... recommended for the Order of the Victoria Cross' survive at the PRO [89] and provide some interesting evidence of

85   *Panmure Papers, passim*
86   *ibid*
87   *ibid* and GEC, *Complete Peerage,* sub Longford
88   VCR, i, p15
89   To be found in WO 98/2, from which all material quoted in this section has been derived, unless otherwise stated

contemporary thinking on the subject. There was a good deal of confusion as to what the distinction was – as will be noted, the official form described it as an order, something that the Queen was to be at pains later to point out that it was not, [90] whereas Col Paulet of the Coldstream Guards spoke of the 'Victoria Medal', whilst to Col Armstrong of the 49th Regt it was the 'Order of Valour'. No procedure had been laid down for selecting the men, despite what had been said earlier about 'juries of comrades', and each CO seems to have adopted his own method. In the 44th Regt the CO had taken a vote of all the DCMs and the Medaille Militaire men in his regiment. Others had circulated the order and invited those who thought they deserved consideration to appear before a regimental board, thus embodying Prince Albert's idea of those considering themselves worthy claiming the decoration. Col Warre of the 57th Regt seems to have taken things to extremes, for he wrote, 'I have taken the liberty of submitting the whole of the names of those men whom after careful examination by myself and a board of officers have been found to have distinguished themselves "above their comrades".

'I do not anticipate that HRH will admit the whole of these claims but it will be a great satisfaction to the claimants to know that their gallantry has been made known, as many if not all of those soldiers would, I am convinced, have been perfectly satisfied with the Cross, unaccompanied by the pecuniary recommendation, which must limit its distribution'.

It is interesting to note that this is Col Warre's one idea as to what might limit the number of crosses distributed – he had, of course, the analogy of the Distinguished Conduct Medal, the distribution of which was limited by the sum of money assigned to provide the pensions and gratuities which accompanied it but, quite plainly, the idea of the high degree of selectivity the new award was to carry had not penetrated to him. Had his letter not been dated 25 Oct one might have suspected that it was the occasion for Gen Peel's letter of 29 Sep, quoted earlier. However, it seems quite conceivable that Col Warre's thinking was by no means untypical of his colleagues and there may well have been other letters expressing similar sentiments received at the Horse Guards.

Curiously enough, Warre's idea of the honour of having participated in the selection for the VC was one that was to be raised by the Admiralty sixty years later. He was, however, logical in his interpretation of the financial limitation, for his letter goes on, 'as there is no pecuniary reward attached to the Cross to be conferred upon officers I have

90   *Panmure Papers*, ii pp398/9

submitted the names of five', and ends, 'I should feel gratified in being permitted to wear a decoration so entirely military and one for which all soldiers will eagerly seek'. Plainly, if he had not grasped the idea of its selectivity, the esteem of the new award had made its impression.

Those familiar with VC citations tend to take the view that it was bestowed somewhat freely in respect of the Crimean War. As Fortescue [91] remarked, 'the Indian Mutiny first gave a real value to the VC'. It is thus of some interest to see what measure of selection took place in considering the names submitted. All the names on the lists have either pencilled ticks or crosses against them and it seems reasonable to suppose that these represent the judgment of Gen Simpson and his board of officers at the Horse Guards. However, by no means all the names which have ticks against them were eventually gazetted. The list of those selected was forwarded to Panmure by Cambridge on 2 Feb 1857 [92] but it was only on 15 Feb that Panmure communicated to the Queen the names of those recommended [93] and it seems highly probable that, during this fortnight, a further examination of the board's recommendations had been undertaken by Cambridge and Panmure, reducing the number of names brought forward very considerably. The original returns show that thirty-two names were submitted from 55th Regt; of these, eight seem to have passed the board and two were gazetted. Warre's list of NCOs and men recommended from 57th Regt comprised thirty-one names, of whom twelve apparently satisfied the Board and two were finally gazetted. The CO of the 77th Regt brought forward no fewer than thirty-eight names, six were approved but only two gazetted. Other cases where all the pruning was done by the Board and their recommendations accepted were 47th Regt [sixteen submitted, one approved], 49th Regt [nine submitted, one approved], and the 68th Regt [twelve submitted, two approved]. Despite this profusion of recommendations from some COs, by no means all were equally enthusiastic, and the Cols of the 42nd, 50th, 56th, 62nd, 71st and 79th Regts all replied that they had no names to bring forward. Considering that the 42nd, 50th and 79th had been engaged at the Battle of the Alma, and the 50th also at Inkermann, there are grounds for suspecting that the difference lay not so much in the conduct of the men as in the energy of their Colonels in undertaking the somewhat tedious task of ascertaining names of men who had distinguished themselves.

The numbers of recipients, as against recommendations, may give the

91   J.W. Fortescue, *A History of the British Army,* xiii p402
92   PRO, WO32/7303
93   *Panmure Papers,* ii, p351

impression that the selectors were working on the principle of one VC per regiment. Col Warre, whose other misapprehensions regarding the new award have already been noted, evidently laboured under a delusion on this point also. On 9 Apr 1857 he wrote from Malta to inform the WO of the death in hospital the previous day of Pte McCorrie, the 57th's Crimea VC, 'I have the honour to request your kind intercession with HRH the Gen CinC in order that the much coveted honour may be given to one of the individuals in the 57th Regt whose names were submitted with that of Pte McCorrie... to continue in the Regt that high distinction of which it has pleased the Almighty so soon to deprive us'.[94] It is true a further VC was gazetted to the 57th, that of George Gardiner on 2 Jun 1858, but the surviving papers make it clear that his was one of the not infrequent cases where an award was deferred pending the submission of fuller details of the deed in question. In this case, the initiative in providing further particulars was taken by Gardiner himself in a letter of 22 Oct 1857, and of Gen Pennefather in forwarding this for favourable consideration of 7 Nov. [95]

Panmure's views on the question of substitution had been plainly stated in July of that year when this solution had been suggested to deal with the problem of a gazetted recipient who had subsequently committed misconduct. His opinion on that occasion had been that, since there was no limit on numbers of recipients, anyone worthy of consideration should have been submitted already and adjudicated independently; there could be no question of a place on a list being filled by any alternative name. [96]

As already mentioned, Cambridge forwarded to Panmure the list of names 'selected from very numerous applications' by his Board of Officers on 2 Feb 1857. After a short delay, during which time it is suggested that a further scrutiny reduced substantially the number of names being brought forward, Panmure wrote to the Queen on 15 Feb. '... to forward for... consideration the list of... those... selected by the Lords of Admiralty and HRH the CinC for the Victoria Cross.

'The list for the Army is incomplete, but as it will take some time to receive the names from the regiments abroad, both HRH the Duke of Cambridge and Lord Panmure think that it is better at once to proceed with this first list.

'As soon as Your Majesty has considered the two lists, Lord Panmure will submit them formally for Your Majesty's approval.' [97]

94 PRO, WO98/2
95 *ibid*
96 VCR, i, p38
97 *Panmure Papers,* ii, pp351/2

Despite the two stages of selection that the list of names had passed through there was to be yet a third, for on 17 Feb the Queen wrote back to Panmure, 'The Queen returns... the recommendations for the VC which she has most carefully gone over. The selection appears to her very well made and with a due regard not to make the decoration too common, and not to recognise the mere performance of duty to the satisfaction of superiors, but to solely volunteer acts.

'There is only one case which the Queen thinks had better be omitted, viz; Pte P. M'Gwire of the 33rd. His deed, although publicly praised and rewarded by Lord Raglan, was one of very doubtful morality, and if pointed out by the Soveriegn as praiseworthy, may lead to the cruel and inhumane practice of never taking prisoners, but always putting to death those who may be overpowered, for fear of their rising on their captors'. [98]

The recommendations from the 33rd Regt are missing from those at the PRO, so that the terms of M'Gwire's citation are not known. The incident is, however, described in a letter from the Crimea of 21 Oct 1854.

'You hear every day of heroic acts of bravery by the soldiers: one I call to mind. A few days ago a private of the 33rd [Duke of Wellington's Regt] was surprised and made prisoner by two Russian soldiers when an advanced sentry. One of these worthies took possession of his musket, and the other of his pouch and marched him between them towards Sebastopol. The Englishman [sic] kept wary watch and, when he fancied his captors off their guard, sprang on the one who carried his musket, seized it and shot dead the other of his foes who carried the pouch as well as his own arms and accoutrements. Meanwhile the Russian from whom our fellow had taken his own musket and who had then fallen to the ground when rising from his recumbent position, fired, missed, and finally had his brains knocked out by the butt-end of the Englishman's musket; after which the man coolly proceeded to take off the Russian accoutrements, etc, with which he returned laden to the post where he had been surprised, fired at by the Russian sentries and received with loud cheers by our own pickets'. [99]

It was in virtue of this exploit that M'Gwire received the French Medaille Militaire. [100]

98   *ibid*, pp354/5

99   *Letters from Headquarters*, by an Officer on the Staff, 1857, Chapter VI. I
      am indebted to Lt-Col W. Skelsey of the Duke of Wellington's Regt for this
      reference

100   *Parliamentary Accounts and Papers 2, 1857, 1st Session*, p233

The Queen's view prevailed and Panmure wrote on 18 Feb to advise HM that, with the concurrence of the CinC, M'Gwire's name had been removed. [101] Two lists were thereupon prepared for formal submission, one of the names of Naval and Marine recipients, [102] the other, those for the Army [103] and, the Queen's signature having been obtained, both were published in the *London Gazette* of 24 Feb 1857.

The procedure thus established has been followed ever since. A formal memorandum is prepared proposing to confer the decoration on the persons named in it for the deeds described in an appended statement, and this document is submitted to, and signed by, the Sovereign — the earliest examples at the PRO have the handwritten addition, 'Approved — Victoria'.

In general, the *London Gazette* published citations as submitted to the Queen, though not universally, as in the case of Assistant-Surgeon Thomas Egerton Hale. The statement submitted to the Queen read, in part, 'For remaining with an officer who was dangerously wounded (Capt. H.M. Jones, 7th Regt) in the fifth parallel during a panic on 8 Sept 1855, when all the men in the immediate neighbourhood retreated...' A marginal note on the papers [104] reads, 'It will probably be desirable in the copy sent to the Gazette of this officer's service that the words "during a panic" should be omitted', and the words do not appear in the *London Gazette* of 5 May 1857 in which his award was announced.

On the subject of the wording of VC citations, there is some correspondence of a much later date between Buckingham Palace and the WO which is of interest both as showing how keenly King George V studied details of such awards and providing evidence of a change in WO practice relating to submissions.

On 6 Nov 1918 Col Wigram wrote on behalf of the King from Buckingham Palace to Lt-Gen Sir F.J. Davies, MS at the WO, '... the King wishes that the statements may be carefully edited before appearing in the Gazette and in the press. HM took especial exception to some of the terms used in the statement of the services of Lt Charles Smith Rutherford and the King does not think that "Hun" is the correct official language for the *London Gazette*.

'HM feels that as these statements will be handed down more or less as official documents, they should be carefully prepared.' To this

101   *Panmure Papers*, ii, p357
102   PRO, WO32/7302
103   PRO, WO32/7303
104   *ibid*

Gen Davies replied the following day, 'I very much regret that HM has occasion to find fault with the form of submission for the VC. I should be glad, however, if you would take an opportunity of explaining to the King that in the submission made to HM the identical words used in the recommendation are followed, but the draft of the statement to go in the *London Gazette*, which is now before me, is carefully edited before it goes forward. For instance, the word "Hun" has been replaced by "enemy". It was a little difficult to know what to do about the word "pill-box" as that expression has become universal and, so far as I know, there is no other expression which describes it. I note that in the draft for the Gazette the term "pill-box" has been put in inverted commas. I should be glad if you would ascertain whether HM approves of that method of expression'.

Col Wigram closed the correspondence on 8 Nov, expressing the King's pleasure and agreement. [105]

An even more recent case shows at how late a stage the wording of citations could be amended. When 2nd Lt Upham was awarded his VC for his conduct in the defence of Crete in 1941 the published citation stated, as a further point of distinction regarding his exploits, that during the whole time he had been suffering from dysentery. This was, indeed, the wording that had gone before King George VI, but only as the result of a manuscript alteration in the typed text submitted for his approval. In all previous documents regarding Upham's exploits, and in the submission as originally typed, the disability from which he was suffering was described more bluntly as diarrhoea. On medical grounds, of course, the word finally used is obviously preferable as identifying the complaint itself, and not merely its symptom, disabling as this might be. [106]

105   VCR, iii, pp341 and 343
106   PRO, WO32/11643

Chapter 6

Presentation

THE WARRANT instituting the Victoria Cross makes no specific
provision as to who should actually bestow the Crosses on the recipients,
though the implication of Clauses 9 and 10 would seem to be that it
should be the Admiral or General Officer Commanding the force with
which the individual concerned had won it. It is perhaps indicative of
how personally involved the Queen had become that Lord Panmure's
letter of 15 Feb 1857, forwarding the list of recipients for informal
approval, should end, 'your Majesty will no doubt be graciously pleased
to decide in what manner the members [sic] are to be decorated'. [107]
Nor can Victoria's reply from Windsor on 17 Feb have come as any
surprise. 'The Queen would wish to confer the distinction in person on
all those who are ready to receive it, but not till later in the season.' [108]
There the matter was allowed to rest until raised by Panmure in a letter
to HM on 8 Jun 1857 in which he enquired 'as to the time when it will
be agreeable to Your Majesty to decorate with the Victoria Cross those
officers and men on whom it has been bestowed. It will take a few days
to get them together after Your Majesty's pleasure is known'. [109] She
replied from Windsor on 12 Jun that she had consulted with the Duke
of Cambridge and '... come to the conclusion that it will be best to have
a Review in Hyde Park, where she would attend on horseback and give
the Crosses to the recipients before the front. That day might be the
26th inst. Thus most people would see it, and the ceremony would still
remain an entirely military one.' [110]

Thus responsibility for the form of the ceremony and its venue were
almost entirely the Queen's. It is interesting to note that it was she, and
not her ministers, who in this instance consulted Cambridge. As CinC he

107   *Panmure Papers*, ii, p352
108   *ibid*, p355
109   *ibid*, p390
110   *ibid*, p391

was the obvious authority on such questions, but the fact that she consulted him direct suggests that she turned to him as her cousin rather than as her CinC on this occasion.

The Queen had given her decision on 12 Jun and the date nominated was 26th. The inefficiency of the 19th century War Office and Horse Guards has frequently been commented on, but the fact that a Review could be marshalled in exactly a fortnight from the time the date was first stated does seem to reflect some credit on those concerned. Cambridge was sent his instructions by Panmure on 13 Jun in a letter referring to '... Friday the 26th instant at a grand parade of the Troops in Hyde Park. I have the honour to request that Your Royal Highness will make the necessary arrangements for this purpose and that you will summon such Officers and Men of the Royal Artillery, Engineers, Foot Guards and the Line as are now in this country to receive at the Queen's hand the decoration to which their valour has entitled them.

'I have caused a communication to be made to the First Lord of the Admiralty desiring him to have in attendance those Officers and Marines of HM Navy who are entitled to the Order... The Queen has signified her intention of attending the Review on horseback. As it is Her Majesty's desire that as many of Her Loyal Subjects as circumstances permit shall be spectators at this most interesting ceremony I need scarcely suggest to Your Royal Highness that every arrangement should be made by the Quartermaster-General's Department to secure HM's comfort on the one hand and the convenience of the public on the other.' [111]

Meanwhile, the lesser but vital matter of how the Queen was actually to pin the crosses on to the recipients was also receiving attention and on 19 Jun Prince Albert wrote to Panmure, 'The pins attached to the VC, as in the specimen submitted, will answer very well. The Queen has tried them and found them to do so.' [112]

The pressure of events in these last few days is evident. On 17 Jun a further list of recipients was approved by the Board, forwarded by Cambridge to Panmure on 19 Jun, and acknowledged on 23 Jun with the request that those included, and now in this country, be summoned for presentation on 26 Jun. However, this was not all that had to be done. On 22 Jun Mr Pennington informed Sir Henry Storks that 'as it is important that no time should be lost in having Crosses engraved for those named (submitted to HM) I have furnished Mr Hancock with the names and told him to get them done out of hand, in order that they

111   VCR, i, pp30/2
112   *Panmure Papers*, ii, p395

may be ready by Friday.' As a result of further correspondence the list
was published in that night's *London Gazette*.[113] and in this somewhat
breakneck fashion all was made ready for the events of the 26th.

For the events of the day itself, no better account can be quoted
than Victoria's own.

'June 26 1857   Buckingham Palace

A thick, heavy morning. — Full of agitation for the coming great
event of the day, viz: the distribution of "Victoria Cross". — Breakfast
early, & ½ p.9 we went down & mounted our horses, I, in my full
uniform, riding "Sunset". The whole was conducted in full state. Several
interesting circumstances combined to make this day, an important one.
It was, in the 1st place, the solemn inauguration of the new and
honourable order of valour, — also the day of Albert's new title
becoming known & the 1st time *I* had ever ridden on horse-back, at a
great Review in London, the 1st time that our 2 Boys rode at a really
great state Review; the 1st time dear little Leopold appeared in public,
& lastly the 1st time Fritz appeared in public with us, as our future son-
in-law. I rode between him & my beloved Albert. It was a beautiful
sight, & every thing admirably arranged. All the Royal Family, including
little Leopold, followed in carriages. The road all along was kept clear,
& there was no pushing or squeezing. Constant cheering, & noises of
every kind, but the horses went beautifully. George & the Staff met
just within the Quadrangle Entrance of the Palace, & preceded us. The
sight in Hyde Park was very fine, — the tribunes & stands, full of
spectators, the Royal one being in the centre. After riding down the
Line the ceremony of giving medals, began. There were 47 in number,
with blue ribbons for the Navy, & red, for the Army. I remained on
horseback, fastening the medals, or rather crosses, on recipient [sic].
Some, were in plain clothes, — one a Gate Keeper & one a Policeman.
Lord Panmure stood to my left, handing me the medals, & to my right,
Sir C. Wood, whilst the naval men were being decorated, & Sir G.
Weatherall, for the soldiers, each, reading the names out, as the men
came up. This over, the march past began. I never saw finer troops, nor
better marching, excepting the Life Guards, who did not come by well,
in quick time. The heat very great, but I felt it less than I had expected.
I was glad to see Sir Colin Campbell in command, & to give the "Victoria
Cross" to young Lieut: Hewitt who had distinguished himself so much
at Balaklava with the one Lancaster gun, — also to Lieut: Knox, Rifle
Brigade, whom I have before mentioned, as having risen from the ranks,

113   PRO, WO32/7304 for the whole of this episode

having been a Sergt:, in the Scotch Fusiliers, — & to Corporal Coffey, of the 34th:, whom I had seen at Aldershot. — Got back at 12, & stopped for a moment below, with Mama, Aunt Cambridge, Mary, & all the children. It was indeed a most proud, gratifying day.' [114]

It is curious that the Queen gives the number decorated as forty-seven, [which is the number of Army recipients] as the number usually accepted is sixty-two, which comes from the report in *The Times* of 27 Jun 1857. From this source the recipient in police uniform can be identified as George Walters, and Robert Shields as the 'gate keeper' — in fact, a park keeper. It appears from this source also that the Queen's decision to remain mounted for the actual presentation came as a surprise, the arrangement of table and dais evidently having been made for her use dismounted, whereas 'with her charger a little in advance of the suite, with the Prince of Prussia on her right hand and the Prince Consort on her left [the Queen] awarded the crosses from her seat on horseback.' [115] [See Frontispiece]

The uniform worn by Queen Victoria on this occasion is in the reserve collection of the London Museum.

At the same time as recipients in England were being decorated, letters dated 26 Jun 1857 were sent to CinCs of various overseas stations, instructing them to confer the enclosed crosses in as public and befitting a manner as possible on the recipients under their command. Those for Lt Lennox, RE, Pte Alexander, 90th, and Lt-Col Bell, 23rd, were sent to Lt-Gen Ashburnham in Hong Kong; those for Ptes Prosser, 1st, McDermond, 47th, and McCorrie, 57th, went to Lt-Gen Pennefather in Malta; those for Lt-Col Maude and Pte Connors, both of 3rd, and Capt Hamilton and Pte Byrne, both of 68th, to Maj-Gen Butler in Corfu; those for Maj Elton and Pte Beach of 55th to Lt-Gen Fergusson in Gibraltar; that for L/Sgt Smith of 17th was sent to Lt-Gen Eyre in Canada; that for Maj Rowlands of 41st to Maj-Gen Cloete in Barbardos, and that for Sgt-Maj Madden of 41st to Maj-Gen Bell in Jamaica. [116]

Each GOC was instructed to report the proceedings taken for the bestowal of the decorations, a procedure that was to be followed on many subsequent occasions and some such reports are preserved at the PRO. The request seems to have led to some difficulty concerning Lord Clyde, for in Apr 1859 Mr Pennington had to call to the attention of his superiors to the fact that the CinC in India had ignored requests

114   Queen Victoria's Journal, Royal Archives
115   *The Times,* 17 Jun 1856
116   VCR, i, pp44/8

PLATE 1(a) — Henry Pelham, Fifth Duke of Newcastle, Secretary of State for War and Colonies, 1852-1855. *(By permission of the National Portrait Gallery)*

PLATE 1(b) — Fox Maule, Lord Panmure and later Earl of Dalhousie, Secretary of State for War, 1855-1858. *(By permission of the National Portrait Gallery)*

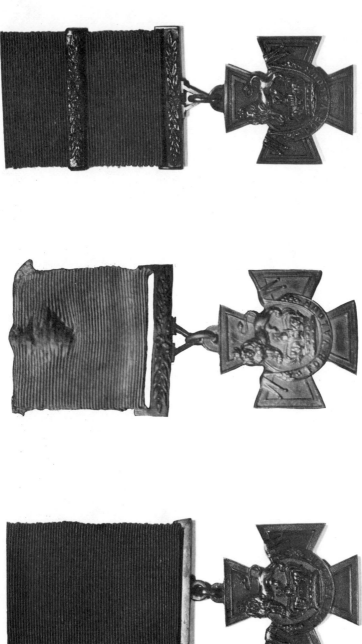

PLATE 2(a) – A forerunner of the final design of the Victoria Cross. From the Royal Collection, Windsor. (*Reproduced by Gracious Permission of Her Majesty The Queen*)

PLATE 2(b) – The original specimen of the Victoria Cross approved by Queen Victoria 3 March 1856. (*By permission of the Curator of the Royal Fusiliers Museum*)

PLATE 2(c) – Specimen Victoria Cross and bar from the Royal Collection, Windsor Castle. (*Reproduced by Gracious Permission of Her Majesty The Queen*)

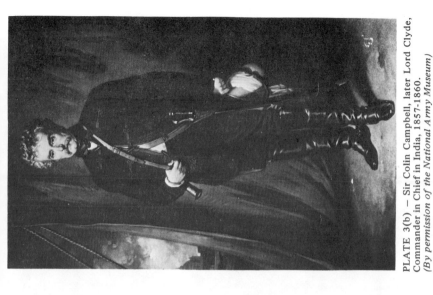

PLATE 3(a) – H.R.H. the Duke of Cambridge,
Commander in Chief of the British Army, 1856-1895.
(By permission of the National Army Museum)

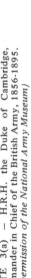

PLATE 3(b) – Sir Colin Campbell, later Lord Clyde,
Commander in Chief in India, 1857-1860.
(By permission of the National Army Museum)

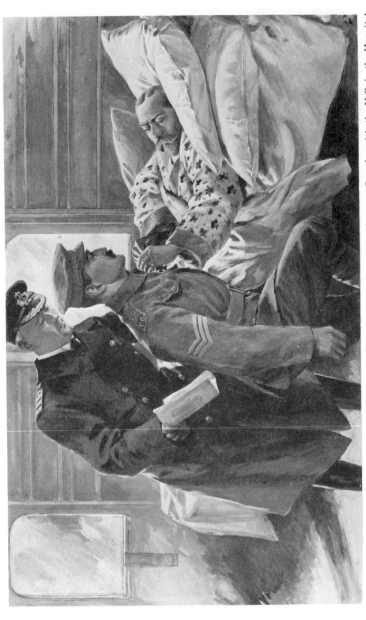

PLATE 4 – H.M.King George V decorating Sergt. Oliver Brooks, 3rd Batt. Coldstream Guards, with the V.C. in the Hospital train at Aire, France, Nov. 1st, 1915.
(Reproduced by Gracious Permission of Her Majesty The Queen)

for reports of the presentation of VCs sent to him for bestowal. A letter was sent to Clyde on 28 Apr and he finally complied on 1 Jul 1859. [117]

He does not seem to have been the only officer deputed to bestow a VC who found the reporting of the proceedings onerous, but Admiral Houston Stewart, when called on to carry out the duty in respect of Able Seaman Hinckley at Devonport in 1863 found a novel way of easing the burden. Instead of forwarding his own report he sent that of the *Western Morning News,* as 'so good an account of the proceedings ... the rain prevented the whole of the programme being carried out.' [118]

It is noted in the VCR for the years 1879/84 that the accounts of the proceedings adopted when VCs were presented by persons other than the Queen were forwarded to Garter King of Arms for his perusal. [119]

A further twelve VCs were presented by the Queen at Portsmouth on 2 Aug 1858,[120] another fifteen at Buckingham Palace on 7 Jun 1859[121] and a further seventeen at a parade of troops in the Home Park, in front of Windsor Castle, held at 9 o'clock on 9 Nov 1860, the Prince of Wales' birthday. [122] Thereafter, no VCs seem to have been presented by the Queen for some fourteen years, all those earned in the interim being presented by the appropriate GOC at home or abroad. This had unfortunate consequences for some who won the VC in India but were home on leave when gazetted, as there was no GOC from whom they could appropriately receive the award, and thus Lts Daunt, Baker and Wood, and Midshipman Mayo all received their VC through the post! Wood's and Daunt's Crosses had originally been sent to the CinC India, but they had already left before these arrived. [123]

A large number of the Indian Mutiny awards of the VC were made provisionally by Lord Clyde as CinC, India, taking very full advantage of Clause 7 which gave GOCs on detached service the right to confer subject to confirmation by the Sovereign. Indeed, although the actual papers do not survive, it seems he asked for a supply of VCs so that he might bestow awards on the spot. Apparently, he twice made such a request, for in Oct 1858 Pennington advised his chief, Sir Edward Lugard, that it would be necessary to take the Queen's pleasure

117   PRO, WO32/7332
118   PRO, WO32/7360
119   VCR, ii *passim*
120   VCR, i, pp117a-c
121   *ibid,* p207a
122   *ibid,* p304
123   *ibid,* pp391/6

regarding any such step and noted that Panmure had not considered it desirable to send out Crosses in this manner. He similarly advised Gen Peel, now SofS for War, that he would be adverse to giving crosses to any CinC for distribution in this way. [124]

Nothing more was heard of this idea, though a certain parallel may be found in the visit of the Prince of Wales [later King George V] to South Africa in 1902, when he took with him a number of unnamed VCs to bestow on such recipients as could conveniently be brought before him in the course of his visit. Three men, Bell, English and Hardham were decorated in this way. In each case a named cross had already been prepared and sent out for the recipient, but they were returned to the WO by the appropriate authorities. [125]

There had been something of a precedent for such duplications in 1881 when a new Cross was prepared for presentation by the Queen in Aug to L/Cpl Farmer, who had returned home whilst the original Cross had been sent to GOC Natal in May. This original was returned and retained by the WO. [126] The same took place in the case of QMS Marshall three years later, the original Cross being sent to Egypt and returned to the WO, a duplicate being prepared for presentation by the Queen in Jul 1884. [127] The unnamed VC which Bell had received was forwarded by him to the WO for naming on 29 Aug [128] that for English was sent by the WO to Hancocks on 11 Sep 1902, [129] but there is no evidence of Hardham's Cross ever having been officially named.

The pattern was thus established of presentation by the Queen or the GOC, rare exceptions being usually to meet the wish of the recipient. One such instance was Capt Ridgeway who wrote that he would be unable to don uniform or travel for another five or six months, as a result of the wounds he had received, and requested his Cross to be sent through the post.[130] Sgt Traynor, whose Cross had been sent to South Africa, requested that it should be sent home since he was suffering from tubercle of the lung and wished to receive it 'Before it was too late'. A special full dress parade was held in York for the presentation on 2 Jul 1902. He was then described as being in very delicate health, but actually survived until October 1954. [131]

124   PRO, WO32/7332
125   VCR, iii, p31
126   VCR, ii, p241
127   ibid, p322
128   VCR, iii, p46
129   ibid, p55
130   PRO, WO32/7395
131   VCR, iii, p41

The CO of the 62nd similarly requested that the Cross won by Sgt Dynon should be sent, since Dynon was seriously ill in hospital, but at Pennington's suggestion it was actually forwarded to the Master of Kilmainham Hospital to make the presentation and here speed was reasonably justified for the Cross was sent on 2 May 1862[132] and Dynon lived only until 16 Feb 1863.[133]

Although the large-scale investitures of the 1850s were not to be repeated by Queen Victoria — and indeed only returned during the First World War — a large number of VCs won during the remainder of her reign were presented by her, often at individual ceremonies, as that of Capt Bell who received a letter from the Queen's Secretary [Sir Henry Ponsonby] to the effect that, 'If Capt Bell will come by the 1.15 train from Paddington (in Uniform) I will send to meet him at the Windsor Station', and the WO papers bear the note over Pennington's initials, 'Presented by HM in the Corridor at Windsor Castle, November 26 [1874].' Clearly the Grand Corridor is referred to here in which the Queen often received her guests after dinner. [134]

Indicative of the Queen's close personal interest is the recommendation of the VC to Lord William Beresford, sent from South Africa to the Horse Guards on 10 Jul 1879. On 22 Aug, Gen Dillon, AMS, wrote to Col Deedes at the WO informing him of the recommendation and of the full concurrence in it of the Duke of Cambridge, the CinC, who was then in Hamburg. A telegram sent the same day to the Duke read, 'Should be glad to receive your recommendation of Lord William Beresford's VC as soon as possible for I wish to confer personally before I go to Scotland which I do on the 26th. — The Queen'. Whether Gen Dillon had already received the Duke's approval before this telegram was sent, or whether he had received a telegram from the Duke as a result of that from the Queen and only then written his letter to Deedes is not clear, but plainly delay was being kept to a minimum. In fact the S of S [Stanley] gave his approval the same day and the recommendation was submitted to the Queen on 23 Aug, being gazetted also that day.

This did not solve all problems, as can be seen from the letter written from Osborne that day, by Sir Henry Ponsonby, the Queen's Private Secretary, to Dillon saying that '... the proverbial difficulty of effecting a satisfactory combined movement is not diminished by the fact of the Queen being here and the Com in Chief at Hamburg. Especially as all is not plain sailing but the VC question is beset with

132　PRO, WO 32/7351
133　Creagh and Humphris, *The VC and DSO,* London [1924], i p77
134　PRO, WO 32/7379. I am indebted to Sir R.C. Mackworth-Young, librarian at Windsor Castle, for elucidation of the significance of the corridor.

difficulties. I am trying to fix Wm. Beresford in London so as to call him here at brief notice. In the mean while, if you will send me the V Cross I shall then have it ready in case he is to be decorated. If not I will not decorate myself with it but will return it to you.' [135]

Although the method of presentation implied by the Warrant was by the GOC, presentation by the Sovereign was frequent and evidently popular, for, on a number of occasions a recipient serving outside Britain [who would clearly have been an appropriate case for bestowal by the local GOC] took occasion to point out that he was about to return home on leave and to express the hope that he might receive his Cross from the Queen. Such was the case with Maj R.B. Adams; in this instance the Cross had already been sent out to India, so instructions were given by the War Office that it should be sent to Adams direct, so that he could bring it with him when he returned to England on leave, and hand it in at the War Office, whence it could be forwarded to the Queen for presentation. [136]

The general policy regarding presentation is made plain in a letter from the Permanent Under-Secretary of the WO [R.Thompson] to the Secretary of the Admiralty in Jun 1884. 'In all cases where decorations have been conferred on officers and men of the Army in recognition of their service before the enemy Her Majesty's wishes are ascertained as to the personal presentation of such decorations to the recipients if they happen to be in this Country.

'Lord Hartington [SofS for War] understands it to be HMs wish that a similar practice should prevail as regards the Naval service but in such cases this Dept has no knowledge of the locality in which a Naval officer or seaman may be serving and Lord Hartington would therefore suggest that when their Lordships have received from this Dept the notification of the grant of a decoration to a Naval officer or Seaman for service before an enemy a semi-official communication should be addressed to HM's Private Secretary, with a view to ascertaining whether HM would wish to present it personally. I am to add that this is the case pursued in Army cases.' [137]

A slight variation from the normal rule took place during the South African War when VCs were presented by Lord Roberts, the CinC then on a tour of inspection. Of the thirteen Crosses Roberts hoped to distribute, seven were presented at a parade in Pretoria on 25 Oct 1900,

135   PRO, WO 32/7382
136   VCR, ii, p395
137   *ibid*, pp325/7

three recipients could not be brought there for the occasion, and three had already returned to England. [138]

The keen interest taken by King George V, coupled with the geographical circumstances of the First World War, resulted in the role of GOCs as presenters of VCs being virtually eliminated. Of the six hundred and twenty six crosses won during that war, more than five hundred were for deeds performed no more than two hundred and fifty miles from London, and with the increasing rapidity of communications it was easy for the King to decorate his troops in the Field or for them to visit London. Presentations frequently took place publicly in the courtyard of Buckingham Palace and there was a large presentation in Hyde Park on the King's birthday, 2 Jun 1917. [139] The reference as to the person responsible for distributing the Cross disappeared from the Warrant when it was redrafted in 1918, and one can now say that it is only presented by the Sovereign or the Sovereign's personal representative, i.e. the Viceroy of India [during the Second World War] or the Governor-General of a Commonwealth country.

The elimination of the presentation role for the GOC led, during the Second World War, to the growth of an additional ceremony, the 'Ribbon Presentation'. This has no sort of official status whatsoever [since anyone can put up the appropriate ribbon, purchaseable from a military tailor, as soon as his reward is gazetted] but by taking the formal presentation of the VC ribbon to the recipient on themselves, the GOCs once more gained a footing in the proceedings. [140]

One rather curious case that arose in these circumstances was that of the Indian, Kamal Ram. He received his Cross, as was customary for Indian troops, from the Viceroy, Lord Wavell, in Delhi on 24 Oct 1944. He had won it in Italy on 12 May of that year; King George VI visited the armies in the field in Italy that July, and had presented Kamal Ram with the ribbon in one of these ceremonies at that time. [141] This is probably a unique case of the minor ceremony being performed by the Sovereign and the major one by his representative.

138 PRO, WO32/7915
139 *The Times History of the War*, passim
140 e.g. F. Gordon Roe, *The Bronze Cross*, London 1945, p101
141 J.G. Smyth, *The Story of the Victoria Cross*, London 1963, p399

Chapter 7

Misconduct

PROVISION FOR the expulsion of members who have in some way disgraced themselves is not unusual in the statutes of an order, and the Duke of Newcastle was no more than following precedent when he made such provision in his draft for the new order which turned into the Victoria Cross. However, when the award changed its form in this way the idea of expulsion remained, despite the fact that it was now much less appropriate. It had, indeed, expanded; under Newcastle's draft, expulsion would only have followed conviction of a serious military offence before a court martial or desertion, whereas under Panmure's Warrant the reference to a court martial was removed, thus making the penalty follow the recipient into civilian life. The only respect in which the original wording was ameliorated was in the removal of the reference to desertion, so that this need not have entailed automatic forfeiture, though whether, as the Warrant now included a reference to 'any infamous crime' of unspecified nature, desertion was held to come within this category, was left open to considerable doubt.

Curiously enough, the first case of disgraceful conduct by a recipient of the VC did not come within the terms of the Warrant. This concerned one of the original Crimea recipients. Panmure's problem in this particular instance was that the private soldier in question, who had committed theft, had been dealt with summarily by his CO so, as he explained in a lengthy letter to Sir Charles Yorke at the Horse Guards on 22 Jun 1857 [142] the man had not been convicted, neither could he now be brought to trial, and without these conditions being fulfilled, the Warrant gave no grounds for witholding the Cross. Yet it was equally repugnant to confer it on a thief, so he suggested that by way of penalty the man should be debarred from receiving the decoration from the Queen's hand. The Duke of Cambridge would have liked to see the Cross go elsewhere or be withheld until the reprobate might have

142   VCR, i, pp34/8

regained his character, but in the view of Sir Henry Storks, the Permanent Secretary, with which Panmure concurred, there was no way in which this could be done,[143] and the Horse Guards were finally informed on 17 Jul that Panmure's suggestion was all that could be undertaken to meet the situation; though it was to be made clear to the recipient why he was not receiving his Cross from the Queen in person.[144]

The first actual case of a warrant of forfeiture arose in 1861, but even here the case was not straightforward as the recipient was a sailor and the immediate cause for forfeiture was his desertion. The Admiralty was, therefore, the prime mover in the case, but all submissions relating to the VC were made by the S of S for War. Did desertion come within Clause 15 of the Warrant to justify the War Office making a submission for forfeiture? It was in these terms that Sir Edward Lugard, successor to Storks at the WO, wrote to the Secretary of the Admiralty on 2 Aug 1861.[145] The Admiralty's reply was to the effect that the man had deserted to evade enquiry into a disgraceful offence [a phrase which the VCR[146] shows to have been drafted almost verbatim into the warrant of erasure] and that, in its view, Clause 15 ('if he be accused of any such offence and doth not after a reasonable time surrender himself to be tried for the same') was applicable. The task of drafting the necessary warrant fell to Mr Pennington, who evidently found it of some difficulty. It will be remembered that a qualification advanced for his employment on work connected with the VC had been previous duties of a similar nature with the Order of the Bath and these apparently stood him in good stead for, in forwarding his draft to Lugard for approval he wrote, 'I have been guided by a similar instrument issued many years ago when the late Sir Eyre Coote was degraded from the Order of the Bath. His case was like the present, a very bad one.' Lugard seems to have found the procedure unnecessarily complicated for his reply to Pennington was, 'I really see no necessity for all this.' But Pennington in his turn finally convinced him that this was as required under the Warrant of institution of the VC.[147]

The actual warrant of forfeiture was signed by Queen Victoria on 4 Sep 1861. It is interesting to note that nowhere in the surviving papers is there any statement as to what accusation the desertion had been

143   PRO, WO32/7313
144   VCR, i, p50
145   *ibid*, pp343/4
146   *ibid*, p350
147   PRO, WO32/7358

undertaken to evade. [148]   Whilst this may be pure chance it seems not impossible that it was deliberate reticence on the part of the 'Silent Service' in order to keep the details of their scandals as far as possible to themselves. It should, however, be noted that a case is recorded of a recipient being convicted of desertion by court martial in 1862, without any question being raised of the expulsion of this recipient.[149]

Expulsion warrants were usually antedated when issued, providing a convenient way of authorising the termination of the VC pension from the actual date of conviction, even though the warrant itself might not be laid before the Queen until some time after. [150]   Another case of desertion provides a curious example of this. Gen Whitmore, MS at the WO, had agreed to the forfeiture of the recipient's annuity [consequent on his desertion in South Africa on 8 May 1881] on 23 Aug,[151] but no further steps in regard to a warrant of erasure were then taken. It was not until 3 Jul following that Whitmore again brought the matter forward, evidently in some perplexity as the recipient did not appear to have been faced with any charge [though in addition to desertion he was liable to a charge of theft, having taken with him his horse, arms and accoutrements on his departure, all of them government property], nor could he be accused of failing to surrender to face any charges, since he was known to have been in touch with the authorities to arrange for his pension to be paid to him in Cape Town.[152] It seems that military discipline was being rather casually enforced in this man's unit, Landrey's Light Horse, but this was not altogether unusual for such locally-raised and largely extemporised units. However, such casualness clearly put the WO in a difficulty when the case of proceeding under Clause 15 of the VC Warrant arose. This was a matter to which Whitmore drew the attention of the CinC South Africa, with which his letter coupled an enquiry as to what steps had been taken to prosecute the man in question.[153] Evidently this galvanised the military authorities in South Africa into action, for on 27 Jul the man was convicted at Kimberley on charges of desertion whilst on active service, and of theft, being sentenced to four months' imprisonment, the rapidity of such action showing how well-known his whereabouts must have been.[154]

148   The probabilities seem to be that it related to drunken behaviour. I am
        indebted to Canon W.M. Lummis for this information.
149   VCR, i, pp400/1
150   See, e.g. VCR, ii, pp298/300
151   *ibid*, p258
152   *ibid*, pp298/300
153   *ibid*, pp301/2
154   *ibid*, pp309/10

There seems to have been some delay in news of this conviction reaching the WO for it was only at the end of Nov 1882 [by which time, incidentally, the man had served his sentence] that steps were finally taken to draw up the warrant of deprivation, this being backdated some twenty months to the actual date of desertion.[155]

It will be noted that the Warrant allows for the restoration to the Register of such individuals as have been expelled. The only occasion on which such action appears to have been attempted is the case of an Irish recipient subsequently convicted of the theft of a cow from his uncle. The case evidently excited local sympathy, for the man's petition for the restoration of his VC was supported by the stipendary magistrate who had committed him for trial, and mitigating circumstances were summarised by a WO official. 'He took the cow in reimbursement of a debt due to him and considered he was merely repaying himself and was not aware of the crime he was committing. He is stated to be "a simple, quiet man and not up to the ways of the world".' On the basis of this report the case was submitted by Pennington to his chief, Lugard, as an appropriate case in which, under the Warrant, the VC might be restored, and Lugard forwarded it to the S of S for War, Lord De Grey, recommending that he should approve the restoration in the circumstances. However, De Grey had also before him a report from the judge who had tried the case, whose views had evidently been sought in the matter. These were very adverse. 'It appears to me,' wrote Mr Justice Hayes, 'that the Board of Superintendance [who had been associated with the petition for restoration] has been misinformed as to a very material fact of the case, viz as to the repayment of the money lent by the prisoner. Upon the evidence given at the trial it appears to me to be a clear case of felony. I see no proper grounds for His Excellency's exercise of the Prerogative of mercy as I do not consider the valour displayed by the prisoner in 1857 any palliative of the felony convicted in 1862.' From this last sentence it is clear that the judge had misunderstood the nature of the petition upon which he had been invited to comment, which did not relate to the pardoning of the offence but only to mitigating one of the consequences. It was, however, decisive for De Grey, and the papers were returned to Lugard with the note, 'See the annexed report of the Judge who tried the case — I cannot sanction the restoration in the face of that document.' [156]

A curious discrepancy in Army Regulations came to light when

155   *ibid*, p307
156   PRO, WO32/7359

another recipient was sentenced by court martial in Feb 1887 to a reduction in rank and forfeiture of medals. Maj-Gen Harman, MS at the WO, thereupon enquired of the Adjutant General the nature of the offence of which the man had been convicted, pointing out that under the VC Warrant the Cross could only be forfeited for certain offences, and that even then special steps would need to be taken, requiring the sanction of Her Majesty, before this could happen. As a result of this enquiry, the AAG pointed out to his chief [at that time Sir Garnet Wolseley] that Article 910 of the Royal Warrant on Pay and Promotions, which laid down the forfeiture of *all* medals and decorations, conflicted with Clause 15 of the VC Warrant, and suggested an amendment to Article 910 which would except the VC from this provision, and have it reserved to be dealt with by a report upon which HMs pleasure might be obtained. Such an amendment was prepared and signed by the Queen at the end of Mar 1887.

Meanwhile, the AAG had given his opinion that the offence, of embezzling money from a comrade, amounted to a felony and a warrant to deprive the culprit of his Cross was prepared. However, it was not well-received on its submission. On 10 April the Queen's Secretary, Ponsonby, wrote to Gen Harman, 'The Queen cannot bring herself to sign this submission. This NCO distinguished himself in South Africa and was conspicuous in his efforts to save Lt Ronald Campbell. For his bravery he was granted the VC. He has now been convicted of embezzlement but apparently of no serious character as his sole punishment is being reduced to the ranks. He is still considered fit to serve the Queen and HM thinks he should retain his VC.' [157]   The Queen may, indeed, have had a point regarding the mildness of sentence, for only three years previously another VC recipient [who had forfeited his decoration in consequence] had been sentenced to twenty-eight days' imprisonment on being court martialled for a somewhat similar offence. [158]   Nor was this all, for a few days later Harman informed Wolseley that the Queen considered it advisable that the man's campaign medals should also be returned to him 'as it would be inconsistent to see a soldier wearing a VC and no War Medals.' [159]   This was, no doubt, a kindly thought by the Queen [though it made the amendment she had signed to the Warrant on Pay and Promotion only three weeks previously a completely dead letter] but it was founded on a misconception, as there were at the time a number of recipients who

157   PRO, WO32/7411
158   VCR, ii, pp334/7
159   PRO, WO32/7411

had won their Crosses in campaigns for which no service medal had been awarded, notably the Boer War of 1881, so that it was by no means impossible to see the VC worn without accompanying war medals.

A point not so far discussed is whether erasure of a recipient's name from the Register entailed surrender of the actual Cross itself. Certainly this was the view originally taken and in almost every case of a man's name being expunged from the VCR there is record of a letter being sent to the appropriate authority [usually governor of the prison where the man was detained] directing him to obtain the VC from the individual and return it to the WO. There is no such record in the case of the naval deserter, but this is almost certainly because his whereabouts were unknown.

In one case, indeed, the VC was not in the recipient's possession, having been pawned by him, but the WO was equal to such a situation. A letter went from the Assistant Under Secretary to the Under Secretary at the Home Office pointing out that '... the Marquess of Lansdowne would desire that the pawnbroker should be asked to surrender the Cross on payment of the amount (8/-) lent upon it, which sum will be repaid to the Metropolitan Police by this Department.' [160]

There was also the curious history of the VC of Frederick Corbett, won by him in 1882 whilst serving in the King's Royal Rifle Corps, sold by him after his discharge [so that he was not at that time subject to the Army Act, under which both vendor and purchaser would have committed an offence] and forfeited by him in 1884 in consequence of conviction for felony by court martial following his re-enlistment in the Royal Artillery.[161] This Cross had, apparently, come in 1903 into the possession of a Mr Mansfield, Clerk of Kingsbury Urban District Council, who approached the WO apparently with a view to restoring it to the recipient or his family. He was, however, informed that '... as the name of Frederick Corbett was erased from the VCR... the cross should not be delivered to him or his representatives.' [162] This reply seems to have worried Mr Mansfield as to whether he was in order in retaining the decoration himself, but a further letter from the WO confirmed that, in view of Corbett's having sold his Cross at a time when he was not subject to the Army Act, Mr Mansfield was entitled to retain it.[163]

In what was to be the last instance of forfeiture of a VC, in 1908, the recipient, George Ravenhill, had been discharged from prison before

160   VCR, ii, p377
161   VCR, iii, p79
162   *ibid,* p67
163   *ibid,* p79

particulars of his conviction were received at the WO and no action was taken at that time to secure the return of the cross. It was, in fact, the advertisement that the man's Cross and medals were to be auctioned at Sotheby's that caused the matter to be looked into though, as the AMS wrote to his chief, 'I can see nothing in the warrant to prevent the man from selling the actual decoration of the VC, but I am not prepared to state definitely that this is the case.' On such a nice point of law the only course open to the WO was to obtain the ruling of the Treasury Solicitor. This was sought on 8 Dec and obtained the following day [the sale was due to take place on 14 Dec]. It was as follows: 'There is no provision for the forfeiture of this decoration which therefore remains the property of the man, or of any purchaser from him. I do not therefore think you can stop the sale. Possibly you might think it proper to inform the auctioneers of the facts of the case; it really is not a genuine VC now.' Apparently the AMS had always been very doubtful whether powers existed under the Warrant by which a holder of the VC could be deprived of the actual decoration, and this view the Treasury Solicitor had now confirmed. He therefore now brought forward the question of giving back the Cross taken from Gunner Collis thirteen years previously but the decision of the MS was that it was unnecessary to take any steps unless or until Collis applied for it. [164]

The first signs of a softening in attitude towards holders of the VC who committed offences may be detected in the views of the Treasury Solicitor and AMS in 1908. Clearly, had any further case of misconduct arisen, even had the recipient suffered the penalty of having his name expunged from the VCR, he would still have been left in physical possession of his Cross. But a further very powerful influence in this direction was to arrive on the scene in the person of King George V. His views were expressed very forcibly in a letter written by his PS, Lord Stamfordham, on 26 Jul 1920. 'The King feels so strongly that, no matter the crime committed by anyone on whom the VC has been conferred, the decoration should not be forfeited. Even were a VC to be sentenced to be hanged for murder, he should be allowed to wear the VC on the scaffold.'[165]

Evidently the Army Council took their cue, for on 24 Nov 1921 a letter was sent from Buckingham Palace concerning their decision in the case of a recipient convicted of common assault. 'The King... while regretting that a man with such a fine war record should have been

164   *ibid,* insert between pp2 and 3
165   *Soldier,* Jan 1956, p13 cites the letter as contained in the VCR. It cannot now be traced there.

convicted of such a horrible crime, is glad that the Army Council do not propose to recommend a submission for the forfeiture of the VC. His Majesty desires me to thank you for keeping him informed of such cases, in which he is always much interested.' [166]

Had matters brought such considerations to the attention of the King a couple of years earlier it seems probable that the expulsion clause might have been reconsidered when the Warrant was under review by the interdepartmental committee which produced the recast Warrant of 1920, but this was not one of the matters to which their attention was directed and the original Clause 15 was reproduced almost verbatim as Clause 12 of the new Warrant, the only alterations being one to improve the grammar, an addition to make all expulsions and restitutions publishable in the *London Gazette*, and the necessary verbal alterations to make women [who were now made eligible for the VC for the first time] equally liable to expulsion. However, the Army Council now acted in the spirit of the King's wishes, regardless of the actual provisions of the Warrant, and no action was taken to deprive of their Crosses any of the several holders who were convicted of various offences in the 1920s. Indeed, in one case, had the old rule been followed, the authorities might have found themselves in a sad dilemma as, the charge being one of murder, the verdict of the jury was 'not guilty due to insanity', the case having been tried in a Dominion which had not followed Britain in changing the form of the finding to 'guilty but insane'. [167] Nor was any action taken in the case of another recipient who was discharged from the Army on account of bad character, and his letter to the WO seeking to 'resign the VC' was not answered. [168]

It was in this climate of opinion that an interdepartmental committee met in the late 1920s to consider the question of forfeiture and restitution of decorations and medals, and it is not surprising, therefore, that their recommendation was that all gallantry awards should now be regarded as irrevocable. Part of the report reads, 'Very exceptional cases of extreme infamy may, however, arise in which it may clearly be undesirable that a gallantry award should be retained, and such cases should be dealt with by recommending approval of forfeiture to His Majesty... It is thought that the cases in which HMs prerogative shall be liable to be sought should be specified and limited to the following offences which, though not referred to in detail in the gallantry

166   VCR, iii, p346
167   *ibid*, p269
168   *ibid*, p318

Warrants, should be established as a standing guide in dealing with cases which may come forward for consideration: (i) Treason (ii) Sedition (iii) Mutiny (iv) Cowardice (v) Desertion during hostilities (vi) Disgraceful conduct of an unnatural kind (in the Army or Air Force under the Army or Air Force Act, Section 18(5)).[169]

This recommendation ran counter to the existing wording of Clause 12 of the 1920 Warrant, which reproduced the 1856 reference to 'Treason, Cowardice, Felony, or of any infamous Crime', and discussions with regard to a revised warrant started in the WO in Jan 1927. The matter seems then to have lapsed for two years. A point upon which clarification was sought by the secretary of the Interdepartmental Committee was the extent to which those no longer serving should be liable to forfeiture, and the reply was given that this could only be in the case of treason and sedition; the remainder would only apply to those serving, and there had been no intention that there should be any liability to forfeiture for analogous offences in civil life. A draft of the new warrant in its final form was prepared on 12 Aug 1929; in this the forfeiture Clause, now numbered 13, was made to read, 'It is ordained that it shall be competent for Us, Our Heirs and Successors, by an Order under Our Sign Manual and on the recommendation to that effect by or through Our First Lord of the Admiralty or one of Our Principal Secretaries of State to cancel and annul the award of the Victoria Cross to any person together with any pension appertaining thereto not already paid, and that thereupon his or her name in the Register shall be erased; but that it shall be competent for Us, Our Heirs or Successors, to restore the Decoration when such recommendation has been withdrawn and with it such pension as may have been forfeited.' And this was the form in which it appeared in the new warrant signed by King George V on 5 Feb 1931.[170]

The Victoria Cross has been forfeited by eight recipients. The offences of which they were guilty can be specified as follows:-

Desertion in order to evade investigation of a disgraceful offence.[171]

Theft of a cow.[172] — Theft of a comrade's medals.[173] — Theft of ten bushels of oats.[174] — Desertion on active service, with theft of a

---

169   PRO, WO32/3442
170   *ibid*
171   VCR, i, p350
172   PRO, WO 32/7359
173   VCR, i, pp466/71
174   VCR, ii, p135

horse, arms and accoutrements.[175] — Theft and embezzlement from an officer.[176] — Bigamy.[177] — Theft of iron.[178]

A number of cases are recorded during the period between George V's strongly expressed disapproval of forfeiture of the VC by offending recipients, and the rewording of the warrant to comply with the recommendations of the Interdepartmental Committee on this subject. The crimes committed were:-

Possession of illicit spirit.[179] — Common assault.[180] — Theft of a postal packet.[181] — Shopbreaking.[182] — Forgery.[183]

There were also the cases already referred to of the holder found not guilty to a charge of murder on the grounds of insanity and of the recipient discharged from the Regular Army on the grounds of bad character. In none of these instances was any action taken to expunge the offender's name from the Register. Comparing these offences with those that did result in expulsion it is very difficult to see how the latter can be held the more heinous, and this plainly illustrates how thinking in this respect has changed. So far as the eight men in question are concerned time has practically annulled their expulsion, since virtually all lists of VC recipients (even including one prepared by the WO itself in 1953) do include the names of these eight, even though the subsequent forfeiture may also be indicated.

The reader will have noted the anonymity in which this chapter is shrouded. This has been done at the express request of the Ministry of Defence, on the very reasonable grounds that there could be descendants of the individuals concerned who might be pained by identifiable disclosure of these matters.

175   *ibid*, p298
176   *ibid*, p335
177   *ibid*, p370
178   VCR, iii, p179
179   *ibid*, p244
180   *ibid*, p264
181   *ibid*, p288
182   *ibid*, p309
183   *ibid*, p19

Chapter 8

Posthumous Awards

A QUESTION to which the Warrant of 1856 gave no explicit answer was whether the VC might be awarded to a deceased person. The issue quickly arose when Mr John Godfrey wrote to the War Office in Apr 1856 seeking the grant of a decoration to his late son. Pennington referred the matter to Lord Panmure for a ruling and was instructed on 2 May to 'Inform Mr G. that in this Order, as in the Bath, the friends of deceased officers cannot have any claim for it as in the case of medals. It is an *order* for the living.' Following the logic of this argument an unidentified official at the WO added the comment, 'The decoration should properly be returned after the decease of the wearer but it will be difficult to enforce this', and nothing more was heard of this idea [184] though, equally, nothing was placed on record in the contrary sense until Mar 1868 when Sir Edward Lugard stated in a letter to the OC, British Honduras, that the Secretary of State approved of the retention by the widow of L/Cpl Samuel Hodge of 4th West India Regt of the VC which belonged to the deceased soldier. [185]

Four years later any idea of recall was evidently completely dead, for in Dec 1872 Sir Henry Storks informed the CO of the 8th Hussars that, in the case of Pte Joseph Ward, VC, who had died without making a will and with no next of kin, there was no objection to the regiment retaining his Cross. [186]

The official reply to Mr Godfrey on 13 Mar 1856 set out Panmure's brief ruling in greater detail. '... this decoration will not be conferred upon the families of deceased officers... it is more in the nature of an order like that of the Bath than of a Medal in commemoration of a campaign or an expedition. In the case of the Crimean Medal, Her Majesty was pleased specifically to command that the medals of those

184   PRO, WO 32/7300
185   VCR, ii, p119
186   *ibid*, p148

PLATE 5 — Record of votes cast to select recipients of the Victoria Cross under Rule 13 of the 1856 Warrant by the 4th Royal Marine Bn for the Zeebrugge Raid 23 April 1918.
(By permission of the Commandant General, Royal Marines)

PLATE 6 — King George V presenting the Victoria Cross to the Revd T. B. Hardy at a field investiture in France, 1918.
(By permission of the Imperial War Museum)

PLATE 7 — Bronze ingot which supplies all the metal used for the casting of Victoria Crosses. Now held at the Central Ordnance Depot, Donnington, this was formerly stored at Woowich Arsenal.
(By permission of the Central Ordnance Depot, Donnington)

PLATE 8(b) – Sir Redvers Buller VC, Quarter Master-General to the Forces 1887-1890, Adjutant-General to the Forces 1890-1897, Commander in Chief in South

PLATE 8(a) – Field Marshal Lord Roberts VC, Field Commander in Afghanistan 1879-1880, Commander in Chief South Africa 1899-1901. Commander

who died should be given to their representatives but it is by survivors only that claims to the VC will be able to be established.' [187]

Thus was laid down the rule that was to govern the situation for the next forty-six years. It did not settle another matter, of the fate of VCs whose recipients had died after the award was gazetted but before receipt of it. This also was a matter upon which a decision had soon to be taken, and on 21 Mar 1857 a letter from the WO to Mrs Elizabeth Taylor read, '... Lord Panmure... has given directions that the VC to which you are entitled as the nearest representative of the late John Taylor be sent to you through the Board of Admiralty as part of his effects, after HM shall have delivered the Cross to those whose names have been already published as deserving of it.' [188]

Mrs Taylor was apparently a women who kept her ears open and must have enquired whether she should attend the Hyde Park parade to receive her husband's Cross, for a further letter from the WO on 25 Jun 1857 reiterated that the Cross would be sent, and that it would not be necessary for her to attend the following day's parade. [189] The Cross was forwarded to the Admiralty for transmission to Mrs Taylor on 8 Jul. [190]

Similar cases on record relate to John Alexander, the Cross being forwarded to his widow on 16 Aug 1858;[191] John Purcell, forwarded to the CO, 9th Lancers on 28 Feb 1859 to be received by his brother James;[192] James R. Roberts, sent to his brother on 21 Sep 1859;[193] Robert Newell, forwarded to CinC East Indies for delivery to his widow, on the application of Assistant Apothecary D.E. Young of the Indian Medical Establishment, whose wife she had become;[194] George B. Chicken, sent to his father, a master mariner of Shadwell on 4 Mar 1862;[195] John Ryan, forwarded to his mother in Ireland;[196] and David Hawkes, sent to his father on 10 Feb 1859.[197]

The Newell and Hawkes cases just mentioned were, although the

187   VCR, i, pp11/12
188   *ibid,* p23
189   *ibid,* pp39/40
190   *ibid,* pp48/9
191   *ibid,* p123
192   *ibid,* p184
193   *ibid,* pp216/7
194   *ibid,* pp357/8
195   *ibid,* pp365/6
196   VCR, ii, pp31/2
197   VCR, i, pp178/9

citations did not reveal it, examples of a slightly different set of circumstances, of which the better known examples are Salkeld, Bankes and
Home. Many of the VCs in the Indian Mutiny were conferred under the
second proviso of the seventh Clause of the 1856 Warrant which gave the
GOC the power to do this, subject to confirmation by the Queen. In all
of these five cases the VC had been so conferred, but in each instance the
recipient had died before the Queen's confirmation. Such awards were
not withheld under Panmure's ruling. Lugard, for the WO, explained to
the MS at the Horse Guards on 17 Jan 1861 that, 'in cases in which the
Cross has been provisionally conferred at the time, but the officer or
soldier has died prior to the confirmation of the grant by HM, the Cross
has, by HM's command, been forwarded to the legal representative, or
nearest relative, with the expression of the satisfaction which it would
have afforded HM to confirm the grant, had such Officer or Soldier
survived'.[198] The text of such letters to Maj-Gen Home and the Revd
Robert Salkeld on 7 Jul 1858,[199] Mrs Bankes on 30 Dec 1858,[200]
and William Hawkes on 10 Feb 1859[201] are all entered in the VCR;
Mrs Newell does not seem to have received any such letter, though a
communication from the WO to the India Office in Feb 1860 [which
gives Newell's date of death as 11 Jul 1858] provides the information
that she was entitled to receive her husband's VC annuity from the date
upon which his Cross had been provisionally conferred [19 Mar 1858]
until his death. [202]

The first cases of confirmation after the recipient's decease were
those of Home and Salkeld, included in a list of thirty-one recommendations submitted by the Governor-General of India to India House and
forwarded thence to the WO in May 1858. As Pennington pointed out to
Storks on 6 May, twenty-four of these had been provisionally conferred
by the various GOCs and the confirmation for these had already been
given in nine cases — some indication of the complication which arose
in India due to the division of responsibility between the British
Government, responsible for its own forces in India, and those alongside
which they were fighting, for which the East India Company was the
administrative power.

As was to be expected, Pennington made particular note that two of
the remaining fifteen were already dead but that confirmation of their

198   *ibid*, p320
199   *ibid*, pp107/8
200   *ibid*, pp155/6
201   *ibid*, pp178/9
202   *ibid*, pp255/6

awards was nonetheless being sought. As the first instances of this nature to have arisen, he drew attention to the analogous position in the case of the Order of the Bath, where a memorandum would have been published stating that the officer would have received the distinction had he survived. He suggested, therefore, that the Duke of Cambridge's attention should be drawn to this point and his opinion sought. On 26 May the Duke replied personally to say that he entirely concurred with such a memorandum being published in the cases of Home and Salkeld [203] though when the citations were actually published in the *London Gazette* the memorandum formula was not used. Instead, the citations began with a parenthesis referring to the provisional award and ended with the sentence, 'Would have been recommended to Her Majesty for confirmation of that high distinction had they survived.'

However, a few months later the procedure of substituting a memorandum for a citation was followed in the case of a recipient who had died before a provisional award could be confirmed. Pennington noted on 1 Dec 1858, 'There is only one case (in the present list of provisional awards for confirmation) to which it is necessary to call attention — that of Cornet Bankes, 7th Hussars. This officer died on 6 Apr last, and the General Order is dated 9 Sep. It must be presumed that the Cross was confirmed on the spot at the time before Bankes' death and that the fact was not notified to the Army until some months afterwards, but this should have been distinctly stated as in the similar cases of Lts Home and Salkeld. Lord Clyde would scarcely have included the name in the General Order if this had not been the case... In Bankes' case the Cross would be sent to the deceased officer's next of kin, as in the cases just referred to.' [204]

As has already been indicated, what appeared in the *London Gazette* of 28 Dec 1858 was a memorandum to the effect that this officer's name would have been submitted to HM for confirmation of the provisional award had he survived. It has often been thought that the appearance of such a memorandum meant that the actual award of the Cross itself was withheld but, in this instance at least, such was not the case; Pennington plainly expected it to be sent to the next of kin and evidence has already been quoted of this being done.

Curiously enough, there was another example in this same list of names to which Pennington might have wished to call attention, that of David Hawkes, who had died on the preceding 14 Aug [205] though

203   PRO, WO32/7317
204   PRO, WO32/7318
205   *The VC and DSO*, i, p52

the fact that, whereas Bankes' Cross was forwarded to his father on the day after the Gazette appeared, Hawkes' Cross was not similarly forwarded until 10 Feb, may indicate that the fact of Hawkes' death did not become known at the WO until after the *Gazette* had appeared. Obviously, no such letter could have been written until the circumstance became known, but it seems reasonable to assume that no time would have been lost [as in the Bankes' case] once it was found to be required.

There remained two other cases relating to the Indian Mutiny where a memorandum was used, on account of the recipient having died before his name could be submitted to the Queen, namely David Spence[206] and Everard Phillipps.[207] In neither case are the circumstances discussed in great detail in the WO papers, but it is fairly clear that there was one vital difference putting these awards into a distinct category. Had they been recommendations to the Queen to confirm a provisional award by a GOC, the memorandum would have stated this and the Crosses would have gone to the next of kin. But they were not; in these cases alone of those of deceased Mutiny recipients, there had been no provisional award, the Queen was being requested to make the grant of the Cross *ab initio*, which Panmure's ruling had put out of court, so that in these two instances there was no Cross sent to the family.

It is fairly clear that the main factor in the somewhat confused situation regarding men who had died before a VC could be conferred arose from two which were peculiar to the Indian Mutiny; long delays in the transmission of news from India to London, and the independence exercised by GOCs in the field. The first factor was one which time, and scientific advances in the methods of communication, was bound to diminish; this in itself was likely to affect the second, but the fact remains that the system by which the VC was awarded was only beginning to evolve. Obviously new factors would arise with experience of dealing with recommendations during campaigns in progress. Those in respect of the Crimea had been awarded after the war, with the benefit of retrospect, and the Mutiny raised new problems. As already noted, Clyde had suggested that a supply of VCs be sent to him so that he could both confer the decoration verbally and pin on the insignia. This suggestion did not, it will be recalled, find favour with the WO — indeed, had it been adopted it is obvious that the Queen's control over her decoration would have been almost completely eliminated — and it may well be that the whole conception of provisional conferment of the VC by a GOC came to be looked at askance as a result of the experience of the Indian Mutiny. Certainly it is a fact that the powers to this effect contained in Clause 7 of the 1856 Warrant were never exercised again.

206   PRO, WO32/7337
207   PRO, WO32/7333

In cases where the person recommended had died before recommendation could be confirmed, the only circumstance open was a
memorandum to the effect that the person would have been
recommended for conferment had he survived, and no VC would go to
the relatives, as in the cases of Spence and Phillipps. Gen Harman, MS
at the WO explained to the Financial Secretary on 15 Nov 1888,
'Ensign Phillipps would have been *recommended* for the VC *had he
survived*, but he was not recommended prior to his decease and, ...there
are only precedents for the issue of the Cross to the relatives of
persons upon whom it had been provisionally conferred, who had been
recommended for it whilst alive.'[208]

This, then, was the doctrine which was to prevail until the end of the
19th century. Nor was even the use of the memorandum entirely liked
at the WO, as is shown in the case of the assault of the Inhlobane
Mountain in Zululand in 1879. Sir Evelyn Wood recommended awards
of the VC to Lt Lysons and Pte Fowler which they received; he also
asked for a memorandum stating that a similar recommendation would
have been made in respect of Capt Ronald Campbell had he survived.
The WO file, however, contains a pencilled note, 'Gen W. [presumably
Wolseley, at that time AG] does not wish this question raised.'[209]
Nothing came of it.

The first instances of the memorandum procedure used after the
Mutiny were in respect of Lts Coghill and Melvill for gallantry at
Isandlhwana in 1879. No recommendation was submitted from the
commander in the field; though Col Glyn's dispatch praised their
conduct in unstinted terms he forebore from suggesting how it might be
honoured and it was left to Cambridge himself to suggest to the S of S
for War that the terms of the dispatch merited the issue of memoranda
to the effect that they would have been recommended to the Queen for
the award of the VC had they survived. [210]

At much the same time there occurred an interesting example of
what might be described as a bending of the regulations to meet
another case of decease between the submission of a recommendation
and its approval. On 15 May 1879 the Government in India forwarded
to the India Office a recommendation for the award of the VC to
Lt Walter Hamilton for his conduct at Futtehabad on 2 Apr, during the
Afghan War. The papers were forwarded by the India Office to the
Horse Guards on 22 Jul, but on 28th Gen Horsford, the MS, wrote to
the PUS at the WO saying Cambridge proposed that the India Office be

208   VCR, ii, pp339/40
209   PRO, WO32/7834
210   PRO, WO32/7390

informed that Hamilton's act did not come within the regulations of the VC and this was approved by the S of S [Stanley] on 6 Aug. The decision was received with regret at the India Office and Lord Cranbrook [S of S for India, whom Stanley had succeeded at the WO only some eighteen months previously] pointed out that the Governor General in Council and the CinC India believed the case of Hamilton very similar to those of Capt John Cook and Lt Reginald Hart who had both been awarded the VC within the previous six months. This appears to have had its effect on Cambridge for on 16 Sep Gen Dillon wrote to the PUS to say that, though the case might be open to exception, it had been recommended and His Royal Highness trusted that the S of S would concur in reconsidering the matter, though Hamilton had now fallen in the defence of the residency at Cabul. To this, Stanley's reply on 19 Sep was, 'If CinC has reason to change his view I have no objection to urge.' The point of particular interest in the present context is the note which was put before Stanley, accompanying the submission to be laid before the Queen. It reads, 'This [i.e. the submission to the Queen] has been dated 1 Sep, two days before Lt Hamilton's death, so as to avoid creating an awkward precedent in giving the decoration after death.' On which Stanley's comment, dated 28 Sep, was, 'Very well.'

The award was gazetted on 7 Oct, bearing the date of 1 Sep, and the Cross forwarded to Hamilton's father with the usual expression of the Queen's regrets on 25 Oct 1879. [211]

No further memoranda cases were to occur until 1897 when Tpr Baxter's conduct in Rhodesia and Lt MacLean's on the NW Frontier came up for consideration. In each case the exploits were closely linked with those of others who survived to receive the VC. Baxter gave up his horse to. allow a colleague to escape the pursuing Matabele, whereas Tpr Henderson, recommended at the same time, aided a similar escape by taking a comrade on to his horse. [212]   MacLean was mortally wounded whilst, with Viscount Fincastle and Lt-Col Adams, bringing a disabled colleague under cover. [213]   There was, therefore, no WO difficulty in agreeing these as memorandum cases, but public reaction indicated that the state of affairs was not regarded as satisfactory, Gen Laurie, MP for Pembroke, asking whether it could be recommended to HM that the VC should be forwarded to the relatives of the late Tpr Baxter. As his parliamentary question was put down for answer on

211   PRO, WO32/7384
212   PRO, WO32/7419
213   PRO, WO32/7421

21 May 1897, and the memorandum had been published only on 7 May, he had obviously wasted no time. The first WO reaction was that 'The VC cannot be forwarded to the relatives of a soldier unless he has been recommended for it or it had been provisionally conferred upon him *whilst alive*.' Gen Grove, the MS, forwarding this view to the PUS on 15 May commented, 'The above represents the established rule, but I do not know on what grounds it was arrived at; or why in the case of a man who dies the day after the recommendation, the VC should be sent to his relatives, while in that of one who dies the day before the recommendation would have been made, it should not. At the same time, under the Statutes, we cannot recommend a dead man and a man cannot get the VC unless he is recommended, so technically we cannot send to his relatives that which he could not get. It is perhaps best to stick to the rule.'

Two days later the PUS was asked for instruction as to the reply to be drafted, and the following day the Parliamentary Secretary, Brodrick, and another whose initials 'A.L.H.' are unidentified, put their view to the S of S, Lord Lansdowne; 'This is a case where one might decide either way were there no precedents to restrain one's decision. You will see from the enclosed copies of letters that we have always refused such requests. The first refusal was in 1859, within three years of the creation of the order. It might give rise to much inconvenience if we were now to reverse such decisions.'

In view of the unanimity of this advice it is hardly surprising that Lansdowne's direction was to refuse. The answer actually given to Laurie was of '... sympathy [with] his wish to commemorate the noble deed of Tpr Baxter but unfortunately the Statutes of the VC do not contain any provision under which a man who is already dead can be recommended for this distinction. Many cases have occurred in which the VC would have been awarded had the soldier or sailor survived but no exception to the rule I have stated has ever been made.' [214] From the evidence which survives it seems that the word 'many' may have been something of an exaggeration, though there is no certainty that papers have been retained in all instances where recommendations were unsuccessful. On the other hand, it may simply have been based on the not unlikely supposition that there were many cases of heroism which had not been reported to the WO since the CO knew it was useless to bring forward the conduct of a man who had not survived his exploit.

There had certainly been something of this nature in the Indian Mutiny where Pte Patrick Cavanagh was the first man to reach a wall

214   VCR, ii, pp384/5

held by the enemy at the battle of Busserutgunge. Havelock described him in a dispatch as 'being hacked to pieces while setting a brilliant example to his comrades', and adding, 'had he survived he should have won the VC which could never have glittered on a braver breast', [215] yet submitted no formal recommendation to this effect.

The case of Lt MacLean, gazetted in Nov 1897, brought an even weightier intervention; an enquiry from Sir Henry Campbell-Bannerman [who had been S of S for War in the preceding Liberal government and was to be the next Liberal Prime Minister], suggesting that the rule refusing the Cross to the relatives of the deceased should be altered. Gen Grove was suitably impressed by the source of the enquiry. In putting it before the PUS he wrote, on 12 Feb 1898, 'The rule as to the non-bestowal of the VC when a man has not been recommended when alive has been discussed so often that I do not enter upon it here. The facts and cases are well known. The last time the question was considered was in May of last year at the instance of Gen Dyson [J.W.] Laurie and the old rule was adhered to. The only reason I submit the case now is because, as a late S of S for War asked that the rule may be reconsidered, I think his request should come before the S of S.' Sir Ralph Knox, the PUS, in forwarding the papers to Lansdowne, commented, 'In no case has the Cross or any decoration been given to anyone who had not been recommended to the Queen before his death [this chapter has shown that statement as by no means correct]. It would be very inconvenient to depart from this course, and I fear it would lead us much further than the grant of a decoration.' Lansdowne's ruling, given on 28 Feb, was, not surprisingly, 'We must adhere', and Grove wrote privately to Campbell-Bannerman two days later to tell him that the matter had been so decided. [216]

There was a pathetic sequel to these events when MacLean's mother enquired of the WO a few weeks later whether she might have a brooch made in the shape of the VC, only half the size and in gold. Neither the CinC nor the S of S saw any objection to this so long as the ornament was made in a different material and in such a form that it could not be mistaken for the VC itself. [217]

With the outbreak of the South African War, cases soon arose to test the rules relating to the award of the VC to the dead. Indeed, the first list of VCs conferred for that war contained the name of one 'since deceased' recipient, Lt F.H.S. Roberts, only son of the CinC South

215   I am indebted to Canon W.M. Lummis for this quotation from Havelock's dispatch.
216   VCR, ii, p392
217   *ibid*

Africa, Lord Roberts. As no official papers appear to survive regarding this award it is impossible to say whether the case received any treatment not strictly in accord with the existing rules though one can understand why, in view of who his father was, the WO might have desired to stretch a point in this instance. It was certainly at Queen Victoria's request that his Cross was forwarded to her for personal presentation to Lord Roberts, instead of being sent by letter as had been done in all similar cases.[218] In any event, as Lt Roberts did not die until two days after his act of gallantry at the battle of Colenso, the criterion for an actual award instead of a memorandum, that the man should have been alive at the time he was recommended, could conceivably have been met.

Certainly, the other cases which arose during the next eighteen months were all treated exactly in accordance with the precedent. In forwarding recommendations in respect of Capt Gordon [who had survived] and Capt Younger [who had not], Gen Smith Dorrien commented that Younger would have richly deserved the VC and would have been recommended had he survived. These recommendations were strongly supported to the WO by Lord Roberts, but drew the comment from the MS's Department, 'all that can be done in his [Younger's] case is a notification in the *London Gazette* that the VC would have been conferred on him had he survived'. The papers were simply endorsed by the CinC, Lord Wolseley, to proceed in both cases and the usual memorandum was gazetted in respect of Capt Younger on 28 Sep 1900. [219]

Exactly the same occurred in the cases of Lt Digby-Jones and Tpr Albrecht on 18 Apr 1901. That there could be no possible doubt about the WO thinking in such matters is shown by the reply given on 16 May 1901 to an enquiry as to whether Digby-Jones might be styled 'VC' on a memorial to be erected to him. The reply given was, 'It would not be in order to put VC after the name of the late Lt Digby-Jones, RE, on a memorial tablet as the decoration was not conferred upon that officer, though he would have been recommended for it had he survived'. [220]

The punctiliousness of the WO in enforcing these rules, and also the logical tangles into which they might lead, are well illustrated by the case of another deceased officer, Lt F.N. Parsons. His conduct was brought to the notice of the CinC on 28 Mar 1900 in respect of the battle of Paardeburg on 18 Feb, but he had been killed on 10 Mar.

218   VCR, iii, p2
219   PRO, WO32/7301
220   VCR, iii, p25

Lord Roberts wrote to the WO on 12 Apr that he 'would have hesitated to recommend the award of the VC for the action had not the conduct of this officer been again brought to my notice for conspicuous gallantry at the engagement at Driefontein on 10 Mar, when I regret to say he was mortally wounded. Though this gallant young officer has not lived to receive it, I would recommend the grant of the decoration which would be much appreciated by his regiment and be some consolation to his relatives'.

The MS's department at the WO made the usual point that the Cross could not be issued unless it had been recommended or provisionally conferred before the man's death, so apparently nothing could be done except a memorandum, and Wolseley did not recommend the case as Parsons was dead before he had been recommended; as he pointed out, on Roberts' own statement the recommendation that Parsons had received while he was alive had not been thought sufficient to merit the award. This view was accepted by the S of S and the matter then dropped. [221]

For some unexplained reason, however, this was *not* the end of the matter for, four months later, Roberts was asked if he recommended the grant of the VC on the basis of the earlier recommendation, and what had been the date of this. Roberts' reply, which is not wholly consistent with what he had written to the WO on 12 Apr, was that the recommendation he had received in respect of Parsons' conduct at Paardeburg had been dated 3 Mar, and that he would have forwarded it with his supporting recommendation had he then been able to deal with it, but the matter did not actually come before him until after Parsons was mortally wounded, when he was again recommended. A WO note on the papers makes the point that the recommendation covered both dates but that Parsons had indubitably been recommended before his death and that the case was one which should be given the benefit of any doubt – which in itself represented a very considerable modification of the line that had up to then been taken. Wolseley gave his recommendation on 7 Nov that the case should be treated as a recommendation made before death, an actual award of the Cross should be gazetted and the decoration given to his relatives. This received the approval of Brodrick, now S of S for War, on 14 Nov, the recommendation went before the Queen on 16 Nov, and the award was duly gazetted on 20 Nov. [222]

As will be seen, the force of circumstances was making the strict

221   PRO, WO32/7445
222   *ibid*

interpretation of the old rules more and more difficult, and evidently the feeling was growing in official circles that evasion of the rule was desirable if at all possible. In Oct 1900 Brodrick, who had as Under-Secretary in 1897, shown himself not entirely opposed to the idea of posthumous VCs, as in the case of Lt MacLean, became S of S for War; and in Jan 1901 Lord Roberts, whose South African recommendations had clearly favoured such awards, became CinC of the British Army. In these circumstances some modification of the previous ruling could well be looked for – indeed, it is a little surprising that nothing of this nature occurred in Apr 1901, when the memoranda cases of Digby-Jones and Albrecht were under consideration but, as this is another instance where no VC file has survived, no explanation can be given for this.

As so often in the history of the VC, it was an individual case that brought about the decisive move. On 22 Jan 1902 a letter[223] was received at the WO from a Mrs Atkinson, forwarding a letter from the Adjutant of the 1st Bn The Yorkshire Regt, concerning the conduct of her son, the late Sgt Alfred Atkinson, at Paardeburg, and quoting the MS of the CinC as regretting that in view of the sergeant's decease before any recommendation had been made he could not be awarded the VC. Mrs Atkinson added, 'I send this copy of my son's bravery and I should be very pleased if you would kindly use your influence to help me get his VC and if there is anything else would you kindly send it me, for my husband is turned seventy years and a cripple and I assure you that we are greatly in need of help.'

The reaction within the MS department at the WO was that 'the rule is invariable that the VC cannot be awarded in the case of a soldier who was not recommended whilst living', though Lord Kitchener had in fact recommended him for the VC in the previous February, just a year after his death. The first suggestion now made was that a Distinguished Conduct Medal might be awarded, which might meet Mrs Atkinson's circumstances since it carried with it a gratuity of £20, and some dozen cases could be quoted in which the DCM had been awarded after the recipient's death. Such a recommendation was accordingly made to the MS, from whence it passed to Lord Roberts who recommended it in his turn to the S of S. Presumably because of the question of the gratuity Brodrick asked the Financial Secretary Lord Stanley [later 17th Earl of Derby] if the award might be made and he, in his turn, asked the department's Accountant-General [Mr Marzials] if there were any financial objections. From here the discussion took a somewhat unexpected turn.

223   PRO, WO32/7478 and for all that follows up to 8 Apr 1902.

The Acct-Gen's reply was: 'There is nothing in the Warrant that says a DCM can only be issued if the recommendation has been made before death – and as a matter of fact such awards have been made in the past – neither do the regulations make any restriction as to the issue of the gratuity that follows the medal. So far as regulations and precedent go, therefore, we are quite free.

'On the other hand, it is only right to point out that posthumous promotion, giving a widow a claim to a higher rate of pension is not allowed, in the case of the officer, unless the promotion has been recommended before death and similarly it is a long-standing rule that the VC shall only be granted if recommended while the soldier was alive. According to strict analogy, therefore, the DCM should not be granted in a posthumous recommendation.

'At the same time, I think this is a hard ruling, so far as the Medal is concerned, if the man has lost his life in the performance of some very gallant act, and not calculated to popularise the Army. I confess I should leave the more liberal existing practice alone. It is not a case in which there is likely to be abuse.'

In other words, a liberal practice was being followed in the case of the DCM, and there was no desire to alter this, whereas in logic the case should be treated on exactly the same basis as the VC. The obvious step to which this reasoning pointed was to reverse the analogy and make the practice in the case of the DCM the pattern for the VC also. This step Stanley took and on 10 Feb he wrote to Brodrick, 'I so entirely agree with the Acct-Gen that I think I would go further and award the VC even after the man is dead. I suppose we must take the Treasury with us, if you agree to the request.'

Brodrick's reply came three days later, 'I agree with the Financial Secretary. Ask Treasury.' Panmure's 'Order for the living' of 1856 was at last forgotten.

So far it was the civil side of the War Department which had been expressing its views. Gen Lord William Seymour, the MS, now sounded a note of caution to the Acct-Gen. 'In the course of many years the question of giving the VC in cases where the individuals were killed in performing acts of valour has come up several times and always with the result that it was decided to adhere to the rule not to give it unless the man was recommended for it whilst alive...

''Though not an Order, the VC is more akin to one than the DCM, which is simply a medal. If the practice as regards the VC is changed, it may perhaps raise the question of a change of practice with regard to orders as the Bath and the DSO. Hitherto the most that has been done in the case of dead men is to notify that they would have been recommended for the dignity had they survived.'

To which Mr Marzials, the Acct-Gen, replied, 'If, as I gather, you wish the decision reconsidered, so far as the VC is concerned, perhaps you would resubmit.'

Seymour's response to this was an attempt to secure allies and, on 5 Mar, he asked the AG, Gen Kelly-Kenny, if he had any remarks to make, adding, 'I would deprecate any alteration in the present rule as regards the VC although I see no harm in reusing the notification, *"that the VC would have been recommended had the individual survived".'*

The AG's reply was, 'I would be very cautious in this. If the Acct-Gen and Financial Secretary's recommendations are adopted you will find that on every single case of officers or men killed, applications for these distinctions will be made. No difference will be considered by the widows, mothers, fathers. They will with much reason say their son had lost his life, sacrificing to the country — this cannot be denied and where are we.'

It was in these circumstances, therefore, that the matter came before the CinC. On the one side were the civil heads of the department arguing in favour of a change, and on the other the military heads who were against it. Some indications of the view Roberts was likely to take on such a question have already been given. Nor were these belied; he came down firmly on the side of the civilians and in favour of the change. On 7 Apr he wrote to the S of S, 'I agree entirely with the Acct-Gen and the Financial Secretary and I am glad to see that their views commend themselves to you and I trust that the relatives of men and of officers and men [sic] who lose their lives in the performance of gallant deeds for which the actions themselves would have been awarded the DSO or the VC had they survived, may be given the medal or Cross with its accompanying advantages. I do not share in the AG's anticipation that trouble will result with the relatives of those who have lost their lives. The question whether the officer and man deserves a special recognition of his services rests in the hands of the COs, and the reply to any application for reward would be in the affirmative or negative as the nature of the case might require.

'I am very pleased the matter has been brought forward, for I have always wished to see it altered in the way I hope it now will be.' To which Brodrick initialled his approval the following day.

It was perhaps as keeping up a rearguard action that the MS pointed out on 26 Apr that the CinC did not propose that the Cross should be conferred in cases of this kind which had occurred during previous campaigns, and on 5 May that a limit should be set for the time within which relatives of deceased soldiers would have to submit their claims. The CinC, he indicated, hoped that no such limit would apply during the current South African campaign, and there would be none [i.e., no awards, not no time limit] for prior campaigns.

A time limit of three months had been suggested, apparently, but this he thought too short to meet the circumstances in East and West Africa, where communications were bad. Brodrick evidently accepted the general implications of this for he replied on 6 May that, 'If a list can now be made of "arrears" cases (from present war) I will accept CinCs views, but we must have a limit in future. I approve six months to cover cases (such as E & W Africa)'. [224]

The list finally produced contained six names. These were Younger, Digby-Jones and Albrecht, in respect of all of whom memoranda had already been published, Sgt Atkinson, from the discussion of whose case the whole business had started, and two others, Lt Coulson and Pte Barry. No distinction between those in respect of whom memoranda had already been published, and those whose names were now being gazetted for the first time was made in the announcement, which appeared on 8 Aug 1902, the formula used being 'The King has been graciously pleased to approve of the decoration of the VC being delivered to the relatives of the undermentioned officers, NCO and men who fell during the recent operations in South Africa in the performance of Acts of Valour which would, in the opinion of the CinC of the forces in the Field, have entitled them to be recommended for that distinction had they survived.' The Crosses were actually sent on 30 Apr 1902, each being accompanied by a letter signed by Lord Roberts.[225]

Despite the change in rule that this involved, and some statements that have appeared to the contrary, no new Warrant was issued to cover this departure. Col Cowan, AMS at the WO, was probably the first to point out in Oct 1902 that, 'The present published regulations for the VC do not state that the decoration can only be awarded in the case of a soldier who is still alive or who was recommended for it before he died, and there would therefore appear to be no necessity to alter them in the manner suggested by the AG', [226] who had, presumably, suggested the drafting of a new Warrant. But this was certainly turning the old view inside out with a vengeance; formerly the absence of any

224   PRO, WO32/7479
225   VCR, iii, pp47/52
226   PRO, WO32/7480

positive statement that a dead man could receive the Cross had been held to debar it, but now the absence of any positive prohibition on this was being held to sanction it.

As was to be expected, concession of the Cross to relatives of the three South Africa memoranda cases raised the question of similar action in respect of the six instances prior to that war. On 17 Sep 1902 Lord Rathmore wrote a lengthy letter to Brodrick referring to nine cases [being unaware that Crosses had been forwarded at the time to relatives of Home, Salkeld and Bankes] and making a special plea on behalf of Sir John Coghill, father of the Lt Coghill who had fallen at Isandhlwana.[227] Brodrick wrote to Roberts the following day, 'I do not like reopening this question again because I fear shoals of applicants. But Lord Rathmore makes out a strong case – if there are only nine such applicants. What do you think?' Evidently the AG's previous reservation about the number of people who might claim a VC for a relative killed in action had some influence on the S of S, but these fears were apparently not universal in the Department, for in the margin against Brodrick's reference to 'shoals of applicants' someone has written the question, 'Why?'.

Roberts answered on 27 Sep saying that when he made his proposal he 'did not think it would be necessary to make the concession have a retrospective effect beyond the present war. In cases, however, such as the one brought forward by Lord Rathmore ... it would be difficult to refuse the request for the VC for it was notified in the *London Gazette* that the VC would have been awarded had the officer survived. I would suggest your acceding to the request and expressing your determination not to consider any case which has not been recorded in the *London Gazette'*.

This letter bears Brodrick's direction to the AMS, 'I am prepared to proceed on the lines proposed by the CinC. Raise the point officially.' At this juncture the papers came before the MS, now Sir Ian Hamilton, and this drew a very full statement of what might be called the case for the Opposition. 'If we can confine this to the nine families,' wrote Sir Ian on 8 Oct, 'all will be well, but I must say I have sad misgivings about the business. Until now it has been the laudable object of a commander to write to the relatives of officers and men who have fallen in terms of unmeasured praise. This could do no harm and was a certain consolation – now all this must stop and a dead man must be measured by the same standard as a living one; or else applications for posthumous

227   PRO, WO32/7478 for this and all that follows up to Nov 1902.

decorations will be the rule and not the exception. The impossibility of arguing with the relatives of a dead man is well shown by the intensely disagreeable and threatening tone of Sir J. Coghill in his letter to the S of S dated 3 Aug 1902'. This last letter has not survived.

These views again attracted marginal disagreement. 'Why not?' against Hamilton's opening remark regarding confinement to the nine cases, and against his remark about posthumous awards becoming the rule and not the exception, 'and if they have already appeared in the Gazette, WHY NOT'. Brodrick's reaction, dated the next day, was, 'I will not resist this proposal though I agree with the MS as to the danger. Submit to the King and at the same time make it perfectly clear that no one will be allowed to participate in the decision who is not one of these nine.'

Three days later the MS was given his orders by the CinC. 'Carry out. I confess I do not share your fears about not being able to confine claims to the nine cases mentioned in the Gazette.' The submission finally prepared to go before the King, dated 20 Oct, actually contains six names as it had evidently come to light in the meantime that although memoranda had been published in the cases of Home, Salkeld and Bankes, Crosses had in fact been sent to their relatives. The submission bears a marginal note in Brodrick's hand that no departure will be made from the rule of allowing this only in the case of the six whose names were published in the *London Gazette*, 'as any departure would cause great difficulties.' Plainly there was a fear that numerous cases might be brought forward, such as that of Pte Cavanagh, mentioned earlier, where some official suggestion had been made that a VC might have been merited, but the matter had been taken no further nor had the case been investigated at the time since no award could be made, and it would now be impossible to assess the merits of the case.

However, all the discussions and labour had been in vain; when the matter was placed before him, King Edward VII said 'No'. As Brodrick recorded on 3 Nov, 'His Majesty at an audience yesterday informed me that he was not disposed to grant the VC in such cases as he feared it would open the door to many recommendations. We must therefore decline the step proposed.'

From the King's refusal the WO seems to have drawn the hardly surprising conclusion that what had happened in the South African War was a once-for-all exercise. Thus, when the US of S enquired later that month as to under what actual conditions posthumous VCs were to be given, and whether these would not apply in future wars, Hamilton's answer was, 'I take it no more posthumous VCs will be given for the

late or for future wars.'[228] Similarly, when a request for a posthumous
VC was forwarded by the Colonial Office in the following May, one of
the grounds given for declining it was 'it having been decided that the
posthumous grant of the decoration must be confined to a certain
limited number of cases which have already been notified in the
London Gazette'.[229]

This position was reiterated by Gen Ewart, the MS, three years later
in reply to a request from Lord Methuen for consideration to be given
to the case of the late Capt Ollivant. 'During the progress of the South
African War it was decided that the VC should be posthumously
conferred and handed to the relatives of officers and men who fell
during operations in South Africa in the performance of acts of valour
which would, in the opinion of the CinC of the Forces in the Field, have
entitled them to be recommended for that distinction had they survived.

'As, however, there had been six cases in campaigns prior to the
South African War, it did not seem very logical to withhold similar
treatment in such cases where an exception had been made for the
South African War. It was accordingly submitted to the King that in
these six specific cases, in campaigns prior to the South African War, ...a
similar concession should be made and that the decoration should be
given to the relations of these soldiers also. For some reason which I do
not understand, however, this was not approved. Consequently we are
still in the position that an exception was made in the case of the South
African instances − not a very logical decision, I admit − but there for
the moment the matter rests. It was, however, decided that in future no
more posthumous VCs or decorations should be conferred at all.' [230]

This letter was written in Apr 1906. At much the same time another
letter under consideration at the WO was touching on the same point.
On 12 Mar of that year, Philip Wilkins, whose name is well known to
students of the VC for his History of the Victoria Cross, published two
years previously, wrote suggesting that the Cross should be delivered to
the relatives of these same six men mentioned in Ewart's letter. The
embarrassment of the Department, and the logical impossibility in
which it found itself, was well summed up in the minute the Assistant
Secretary wrote to the S of S on this letter on 30 Mar. 'If there had been
a consistent refusal to grant the decoration to the relatives... we should
be on perfectly clear ground. The decision, however, in the six cases

228   VCR, iii, p61
229   ibid, p81
230   ibid, p128

during the South African War naturally lead to a demand for the same treatment in the case of similar Gazette notices for previous campaigns, the decision in the papers in which it was proposed that the Cross should be delivered to the relatives of those who fell in previous wars seems to lead to the inference that it was thought that this concession would open the door to many other applications, but as it has never been proposed to grant the VC except in those specific cases where a Gazette notice has actually been published we know for a fact that not more than six similar cases exist altogether. The Army Council may possibly feel disinclined to resubmit the matter to the King but it seems only too certain that the relatives of the six officers and men killed in campaigns prior to the South African War will continue to consider that an unfair and illogical decision is being maintained and to contrast their own treatment very unfavourably with that accorded to the relatives of the dead heroes of South Africa.'

The PUS, Col Sir E.W.D. Ward, commented to the AG, Gen Douglas, the following day, 'I fear that in view of the very explicit statement of HMs decision contained in 012/2066 we cannot reopen the question with him.' However, Gen Douglas thought something should be attempted and replied on 3 Apr, 'This is a very unsatisfactory state of affairs. I do not think that we can approach the King again officially, but possibly something might be done by approaching Lord Knollys [the King's PS] unofficially.' This was indeed done, but with no better result.

On 31 May, Gen Sir N.G. Lyttleton, the CGS, wrote to the MS, 'I saw Lord Knollys unofficially about this and he has written to me that "HM thinks that, with two exceptions, the acts of gallantry were so long ago that it would hardly be understood were the VC to be given to the representatives of the dead officers and men after the lapse of so many years. *HM thinks that in future the decoration should be given at once or not at all.*" This settles the question.'

The only question that it did not settle was what reply could be sent to Mr Wilkins. As an embarrassed note from the MS to the PUS put it, 'We can hardly mention the King, or even Lord Knollys. The distinction made is very difficult to defend in writing.' It was no doubt this difficulty which caused the delay of four weeks between the receipt of Knollys' letter and the final sending of a reply to Wilkins dated 27 Jun. This was sent over the signature of the PUS and read, quite simply, 'With reference to your letter of 12 Mar last I am commanded to acquaint you that the cases of the officers and men brought to notice have been carefully considered but after the lapse of so many years since the acts of gallantry were performed by them it is regretted that it has not been found possible to make an exception to the rule that the VC cannot be delivered to the relatives of a deceased soldier unless he had been recommended for it, or it had been provisionally conferred upon him before his death.

'I have to add that in the cases of Lts Home and Salkeld and Cornet Bankes to which you refer, the Cross was provisionally conferred while they were alive, see extracts from the *London Gazette* herewith.'[231]

Which, in fact, based itself pretty firmly on the main point of King Edward's objection. Wilkins's reaction to this letter was to ask for an interview with Lord Haldane, then S of S for War[232] but there is no evidence as to whether his request was granted. Knowing how acutely embarrassed was the WO in defending the highly illogical position in which it had been placed by the King, it seems unlikely that Wilkins would have been given any additional opportunity to expose its weaknesses.

By June of 1906 the King had twice declined to accept the WO proposal that VCs should be forwarded to the families of the six admitted in the *London Gazette* to have merited such award prior to the South African War. All official attempts to persuade him otherwise had failed and all the urgings made on behalf of the families appeared to have got absolutely nowhere. The campaign had, it would seem, ended in utter failure. Yet, on 15 Jan 1907, it was announced in the *London Gazette* that, 'The King has been graciously pleased to approve of the decoration of the VC being delivered to the relatives of the under-mentioned officers and men who fell in the performance of Acts of Valour, and with reference to whom it was notified in the *London Gazette* that they would have been recommended to Her late Majesty for the VC had they survived.'

This was complete victory. How had this entire *volte-face* come about? The answer is very simple. Mrs Melvill, widow of Lt Teignmouth Melvill, one of the 'memorandum cases' of Isandlhwana, had petitioned the King direct, and she succeeded in moving King Edward where official approaches had failed. A letter, which does not survive, went from Sir Arthur Davidson at Sandringham to Gen Wynne, MS at the WO, who wrote on 6 Dec 1906, 'In reply to your letter of 3rd instant regarding Mrs Melvill's petition to the King for the VC which would have been awarded to her late husband, had he survived, the grant would

231   *ibid,* pp131/3
232   PRO, WO32/7499

be in accordance with the precedent in similar cases during the South African War, but His Majesty has twice decided that the precedent is not to apply to cases which occurred prior to that war.

'Of such cases there are six only and the case of Lt Melvill is one... It would seem, therefore, that Melvill's case could hardly be considered apart from the other five. Judging from your letter of 3rd instant HM might be disposed to concede the six pre-South African cases. If so and on hearing from you I will have submissions prepared.' [233]

Two days later Davidson wrote again from Sandringham, 'The King has been pleased to reconsider his decision in reference to the six cases where the VC was posthumously awarded [sic]. Having regard to all the circumstances, HM directs that the decoration of the VC should be handed to the nearest representative of the six recipients in question... on the strict understanding that no other cases are involved in this decision. It will, perhaps, be best to send in a formal submission for the King's signature.'

This formal submission went forward from the WO on 7 Jan and the King's decision was announced in the *London Gazette* of 15 Jan, so that at long last the relatives of Edward Spence, E.A. Lisle Phillipps, Teignmouth Melvill, Neville Coghill, Frank Baxter and Hector MacLean received their VCs, the first two almost fifty years after the decease of the person honoured. Crosses for Phillipps and Coghill were sent to brothers, for MacLean and Baxter to their fathers, and for Melvill to the widow who had, of course, been the cause of the final proceedings. All had been located and the Crosses dispatched by early Feb, but the tracing of any person to whom Spence's Cross could be sent proved much more difficult. It was known he had some connection with Dumfries, but local advertisements and searches of parish registers proved fruitless. A claimant, Richard Lyn, finally came forward in Hawick, and the Provost forwarded a genealogical table prepared by the claimant's uncle and checked against entries in local registers. This showed a Berwickshire fisherman named Ogilvie to have had two daughters. One, Catherine, married a Spence and was mother of Edward whose VC was now being claimed; the other, Isabella, married Richard Lyn and had a son, also Richard. It was the son of this second Richard who claimed the Cross awarded to his father's cousin, and who eventually received it in July.

The sending of Phillipps' VC to his brother also involved the WO in some correspondence, as two female members of the family wrote to

233   PRO, WO32/7500 for this and the remainder of the 1907 correspondence.

the Department requesting that it be transferred to his nephew, the son of his elder brother, now regarded as head of the family. This letter in its turn produced one from another member of the family demanding that no such thing be done because of a scandal involving this nephew who had, apparently, announced his intention of leaving his entire estate to his natural son by one of the household maids whom he had married after she was divorced by her valet husband. The WO declined to be drawn into this family feud — as Gen Wynne pointed out, the Crosses had been delivered to the next of kin as defined in King's Regulations, and that settled the question so far as they were concerned.

From this point onwards there was no obstacle in the way of posthumous awards of the VC. The principle had been conceded in the South African War and the decision that there should be no more posthumous awards after the first list of 1902 stemmed directly from King Edward's refusal to sanction the transmission of the Cross in the case of the six individuals of earlier campaigns. With the withdrawal of this objection the WO could go back with no reservations to the position established at Stanley's instance in 1902 and accept recommendations in respect of the dead. But there was no written authorisation to this effect, and at the outbreak of war in 1914 the position was by no means clearly understood, outside the WO at least.

Thus in the papers relating to the first batch of First World War awards recommended by Sir John French, Gen Briggs, commanding the 1st Cavalry Brigade, commented in connection with the famous stand of L Battery at Nery, 'Capt Bradbury... I should have recommended for the VC had he lived.'[234] Presumably other field commanders were better aware of the actual situation, for a number of other deceased soldiers were recommended at this time and, among the queries telegraphed by the WO to French's MS was, 'Why Capt Bradbury, L Batt RHA, was not recommended for posthumous decoration as were Capt T.E. Wright, RE, and Lt Dease, 4 R Fus.'[235] His VC was, in fact, gazetted a fortnight after these other two.

The only authority therefore upon which the many posthumous VCs of the First World War were awarded was that there was nothing in the rules that precluded it. The Warrant still said nothing that could be quoted as clearly sanctioning the practice, so that when an interdepartmental committee was set up in Jul 1918 to consider its revision, this was an obvious matter to lay before it, and Clause (f) of its terms of

234   PRO, WO32/4993
235   *ibid*

reference read, 'To consider and advise on a new clause to support posthumous award of the VC as the existing Warrant does not legislate for such awards.'[236]

The point was dealt with at the first meeting of the committee on 30 Aug 1918 and it is interesting to note that Col Graham, representing the WO, referred to the case of Lt Roberts as the first in the South African War, noted that he died two days after his exploit and commented that it was not clear what circumstances had brought about an actual award of the Cross as distinct from a 'Would have been recommended' note. The 'custom' of such awards had been carried into the 1914-18 war with nothing to justify it; there was nothing in the Warrant to forbid it, but its wording followed the practice of orders, where this did not happen. Admiral Everett, the naval representative, suggested that a man must be honoured in all cases where he died between a recommendation being made and its being published [which had been the accepted practice for the VC all along] but was faced with the query as to what should be done if the man died before his CO had time to make his recommendation. Sir Frederick Ponsonby, chairing the committee, then made an astonishing remark which was about eighteen years out of date in practice. 'No man,' he said, 'can get the VC when he is killed during the action in which he earns the decoration.' This Graham corrected by pointing out that the recipient had to be alive at the time of recommendation for all other decorations; the illogicality was that the VC was being awarded posthumously when all the others were not. The committee was, however, generally agreed that a clause should be put in the Warrant to sanction this. This appears to have been drafted by the committee's secretary, R. U. Morgan of the WO, and took the form of a simple sentence, 'It is ordained that the Cross may be awarded posthumously.'

With the publication of the new Warrant, of which this was the fourth Clause, in 1920 this aspect of the evolution of the Victoria Cross reached its conclusion.

236   PRO, WO 32/3443 for all that follows.

Chapter 9

Bars

THE PROVISION of a bar to be worn on the ribbon of the VC by anyone who, after having received the Cross, should perform a further act which would have merited the award had he not already received it, was a fairly novel idea at the time the VC was instituted, though not without precedent. It revived the system adopted in connection with the bestowal of the Peninsular Gold Medals and Crosses, promulgated in Oct 1813. This was indeed the first occasion upon which a token to be worn on the ribbon by which the original award was suspended was substituted for the wearing of a second specimen of the same award when again merited. Thus, just as the design of the Peninsular Gold Cross had clearly influenced the appearance of the VC, so had the conditions of award influenced the latter in one respect at least.

However, despite mention of such a bar in the VC Warrant, the requirement went unnoticed when the design of the Cross was being decided upon and the deficiency was to remain until the matter was rendered urgent by the gazetting on 18 Feb 1915 of the award of a bar to Lt A. Martin-Leake, VC. Even so, it was only after the WO had asked that officer on 20 Feb 1915 to forward his Cross for the addition of a bar, and Messrs Hancocks had sought direction as to the design the bar should take, that anyone seems to have realised that no design had ever been approved for such bar.[237]

At the same time that they made this enquiry, Hancocks offered two suggestions of their own as to possible designs for the bar, and their drawings for it are preserved in the WO file. Both show a second laureated bar, closely resembling the suspender of the Cross; in one case the ribbon appears to finish at the upper bar, which is connected to the suspender by terminal links, whilst in the other the ribbon clearly goes to the lower suspender, to which the bar is linked by a central circular laurel wreath. In referring the matter to the Military Secretary

---

237   PRO, WO 32/4992 is the source for the whole of this section.

for decision, Lt-Col B.R. James, head of MS3, the section of the WO responsible for VC matters which it remains to this day, observed, 'The circular wreath... seems neither beautiful nor necessary', and this view was evidently shared by his superior for the decision given, over the signature of the MS, Maj-Gen Sir Frederick Robb, was, 'I think the bar should be an exact copy of the already existing one', [i.e. the suspender] .

Once noted the deficiency was promptly dealt with. Martin-Leake's VC was forwarded by his brother to the WO on 31 Mar; Col James put the matter to the MS on 16 Apr and his decision was given the same day. The VC involved was also sent to Hancocks that day, followed on the next by a letter from James which read, 'I am directed to inform you that the "bar" for the VC belonging to Lt A. Martin-Leake, RAMC, should be exactly like the bar from which the ribbon is suspended, the dates of the acts of bravery being engraved on the back'.

Hancocks acknowledged this letter, sought confirmation for the inscription proposed for the new bar on 19 Apr, and received WO approval in a letter of 20 Apr.

A great deal of misplaced ingenuity seems to have been expended on attributions of VC bars to men who fought in the Crimea.[238] However, if the exact wording of the Warrant is studied, it at once appears that all such claims must have been impossible, for by the fourth clause of the Warrant, the bar was to be available to 'anyone who, *after having received the Cross* [our italics] shall again perform an act of bravery...' In other words, it was not a case of one award per act of bravery, but of a further act of bravery after the VC [which could be regarded as conferred in respect of all that had gone before] had actually been pinned on the man in question. And as all the awards of the VC for the Crimean War were made after the war was over, there would have been no case for a Crimean bar which would have fallen within the terms of the Warrant. In fact, no fewer than twenty-nine Crimea cases made reference to conduct displayed on more than one occasion. Most referred to two, six cases mentioned three dates, Sgt John Park's citation named five occasions upon which his conduct had been noteworthy, whilst for Lt Gerald Graham, after quoting the specific case of the storming of the Redan, the citation went on to refer to 'devoted heroism... on numerous occasions...' An instance where misunderstanding is explicable is that of Sgt-Maj Berryman, whose citation amounts virtually to a summary of his extensive service in the Crimea. After listing the engagements in which he took part and distinguished himself

238   See, e.g. S.C. Johnson, *The Medal Collector,* London 1921, pp 218/9

it ends, 'He has also a clasp for Inkerman', but this can only be read as referring to the clasp he bore on his *Crimea* medal, and not his VC.

Many similar cases of numerous acts of heroism being recompensed by the single award of a VC occurred in the Indian Mutiny. That of Lt Daunt is of particular interest because about a year after his award was gazetted he appears to have written to the WO claiming that he should have received both Cross and bar by virtue of his award having been in respect of gallantry on two occasions. The reply, informing him that the case did not come within the statutes, contains the remark that 'no person is entitled to a bar unless, *after having received the cross,* he shall again perform an act of bravery'.[239]

Curiously enough, the only other cases on record of VC recipients claiming that they should be granted a bar in addition were men whose citations had only referred to a single exploit. The men were Pte John McGovern whose award dated from 1859, and on whose behalf a claim to a bar was advanced in 1879,[240] and Lt William Hope, a Crimea recipient whose second claim was put forward in 1893![241] At that distance in time the refusal of the WO to look into the matter was automatic and in each case the recipient's champion [in neither case was the approach made by the man himself] was so informed. In Hope's case a statement was added that he would in any case be ineligible under Clause 4 of the Warrant, which may be taken as confirming what has been argued above regarding the impossibility of bars being awarded for service in the Crimea. In neither case has the original correspondence survived, but there does seem to be evidence that both men had performed creditable exploits not mentioned in their citations. Hope's VC was awarded for his conduct at the attack on the Redan on 18 Jun 1855, but he also distinguished himself at the explosion of a magazine in the following November, for which he was publicly thanked by Gen Straubenzee and his own colonel.[242] McGovern's award was 'for gallant conduct during the operations before Delhi, but more especially on 23 Jun 1857', but there was evidently a strong regimental tradition that he earned it once more by his exploits at the battle of Markoul on 16 Dec following.[243]

A question bound to arise sooner or later was the course to be taken in the event of a second recommendation for the VC award received

239   PRO, WO 32/4991
240   VCR, ii p170
241   *ibid,* p364
242   *The Daily News,* quoted in *The VC and DSO,* i, p27
243   *The Munster Fusiliers' Regimental Annual for 1912,* p44 quoted in *ibid* p61

whilst the first was still 'in the pipeline'. Under a strict interpretation of the Warrant, the first award would not have been conferred at that time, so there would be no case for the bestowal of the bar. In the event, the first time it occurred the circumstances were such that the WO had every inducement to insist upon such strictness in interpretation. On 17 Oct 1857 Field Force Orders had been submitted for confirmation, as follows; 'The Brig-Gen [Henry Havelock] has on Sir James' [Outram] recommendation awarded this decoration [the VC] to Lt Henry Marshman Havelock...'[244] This provisional award had been backed by the President of the Board of Control and had been submitted by Lord Panmure to the Queen for confirmation in December, it being actually published in the *London Gazette* on 15 Jan 1858. The fact that this was, to all intents and purposes, a father conferring the VC on his own son had not gone unremarked in Army circles in India — Havelock himself appears to have had some qualms on the point, for his Field Force Order relating to the award concludes, 'On the spontaneous statement of the Maj-Gen, the Brig-Gen consents to award the Cross to the officer which act if originating with himself and from the near relation Lt Havelock bears to him would assume the appearance of undue partiality'.

It must have been with some consternation that the WO received a list of new recommendations for the VC, forwarded by East India House from the Governor-General in Council in May 1858, which brought forward the name of Havelock a second time. This was a point to which it was obviously desirable to draw the attention of the Duke of Cambridge and on 1 Jun a letter from the WO to the Horse Guards put the question of whether, in views of Havelock's having already received the VC for a previous act of gallantry, was the act now reported such as to entitle him to a bar? Cambridge's reply of 7 Jun shows that he was well aware of the difficulty of the situation for this contained the comment '... considering the feeling... excited in India by the terms in which the act of gallantry was described in the Gazette for which the VC was awarded on the former occasion to Sir Henry [Marshman] Havelock... it appears to me desirable that the case should be referred to Sir Colin Campbell before any decision is come to respecting it'.

Pennington's observations in forwarding this letter to Sir Henry Storks at the WO on 10 Jun made the embarrassment of the position even more clear. 'I suppose,' he wrote, 'that Gen Peel [then S of S for War] will not object to the proposed reference to Campbell with regard to the question whether a bar should be granted to Havelock in addition

244 PRO, WO 32/7317 for all that follows

to the Cross which he has already received on the recommendation of his late father. The terms... were in the late General's own words which have been the subject of comment in the letter from Sir Colin recently laid before Parliament.' Campbell's views were sought and he set about enquiring into the matter by means of a specially constituted Board of Officers, a commonly adopted procedure for enquiries into exploits which might merit the award of the VC.

His reply of 17 Sep 1858 was, 'The Board of Field Officers assembled under the instructions contained in your letter of 4 Jun last [sic, but obviously incorrect, since this letter must clearly have been subsequent to Pennington's note of 10 Jun] after a careful reconsideration of the subject, has recommended that the bar should not be conferred on that officer as it was not known in this country [i.e. India] at the time the recommendation was made that the decoration had already been conferred in England, for another service, in which opinion I concur'. Pennington was quick to point out the flaw in this reasoning, in an observation to Storks on 12 Nov. [The delay being due to the time for travel from India of the views of Campbell, by now Lord Clyde.] 'I confess I do not see the force of this reason; because the fact of the Cross having been conferred for the first act... even it if had been known at the time [he] was recommended for the second act, might not have precluded the last recommendation being made if the claim was really established. It seems like saying "you were not entitled to it for the first act, but you got it, and you must consider *that* as your reward for the second act" '. Which was, no doubt, almost exactly what the Army in India was saying.

Pennington presumed, therefore, that the opinion of CinC India would have to be paramount and that the matter would have to drop. Storks, laying the papers before the S of S two days later, commented, 'It is quite clear that the feeling of the Army in India was that Bt-Maj Sir H. Havelock had not won the Cross when conferred on him by his father. The reasoning is bad − but the decision as it stands must be accepted'. To which Peel replied on 15 Nov 1858, 'This having been referred to Lord Clyde I must abide by his decision'.

As a result of the Havelock case the WO was committed to an extremely rigid interpretation of the exact words of Clause 4 of the Warrant. This may well have had a much later victim in the person of Cpl John McKay in South Africa. He was recommended for the Cross by Lord Roberts on 25 Jun 1900, for an exploit performed on 20 May. The award was recommended by Wolseley, CinC at the WO, on 27 Jul, approved by the S of S on 31st, submitted to the Queen on 4 Aug and gazetted on 10 Aug 1900. He was then recommended for a bar to his Cross for an exploit performed on 11 Jul 1900; the WO argument was, therefore, that although he performed the second act of valour after he was recommended for the VC by the CinC South Africa, the recommendation was not approved until after the date of the second act and so he could not be considered as entitled to a bar under the terms of the Warrant. This opinion was endorsed by Sir Ian Hamilton on 31 Aug 1901, with the brief comment in regard to the award of a bar, 'Cannot be done'.[245]

No such objection could be raised in the case of Martin-Leake, already mentioned as the first man to be awarded a bar to his VC, for his Cross had been won in 1902 and the recommendation for the bar did not follow until thirteen years later when he was clearly a person who performed a further act of bravery 'after having received the Cross' as required by the Warrant. So, also, had Capt Noel Chavasse actually received the Cross awarded him in Oct 1916 before earning, in Aug 1917, the bar for which he was posthumously gazetted in Sep of that year. However, in view of the almost complete destruction of the WO files relating to the award of the VC during the Great War, one cannot assume that no further cases such as that of Cpl McKay arose.

Although the wording of the clause on bars was not drawn to the attention of the 1918 Committee, nor was it discussed at its two meetings, there is evidence of official dissatisfaction with its drafting for it emerged in the new Warrant of 1920 in a subtly revised form which has persisted in all subsequent Warrants. Instead of eligibility for the bar being restricted to 'anyone who, after having *received* the cross shall again perform an act of bravery...' the reading is 'if any *recipient* of the cross shall again perform an act of bravery...'. This is obviously a broader wording for, whilst the actual wording of the earlier Warrant makes the physical possession of the Cross essential, it can be argued that the second form of words is compatible with a certain element of futurity and that in a case such as that of Cpl McKay he could be considered a 'recipient' from the time the first recommendation was made by the CinC, South Africa, and it is not impossible that the new wording was drafted with that case in mind.

As has been said, this particular piece of drafting did not engage the attention of the Committee itself, so the credit for it must go to the person responsible for the drafting of the new Warrant as a whole, namely the Committee's secretary, Mr R.U. Morgan of the WO.

245   VCR, iii pp402/3

Quite apart from the McKay case there is also the example of the procedure which had been followed with the DSO, for which, during the 1914-18 war, more than one recommendation for the same individual had been allowed to go through the pipeline simultaneously, so that on a number of occasions the award of both the original decoration and of a bar to the same individual had appeared in the same *London Gazette,* which would have been completely impossible under the original wording of the VC Warrant. Too much should not be made of this particular redrafting of the Warrant, perhaps, for the only subsequent award of a bar to the VC to date is that to Capt Charles Upham in the 1939-45 war, and as he received his Cross on 11 May 1945 and had only been gazetted for the bar on 26 Sep 1945[246] he would clearly have qualified for his second award even under the previous terms of the Warrant.

A feature deserving of comment in this case is the lapse of time between the exploit by which Upham earned his bar [Jul 1942] and its gazetting. Two factors were evident, one a certain apprehension regarding making any recommendation at all for a VC bar; as the papers[247] show, the DMS at Middle East HQ had clearly advised that there was little chance of such a recommendation succeeding, though equally clearly it emerges when the case was reconsidered later that the DMS had no business to advise at his level on any such submission being made. This objection would not have precluded a recommendation for the DSO, but here the second factor came into consideration, that Capt Upham had ended his exploit as a prisoner of war. This was a matter which had exercised the minds of the Army Council on several occasions in the past and had caused particular difficulties in connection with First World War operations at Kut-el-Amara, which culminated in the capitulation of Gen Townshend's force to the Turks. The Army Council had ruled in 1917 that an award could be made to a POW provided the act for which he was recommended was unconnected with the circumstances in which he had been taken prisoner for, theoretically, every soldier taken prisoner was liable to have an enquiry held into his conduct, to establish whether he was blameworthy for having fallen into enemy hands. Gen Ruggles-Brise, the MS at GHQ in France in 1918, had pointed out the lack of reality in this situation; if a company commander were ordered to hold out to the last, and did so, his ultimate fate might well be unknown when it was wished to honour his service.

---

246   VCR, iv p30
247   PRO, WO 32/11644

Had he been killed there would be no argument about a posthumous VC, yet had he survived as a POW and had been awarded the VC the award might have been in breach of the regulations.[248]

That these reservations were still present in the Second World War is clearly shown when the question of awards to POWs was considered by the Committee on the Grant of Honours, Decorations and Medals in Time of War, at its meeting on 18 Jul 1940. Although it was then agreed that such awards could be made, Gen Floyer Acland thought that the WO would not wish to use the power, whilst his Air Ministry and Admiralty colleagues, Air-Marshal Gossage and Rear-Admiral Syfret both agreed that such recommendations should not be invited, though any that were submitted could receive consideration. It came out clearly in these discussions that a difficulty in trying to enforce the earlier rule of 'no award before a court of enquiry' was that, by the time POWs had been repatriated and courts of enquiry held, it was extremely difficult to obtain satisfactory evidence of the act it was proposed to reward.

A further point raised in connection with POWs was whether the captor power might retaliate against prisoners so honoured, but the Deputy Director of Military Intelligence, whose advice was sought on this point, thought it unlikely.[249]

It was in Jul 1945, when Capt Upham had been released and repatriated, that Gen Freyberg, through whose hands as Divisional Commander the 1942 recommendation had passed, but who had been in hospital recovering from wounds when it was originally under examination, and therefore unable to pursue matters at that time, sought to have the case reopened.[250] Gen McCreery, Commander of the Eighth Army, agreed with his predecessor, Gen Alexander, that a DSO would be appropriate but saw to it that the papers, for the first time, went forward to London for adjudication. At the same time an additional witness statement was added to the original testimony: and it is interesting to note that this was made as a sworn statement before Maj-Gen Kippenberger who, as a battalion commander, had taken the sworn statements of the witnesses of Upham's earlier exploits in Crete.[251]

These papers came before the MS, Gen Wemyss, on 7 Sep, who supported the award of a bar to the VC, as did also the Supreme Allied Commander. On 14 Sep Wemyss wrote to Sir Alan Lascelles, the King's

248   PRO, WO 32/5396
249   PRO, WO 32/9957
250   PRO, WO 32/11644 for all that follows except as indicated
251   PRO, WO 32/11643

PS, to give King George VI details of the two previous cases of bars to the VC, and the S of S's submission of the third followed on 18 Sep. When Lascelles returned the submission on 19th, his letter added, 'If there is any likelihood of Upham being in London, so that HM could see him, perhaps you would let me know'. This did not materialise and Upham actually received his VC and bar from the Governor of New Zealand in the Civic Theatre of Christchurch on 25 Mar 1946.

Curiously, in their original instructions regarding the insignia, Hancocks were told to add a bar to the original Cross and alter the inscription on the reverse of the Cross so that both the May 1941 and the Jul 1942 dates should appear there, which would not seem to correspond with the treatment of previous Crosses in bar cases. However, as it appears that in the final outcome the original Cross never returned to Hancocks, no such alteration was made.

Chapter 10

Awards by Ballot

ONE OF THE provisions of the Victoria Cross Warrant of 1856 which is most clearly attributable to the influence of Prince Albert was that of Clause 13, under which, in any case where a gallant act had been performed by a body of men, in such manner that all had distinguished themselves equally and the officer commanding felt that no special selection could be made, then those involved should make their own selection, one officer being chosen by the officers, one non-commissioned officer by the NCOs and two privates by the privates, which followed very closely Albert's suggestion in his memorandum of 22 Jan 1855 'that in the cases of general actions it be given in certain quantities to particular Regiments, so many to the Officers, so many to the sergeants, so many to the men (of the last say 1 per Company) and that their distribution be left to a jury of the same rank as the person to be rewarded'.[252] The type of exploit that Albert had in mind was fairly clearly some such as the charge of the Light Brigade at Balaclava, and indeed his memorandum refers to this as a case of special difficulty ('How is a distinction to be made, for instance, between the individual services of the 200 survivors of Ld Cardigan's Charge? If you reward them all it becomes merely a medal for Balaclava, to which the Heavy Brigade and the 93d have equal claims.') But, in fact, the recipients for the VC for this exploit were selected without recourse to the procedure of Clause 13, nor was it invoked at all for the Crimean campaign, even though some regimental commanders made use of votes among their men to draw up their list of names for submission.[253]

The Indian Mutiny first saw the operation of the VC ballot and, since of the 46 VCs that have been awarded in this way to date no fewer than 29 relate to this campaign, it is plain that the events of the Mutiny must bulk very large in any consideration of its operation. Four incidents

252   See Appendix II
253   See Chapter 5

were involved. VCs were bestowed by ballot on the 60th Foot for their part in the Siege of Delhi, those selected being Lt A.S. Heathcote, Colour-Sgt G. Waller, Bugler W. Sutton, Pte J. Divane and Pte J. Thompson. The 84th similarly selected recipients for the VC for their part in the Siege of Lucknow, L/Cpl J. Sinnott and Pte P. Mylott being the recipients, and the charge of the 8th Hussars at Gwalior was similarly rewarded, the selection in this case being Capt C.W. Heneage, Sgt J. Ward, Farrier G. Hollis and Pte J. Pearson. All the remaining awards related to the relief of Lucknow, and were distributed as follows: Bengal Artillery: Lt H.E. Harrington, Rough-Rider E. Jennings, Gunners T. Laughnan, H. McInnes and J. Park. 53rd Foot: Lt A.K. ffrench, Sgt-Maj C. Pye, Ptes C. Irwin and J. Kenny. 90th Foot: Maj J.C. Guise, Sgt S. Hill, Pte P. Graham. 93rd Foot: Capt W.G.D. Stewart, Sgt J. Paton, L/Cpl J. Dunley, Ptes P. Grant and D. Mackay. 1st Madras Fusiliers: Pte J. Smith.

The most striking thing about this list is how widely it departs from the terms of the Warrant. Of the eight units involved, in only two cases do the number of recipients correspond with the regulation four – one officer, one NCO and two privates; three units had five recipients accepted and three submitted fewer recipients – indeed in the case of the 84th Foot and the 1st Madras Fusiliers the citations appear to imply that only the privates of the regiments participated. So far as the three cases where more than the 'ration' of Crosses had been granted – those to the 60th, 93rd and Bengal Artillery, a possible clue as to its justification may be provided in the citation for the five artillerymen, which reads 'Elected respectively, under the thirteenth clause of the Royal Warrant of 29 Jan 1856, by the officers and non-commissioned officers generally, and by the private soldiers of each troop or battery'. However, this is still a puzzle, for there is no equivalent statement that the extra ranker in the other two regiments had also arisen from a 'one per company' ballot, and even if this explained the procedure, it still does not explain how the five names had been accepted, for there is nothing in the wording of Clause 13 to justify the 'one private per battery' of the Bengal Artillery. This is exactly the sort of point upon which one would have expected a comment from Mr Pennington, but in no case – that of the 60th,[254] of the 93rd[255] or of the Bengal Artillery[256] – is this point raised. Indeed, in the submission which included those for the

254   PRO, WO 32/7338
255   PRO, WO 32/7317
256   PRO, WO 32/7320

93rd [in each case the submissions cover a considerable number of other recommendations in addition to those awarded under Clause 13], Pennington comments, 'There is only one case to which it is necessary to call attention — that of Cornet Bankes' — which raised a very different matter. Moreover, Gen Peel, the S of S for War, commented on the Bengal Artillery election cases 'As I read the warrant Lord Clyde would have been justified in allowing the election of *two men* per troop instead of one for the honour'.

However, the tendency of Clyde to treat somewhat cavalierly the actual requirements of the VC Warrant has been made apparent earlier. If one is to accept the word of Col Maude, himself a Mutiny VC, though admittedly writing nearly forty years later, it seems that the ways in which selection was carried out by no means coincided with the provisions of the Warrant. He quotes, for example, from a letter written by Capt Willis of the 84th Regiment, written from Lucknow in Nov 1857, 'An order came out for names to be sent in from each corps — one officer, one NC Officer, and one private, for the Victoria Cross — this was afterwards altered to one man from each corps — but other regiments had already sent in the names of officers in accordance with the first order, and left it so, and they have all been recommended for the Cross'.[257] If this evidence is accepted then, clearly, the selection was not being made on the numerical basis laid down by the Warrant.

A story which Maude himself relates implies yet another irregularity. 'The following conversation, which was overheard upon the subject, and repeated to the writer at the time, shows in what light the question was regarded by the private soldiers, of — never mind what corps. "Well," said one to his comrade, "who are you going to vote for?" The answer was "So and so, and who are you going to vote for yourself?" "Well," replied the first questioner, "I think I shall vote for our Doctor." The others became curious to know why his choice had fallen on the Doctor. "Because," said the soldier, "I think he's the most likely man among us to live to wear it." The others asked in an amused tone "What makes you think that?" "Because" was the reply, embellished with the usual affidavit, "he takes such.....good care of hisself!" '[258] If there was any truth in this story then, clearly, all ranks were being asked to vote for all ranks, which was certainly contrary to the terms of the Warrant. It is, perhaps, worth mentioning in connection with the last

257   F.C. Maude and J.W. Shearer, *Memories of the Mutiny*, London 1894,
        vol ii, p536
258   *ibid*, p328

anecdote that although a number of Medical Officers were awarded the VC during the Mutiny, none in fact received it under Clause 13!

However, too much reliance should not be placed on Maude, as may be shown in his use of the story of the 78th Regiment to demonstrate the disrepute into which Gen Havelock had brought his VC recommendations. 'The truest and keenest perception of the matter seems to have lain with the 78th (Ross-shire Buffs, or Seaforth Highlanders, as they are now called) who, although repeatedly called upon by Havelock to name some one for distinction, steadily but respectfully refused; saying that, in their opinion, no one of their number had more particularly distinguished himself than another. At last it was represented to them by the General that if such a distinguished Regiment as the 78th persisted in this course, he could not conscientiously recommend anyone else. Upon which they grimly sent in the name of one of their medical officers, who, doubtless, was thoroughly deserving of the decoration.'[259] Unfortunately for the story the 78th received eight VCs in the course of the Mutiny; nor can it even be argued that, having relented and made the one recommendation of their MO, they allowed the others to go forward, since their first Cross to be gazetted was to Lt Crowe, on 15 Jan 1858; their Assistant Surgeon, McMaster, did come next, chronologically speaking, his award being gazetted on 18 Jun of the same year, but simultaneously with three others to the 78th; whereas if Surgeon Jee is meant, his was the Regiment's last, not being gazetted until 8 Nov 1860.

Certainly, Lord Clyde treated the matter of the VC in a very off-hand manner. Referring to what appears to be the case of Pte Joel Holmes, who received the Cross, Capt Willis wrote from Lucknow, 'Maude's guns came up, and two were brought into action, and for about ten minutes it was a question of give and take; at one of our guns five men were knocked over. I am happy to say one of my old company volunteered as a number at the gun in the poor fellow's place who had been killed, and he remained working at it until it limbered up, for which I recommended him for distinguished conduct, expecting he would get a medal and gratuity, but to my surprise he is in orders as recommended for the VC (which is a mistake, I think)'.[260] There is also the evidence of someone whom Maude describes as 'a distinguished General of Lord Clyde's Relieving Force':-

'With regard to the Victoria Cross, I know Lord Clyde was much

259   *ibid*, pp330/1
260   *ibid*, pp533/4

opposed to this decoration, and looked upon it as quite unnecessary in
the British Army, the soldiers of which, he thought, rather required
restraining than egging on to gallant deeds. After the Relief of Lucknow,
many recommendations of officers and men for the VC were made from
some regiments, on whom the brunt of the fighting had fallen; whereas
other regiments, which had not been engaged, had nobody to
recommend for it. Lord Clyde, NOTWITHSTANDING (!) sent four
Crosses to each Regiment of his force, 1 for the officers, 1 for the non-
commissioned officers, and two for the privates. The 9th Lancers had
been left to keep open communications with the Alum Bagh, *and had
not been engaged with the enemy,* so had no one to recommend for the
Cross. It was reported at the time that they were ordered, by Lord
Clyde, to award the Cross, *nevertheless,* and that they selected one of
their regimental 'Bheesties' (water-carriers) for the honour; at which
his Lordship was very wroth.'[261] How much truth there is in this story
is difficult to say. Some of the details are plainly erroneous; Clyde did
not have any Crosses to send to anybody, but that he was treating with
contempt a decoration which, according to Parry, he never seems
thoroughly to have understood or to have appreciated,[262] may well be
true. It has already been shown[263] that he did indeed ask if he could
have a supply of Crosses available for distribution, and the WO's refusal
may well have been due to their fearing circumstances of the type
described here arising if he were given too free a hand. Also it is on
record that the Duke of Cambridge had occasion to question whether
Clyde's recommendations were strictly complying with the terms of the
Warrant, and his suggestion that Clyde might be written to drawing his
attention to these was endorsed by the S of S.[264]

The use of the Clause 13 procedure gave the GOC a very free hand
anyway, for once he had decided to put a unit to the ballot the WO was
placed in a very difficult position indeed. It could hardly say that the
action as a whole did not merit any awards of the VC, for this would
indicate a very grave censure of the judgment of the General
responsible, nor could it exercise its normal powers of adjudicating as
to the fitness of the individual recipients, for, to question the names
brought forward would mean challenging the outcome of the ballot and
the judgment of the participants. However, when the Bengal Artillery

---

261   *ibid,* pp332/3
262   *The VC, Its Heroes and Their Valour,* p193
263   See p53
264   PRO, WO 32/7338

selections were put forward without any supporting justification whatsoever — they were gazetted simply 'for conspicuous gallantry at the
Relief of Lucknow, from the 14th to the 22nd November, 1857' — the
Duke of Cambridge was moved to comment that in all elections, the
special service of the corps participating should be distinctly described
and suggested that an instruction should be issued to that effect.[265]
Such a letter was indeed sent to Clyde on 20 Dec 1858, presumably
with effect, for no subsequent cases of elected VCs had to be gazetted
with such vague particulars.

One slightly curious situation that could arise in circumstances such
as the Mutiny, where so many regiments were given the chance of
selecting recipients for the Cross by ballot, was that a sense of grievance
could be felt by those regiments not given this opportunity. In bringing
to notice the claims of Pte Denis Dempsey, the CO of the 10th Regt
made the point that, despite the regiment's distinguished service in
India, it had not been 'allowed a ballot'.[266] Dempsey's case was
considered to be a good one, and his claim to a VC as an individual
recipient was allowed, so that the point raised by the CO did not receive
any particular attention. Had it been raised as a point of more substance
there can be little doubt that it would have been resisted by the WO;
ballotted Crosses were uncomfortably out of the control of the home
authorities and there was no likelihood that they would have countenanced any claim by individual units to any right to be allowed to avail
themselves of the procedure of Clause 13.

There was one unsuspected disadvantage resulting from the use of
the Clause 13 procedure: once it had been invoked, and the recipients
selected by ballot, it became impossible for any other claims to be
entertained from the same regiment on the same occasion, which
conflicted somewhat with the then normally accepted doctrine of the
legitimacy of claims to the Cross by individuals. There is one clear
case of this on record, in respect of the 93rd Regt at Lucknow. On
15 Feb 1860 Sidney Herbert, then S of S for War, wrote to the Duke of
Cambridge, regarding claims to the VC submitted by Capt and Bt-Maj
Burroughs and Capt Cooper of the 93rd. As he pointed out, these
claims would appear to be inadmissible, as the officers of the regiment
had been instructed to elect a recipient under Clause 13 of the Warrant
for service at the Relief of Lucknow, and had selected Capt Stewart.

265   PRO, WO 32/7320
266   PRO, WO 32/7339

However, Capt Stewart's Cross had been awarded for conduct in another part of the action, so the S of S felt that the claims of these two officers should be investigated by the CinC, in consultation with Lord Clyde.[267] It may appear a little surprising that Herbert was prepared to go even this far, since it is logical to assume that the officers would have considered the whole of the action at Lucknow in making their choice, and that wherever the deeds of the selected recipient had been performed there would always be other disappointed claimants whose service was elsewhere, though within the scope of the same action. No further correspondence is on record to show how the discussion progressed but apparently the claims of the two officers were not allowed, since neither received the Cross. It was evident, many years later, that Gen Sir Ian Hamilton had the problem of the 'blanketing effect' of a Clause 13 recommendation much in mind when, after Gallipoli, he took care to make it clear that the landing, in respect of which he was recommending Corporal Cosgrove for an individual VC, was quite apart from that for which a collective recommendation was being made for the Lancashire Fusiliers.[268]

After the conclusion of the Indian Mutiny no further case arose of the ballot for selection of VC recipients until the ambushing of Q Battery, Royal Horse Artillery, at Sanna's Post, Korn Spruit, in South Africa, on 31 Mar 1900. The recipients here were Maj E.J. Phipps-Hornby, Sgt C.E.H. Parker, Gunner I. Lodge and Driver H.H. Glasock. As will be seen from the number of names, this was an entirely orthodox application of the terms of Clause 13, and as the citation states 'After full consideration of the circumstances of the case, the Field Marshal Commanding-in-Chief in South Africa formed the opinion that the conduct of all ranks of 'Q' Battery, Royal Horse Artillery, was conspicuously gallant and daring, but that all were equally brave and devoted in their behaviour. He therefore decided to treat the case of the battery as one of collective gallantry, under Rule 13 of the Victoria Cross Warrant...' However, a further inherent weakness in the rule was brought to light on this occasion, as the citation goes on to explain. 'A difficulty arose with regard to the officer, owing to the fact that there were only two officers — Phipps-Hornby and Humphreys — available for the work of saving the guns, and both of these had been conspicuous by their gallantry and by the fearless manner in which they exposed themselves, and each of them nominated the other for the decoration.

267   VCR, i pp258/61
268   PRO, WO 32/4995

It was ultimately decided in favour of Phipps-Hornby, as having been the senior concerned.'

Since it was only the men of the artillery battery who participated in the ballot, the award of these collective VCs should not have prejudiced the granting of the same award to men of any other units who took part in the action. On 29 Apr 1900, Lord Roberts wrote from South Africa announcing the provisional conferment of the VC on the four gunners selected in the ballot, and then continued, 'As regards the officers and men not belonging to the battery who volunteered their assistance in saving the guns I have selected the following as having shown the greatest gallantry and disregard for danger in carrying out their self-imposed duty, and I recommend them for the decoration of the VC:- Lt Francis Aylmer Maxwell, DSO, 18th Bengal Lancers; Lt William John Ainsworth, 2nd Durham Light Infantry; Lt George Murray Haine Stirling, 2/Essex Regt.'[269] The WO reaction to these further recommendations showed an unexpected factor being taken into consideration. On 30 Jun Roberts was informed, in a letter over the signature of the MS, 'Taking, however, into consideration the fact that the affair at Korn Spruit taken as a whole was not of a nature to reflect credit on our Army, the CinC [at that time Lord Wolseley] is of opinion that the four Crosses given by you [sic] will be a sufficient recognition of services rendered, and feels precluded from recommending to HM the three additional proposed in your letter under reply'.[270]

There the matter might have ended, but for a letter which Maxwell's sister wrote on 16 Oct 1900 to a Mrs South. This read in part 'We have had a great disappointment about our brother Frank, the one who has been attached to Roberts' Horse. He was recommended for the VC for saving a man's life at Sanners [sic] Post but owing to so many persons being sent in for the VC in that particular occasion his name has been passed over and he is not to get it. This is the *second* time he has been recommended for it and not got it so you can imagine how dreadfully disappointed we are'.[271] Presumably Mrs South was a lady at court, for on 10 Nov another letter was sent, this time from Sir Arthur Bigge, the Queen's PS, at Windsor Castle to Gen Grove, the MS at the WO:- 'The Queen is greatly interested in the family of Maxwell's splendid record of six sons in the Army and five fighting at the front. Miss Maxwell's letter was read to Her Majesty who is much struck at the fact

269   PRO, WO 32/7452
270   VCR, iii p5
271   PRO, WO 32/7452 for this letter and the remainder of this episode.

that one brother Frank has been twice recommended for the VC and HM cannot help thinking that if this really is the case his claim to the coveted honour is a strong one. Of course Her Majesty does not wish to issue any special orders on the subject but if the Commander in Chief was subsequently able to recommend this officer for the VC she would gladly approve'.

The result of this letter was to cause the Maxwell papers to be re-examined, and although no trace could be found of any recommend-ation other than that of Roberts' letter of 29 Apr, a note was made on 16 Feb 1901, that the CinC considered that Lt Maxwell should be selected in view of the previous recommendation — a decision that was only to be expected, as since January of that year the post had been held by Lord Roberts himself! Brodrick, S of S for War approved the submission on 20 Feb, and it was duly submitted on the 26th; this provided the only rather sad feature of the whole story, for Queen Victoria had died just five weeks before, thus making his one of the first VC recommendations to be approved by King Edward VII. The award itself was actually gazetted on 8 Mar 1901. Maxwell was singularly fortunate, for nothing more was heard of VCs for either Ainsworth or Stirling, neither of whom, perhaps, were blessed with sisters who were such able correspondents! Though it may be added that both ended the South African War with DSOs, as also did Capt Humphreys.

This episode did have one other feature of interest, for at the end of 1901 the suggestion was made that when a unit such as a battery had participated in a VC ballot, the battery itself should be granted some permanent badge.[272] The first form suggested for this was a cloth badge with a facsimile of the Cross on it, but on 3 Jan 1902 it was ruled that the idea was not to be entertained. On the 26th of that month the AAG suggested as an alternative that the emblem of the VC might be added to the colours, or worn by the staff sergeants and sergeants in the case of the Artillery, where there would be no colour. However the AG, Lt-Gen Kelly-Kenny, expressed himself averse to the whole idea — 'The VC if possible should be a purely personal distinction' and with Roberts' agreement to this view on 29 Jan the whole idea came to an end.

To find the next use of a ballot for the choice of recipients of the VC, at least on the evidence of what appeared in the *London Gazette* one must move fifteen years to the occasion of the landings in Gallipoli, although despite what was published in the citations, certain doubts must remain.

272   PRO, WO 32/7474

On 25 Apr 1915, three companies and the HQ of the 1st Bn Lancashire Fusiliers landed to the West of Cape Helles, on the Gallipoli
Peninsula, in the face of intense fire which caused many casualities, the
survivors displaying great heroism in effecting a landing. On 15 May
Maj-Gen Hunter Weston, commanding the 29th Division, wrote to the
DAG at GHQ, Gallipoli: 'The landing... is a deed of heroism that has
seldom been equalled and I strongly recommend that the gallantry of
the deed may be recognised by the bestowal of six VCs on the two most
distinguished officers and the four most distinguished NCOs and men',
namely Capt C. Bromley, Capt R.R. Willis, Sgt A. Richards, Sgt F.E.
Stubbs, Cpl J. Grimshaw, and Pte W. Keneally. 'Their deeds of heroism
took place under my own eyes... Where all did so marvellously it is
difficult to discriminate, but the opinion of the battalion is that Bromley
and Willis are the officers, and Stubbs, Richards, Grimshaw and Keneally
are the NCOs and men to whom perhaps the greatest credit is due. As
the representatives, therefore, of the Battalion, as well as for the deeds
of great gallantry performed by them themselves under my own eyes,
I strongly recommend these officers, NCOs and men for the VC'.[273]

To this Gen Sir Ian Hamilton added his endorsement as GOC of the
Mediterranean Expeditionary Force: 'Recommended. These six
Decorations for one battalion may seem to those who have not seen,
excessive. But only one other VC recommendation has been made for
all the Southern landing'. A separate account of the landings, detailing
the part played by each of the VC recommendations [the other being
Cpl Cosgrove], dated 13 May 1915, is appended to the recommendations
in the WO file, though it appears to have been forwarded only on
20 May, after Hunter Weston's recommendation, supported by Sir Ian,
had gone forward. As will be seen, Hunter Weston's recommendation
implies that some sort of consultation and selection had taken place
within the battalion, but there is no suggestion of a formal ballot having
been held. The first suggestion of any such thing occurred when the
documents reached the WO. On 5 Jun Gen Robb minuted the Deputy
Permanent Secretary 'Do you concur that we should ask the CinC to
apply the provision of the thirteenth condition in the R. Warrant
instituting the VC?', a course of action which was agreed the following
day. On the 7th Robb instructed WO, section MS3, 'Please return this
application to the CinC Med Force and ask whether the selection of the
individuals was made as laid down in the 13th part of the VC Warrant
and, if it was not, ask that this procedure may be resorted to unless such

273   PRO, WO 32/4994 for this and all that follows.

specific act of bravery can be recorded against each of those recommended that each can be considered on its merits. Possibly the GOC has not a copy of the Warrant, so it will be as well to forward one.'

The requested letter was sent to Hamilton on 11 Jun.[274] A reply came from Gen Hunter Weston on 14 Jul saying that this was indeed a collective act for which the whole battalion should be honoured. He had therefore taken action under paragraph 13; Capt Willis had been selected by the officers, Sgt Richards by the NCOs, and Pte Keneally by the privates. The latter had expressed a wish to nominate Cpl Grimshaw in place of a second private and Hunter Weston hoped this request might be acceded to. Accompanying papers showed that Gen Wolley Dod, commanding the 86th Brigade, had mentioned a difficulty which had been experienced in obtaining the necessary decision as so few of any rank were now serving with the battalion who had been present on 25 Apr. His NCOs had in fact attempted to put forward both the sergeants, and the name of Sgt Richards had only been settled on after the matter had been submitted to them for reconsideration. Gen Dod had also urged that both Capt Bromley and Sgt Stubbs should be submitted for other awards if they were not to be allowed the VC.

Hamilton's reply was: 'The GOC Mediterranean Expeditionary Force now recommends: Capt R.R. Willis, No.1293 Sgt H. Richards, No.1809 Pte W. Keneally all 1st Bn Lancs Fus for the VC under Article 13 of the Warrant', and he also recommended Cpl Cosgrove for a specific personal act. Gen Robb put these revised recommendations forward for approval on 7 Aug, obtained this at various levels on 9th and 12th, on which date he instructed MS3 to prepare the necessary submission, that for Cosgrove going to King George V over Kitchener's signature on 14 Aug, and for the other three on 23rd. The submission now stated 'Amongst the many very gallant officers and men engaged in this most hazardous undertaking, Capt Willis, Sgt Richards and Pte Keneally have been selected by their comrades as having performed the most signal acts of bravery and devotion to duty', in which terms their awards were gazetted the following day.

The request by Hunter Weston for the substitution of Cpl Grimshaw for the second allowable private does not seem to have been pressed by Hamilton, though he was awarded a DCM in the *London Gazette* of 16 Nov 1915.

This was how matters stood until in the early part of 1917 Gen

274   PRO, WO 32/4995

Wolley Dod raised once more the question of the awards for Gallipoli. On 26 Feb the MS, Lt-Gen Sir F.J. Davies submitted to the Deputy CIGS, Maj-Gen Sir R.D. Whigham, a minute examining Dod's representation. Evidently he found a good deal of substance in it, and that the cases deserved reconsideration. He noted Hunter Weston's reference to the deeds being performed 'under my very eyes' which suggested that he had had Clause 7 of the Warrant in mind. It had been the WO who had decided to treat the matter as a case of collective gallantry, and this had been interpreted by Hamilton's staff as authorising the award to one officer, one NCO and two privates per *battalion,* whereas this scale was laid down in Clause 13 as applying per *company,* and more than one company had taken part in the exploit. Three of those originally recommended had been excluded on this basis; of these, Capt Bromley, subsequently drowned in the sinking of the *Royal Edward* on 13 Aug 1915, had received no award, and Cpl Grimshaw had received the DCM. The MS now suggested that it was open to consideration whether Grimshaw and possibly Bromley might not be recommended for the VC. The reply given on 28 Feb was that the DCIGS was strongly inclined to recommend the award of the VC to both. On the following day the matter came before Sir R.H. Brade, the PUS, who gave his opinion, 'If more than one Co. then additional 1 officer, 1 NCO and 2 privates, or rather 3 privates as only one has been recommended so far. There evidently was more than one Co. But we are asked to give 1 Officer — 2 NCOs (i.e. Stubbs as well as Grimshaw). The only point is can we give the 1 extra NCO in place of the 3 privates. This is a question of strictness in the interpretation of the Warrant. I think we can get over this — if necessary by adding the second NCO as a case of individual act. If we can't do this then we have to choose between Stubbs and Grimshaw, and in that case I think the latter gets it. But I would give them both.'

It is interesting to try to calculate at how many points the PUS's very commonsensical view was in breach of the strict letter of Clause 13. Obviously it was disregarding the strict application of the numerical distribution of Crosses. But, perhaps more strikingly, it was breaching the whole principle of award by ballot. If any additional names were to be put forward, this could only be done in strict logic by going back to the original participants, and asking them to vote again. In fact the list was now reverting to the original six names put forward by Hunter Weston, which he had clearly arrived at before any formal ballot had been held. However, strict logic was not followed here, and on 2 Mar the AMS wrote to the DCIGS, seeking his advice, drawing the reply two days later that he supported all three.

A submission to King George V naturally followed, and in this the names of Bromley, Stubbs and Grimshaw were put forward as equally deserving with those already approved, with the further recommendation that Cpl Grimshaw's DCM should be cancelled in consequence. This was put forward on 8 Mar, signed by the King and the awards gazetted on 15 Mar. In this *Gazette* the citation that had appeared on 24 Aug 1915 with the earlier Gallipoli awards was reprinted, with a note that these three names were to be read in conjunction with the earlier ones.

Since the episode of Gallipoli there have been no further instances of VCs awarded by ballot for any action by the Army. There were, however, to be seven more such awards, relating to three further incidents during the 1914-18 War involving the Royal Navy and Royal Marines. The first of these concerned the action between the 'Q Ship' HMS *Pargust* and the UC29, on 7 Jun 1917, under the command of Commander Gordon Campbell, who had already been awarded the VC for a personal act of gallantry as commander in another 'Q Ship' action on the previous 17 Feb. It appears that upon this later occasion the Admiralty had found it difficult to decide, on the basis of Campbell's report, upon whom the VC should be conferred, and therefore referred the matter to the King, who had approved the selection of one officer and one seaman by ballot, those chosen being Lt R.N. Stuart, the First Lieutenant, and Seaman W. Williams.[275] For the guidance of the 1918 Interdepartmental Committee on the VC, Campbell gave a report of how he had then proceeded. 'I read out the award to the officers and men and gave 24 hours notice for the ballot. I got an officer from the office at Plymouth to superintend the ballot. Each officer wrote the name of an officer on a chit, and each rating wrote the name of a rating on a chit. Personally I took no part in the voting, beyond noting down the name of an officer and man which were only to be used in the event of an even draw. Neither was necessary. The balloting officer only gave out the names of the selected ones so that no one should know how near he might have been. Of course as Captain of the ship I made it clear that I was not included in the vote or the position would be impossible and I do not consider that was their Lordships' intention. I do not think there is anything else I can tell you about it.'[276] In his book *My Mystery Ships,* Campbell added to this information 'My officers did me the honour of expressing their wish that I should be the officer recipient,

275   PRO, WO 32/3443
276   *ibid*

but I, of course, could not agree to this, as I already felt that the VC I wore was on behalf of my crew and through no special act of my own.'[277]

It would appear that a similar scale of awards was decided on in consequence of Campbell's further 'Q Ship' exploit in the *Dunraven* against the UC 71 on 8 Aug 1917. Here there appears to have been no question regarding the selection of the officer recipient, Lt Bonner, Campbell's First Lieutenant in the action receiving the Cross as a personal award. For the other recipient a somewhat unusually restricted ballot was held, Petty Officer Ernest Pitcher's award being gazetted as 'selected by the crew of a gun... to receive the VC under Rule 13 of the Royal Warrant'. A ballot of this nature appears to have been stretching the terms of the Warrant, but as the events of the Gallipoli awards show, such things were not ruled out at that time. Certainly the circumstances were such that, even within the context of a 'Q Ship' action, Campbell had a collective act of heroism to deal with, in which he might well have found it impossible to single out any one man as more deserving than any other, for the events of the action required a gun crew to remain in concealment on the poop, which was on fire and, since it contained the magazine, was certain to blow up. By a remarkable piece of good luck, when the explosion did take place, and the entire gun's crew was blown in the air, their fall back on to the deck of the ship was broken by a number of dummy railway waggons constructed of wood and canvas, as part of the ship's disguise, so that no lives were lost. This was the crew that took part in the ballot, selecting the captain of the gun, all the remaining members receiving the CGM.[278]

The one remaining occasion upon which the selection of VC recipients has so far been made by ballot was for the assault upon Zeebrugge on 22/23 Apr 1918. Here two separate ballots were held, one for the Royal Navy participants, and the other for those of the Royal Marines, the voting being deliberately held in this way to prevent the formation with the greater number of survivors outvoting any selection from the other.[279] It would appear that the decision taken as to the number of recipients in the case of the *Pargust* was again invoked by the Admiralty, for the number selected by each force was two, one officer and one other, despite the fact that this number is at considerable

277   Rear-Admiral Gordon Campbell, *My Mystery Ships,* London 1928, p228
278   *ibid,* p258
279   PRO, WO 32/3443

variance with the terms of Clause 13. The selection of the Naval participants, from HMS *Vindictive, Iris II* and *Royal Daffodil* and the naval assaulting force was Commander A.F.B. Carpenter and Able Seaman A.E. McKenzie; for the Marines, Capt E. Bamford, RMLI, and Sgt N.A. Finch, RMA, it being a matter for comment in the citation that a member of the Royal Marine Artillery should have been so selected by a unit the majority of whom were from the Royal Marine Light Infantry. The original record of the Marine ballot, although not listed in the catalogue, was exhibited in the Victoria Cross Centenary Exhibition, held at Marlborough House in 1956. It consists of a scrap of flimsy yellow paper, with all the names mentioned in the voting written on it in blue crayon, with lines of ticks by each recording the individual votes received, and is illustrated as Plate 5. As will be seen about a score of names were mentioned, but the preponderence of ticks against the two chosen appears quite overwhelming. Sgt Finch was heard to say in a radio interview, apropos the Cross he wore 'This isn't really mine; I'm only selected to wear it on behalf of the Regiment, and when I die it will have to be returned to the Regiment.' There seems to be no foundation for such a remark, for nothing has ever appeared in any official document to suggest that the Cross of a recipient selected by ballot is any less his personal property than one awarded for an individual act.

There is one curious circumstance in relation to the Zeebrugge awards. As has been pointed out earlier, the holding of a ballot did not prevent the award of a Cross for an individual act of heroism in the same operation, provided it could be regarded as a distinct episode; therefore no problems are raised by the award of the VC to Lt R.D. Sandford, RN, who won his Cross for placing a submarine filled with explosive against the railway viaduct in the harbour, or the several given to the men of the motor launches who went in to take off the survivors of the assault. However, it is difficult to see how the two posthumous awards gazetted on 17 Mar 1919 to Lt-Commanders G.N. Bradford and A.L. Harrison can have been sanctioned, since both received the Cross for their part in command of the naval storming parties from *Iris II* and *Vindictive,* services which would appear to have been entirely within the scope of the exploit for which the recipients had been selected by ballot.

When an interdepartmental working party was set up at the end of July 1918 to consider the revision of the VC Warrants, one of its terms of reference was, 'What amplification, if any, is necessary to facilitate the interpretation of Clause XIII'.[280] In the discussion of this question, Col Graham, the DMS made a number of interesting statements, mainly in support of the view that, in the conditions of modern war, the conduct of a ballot was largely impracticable. 'In the case of the landing of the Lancashire Fusiliers at Gallipoli, no ballot could possibly have been applied there. They landed and most of them got killed, and eventually they began to sum up things, and people who watched the operation from trawlers and ships and had possibly seen things through glasses, and were able to identify certain people doing certain things made reports, and after a long period of time it was evident that the particular people seen doing were so-and-so and so-and-so... I think it impossible that any large proportion of the survivors had a say in the matter at all... It was really that the survivors were asked to state their opinion, but the survivors were very few in number, and no officer survived at all. The officer cases always wash out, and in a forlorn hope in which you have elected VCs it is very seldom that there is any officer left to vote.' Graham was evidently not an altogether reliable witness – he was in error in saying that no officer from the Lancashire Fusiliers survived the landing, and the evidence of his work in the WO papers shows that he often misunderstood the paperwork on earlier VC awards, but there does seem to be an inherent probability in what he is here describing. He had another point to make also. 'We have used the elective principle in many cases in this war without its being done regularly. Practically every high distinction is given more or less on this elective principle, that is to say the Commanding Officer consults his officers, but it is not done on the terms laid down here.' It is fairly clear that it was arguments such as these which led to the somewhat less strict rules for the conduct of the ballot 'in such manner as shall be determined... by the Officer directing the selection to be made',[281] in the Warrant of 1920.

Another question to engage the attention of the Committee was that of numbers. When the 1856 Warrant was drawn up, a company [the unit upon which the selection was based] had comprised sixty or seventy men, whereas in the First World War, it numbered two hundred and fifty rifles. The Admiralty clearly favoured a more generous distribution, with a sliding scale starting at four [on the old basis] for a party of twenty-four seamen. As the WO representative pointed out this would apply to any boarding party, and the general view was that this

280   *ibid*, for all that follows.
281   See Appendix XII

was too lavish. A suggestion that brigades should be included in the terms for collective awards was rejected, since it was too big a unit, and eventually Mr Morgan, the secretary to the working party, suggested the scale that was finally adopted, namely one officer, one NCO, and one private for a body of one hundred, a second private if the body was between one and two hundred, and special consideration if the number was over two hundred. It was at this point in the discussions that it was also settled that the holding of the ballot should be as determined by the circumstances. This was all finally incorporated as the ninth article of the new Warrant, which represents the terms still operating, even though they have never been invoked.

Between the two meetings of the 1918 working party the Admiralty had suggested that the new Warrant should contain a provision that participation in a VC ballot be noted in the records of those taking part, with a corresponding provision for deletion of this in similar circumstances to those that would entail forfeiture of the Cross.[282] This suggestion was not pursued at the time, but in Jan 1919 a letter went from the Army Council to the Admiralty, saying that while they accepted that such record of participation was desirable it was thought that this was a matter that could be more appropriately dealt with in King's Regulations than in the Warrant itself.[283] Nothing more was heard of the matter for another four years. On 18 May 1923, a further letter went from the WO to the Admiralty on the same subject. This noted that the Admiralty had issued an instruction for such a record to be placed in the service certificate of their personnel. However, so far as the Army was concerned, only Other Ranks had records of service in which such an item could be entered and subsequently exhibited, whereas the equivalent records of officers remained with the authority. The military authorities felt that such entries might lead to the supposition that the individual concerned should have received the VC, and this might tend to the regard of the decoration being cheapened. In their view there should be no entry made for use in civil affairs, but it should be confined to military documents.[284] Nothing more has ever been done on this point by the WO though, according to Gordon Campbell[285] such a note was inserted by the Admiralty on each man's certificate of service.

282   PRO, WO 32/3443
283   VCR, iii p344
284   *ibid*, p348
285   *My Mystery Ships*, p228

Chapter 11

Awards to the Indian Services

THE INDIAN MUTINY was, in many ways, crucial for the development
of the Victoria Cross. One aspect of this, the extent to which general
officers commanding in the field might arrogate to themselves the right
of bestowing the Cross, has already been discussed in previous chapters.
But one problem of eligibility became immediately apparent, for the
British forces engaged were made up of two distinct entities; on the one
hand those who were, in the fullest sense, 'soldiers of the Queen', and
on the other those who were technically servants of the East India
Company, even though the employment of the one was just as fully
military as the other; for the East India Company's soldiers were in no
sense part of the British Army. On a broad interpretation of the Warrant
the point may be thought of little substance, but the arbiter of such
points of interpretation at this time was Lord Panmure, and broad
interpretations were things that he was evidently incapable of giving.
'As for Panmure', wrote an exasperated Lord Clarendon to his wife on
1 Oct 1857, following a Cabinet meeting at which both men had been
present, 'with his foolish red-tape objections, I could have knocked him
down' — and the point under discussion which provoked this outburst
seems, curiously enough, to have been the question of providing
military assistance against the mutineers in India.[286] However, if the
view was taken that the 1856 Warrant did not cover the East India
Company troops, there could have been little objection to drawing up a
new Warrant, to remedy the deficiency. All precedents pointed in the
same direction. Since 1815 awards of the Order of the Bath had been
made to reward military service in the Company's forces and even
though the statutes did not formally render them eligible for grades
other than that of CB and KCB until 1847, GCBs had in fact been
conferred on them since 1818, whilst for the last fifteen years there had

---

286 Sir Herbert Maxwell, Bart. *The Life and Letters of the Fourth Earl
of Clarendon,* London 1913, ii p153

been a reciprocity in campaign awards, so that the Queen's troops had regularly been authorised to receive and wear the medals issued by the Company when fighting alongside its forces, as in the First Afghan War, whereas in the First China War of 1842, when the roles had been reversed, the British Government's medal had equally gone to both. So, although no papers are extant regarding the preparation of a new warrant, it may be assumed that its production did not entail any very prolonged discussion, and the new instrument, extending eligibility for the VC to the officers and men of the naval and military service of the East India Company was signed by Queen Victoria on 29 Oct 1857.[287] But though there had been no obstacle in the way of making this extension, the policy had been established that the Warrant of 1856 was to be construed in its narrowest terms, and this despite the widely [and wisely] drawn wording of Clause 12, 'It is ordained that as cases may arise not falling within the rules above specified... We will... confer the decoration...' and it was only the ignoring of this discretionary power which had alone made a new warrant necessary. This attitude can only be considered to have constituted an unfortunate precedent in the later history of the Cross.

The new Warrant may have settled one problem, but it left open [or at least made no mention of] another. Just as there was a dichotomy between the forces of the Crown and of the Company in India, so there was a dichotomy within the forces of the Company itself, which were divided racially into Europeans, who only served in the ranks in their own units but led the native Indian units, and Indians, who provided the rank and file and junior commanders only of their own units, so that no European was ever under the command of an Indian. Much may be deduced of the attitude of the Company to its Indian officers from one of the reasons given to the Court of Directors in 1834 by the Government of India in connection with a proposal to establish a number of decorations for Indian soldiers — 'To increase the respectability and improve the prospects of the Native Commissioned Officers, by placing within their reach honors, [sic] distinctions and superior emoluments, without imparting to them such additional power or influence over the Native Soldiery as might be injurious to the authority, which, in consideration of the composition of the Indian Army, it has hitherto been deemed necessary to vest exclusively in the European Officers'.[288] But this distinction between Indian and European had been given no

---

287   See Appendix V
288   *Medals and Decorations of the British Army and Navy,* ii pp533/4

recognition in the new Warrant. The point was soon to be put to the test for when, on 31 Oct 1857, the Company brought forward the name of Lt W.A. Kerr as meriting the VC [a recommendation which must have originated in India before the new Warrant had been signed, so evidently it had not occurred to the Company's officials there that the 1856 Warrant did not cover their own troops] for his gallantry in tackling a fort held by sepoys following the outbreak of mutiny at Kolapore, it joined with it the name of his leading aide, Daffadar Gunput Rao Derkur, as this was the form in which the original recommendation had been made by the Government of Bombay. In doing this, however, the Company observed that they did not recommend the extension of the Cross to Indian troops since they were already eligible for the Indian Order of Merit. This was hardly surprising, in view of what has already been said about the attitude of the Company to its Indian troops − perhaps more surprising was the attitude of the Bombay government in having recommended the Daffadar in the first place − but there was some substance in their objection, since with the existence of the Indian Order of Merit, [admission to which was confined to Indians, was earned by conspicuous gallantry, and by successive promotion through its three grades up to double pay could be obtained by the recipient] it could be argued that the Indian soldier was already better provided for in the way of gallantry awards than was his British equivalent, and that it would hardly be fair for the Indian soldier to be eligible for both when his European colleague could only earn the one. This reasoning did not, apparently, appeal to Sir Henry Storks, who commented that he was unable to see on what grounds the Governor-General in Council objected to Indians being eligible for the VC: the Indian Order of Merit was no bar, since British troops were eligible for a medal with pension as well [by which he presumably meant the DCM, though its financial provisions were much more modest] , and he added what might have been a more telling point, that the French gave their Legion of Honour to their non-European troops. It is of interest that this was one of the very few points of interpretation of the VC warrants which Panmure was not prepared to settle on his own responsibility. On 14 Dec 1857 he agreed to put the matter forward for consideration and on 16th he noted on the papers, 'It is the opinion of the Cabinet that the natives had better be dealt with as Lord Canning suggests.' i.e. by the award of the Indian Order of Merit and not the VC. It may, perhaps, be added that the recommendation in respect of Lt Kerr did not succeed either on this occasion; though he was eventually awarded the Cross for this exploit it was only when renewed representations were made by the Court of Directors of the East India Company in April 1858.[289]

The point at issue, it should be stressed, was not simply that of race, but the particular circumstances of the Indian Army. Effective demonstration that there was no policy of confining the VC to Europeans is provided by the fact that the VC was bestowed at this very time — the actual date of gazetting being 1 Feb 1859 — on William Hall who was a Nova Scotian negro serving in the Royal Navy, and further evidence is provided by the awards of Crosses to Samuel Hodge in 1867 and W.J. Gordon in 1892, both of whom were negroes serving in the ranks of the West India Regiment.

The position, as ruled by the Cabinet in 1857, appears to have remained unchallenged for some forty years, though when a recommendation was submitted to the Queen in Dec 1893 for the award of the VC to Surgeon Lloyd for his conduct at Fort Sima, the Queen was moved to enquire whether anything was being done for Subadar Mateb Singh, who had also played a prominent part in the exploit, and expressed herself glad to hear that he was to receive the Third Class of the Indian Order of Merit as were another five sepoys who also participated.[290] Apart from the Queen's enquiry, there does not seem to have been any comment on this occasion regarding the treatment of the two races in the Indian Army. This was not the case four years later, when the VC was awarded to Maj Adams and Lt Fincastle, and the Indian Order of Merit to five men of the Corps of Guides for their action at Nawa Kili.[291] These awards were gazetted on 9 Nov 1897 and there can be little doubt that this is what inspired Mr Brookfield, MP for Rye, to put down a parliamentary question for answer by the S of S for India on 3 Mar 1898, 'Whether it is the case that Native Officers and soldiers of the Indian Army are at present ineligible for the decoration of the VC, and whether, in view of the many signal acts of valour and devotion for which these subjects of HM have been distinguished since the VC was first instituted, he will consider the expediency of advising an alteration in the present conditions of winning the VC so as to make all officers and soldiers in HM's service eligible for this reward for distinguished bravery in the field.'[292] It will be noted that the question was addressed to the

Secretary for India, and not to the WO; in fact the constitutional position was a little curious, for the Indian Army was most certainly a subject to be dealt with by the former department, yet the WO was the department charged with the responsibility for matters relating to the VC. It was obviously going to take a very close interest in the matter that had been raised, and evidently the question quickly caught the attention of Lord Wolseley, the CinC, for on 2 Mar Gen Grove, the MS, wrote to the PUS, 'The view of the CinC is that the VC may fairly be thrown open to Native Officers and Soldiers of the Indian Army. He presumes however that the India Office will be consulted – in fact the question is addressed to them.' In forwarding this opinion to the S of S Lord Lansdowne, Brodrick, at that time his US of S but eventual successor, added his own view 'I am sure the CinC's proposal will be most popular.' Despite these opinions, and evidently conscious of the proprieties as between the two departments of state, Landowne's reply was 'We must not intervene unless we are asked. I have myself great doubts whether it would be wise to give the VC to natives. The change might lead to much discontent in the native army, and to all sorts of invidious comparisons'.[293] And despite the statement by R.C.K. Ensor that 'Lord Lansdowne... was no match for the masterful Wolseley',[294] it was the S of S's view that, on this occasion, prevailed for the reply Lord George Hamilton, S of S for India, gave to Mr Brookfield was 'My hon. friend is perhaps unaware that the officers and soldiers of the native Army, who are ineligible for the Victoria Cross, have an order of their own, the Order of Merit, for which they alone are eligible. This order is given as a reward for personal bravery. It consists of three classes and carries with it additional pay – In the 3rd class one third, in the second class two thirds, in the first class the equivalent of the recipient's net pay. In the lower ranks the additional pay is less than the £10 attached to the Victoria Cross, in the higher ranks it is more. The order is highly valued by the native Army and I see great objections to an alteration in the existing arrangement.' To this Mr Brookfield's obvious rejoinder was 'Does the noble lord mean the House to understand that the Order of Merit referred to is regarded as a full equivalent to the Victoria Cross?' The best reply Hamilton could make to this was 'Yes Sir, it is an equivalent so far as the native Army is concerned. It is perhaps given on a somewhat more liberal scale than the VC, but it is an equivalent'. Here Mr Redmond, the Irish Nationalist, evidently saw the

293   VCR, ii p393
294   R.C.K. Ensor, *England 1870-1914,* Oxford 1936, p292

opportunity of making some mischief, for he intervened to ask, 'Is there any general disposition amongst the soldiers of the native Army to become eligible for the VC, and if so, whether arrangements could be made whereby they might obtain it as well as white soldiers?' and Hamilton's reply to this, 'The existing arrangements, I think, are more favourable to the native soldiers than if they were eligible for the VC' simply drew from Redmond the retort 'May I ask the noble lord to answer the question put to him?' Hamilton's final answer was 'I cannot give any other answer than that which I have already given', and Redmond concluded with the threat, 'I beg to give notice that I will put several questions on this subject' – a threat that he did not in fact carry out.[295]

Evidently, from the attitude taken by the S of S for India, there was no likelihood of any approach being made to the WO from the India Office, which Lansdowne had laid down as the prerequisite for any alteration in the Warrant in favour of Indian troops. After one final set of VC awards in respect of Dargai and Bilot, which were gazetted on 20 May following, the North West Frontier seems to have settled down into a somewhat quieter period – at least no more VCs were to be won there for another seventeen years, so there was nothing to bring the point of the Indian ineligibility to public notice, for the May 1898 awards came too soon after the negative parliamentary response of March to reopen the question. But it was perhaps evidence that official opinion was not altogether unready for a change that both the CinC and the Under S of S had reacted favourably to the possibility in 1898. It is, however, strange that Brodrick himself took no steps in the matter when he became Secretary for War, nor even [since Lansdowne had laid down the doctrine that it was a matter for the initiative of the India Office], when Brodrick succeeded Lord George Hamilton as Secretary of State for India in 1903 and had, as virtually the only military occurrence during his tenure of it, the case of the action at Gyantse, Tibet, for which Lt Grant was awarded the VC and his Gurkha companion, Havildar Karbir Pun, the Indian Order of Merit. However, events were soon to reach their climax, and on 21 Oct 1911 a Warrant extending eligibility for the VC to the native officers, non-commissioned officers and men of the Indian Army was at last signed by King George V.[296] Both the previous supporters of the move – Wolseley and Brodrick – had now disappeared from the scene, and no direct evidence survives of

295   *Hansard,* 4th Series, liv cols 469/70
296   See Appendix XI

the detailed events which brought it into being.[297] But, bearing in mind what had been previously laid down about the direction from which such a move was required to come, and noting the date of the new Warrant, there seems a very strong probability as to what had produced it. The Warrant was dated just three weeks before the King sailed on his Durbar visit to India, and it is as part of the public relations exercise for this that it must surely be read.

An India Office initiative had been required by Lansdowne, and of all circumstances the visit of the King Emperor to his Coronation Durbar in India seems one that would have been most likely to produce such an initiative, Brodrick having remarked thirteen years previously how popular such a measure would be. So it seems virtually certain that it was the India Office that started the first move to produce the 1911 Warrant though, again harking back to the events of 1898, it does not look as if there would have been any great unwillingness at the WO to move in this direction. It is just possible that the source of the initiative within the India Office can be identified, for it is on record that the planning of the Delhi Durbar was the work of the Marquess of Crewe, the S of S for India.[298] There appears, therefore, at least a very strong possibility that it was on his initiative that the matter was raised with the WO. The fact that Crewe himself stood high in the confidence of the Royal Family would undoubtedly have strengthened his hand in such a matter.

The old question of the relationship of the Cross to the Order of Merit was dealt with very simply, and in the obvious way. As from 12 Dec 1911 the First Class of the Indian decoration was abolished and the old Second and Third Classes redesignated First and Second Class respectively, but without prejudice to the interests — particularly financial — of those who had been admitted to the Order on its old basis.[299] In the case of Indian recipients alone, all ranks were made eligible for the VC pension, and these pensions were to continue to the widows of such recipients. Evidently the reference to native officers in this Warrant had not been very carefully thought over, for in the 1920 Warrant the wording was altered to make it clear that only Viceroy

---

297   An index of WO Series 012 files at the PRO shows that such a file did exist, but has now been destroyed, which seems an unforgivable piece of 'weeding'. No papers exist in the India Office library, and the episode is not referred to in the autobiography of Lord Haldane, S of S for War at the time, nor do there appear to be any papers on the subject in the Royal Archives.

298   *Dictionary of National Biography,* sub Crewe

299   *The VC, Its Heroes and Their Valour,* p418

Commissioned Officers were intended. To some extent, therefore, it could be said that the native Indian soldier was at an advantage over his European colleague but, by and large, it could now be said that both races had been placed on an equal footing as regards the highest honour, and also as regards to lesser honours, even though they retained their distinctive and separate awards at the lower levels.

It was somewhat ironic that, after all that had gone before, the first VC awarded to Indian soldiers should have been won many thousands of miles from the North West Frontier, these being earned by Naik Darwan Singh Negi and Sepoy Khudad Khan and gazetted together on 7 Dec 1914, for services with the British Expeditionary Force in Flanders. Nevertheless, it may be held fortunate that the new Warrant was produced in time for the 1914-18 War, for the circumstance of native Indians, fighting in what was essentially a European conflict and yet unable to share in the rewards of their English fellow-soldiers, could not have been other than distasteful.

With the issue of the 1911 Warrant little more remains to be said of the separate concern of Indian troops with the VC, for they were thenceforth embodied in its provisions, and all subsequent warrants took the necessary account of any particular circumstance that had to be catered for to comprise them in its terms. A few other specifically 'Indian' points may be mentioned. A detail in which the coverage of the 1911 Warrant was incomplete was dealt with in that of 1920, which for the first time included men serving in the forces of the Native States as among those eligible for the Cross.[300] On 1 Apr 1937 Burma ceased to be part of the Indian Empire, and a further Warrant was therefore issued on 9 May 1938, to make members of the Burma forces eligible in their own right for the Cross[301] and the same action was taken by a Warrant of 25 Jan 1941, to include the members of the newly created Indian Air Force among those listed as eligible,[302] though in neither case were any members of these forces ever awarded the Cross. Finally, a Warrant of 31 Dec 1942 took out any specific reference to the amount of the financial provision for Indian and Burman holders of the Cross, making these matters to be dealt with by the regulations of the administrations of those countries, and the money to be provided from their own revenues.[303]

---

300   See Appendix XII
301   See Appendix XIV
302   See Appendix XVI
303   See Appendix XVII

With the ending of the Indian Empire in 1947 one part of that
country's forces remained as part of those of the United Kingdom,
namely the Brigade of Gurkhas, these being henceforth part of the
British Army, in exactly the same way as the old West India Regiments
had been. For their benefit the provisions of the old clause regarding
pensions to the widows of VC recipients have been continued, and still
find a place in the latest Victoria Cross Warrant, that of 1961.[304]

304   See Appendix XVIII

Chapter 12

Awards to Civilians

TO TRACE TO its origin yet one more theme in the evolution of the Victoria Cross it is again necessary to go back to the Indian Mutiny, since the circumstances of these operations provided yet one more field in which the conditions of award, based on the events and experiences of the Crimean War, were found wanting. In the circumstances of the Mutiny there could be no entirely non-combatant role for any male European in the areas where fighting broke out, and it was common for various non-military persons to bear arms alongside regular soldiers; indeed, considering the limited numbers of European soldiers in India, operations would have been much restricted if the soldiery had not been aided by civilian volunteers and, in such circumstances as the siege of the Residency at Lucknow, when even schoolboys helped man the defences, to attempt to distinguish soldier from civilian would have been impossible. That a demand should arise for the VC to be made available to such non-military persons in these circumstances was therefore only to be expected.

The detailed steps which led to the issue of a Royal Warrant to widen the availability of the VC in this way cannot be entirely reconstructed since no War Office file now exists on the subject of the gazetting of the award to Thomas Kavanagh and R.L. Mangles, the first two men to benefit under it. But bearing in mind that both were, as members of the Indian Civil Service, in the employ of the East India Company, and that the Company was responsible for submitting a large number of recommendations for the VC to military personnel [often, in fact, duplicating recommendations already made or in the process of being made by the CinC India and thereby causing much administrative complication at the WO], it seems likely that it was the Company which pressed their claim, so that similar conduct on the part of both its civil and military servants could receive an equal reward. As will have been noted from the previous chapter, the Company had not bothered itself overmuch about the exact wording of the Warrants when the question was raised of conferring the Cross on a native Indian soldier. And, certainly, Kavanagh, in submitting his account of his exploits, did not think he was debarred from claiming the VC as his just reward for them. [305] Confirmation that this was the course of events seems to be provided by the one surviving document in the case, a letter from Gen Storks at the WO to Mr J.C. Melvill at East India House on 13 Nov 1858. In this, Storks refers to the claims of Kavanagh and Mangles and informs Melvill that the Queen has approved, on the recommendation of Gen Peel, the S of S for War, that all civilians who have borne arms as volunteers under the orders of an officer in command of troops in the field, shall be eligible for the VC.[306] The Warrant to this effect was signed by the Queen on 13 Dec,[307] so that the WO letter had anticipated the official action of the Royal Warrant by exactly a month, and it is unthinkable that such a letter would have been sent to anyone who was not concerned in the most intimate way with the matters to which it related. To read it as the WO confirmation to the prime mover that a desired course of action was to be adopted, is the only interpretation which seems to fit the facts.

The logic of treating non-military persons on the same basis as regular soldiers, in the circumstances of the Indian Mutiny, must have been so overwhelming as to preclude much official argument over the propriety of such a step, and, since the proposal seems to have arisen out of the specific cases of Kavanagh and Mangles [most of the Victorian amending warrants did arise as the result of consideration of specific cases], matters must have been helped by the fact that Sir Colin Campbell was already on record as speaking in the highest terms of Kavanagh's conduct, 'one of the most daring feats ever attempted'.[308] However, one note of WO caution may be discerned in the stipulation in the new Warrant, requiring it to be established that the non-military person in question 'was serving under the orders of a General or other officer in command of troops in the field'. In this way the exploit would always be performed in a situation where there would be a military commander competent to adjudicate on its merit, though at the cost of rendering ineligible the isolated magistrate who might have acquitted himself well when threatened by mutineers on his station. Despite the

---

305 P.A. Wilkins, *The History of the VC,* London 1904, p134
306 VCR, i pp 138/41
307 See Appendix XII
308 Quoted in *The VC and DSO,* i p62

clarity of the situation regarding the new Warrant and the two men
whose claims had given rise to it, the gazetting of the Crosses was by no
means immediate, for it was only on 6 Jul 1859, almost seven months
after the Warrant had been signed, that the official announcement of
their conferment appeared. The next such award followed at the
beginning of 1860, when the India Office brought forward the name of
another member of the Bengal Civil Service, Mr W.F. McDonell, who
had been recommended to them by the Government of India, with the
support of Lord Clyde. It may be taken as confirmation of what was said
earlier about the Indian Government's lack of concern with the niceties
of the Warrants, that the same dispatch also included recommendations
for two of its military servants, Capt Cafe and Lt F.D.M. Brown, without
taking any account of the differing Warrants needing to be invoked.
These recommendations were forwarded by the India Office to the
Horse Guards on 29 Jan, and by the Duke of Cambridge to Sidney
Herbert, now S of S for War, on 4 Feb. Mr Pennington, in giving his
usual appraisal of the recommendations in the terms of the Warrant,
commented to Sir Edward Lugard, PUS, on the 9th, that the two
officers were clearly unobjectionable, but that it was not clearly stated
that McDonell was serving under the orders of an officer, as the Warrant
required, though he thought this might be fairly assumed. That
Pennington need not have entertained any doubts on this score is
shown by the PUS's note in forwarding the papers to Herbert, which
provided the almost perfect answer. 'I know that Mr McDonell was
attached to troops, as he was attached to me as Special Commr. throughout my subsequent operations'. All three names were approved by the
Secretary of War on 13 Feb, went to the Queen on 15 Feb and were
published in the *London Gazette* on the 17th.[309]

There was to be one further civilian VC in the Mutiny – George Bell
Chicken, whose name is frequently, but wrongly, listed among the
naval recipients of the Cross, which no doubt arises from the fact that
he was serving with the Naval Brigade at the time of his exploit. The
error was originated very early in the story of Chicken's recommendation,
in fact occurring in the original papers received from Clyde via the
Government of India, and which the India Office forwarded to the
Horse Guards on 5 Mar 1860. A marginal note was, however, made on
them by Pennington, 'This is a mistake. I have ascertained that he is not
in the Indian Navy'[310] and, as is quite clearly stated in the *London*

309   PRO, WO 32/7340
310   PRO, WO 32/7342

Gazette of 27 Apr 1860, announcing the award of the VC to Mr Chicken, this was done under the terms of the Warrant of 13 Dec 1858. Another name was put forward in the same papers from India, that of Lt C.G. Baker, who did eventually receive the Cross, but not for nearly another two years, the recommendation on this occasion being held insufficient as not relating to any specific act of gallantry. What had evidently caused Pennington most trouble was the question of Baker's status, as a lieutenant in the Bengal Police Bn, and this is a good illustration of the complexity of distinguishing military from non-military persons in the circumstances of the Mutiny. A document in the WO file, which has no indication of its source but may be presumed to be the India Office's answer to Pennington's enquiries, reads, 'Mr Baker is not a military man but was appointed to the Bengal Police Battalion, a Corps having much of military organisation, which was raised for the protection of the Sonthal District, but on the outbreak of the disturbances was sent to protect the Bihar province, and did so in a very providential manner. He was there in the field during the whole of the disturbances and was employed uniformly with troops of the line when such were present. Baker was not a volunteer, but in virtue of his appointment, of course accompanied his Battalion' – which led Pennington to observe to Lugard, in putting forward the names of Chicken and Baker on 19 Mar that Baker was not a military person but *not* a volunteer, and that there might be a question of bringing the case within the Warrant.[311] As already remarked, Baker's name did not go forward upon this occasion, but when it finally did do so it was gazetted as a straightforward military award. Chicken, incidentally, never lived to receive his Cross, which was forwarded to his father, Mr George Chicken, Master Mariner, of 35 King David Lane, Shadwell, in Mar 1862.[312]

Chicken's Cross was the last to be awarded under the terms of the 1858 Warrant. On a narrow interpretation of the wording it could be read as spent with the ending of the Mutiny, by taking the 'such persons as aforesaid', whom it had made eligible, as referring to those who had borne arms 'against the mutineers', and as has been shown in other contexts, the interpretation given to the Warrants tended to be a narrow one. Certainly it was the narrow interpretation upon which Lt-Gen Whitmore, the then MS, based the WO letter to the India Office on 26 Mar 1881. 'The Revd J.W. Adams is not eligible for the decoration in question as it appears that he holds no Military Commission. The

311   *ibid*
312   VCR, i pp365/6

cases of Kavanagh, Mangles and McDonell quoted in your letter of
27 Jul 1880 do not constitute a precedent inasmuch as the decoration
was conferred on these gentlemen by a special Warrant which had
reference only to the Indian Mutiny'.[313] The case of the Rev J.W.
Adams, a chaplain accompanying the Kabul Field Force in the Second
Afghan War, is the next matter to require attention in the relation of
civilians to the VC. Concerning him, Sir Frederick Roberts wrote to the
AG in India on 29 Jan 1880,[314] 'I have no hesitation in saying that
were Mr Adams a combatant officer, I would recommend him for the
VC; but in the absence of any precedent for a clergyman receiving a
distinction of this nature, I content myself with submitting the
circumstances for His Excellency's information, as an official record of
a most chivalrous act'. Evidently the CinC was much of the same mind,
for on 17 Apr the AG wrote in his turn to the Military Department of
the Government of India, 'His Excellency [the CinC in India] is not
aware whether it is possible to bring it under the rules for the grant of
the Victoria Cross; there is, however, no question but that Mr Adams'
conduct was conspicuously gallant'. To this the Government replied on
11 May '... in the opinion of the Government of India the precedents
established in 1857 when the VC was conferred on Messrs Mangles and
McDonell of the Civil Service and Mr Kavanagh of the uncovenanted
Civil Service, would be applicable to the case of Mr Adams.

'...The circumstance of that gentleman's position as a non-combatant
and a clergyman do, in the opinion of the Government, mark the
character of his gallantry in a special and remarkable manner.

'Should His Excellency the Commander in Chief concur in this view
and consider that Mr Adams' services have established for him a
legitimate claim to the distinction, the Governor-General in Council
will have pleasure in forwarding for the favourable consideration of Her
Majesty's Government, any recommendation to that effect which His
Excellency may see fit to make'.

A letter from the AG followed on the 19th of that month, making
clear that the CinC did indeed concur, and containing the necessary
recommendation. The Government of India made its submission to the
S of S for India on 1 Jun, and it was the India Office's submission to the
WO on 27 Jul to which Gen Whitmore's reply has already been quoted.

The Government of India did not, of course, have the authority to
make any interpretation of the terms of the VC Warrants, which was

313   VCR, ii p236
314   PRO, WO 32/7399 for all that follows.

clearly the responsibility of the WO; nevertheless their rather casual regard for their exact wording [as against the pedantry of the WO] was very much in keeping with the events of twenty years previously, when their predecessors had put forward a number of cases which they felt deserving of the decoration, regardless of whether the persons recommended fell within the categories covered by the Warrants, such as soldiers serving in the East India Company's forces, civilians [both of which categories were brought in by extensions of the Warrant] and native Indian soldiers [who were not]. However, past experience had shown that if their recommendations had not always been within the Warrants as they originally stood, there were ways of dealing with such a situation. On 16 May 1881, not quite two months after Whitmore's unfavourable reply to the India Office, Sir Frederick Roberts wrote to the MS at the WO, using the cases of Kavanagh, Mangles and McDonell in a subtly different way. If the Warrant as it stood did not allow Mr Adams to receive the VC, why should a new warrant not be drawn up, '... as was done when certain civilian gentlemen received the VC for deeds of bravery performed by them during the Mutiny in India?' This seems to have been the first time this particular proposal had been made and, although Cambridge did not see the necessity for a new Warrant [one may presume he shared the Indian Government's broader interpretation of the December 1858 Warrant] he was evidently in no doubt of the worth of Adams' case, for the India Office's formal submission bears a note 'This seems an excellent case for the VC', which is signed George. However, the Warrant which was prepared was couched in very narrow terms, and the papers in the file make it abundantly clear that it was drawn up expressly to meet this one case. The memorandum from the WO asking the Queen to agree to it stated the whole point of the matter 'The Indian Ecclesiastical Establishment is a Civil Department', and this was the entire extent of the widening of the VC's availability. This memorandum went to Queen Victoria on 30 Jul, the new Warrant[315] was dated 6 Aug and Adams' award was notified in the London Gazette of 20th. As will be noted, the Warrant repeated the stipulation of the 1858 Warrant that the person recommended should be serving under the command of an officer commanding troops in the field, so that the WO was again asserting the necessity of military supervision for an act of civilian bravery to qualify for the award.

It is hardly surprising that under the very limited extension of the 1882 Warrant, Mr Adams was the sole beneficiary. The act of

315   See Appendix X

Mr Kavanagh, who had made his way in disguise through the lines of the mutineers to carry information of the besieged in Lucknow to the relieving force under Sir Colin Campbell, was to be invoked on at least two other occasions when the claims of a civilian to the VC was being urged. In 1879 a suggestion seems to have been made in some quarters that Mr Forbes, a war correspondent, merited this reward for carrying official dispatches reporting the victory at Ulundi through Zulu territory to a telegraph station[316] though this appears never to have received any official backing. The second case is more interesting. Although no file survives, a WO index handed over to the PRO shows that these files once contained one discussing the possibility of the award of the VC to a civilian for service in the Boxer Rising. There can, however, be very little doubt of the exploit which was under discussion. The first attempt to send a force inland to the relief of those besieged in the legations at Pekin had led to the relief force in their turn being besieged in Tientsin, a fact of which the Allied forces on the coast were unaware, or at least were taking no steps to remedy. On 20 Jun 1900 a young English civilian, James Watts, who was a member of the Tientsin Volunteer Corps, volunteered to ride from the besieged Tientsin to Taku, where the Allied force was, with news of their almost desperate situation; he was an excellent horseman, and knew the country well. He set out at night, taking an escort of three Cossacks from the Allied contingent in Tientsin, and one spare pony. They charged at full gallop through the villages and over the little hump-backed bridges which were a feature of the countryside where these danger points could not be by-passed, for the whole of the countryside through which the ride was being made was more or less hostile, Watts having one pony shot under him. They were favoured by a sea mist as they approached the coast, and on the morning of 21 June Watts delivered to the naval authorities information, in the light of which yet another relief expedition was mounted.[317] Admiral Seymour is certainly believed to have recommended Watts for a decoration,[318] and the belief was held in Watts' family that had he been a regular soldier, he would have received the VC.[319] He was in fact decorated by both the German Emperor and by the King of the Belgians, which led to a question being asked in Parliament on 2 Apr 1901. Lord Cranbourne's reply to this was that,

316   VCR, ii, insert between pp187/8
317   See Peter Fleming, *The Siege at Peking,* p85
318   Private information from Mr Erik Watts, nephew of James Watts.
319   See O.D. Rasmussen, *Tientsin, An Illustrated Outline History,* Tientsin 1925,
       I am indebted to Mr Erik Watts for bringing this material to my notice.

while HM Government had expressed high appreciation of the gallant and distinguished services of Mr Watts, he was unfortunately not eligible by existing warrants for any British order of merit. This reply raised a storm of protest in the British press, notably in the *Pall Mall Gazette,* which commented the following day, 'That this country should have to be taught by a foreign sovereign how a British subject ought to be rewarded for an act of distinguished gallantry, is not creditable to us, however much it is to the Kaiser. How long is this sort of stupid snobbery — which cannot recognise bravery in a civilian — to be tolerated?' Somewhat unusually such outcry seems to have had an effect, for on 13 May 1901 it was announced that a companionship of the Order of St Michael and St George had been conferred on Mr Watts in recognition of these services.[320] This may seem a curious circumstance for the bestowal of the CMG, but there was a precedent of some fifteen years previously when Capt J.R. Beech [who enters the VC story at another point also] received the same award for the similar service of carrying alone a letter from Queen Victoria to King John of Abyssinia, through most difficult and hostile country.[321]

The point at issue in this chapter so far is that of civilians who were serving as soldiers. When Viscount Fincastle [later the Earl of Dunmore] was recommended for the VC the position was rather the reverse. Sir Bindon Blood had recommended him with Maj and Brevet Lt-Col R.B. Adams, and would also have recommended Lt H.L.S. MacLean had he survived, for a joint act of bravery in the attempted rescue of a wounded fellow officer at Nawa Kili, on the North West Frontier of India; but in forwarding his name to the WO on 13 Sep 1897 the CinC India was forced to point out that Fincastle was not, in fact, serving under Sir Bindon — he was actually on leave from his own unit, and accompanying the expedition as special correspondent of *The Times.* To this the AMS, forwarding the papers to the PUS, added that he had only been allowed to accompany the expedition on condition that he should in no way belong to it, should not be on duty, and should not be eligible for any medal, gratuity or other reward that might afterwards be sanctioned for it. It was, he thought, curious that if he were a non-military person he would have been required, under the terms of the 1858 Warrant, to have been serving under the command of an officer in command of troops in the field which Fincastle most clearly was not whereas there was no requirement that any officer or member of the Army should be serving

320   Rasmussen, *op cit*
321   *The VC and DSO,* ii p44

under anyone's orders. It was perhaps fortunate that the CinC was prepared to overrule all this debate on the ground that Fincastle fulfilled the prime condition of performing a signal act in the presence of the enemy. Lord Lansdowne, the S of S, in approving on 11 Oct the submission of Fincastle's name to the Queen, commented, 'The warrants are not very distinct but the interpretation placed upon them by the CinC seems to me reasonable'[322] and Viscount Fincastle's award was duly gazetted on 9 Nov 1897.

The only other case on record in which the status of the person recommended was an issue, and also where a VC was sought officially for someone who might be reasonably considered a civilian, occurred at much the same time as the Fincastle episode. In December 1897 the Colonial Office approached the WO on the possibility of the award of a VC or DSO for Lt Henderson, a retired naval officer, who had displayed gallant conduct whilst employed in the essentially civilian post of Travelling Commissioner on the Gold Coast, and it was also made known to the WO that the Queen was interested in the case. The MS observed to the PUS that a retired Army officer would not be regarded as eligible for either decoration, but he had ascertained that the Admiralty would consider him as coming within the Warrant of the DSO, in virtue of his status as a retired naval officer [which is an interesting example of divergence of practice between the two service departments]. The MS commented that it was rather difficult to see what the WO had to do with the case of a retired naval officer employed by the Colonial Office — in this he was being obtuse; it was fairly clear that the WO was approached as the department responsible for the administration of the VC — but he suggested the case might be referred to the Admiralty as the more appropriate department to deal with it, and also, evidently one that was likely to give it a more favourable hearing. The Colonial Office was indeed informed in these terms on 22 Dec 1897, evidently with good effect, for on 8 Mar 1898 the award of a DSO to Henderson for his services in West Africa was duly gazetted.[323]

The main way in which the question of military awards to civilians came to be an issue in the 1914-18 War was in respect of gallant acts performed by members of the Merchant Navy. In the course of the discussions of the 1918 Interdepartmental Committee, which met to consider the drawing up of a new VC Warrant, it emerged that the Admiralty had adopted a typically sailorly method of dealing with this situation, which was to confer on any Merchant Navy officer who appeared to merit a DSO or DSC a Naval Reserve commission antedated to the day before his act of gallantry.[324] There had evidently been some doubt of the propriety of this course in respect of the VC, and it was principally on account of the conduct of Archibald Bissett Smith, when his ship, the *SS Otaki*, was attacked by the German raider *Moewe*, which was universally agreed merited a VC, that the Admiralty took the opportunity to press for the inclusion of the Merchant Navy in the new Warrant, a suggestion which was generally acceptable to the Committee.[325] The new Warrant was drawn up, following the Committee's discussions, early in 1919 and signed by King George V at the beginning of March of that year, but publication was delayed at HM's request, until the formal ending of Britain's state of war.[326] The Admiralty seem, however, to have decided that there was no need to wait for formal publication before bringing forward the two pending cases of VCs for Mercantile Marine officers and the awards to Frederick Parslow, who had lost his life in command of the *Anglo-Californian* on 4 Jul 1915, when attacked by a German submarine, and to Archibald Bissett Smith, which has been already mentioned and which dated back to 10 Mar 1917, were both gazetted on 24 May 1919.

One of the objects of the 1918 Committee was to draw up a draft warrant which would consolidate into one both the Warrant of 1856 and five supplementary Warrants. One of these was the Warrant extending the VC to civilian volunteers, which was now stated expressly to have related only to the Indian Mutiny. With the instruction to produce a consolidating Warrant and information before them showing that civilians had been included within the terms of the VC Warrant in certain circumstances, this conception was drafted into the new document, and so made generally applicable, without anyone appearing to notice that the eligibility of civilians had never previously been conceded outside the events of the Mutiny. Indeed, the only discussion which took place at this point was on whether or not there should be reference to civilians of both sexes. In this way the general eligibility of civilians was made part of the new Warrant, though the old idea of military supervision was retained in the new draft – 'Civilians of either sex serving regularly or temporarily under the orders, direction or supervision of any of the above-mentioned forces'.[327] However, the

324   PRO, WO 32/3443
325   *ibid*
326   *ibid*
327   *ibid*

point has now become largely academic, for it seems certain, following the institution of the George Cross in 1940, that this latter award will now always be used in preference to the VC when the deed of heroism has been performed by a non-military person. This would seem to be proved by the fact that it was the George and not the Victoria Cross which was bestowed in 1951 on a Malayan jungle tracker, Awang anak Rawang, for his conduct in operations against Communist bandits.[328] There were all that one would have thought were the essential ingredients for the award of the military decoration — Rawang was acting under military orders, in leading a section of the Worcestershire Regt through the jungle, he was under enemy fire from the Chinese guerrillas, and he was militarily engaged, using rifle and grenade against his opponents. It seems, therefore, that it can only have been his status that decided which award he should be granted, and if the decision was that as a civilian he should receive the essentially civilian award, that part of the VC Warrant which specifies otherwise must be regarded as negated in practice. Similarly, it was the GC and not the VC that was awarded to Capt D.W. Mason of the Merchant Navy for his conduct in taking his tanker to Malta under intense enemy air attacks in 1942,[329] despite the express eligibility that the 1920 Warrant conferred on the Merchant Navy, and which is still contained in the 1961 Warrant, as also is that relating to civilians, despite the fact that both provisions now appear to be dead letters.[330]

328   *The George Cross,* p230
329   *ibid,* p131
330   See Appendices XII and XVIII and Chapter 16

Chapter 13

Not in the Prescence of the Enemy

ON 11 NOVEMBER 1857 the troopship *Sarah Sands,* bound for India with a large detachment of the 54th Foot to help quell the Mutiny, caught fire some 800 miles off Mauritius. Most of the crew took to the boats and the fact that the fire was quelled after eighteen hours of very considerable danger [for the holds were loaded with military stores, including barrels of gunpowder, which had to be thrown overboard for safety], and the ship safely got to Mauritius, was very largely due to the efforts of the soldiers on board. This epic created much excitement in Britain, where a special order describing the courage of the 54th was read to every regiment in the Army, and, in fact, the anniversary of the exploit is still kept as *Sarah Sands* Day by the Devonshire and Dorset Regiment, the present successors of the old 54th [which became the 2nd Bn the Dorsetshire Regt under Cardwell's army reforms though its previous territorial designation had been the West Norfolk Regt].

On 29 Jan 1858 Gen Sir Colin Campbell wrote to the Horse Guards drawing attention to the incident. 'I am not sure', he wrote, 'that the Statutes of the Victoria Cross admit of officers and men whom he [Brett] recommends being honored with that Decoration. I am sure however that no men in conflict with an enemy have ever deserved to be more conspicuously marked out than those composing the 54th Regt where, to use the words of Major Brett, they determined to fight the fire inch by inch in the burning ship.'[331] The reaction of the Horse Guards to this letter is shown by that which Col Yorke, the Military Secretary, thereupon wrote to Sir Henry Storks at the War Office. 'It has been considered that the statutes of the Victoria Cross do not admit of that honour being conferred except for acts of Valour performed in action with the enemy but His Royal Highness entirely concurs with Sir Colin

331   PRO, WO 32/7345

Campbell that it is not possible for men in conflict with an enemy to be more conspicuously marked out than the Officers and Men whom Major Brett has recommended for special service... His Royal Highness will only add that if Secretary Maj-Gen Peel should consider that Her Majesty could be recommended to relax the statutes of the VC in order to confer it upon men who have displayed under circumstances of the greatest danger and sore discouragement, every quality most honorable to soldiers, though not in presence of the enemy, there could be no more fitting occasion than the present to take that course.'[332]

A letter in these terms was obviously one upon which Mr Pennington would be asked for his views, and on 9 Apr he gave these to his chief, Sir Henry Storks. He first rehearsed the sixth clause of the Warrant which set out that no 'circumstance or condition whatever save the merit of conspicuous bravery shall be held to establish a sufficient claim to the honour'. He continued 'The question here raised is whether it would be expedient to relax the rules so far as to include such cases of courage as those displayed on the occasion of the burning of the *Sarah Sands* transport, or for instance cases of daring which may occur on the occasion of the accidental blowing up of a powder magazine. Such cases are not of infrequent occurrence, although they do not come within the meaning of the Royal Warrant, and I think actually did occur in the Crimea,[333] and it was animadverted upon at the time that they could not be rewarded by the bestowal of the VC because they were not deeds of gallantry performed *before the enemy*. Should it be deemed desirable to entertain the question the Adjutant-General might be asked to frame such rules on the question as might be embodied in a Royal Warrant.'[334] This document was forwarded by Storks to the S of S on the following day, with a note 'This is for your consideration and decision. There is no doubt that the "conspicuous bravery" displayed by the Officers and Men on board the *Sarah Sands* is deserving of the honour proposed to be conferred. Submit to the Queen that the Statutes of the VC be amended to permit its being awarded for such acts of "conspicuous bravery" as those under consideration?' and he received Gen Peel's approval on the 12th of that month.[335] A submission to the Queen was drawn up by Pennington on 16 Apr and sent forward on the 20th of that month, Sir Charles Yorke at the Horse Guards being informed that this was being done the following day.

332   *ibid*
333   See p93
334   PRO, WO 32/7345
335   *ibid*

The document that went to the Queen proposing the issue of a new Warrant made clear that it was specifically to meet the case of the *Sarah Sands* 'deserving such a mark of Your Majesty's gracious favour',[336] and in his first public announcement Peel repeated this. In a discussion initiated by Lord Elcho, in the House of Commons on 30 Jul 1858, calling attention to the limitations of the award of the Order of the Bath as then constituted to field officers, the S of S for War remarked that it had been justly stated that the VC was instituted as an extension of, or rather as a substitute for the Order of the Bath. He would not say that the present constitution of the VC might not be improved. At present it was requisite that some extraordinary proof of valour should be given in the presence of the enemy. There were, however, instances of valour exhibited not in the presence of the enemy that ought to be rewarded, such for example as the case of the men on board the *Sarah Sands*. He was happy to say that he had received the sanction of Her Majesty to such an extension of that order as would include them and persons in similar situations.[337]

It was a few days prior to this that Pennington pointed out that no distinct recommendation had been received of the person who would be entitled to the decoration in connection with the incident; all the WO had received had been the Horse Guards' General Order, based on the report of Maj Brett, the officer commanding the detachment of the 54th on board the ship, and that had singled out twenty-five individuals for mention by name. This point, he was told by Storks, could stand over until the Warrant was actually signed[338] which it duly was on 10 Aug 1858, in the terms drafted by Pennington in April.[339] And now, for the first time, a note of hesitation appears. On 11 Aug Pennington drew his chief's attention to the fact that the Warrant had now been signed; was it now to be published in the *London Gazette*, which he thought scarcely advisable, and was anything to be done in connection with the *Sarah Sands*, the time for which he thought now somewhat late?[340] And there, as far as the WO was concerned, the matter was left to rest.

It was reopened from the military end with the return to England in Jul 1860 of Lt-Col Brett, who had been in command of the men of the 54th on board the *Sarah Sands*, and who took the opportunity to have an interview with the AG, in which he stated 'I had hoped, in

336   *ibid*
337   *Hansard*, 3rd series, vol CLI, cols 2366/7
338   PRO, WO 32/7345
339   See Appendix VI
340   PRO, WO 32/7345

consequence of the unparallelled exertions of the Regiment... a VC
would have been conferred on the Regiment', and in support of which
hope he cited Gen Peel's remarks in the Commons, which he had read
in *The Times* and on being informed that any application which he
wished to submit on behalf of his regiment should be made through its
CO, he wrote to Col Michel to this effect on 16 Jul 1860.[341] Michel
forwarded this letter to the AG on the 20th, strongly endorsing its
terms, and appealing in his turn to Peel's apparent promise of the VC
for the exploit. So far neither he nor Brett had met the point raised by
Pennington, regarding the mention of a specific name for the award, but
Michel evidently had an idea that something of this nature would be
required, for his letter concluded 'Should His Royal Highness be
desirous of further special recommendation I will communicate with
Lt-Col Brett and obtain the names of those men, whom he as the officer
in command at this time may consider most deserving of such a high
mark of Royal Approbation'.[342] It seems a little odd that Col Michel
did not take the step of getting names from Lt-Col Brett before writing
to the Horse Guards, for he was entirely correct in his supposition that
this was what would be required of him; in fact his letter has been
endorsed by someone at the Horse Guards, 'A *special application* must
be made on behalf of an *individual* before the case can be brought
before the Board of General Officers'. Evidently a letter was sent to him
in these terms on 26 Jul, for on 13 Aug Brett wrote to Michel, in reply
to the latter's request of 2 Aug for a specific recommendation, with
which a copy of such a letter had been enclosed. Col Brett's letter read
as follows:- 'I have the honour to inform you that I recommend
No.3190 Andrew Walsh Private 54th Regiment for the decoration of
the Victoria Cross. No.3190 Andrew Walsh Private 54th Regiment was
most conspicuous for daring and valour during the burning of the Steam
Transport *Sarah Sands* at Sea on 11th Novr. 1857, in the following
instances —

1. For having, soon after the outbreak of the Fire, when volunteers
were called for to clear the Powder Magazine, entered the Powder
Magazine and with other soldiers of the 54th Regiment succeeded
in clearing it of the greater portion of the powder. He did not
quit the Magazine 'til, from fire and smoke it was impossible to
remain, thus rendering invaluable service.

II. For having, in company with Mr Welch (Chief Officer of the

341   PRO, WO 98/2
342   *ibid*

Sarah Sands) gone aloft with wet blankets, and succeeded in extinguishing the fire at the maintopsail yard (the yard and mast being on fire) a service of great peril and risk, the ship at the time rolling heavily and being as stated by Capt Castle in his report "one body of flame from the stern to the main rigging".

'And generally — after the imminent danger during the many hours the fire lasted had been overcome — for general conduct and example during the twelve days (a period of great anxiety & danger) the wreck was at sea before reaching Mauritius.'[343]

On 18 Aug Col Michel wrote again to the AG: 'In reply to your Communication of the 26th July 1860 informing me that His Royal Highness the General Commanding in Chief would be willing to submit, to the Board of General Officers, the name of the Officer or Soldier of the 54th Regt who most distinguished himself on the occasion of the burning of the Transport *Sarah Sands* on the 11th Novr. 1857, I have now the honor to forward a letter from Major and Bt Lt-Col Brett, the Officer in Command on Board during the fire, with a detailed statement of the act of Valour of No.3190 Private Andrew Walsh, 54th Regt, and beg to recommend him to the favourable notice of His Royal Highness with a view to his case being submitted for consideration as above.'[344] Obviously, from the terms in which Michel had been invited to make a recommendation, the Horse Guards were entirely in favour of this request for the VC. But interpretation of VC warrants was not a matter for them, but for the civil servants at the WO. The first approach to the WO was made on 21 Aug,[345] and was met by a request on 29 Aug for the further views of the CinC before any decision was taken.[346] The Horse Guards' reply of 4 Sep was that HRH was of the opinion that Walsh had displayed conspicuous bravery; the case was exceptional and the Warrant should be retrospective — which is the only hint of the ground upon which the Duke of Cambridge had been asked for his further views — as this was the occasion which gave rise to the 1858 Warrant, a statement which there is ample evidence to prove.[347] Pennington now gave his advice to Sir Edward Lugard, the PUS. The Warrant was to deal with such instances as might be displayed hereafter, and had no retrospective effect. It did not exist at the time of the service in question, which could only be judged by the law as it then

343 *ibid*
344 *ibid*
345 PRO, WO 32/7345
346 *ibid*
347 *ibid*

stood, under which nothing further could be done. To do anything would need a new instrument, and it was questionable whether it was desirable that anything should now be done after the lapse of time since the occurrence of the incident; it would also be an inconvenient precedent to have a new Warrant to provide for an isolated case.[348] Lugard accepted this advice, and a reply along these lines was prepared for the MS at the Horse Guards, with, however, the addition of a paragraph commending Walsh's conduct. 'The Royal Warrant of 10th of August 1858, under the provisions of which it is suggested that Her Majesty should be advised to confer this high distinction upon Private Walsh, has, as was explained in my letter of the 29th August last, no retrospective effect' ran Lugard's letter of 9 Feb 1861, 'there is, therefore, no instrument in existence under the provisions of which Her Majesty could be advised to confer this honor upon the soldier in question. This being the case, it appears to the Secretary of State that it would not be desirable, at this distance of time, to advise Her Majesty to extend retrospectively, as proposed in your letter, the provisions of the Warrant in question, for the purpose of conferring the Victoria Cross on Private Walsh'.[349] An attempt was made by Lt-Gen Breton to renew the application in Oct 1863, but to this the CinC could only repeat the ruling of the S of S for War as given in this letter.[350]

So the WO had said 'No'. But, more precisely than this, it was Pennington's advice to his chief which had made the refusal certain. However, if one compares what he said about the terms of the 1858 Warrant with the Warrant itself, something very startling emerges, for there is nothing in it about acts to be performed hereafter. and in saying this Pennington was flatly contradicting what had earlier been stated in the House of Commons by Gen Peel as S of S for War. Now, as Pennington had himself prepared the draft of the Warrant, it was unlikely that he would be mistaken as to its terms, so it can only be concluded that his modification of its import was deliberate. That it was an unpopular Warrant among the civil servants in the WO is fairly obvious, for when Pennington had suggested withholding of publication in the *London Gazette* and had shown a reluctance to do anything for the *Sarah Sands* under it in August 1858, Sir Henry Storks had shown no wish to push him to act otherwise. The most likely explanation of the situation seems to be that this new Warrant was a scheme of Peel's,

348   *ibid*
349   PRO, WO 98/2
350   *ibid*

and, that while his civil servants could not refuse to draw up a document in the terms he wished, they had no enthusiasm for it, and would gladly have turned this document into a dead letter. It is, in fact, noted on Maj Brett's first letter, against the reference to a new Warrant quoted from Peel's remarks 'No copy of this extension of the Warrant has been forwarded to HRH'. The important difference between the situation in 1858, when the Warrant was produced, and 1860, when the Horse Guards were urging that action should be taken upon it, was that Gen Peel had ceased, with the fall of the Derby-Disraeli Ministry in June 1859, to be S of S for War. Had he still been at the head of the department, Pennington could hardly have got away with his interpretation but, as it was, he was virtually the only man with any knowledge of the subject, for there had also been a change in the Permanent Under Secretaryship, Sir Edward Lugard having replaced Sir Henry Storks. Events which will be related shortly seem to confirm the role of Peel in the matter. However, as far as Andrew Walsh was concerned, this was the end of the story.

Despite the attempt of the WO to keep the existence of the 1858 Warrant as some sort of guilty secret, knowledge of it must have leaked out, for in 1862 Lt-Col Bourchier brought forward the case of Ensign Bourke, of the 1st West India Regt, on the occasion of a fire at Fort Charlotte in the Bahamas, on 10 Jan 1860.[351] Pennington's comment on this case may possibly give the clue to his reluctance to act previously under this Warrant, that it 'would be making the Victoria Cross too cheap to grant it', and his first reaction was that the claim had not been given any encouragement by the Horse Guards, and that any reply should come through them. However, a letter dated 19 Jul from the Horse Guards, submitting one from Ensign Bourke, and enquiring whether the case did come within the 1858 Warrant, forced the WO to make an official reply. This very largely followed the lines of Pennington's minute to Lugard of 25 Jul, in which he remarks that the 1858 Warrant is a dead letter. Lugard's reply to the Horse Guards, dated 30 Jul, was that the case appeared to come to some extent within the terms of the Warrant, but that it could not be entertained without the recommendation of the CO and of a board of officers. Nothing more was then heard of the matter until a further letter was received from the Horse Guards, dated 17 Mar 1863, informing them [no doubt to everyone's relief] that a board of officers had sat to consider the claims of Bourke and had found that his services did not entitle him to the award of the VC under the 1858 Warrant.

351   PRO, WO 32/7345

In Jul 1866 the Horse Guards brought forward yet another case' as coming under the terms of the 1858 Warrant, that of Pte Timothy O'Hea, who had displayed conspicuous conduct when fire broke out in an ammunition car at Danville Station in Canada, on 9 Jun 1866. Pennington's reaction on this occasion, in a minute dated 20 Jul, was 'His conduct, no doubt, was praiseworthy, under trying circumstances, and worthy of commendation; how far it would justify the bestowal of the Victoria Cross, for which he is recommended by the Horse Guards, is however another question. It will be seen that the General Commanding does not recommend, or even suggest, that this distinction should be conferred, but simply brings the man's conduct under the notice of His Royal Highness. It would be contrary to established rule to confer this distinction without such recommendation... If the case is submitted as coming within the provisions of the Warrant of the 10th August 1858 (which has never been acted upon) it should first be submitted for the careful investigation of a Board of Officers on the spot'.[352] Pennington was evidently trying to produce all possible arguments against acting under the 1858 Warrant; other points he brought forward were the fact that the financial reward of £10 a year was no mean sum for a private, that the terms of the Warrant had never been communicated to the Admiralty, and that O'Hea's act might be considered an act of duty, and acts of duty were never held to merit the VC. A draft letter was prepared on his advice, to point out to the Horse Guards that the 1858 Warrant had never been acted upon and to revive it after this interval might constitute an inconvenient precedent, particularly as it had never been published. But this letter was never sent, for the Board of Officers had met and had reported favourably and, perhaps most significant of all, Gen Peel, whom Queen Victoria later described as 'the best and strongest Minister for War we ever had'[353] was back at the WO as S of S, so that the Warrant which had been drawn up under his direction was to be implemented under it also. He did confer with Cambridge before the matter finally went forward, but from their past attitudes it seems unlikely that either would have wished to hold it back. A recommendation went to the Queen on 22 Dec, and the award of the Victoria Cross to O'Hea was gazetted on New Year's Day, 1867.

352 PRO, WO 32/7372
353 This was in conversation with Marie Mallet on 15 Feb 1900; the Queen was developing the theme that civilians *cannot* understand military matters, *Life with Queen Victoria; Marie Mallet's Letters from Court, 1887-1901,* edited by Victor Mallet, London 1968, p186.

It was very soon after this that the only other incident dealt with under the 1858 Warrant took place. The commander and seven members of the crew of the *Assam Valley* had landed on the island of Little Andaman, where they were supposed to have been murdered by the natives. An expedition was landed there to ascertain their fate but, when it was sought to re-embark a party of seventeen officers and men, it was found they were cut off by dangerous surf, so that they were in very great danger of attack from the natives. It was the conduct of Dr Douglas and four men of the 24th Regiment in taking a boat through this surf to rescue their comrades that was brought to notice by Sir William Mansfield, CinC in the East Indies, and strongly recommended by him and by the Horse Guards to the WO. Pennington was left to assume, in his minute of 9 Nov 1867 to Lugard, that this was a recommendation under the 1858 Warrant, as no other seemed applicable, and the point had not been made clear by the Horse Guards. He did not think that life had certainly been saved, and thought a Board of Officers should be set up to investigate. Lugard, however, disagreed. Mansfield was clearly of opinion that it had been established that the lives of the party on shore would have been gravely endangered had they not been taken off, and he supported a strong recommendation to the S of S, who was now Sir John Pakington. The Secretary's reply was 'I quite concur in the view taken of the gallant act by HRH the Commander in Chief and Sir Ed. Lugard' and the recommendation of the five VCs was put to the Queen for approval on 10 Dec 1867.[353a] Curiously enough, although the notice in the *London Gazette* of the award to O'Hea referred to this being made under the 1858 Warrant, no such mention was made when these five awards were published in the *Gazette* of 17 Dec 1867. This may explain why it is often stated that O'Hea's was the only Cross to be awarded under the 1858 Warrant; the first source in which it appears seems to be J.H. Mayo's *Medals and Decorations of the British Army and Navy*, but he is hardly to be blamed for the error, since the VCR shows that a letter was sent to him from the WO in 1895, making the specific [but incorrect] statement that 'the only case of the grant of the VC under the Warrant of 10 August 1858 is that of Private Timothy O'Hea'.[354]

The only other attempt to invoke the 1858 Warrant was also in 1867. In March of that year Lugard wrote to the CO, British Forces in North America, declining to forward a copy of the 1858 Warrant, on the

353a PRO, WO 32/7373
354   VCR, ii p367

grounds that 'the Warrant in question has never been printed, or published in the *London Gazette,* and that it was not deemed expedient to circulate it'.[355] What lay behind this request from North America seems to have been an attempt by the 1st Bn The Rifle Brigade to exploit their success over Pte O'Hea [who was serving with it] by producing yet another claimant, for a few days later Lugard was writing to the MS at the Horse Guards 'the case of Pte William Berry, of the 1st Bn of the Rifle Brigade, which has been submitted for the VC, in consideration of his having saved the life of a child at the risk of his own, on the occasion of a Fire at Quebec on the 14th October last... although no doubt very praiseworthy, was scarcely one which should be rewarded by the bestowal of this high Distinction'.[356]

The refusal to circulate the text of the 1858 Warrant seems to have been automatic, for Lugard was to decline the same request in almost the same words as quoted above, when it was made from the CinC India some three months later,[357] a request which almost certainly relates to the submission of the Andaman recommendations in the following November.

If the coming into existence of the 1858 Warrant was an official embarrassment, and its continued existence a kind of guilty secret, then the circumstances in which it was brought to an end were truly in keeping with its life history. On 24 Apr 1881 a new VC Warrant was signed, which stated 'Our Will and Pleasure is that the qualification [for the award of the Victoria Cross] shall be "conspicuous bravery of devotion to the country in the presence of the enemy"'. Plainly, the terms of the 1858 Warrant were quite incompatible with such a definition, and no more awards of the VC could be made under its terms. Many people have concluded that the main purpose of the 1881 Warrant was to rescind that of 1858,[358] but, as the detailed story of the drawing up of this new Warrant shows[359] the purpose being aimed at was quite different; the terms of the 1858 Warrant [which had always been regarded more or less as a dead letter] were not consciously in the minds of those drawing the new Warrant, and the fact that it did have this effect was virtually fortuitous.

Though there were no more awards of the VC 'not in the presence of the enemy' after 1881, there were a number of awards during the

355   *ibid,* p103
356   *ibid,* pp104/5
357   *ibid,* p107
358   See e.g. *The Medal Collector,* p316
359   See Chapter 15

1914-18 War where the presence of the enemy was virtually irrelevant to the nature of the act of heroism for which the VC was awarded. Some eight or possibly ten cases of this nature can be identified, the features of all but one being very similar – the protection of fellow soldiers from the effects of an explosion not directly produced by hostile malice. The instances in question are those of 2/Lt A.V. Smith, who flung himself on a grenade he had dropped in the act of throwing; Pte W.F. McFadzean, who flung himself on a box of bombs which fell into a trench whilst being opened; Pte D.R. Lauder, who put his foot on a bomb which he had thrown but which had failed to clear the parapet and fell back amongst his own party; 2/Lt G.E. Cates, who put his foot on a bomb which was uncovered whilst a captured trench was being deepened; Sgt W. Gosling who defused a mortar bomb when, owing to a defective cartridge, the bomb fell only ten yards from his mortar, from which it had been fired; Sgt J. Carmichael, who smothered a grenade, uncovered whilst a trench was being excavated, by covering it with his steel helmet and standing on it; and Pte W.B. Butler, who, when one of the shells of the Stokes gun he was in charge of accidentally fired into the emplacement, picked it up and threw it out of the trench. The two cases that are debatably within this group are those of Cpl G. Jarratt and Pte T.H. Sage. Jarratt had, with a number of wounded men, been taken prisoner and was under guard in a German dugout, when the German front line was driven back by a British attack; in the course of this attack a grenade rolled into the dugout, which Jarratt smothered by standing on it. Sage smothered a bomb which fell into the shellhole in which he was when one of his comrades there was shot in the act of throwing it. The one case which clearly comes within this category, but where the circumstances were quite different, was that of Sapper Hackett, who refused to leave an injured colleague, when his party was extricated after being entombed in a mining gallery following the explosion of an enemy mine, and thus failed to escape before the rescue tunnel which had been dug to them collapsed. As none of the WO files on these awards have been preserved [this is true of almost all 1914-18 VC papers] it is not possible to say whether any discussion took place as to the applicability of the VC Warrant to these cases. It may, however, be significant that all the awards just mentioned were gazetted within quite a short period, the first [Smith] being published on 3 Mar 1916 and the last [Sage] on 18 Dec 1917. It seems reasonable to assume that in present circumstances these exploits would be rewarded by the GC instead of the VC. Markedly similar exploits for which the former has been awarded include those of Lt W. Foster,

Maj A.G. Kempster and Sgt J. Rennie, who each gave their lives smothering misthrown grenades which had rolled back among the throwers on practice ranges; Ptes C.A. Duncan and J.A. Silk, and Lance-Naik Islam-ud-Din who each performed the same act when grenades were dropped with the pins out among parties of men; whilst Naik Kirpa Ram similarly attempted to dispose of a grenade which fell short after being fired from a discharger on a field during exercise and Subedar Subramanian smothered a Schumine activated by a fellow soldier whilst they were clearing a minefield in Italy. The nearest recent parallel to the case of Sapper Hackett seems also to be provided by the award of the GC to the Reverend H.C. Pugh who, when the troopship *Anselm* was torpedoed, insisted on being lowered into the damaged part of the ship where a number of airmen were trapped and the ship on the point of sinking, remaining with them in prayer as the ship finally went down with all of them. [One other point of comparison may perhaps also be made in this case. Sir Evelyn Wood, the Mutiny VC and Crimea hero, is on record as saying 'The most divine-like act of self-sacrifice of which I have read was that of the late Sapper William Hackett', whereas in the opinion of the present writer, of all the courageous deeds of which he has read in his researches on this subject he would consider that of Mr Pugh the most moving in its frightening and absolute heroism.]

Chapter 14

The Warrant of 1867

AS WILL ALREADY have become apparent, the occasions which have given rise to the production of new warrants extending the availability of the Victoria Cross have usually been quite specific; a recommendation has been made to the War Office for an individual who, on the narrow reading which was invariably applied in the 19th century, was found to fall outside the terms of the existing Warrant, and after greater or lesser hesitation by the authorities, the necessary extension to the Warrant has followed. One reason for this piecemeal approach will become apparent when the Apr 1881 Warrant is discussed, but in the meantime the history of the extension of the VC to local colonial forces provides a further illustration of the way in which such things came about.

In the 1860s a further outbreak of disturbances took place between the European settlers and the native Maoris in New Zealand, as they had previously done in the 1840s. The forces involved on the settlers' side included sailors from the Royal Navy, regular units of the British Army, and locally raised militia units. So far as the regular units were concerned, claims to the VC were unexceptionable and a number had already been awarded to both services when, on 22 Dec 1864 Sir George Grey, the Governor General, wrote to Cardwell [later to become famous for his army reforms as S of S for War, but at this time Colonial Secretary], transmitting recommendations made by Maj-Gen Galloway for the award of the VC to two members of the local forces, Maj Heaphy and Sgt Kenrick.[360] The papers in the case came before Mr Pennington at the WO in Mar 1865. His reaction was, as might be expected, to minute the PUS, Sir Edward Lugard, on the 11th, that the extension of the VC to civilians serving under military orders was the only case where the Warrant had gone outside its original limitation to the Army and Navy. The Queen had not extended its grant to the Colonial Militia and it was a matter for consideration whether it should be so extended.

360   PRO, WO 32/7370 for all that follows, unless otherwise indicated.

Lugard, in his minute to the S of S, Lord de Grey, of 21 Mar, was clearly opposed to such action. He thought that the course adopted in the Mutiny had been a mistake and it had not been one advocated by the Indian Government. Furthermore, the arguments in its favour on that occasion did not now apply as the volunteers in question were not under martial law. The Colonial Government was in a position to reward its volunteers in some material way, whereas the only reward for anyone in the Regular Army was a decoration. In the case of Mr Kavanagh, when his application for the VC had been turned down, he had received a grant of 20,000 rupees from the Indian Government, but had then gone on to apply to the WO and got the Warrant extended, so that he had both Cross and reward. [This, one may assume, was what caused Lugard to hold the view he did on the extension of the Warrant – it will be recalled that he had himself served in the Mutiny.] The New Zealand Government could do something similar, so why should the decoration be given as well? The New Zealand Government was not giving anything to the British troops, so why should the British Government give anything to the New Zealand forces? It should be kept for the Regular Army alone.

The letter that Lugard was authorised to send to the Colonial Office followed his minute very closely. This, sent on 26 Apr, read, in part, 'I am directed to request you will observe to Mr Secretary Cardwell that the Royal Warrant instituting this decoration limits the grant of it to the Army and Navy, and as Major Heaphy is an Officer of the Colonial Militia Corps, his Lordship is precluded from recommending Her Majesty to confer the Victoria Cross upon him.

'I am to add that Lord de Grey is of opinion that it would not be advisable that the provisions of the Royal Warrant should be extended to meet such cases as the one under consideration. It should be borne in mind that an Officer of a Militia or Volunteer Corps, who may render good and gallant service in a Colony, can receive a substantial reward either in land or otherwise, from the Government of the Colony whose servant he is, which advantage is not enjoyed by an Officer or Soldier of the Army, and on this account alone, Lord de Grey considers that this high distinction should be reserved for the Regular Army.'[361] So Lugard had carried the whole of his objections with his Minister.

The decision was, of course, unpopular. The first reaction to it was a letter of appeal by Maj Heaphy, who made the not unreasonable point that the phrase 'Our military and naval forces' in the Warrant might well

361   VCR, ii pp41/2

be considered to include members of the militia on active service, and forwarding a letter in support from Gen Cameron, the Regular field officer commanding, who made the further point that Heaphy was not acting in support of Regular troops, but was exercising command in his own authority. These arguments did not impress Pennington, who minuted that the original decision should be adhered to. But the matter did not end there. Governmental opinion in New Zealand was clearly incensed by what had been conveyed to them of the reasons for rejecting Heaphy's claim, and on 11 Aug 1865 a memorandum on the subject was presented to both houses of the General Assembly of New Zealand by command of His Excellency the Governor. This stated that 'Ministers express their regret that technical rules prevent a recommendation to Her Majesty to confer an honorable distinction on officers and men of a Colonial Militia'. Great indignation was evidently felt over the suggestion that such services could be rewarded by a grant of land; the Militiaman's 'sense of pain at his exclusion from a share of such honorary awards is unnecessarily embittered when such exclusion is intimated to him in terms which indirectly convey an imputation of sordid motives'. All these papers were forwarded by the Colonial Office to the WO, including an appeal from the New Zealand Government for an extension to the Warrant. At the same time it was pointed out to the WO – thus cutting most of the ground from under Lugard's feet – that in fact Militia officers had no greater facilities for grants of land than had home Regulars. The Colonial Office letter, dated 22 Nov 1865, made it clear that Cardwell was backing the New Zealand Government in this; also forwarded was a letter, written by Sir George Grey, which contained the further information that 'Had it been possible to confer this distinction on officers and men of Her Majesty's Colonial Forces, I had intended to recommend two other persons besides Major Heaphy as being worthy to receive it, one of whom is a native, and who has, by his gallantry, established unusual claims to some such distinction'. Nor had Heaphy himself been backward in pressing his own claims, for among the WO papers is a letter he had written on 28 Aug 1865, to Lord Palmerston [who died on 18 Oct, probably without having received it] recalling an acquaintanceship between the British Prime Minister and Heaphy's father, and inviting Palmerston's support in urging the Major's case. Against this weight of artillery Pennington became conciliatory. 'It would I venture to think', he minuted Lugard on 23 Nov, 'be impolitic to act against the wishes of the Colonial Government in this matter'. At this point the S of S came into the discussion. 'I have learnt with great regret from the representatives of the Colonial Ministers'

Lord de Grey wrote, 'the nature of the letter which was written to the Colonial Office in April last. It is not in accordance with my minute and if I had seen it I should certainly have struck out the last part.' Sir Edward Lugard did not see this note until some months later, when he added a comment that he recollected that he did alter the draft of his letter, as indeed the papers show, but the alteration was not in fact to this part. The result of all this was a letter from the WO to the Colonial Office [over the signature, interestingly enough, not of Sir Edward, but of Mr Galton] on 25 Nov, expressing regret that the previous suggestion regarding an appropriate reward had been taken amiss and disparaging to Maj Heaphy's gallantry, but going on to say that an extension of the Warrant would be a matter requiring serious and careful consideration by Lord de Grey.[362]

The next document in the case is a memorandum prepared by Pennington on 18 Apr 1866 in which he rehearsed the history of the VC Warrant to that date. The 1856 Warrant was, he noted '...drawn up by the Earl of Dalhousie [as Panmure later became], and Lord Halifax, then First Lord of the Admiralty [and at that time Sir Charles Wood] in immediate communication with Her Majesty and the Late Prince Consort... but there are no minutes or memoranda on record on the subject of these rules'. For some reason, the logic of which does not appear in his memorandum, he went on 'It is fair to infer that it could not have been contemplated that the distinction should be extended to other services at any future period', which seems rather contrary to the comprehensive tone of Clause 12 of the Warrant. He admits that extensions have been made to this Warrant in the case of the officers and men of the East India Company's army and navy, and for civilians bearing arms under military command, during the Mutiny 'but the cases in which the Cross has been granted under this Warrant are very few. A Warrant was also instituted in 1858 in which the original intention of limiting the Cross to cases of courage displayed *before an enemy* was departed from — No person has ever received the Cross under this Warrant so it has practically remained a dead letter. These are the only cases in which the provisions of the original Warrant have been extended, and such extensions being now practically void, the occasions which give rise to them being passed away, it will be seen that the grant of the Cross is now limited, as at its original institution, to the Army and Navy alone.

'Whether it would be expedient', he continued, 'after the lapse of

362   *ibid*, pp51/5

years (for it is nearly ten years since the decoration was first instituted) to make a fresh extension of it to the cases of the Colonial forces in the several colonies is a question which seems to deserve serious consideration. It is in the limitation of an honour and in making the attainment of it difficult that its real value consists; whereas on the other hand, to extend it as proposed might possibly tend to depreciate the value of it to the Army and Navy, and would be an act of injustice to those services for which it was originally intended.' He also mentioned the practical difficulty of securing tribunals to vet the claims that might arise within the colonies, and added that there seemed little real occasion for the extension apart from the troubles in New Zealand and the petty warfare in West Africa.

It is hardly surprising, in the face of this liberal outpouring of cold water by his officials, that Lord de Grey does not seem to have taken the matter any further himself and in Feb 1866 he left the WO for the India Office. However, the Duke of Somerset had also been brought into the discussion as First Lord of the Admiralty. He had not been subjected to the same measure of official discouragement, and he now came forward with a suggestion [which did seem to meet some of the difficulties envisaged] that an extension of the VC should be made to colonial militia and volunteer units called out for service under proper military authority; he had also made an alternative suggestion [which would have dealt with Pennington's 'cheapening' objections] that a new decoration might be instituted to reward acts of valour by colonial soldiers in the presence of the enemy. Pennington was to be found dealing with this new proposal on 10 May 1866, and the Duke of Cambridge was also brought in. The latter concurred with Somerset's proposal for the extension of the Cross, though he thought it should be required that the occasion should be one of advantage to the Empire as well as the colony, and that the recommendation should be made by Regular officers or HM's representatives in the Colony. He pointed out, however, that this extension would mean a similar one to the Militia and Volunteer forces at home, if not to native troops in India also. So far as this last point was concerned, Pennington was able to cite the correspondence of 1857 with the Bombay Government, and the Cabinet decision that had then been taken,[363] but the main problem he foresaw was how one was to adhere to the criterion of the 'presence of the enemy', as the whole point of a home Militia was that it took the place at home of Regular troops sent to a seat of war, or to aid in quelling

363   See p119

insurrection at home. He thought that Cambridge's conception of benefit to the Empire as well as to the colony would be very difficult of determination particularly for a civilian Governor. In fact, Pennington thought the whole question was so difficult that he suggested it should be one for consideration and determination by the Cabinet; the troubles in New Zealand were practically over so the question was hardly pressing, and the views of the other colonies had not been ascertained — which sounds suspiciously like an attempt to postpone the whole matter out of mind.

Whatever Pennington's intentions may have been, discussion was certainly brought to a halt on this occasion by a change of government which took place the next month. It was revived in the following November. The department chiefly concerned with the outcome of the proposal for this extension of the VC was the Colonial Office and on 21st of that month Lord Carnarvon, the new Colonial Secretary, wrote to the WO to know if there was any outcome to the proposal for an alteration to the rules. Pennington's reply to this was that both Lord de Grey and his successor as S of S, Lord Hartington, had come to no conclusion in the matter, but the PUS in recapitulating the past history to his new chief, General Peel, on 5 Dec, gave as his own view that of the Duke of Somerset in the previous April 'It appears to me time that we should endeavour to meet the wishes of the colonials'. To which Peel replied on the 7th 'I am of opinion that at all events under certain circumstances it should be granted'.

Gen Peel's role in connection with the VC has already appeared in the previous chapter. With him at the head of the department when this other question came up for final determination there could be little doubt that a favourable answer would be given, or that the matter should be brought to a vigorous conclusion. A draft, which corresponds almost exactly with the approved text, was prepared by Pennington; the only divergence being that the last eight words in the Warrant as signed — 'or for repelling invasion by a foreign enemy' — were added to the draft in what looks like Lugard's hand. Despite the logic of Cambridge's earlier remark that the extension would require to be made also to the Home Militia and Volunteer forces, this was not done; the terms of the extension were obviously made as narrow as might be. Pennington, in putting his draft forward, drew attention to the fact that he had laid it down that any recommendation should come through the Regular officer in command as a safeguard against abuse. The draft was submitted for Victoria's approval on 22 Dec 1866 and the formal

Warrant signed by the Queen on 1 Jan.[364] One wonders if Lugard feared any repetition of the *Sarah Sands* episode, for on 19 Jan he enquired of Pennington 'I presume there can be no doubt that we can make a retrospective grant?', to which Pennington replied 'Yes, but only for cases arising out of the disturbances in N.Zealand' which rather indicates how little his heart was in the principle of the extension.

As Pennington had been forced to include the circumstances of New Zealand in his draft Warrant, Maj Heaphy was to fare better than Walsh of the *Sarah Sands*. On 8 Jan a letter was sent to the Colonial Office informing them of the new Warrant,[365] to which the reply noted that the news had been received with much pleasure by Lord Carnarvon. On the 21st Pennington pointed out to Lugard that the previous recommendation Heaphy had obtained from Gen Cameron brought his case within the terms of the new Warrant [and also explains, presumably, why nothing more was heard of that of Sgt Kenrick, of whom Cameron had never spoken], and suggested that the case should go to the Horse Guards for formal recommendation with a view to submission to the Queen. Lugard so forwarded it on 25 Jan,[366] submission was made to the Queen on 4 Feb, and the award of the VC finally announced in the *London Gazette* of 8 Feb 1867, though the WO did not write to tell the Colonial Office that the award had been approved until 22nd of that month.[367]

Although it is not expressly referred to in the papers, the existence of the 1867 Warrant must have been of considerable assistance when, in the course of the Basuto and First Boer Wars, the award of the VC was recommended to members of such units as Nourse's Horse, the Cape Mounted Rifles and the Cape Mounted Yeomanry — the last being such a transient volunteer unit that it was impossible to present its VC winner, Surgeon McCrea, with his decoration before his unit drawn up on parade, since it had already been disbanded.[368] Evidently, however, the existence of the 1867 Warrant was not very well known throughout the Colonies, for Col Brabant explained the two year delay he had made in submitting his recommendation of Surgeon-Maj Hartley, of the Cape Mounted Rifles, for the VC for his action in Basutoland in 1879, by the fact that until he had heard of the awards to Tpr Brown and Sgt Scott

364   See Appendix VIII
365   VCR, ii pp81/3
366   *ibid,* pp91/3
367   *ibid,* pp93/5
368   PRO, WO 32/7403

of the same unit, which had been gazetted in April and October 1880, he [Col Brabant] had been unaware of the eligibility of Colonial units for the decoration.[369] In the case of these operations the stipulation of service by local units with 'Our' troops, i.e Regular units, fell into general disregard. The point was raised in connection with the award of the VC to Tpr Henderson of the Buluwayo Field Force, for his gallantry in Rhodesia in the course of the Matabele Rebellion of 1896, a recommendation which was submitted to the WO by the directors of the Rhodesia Company, together with the request for posthumous recognition of the similar conduct of the late Tpr Baxter. In the WO discussion of their eligibility this was the Warrant cited as the relevant one, and the previous liberality of its application where no British troops had been involved noted, with particular reference to the case of Surgeon McCrea. One final doubt was voiced over its application to the Protectorates, the point having been raised by Joseph Chamberlain, as Colonial Secretary, that under the exact wording of the Warrant they were not strictly in. But in thirty years the strictness of interpretation had evidently changed much; the point was not pursued and no hindrance was put in the way of the award going forward.[370]

369   PRO, WO 32/7404
370   PRO, WO 32/7419

Chapter 15

The Warrant of April 1881 and The Act of Duty

FOR THE FIRST quarter of a century of the existence of the Victoria Cross, there was one point upon which official doctrine was quite clear that an act of duty, no matter how gallantly performed, did not constitute a claim to the decoration. On the first occasion that Sir Fenwick Williams recommended his aide-de-camp Lt Teesdale for the Cross on account of his conduct in the defence of Kars, Lord Panmure wrote to Sir Fenwick to inform him that, although Teesdale had shown great gallantry he [Panmure] did not consider that *duties* there performed came within the Warrant, though he subsequently allowed the recommendation to go forward in view of the very decided terms in which Teesdale was again recommended by the CinC.[371] The Admiralty, too, declined to put forward a recommendation in respect of Commander Rennie, for his part in the Persian War of 1857, on the grounds that his acts in taking a mortar battery on a raft under the Persian batteries, taking a boat through fire in order to accelerate the advance of the troops, and leading an expedition which destroyed stores in the face of a large enemy army on the opposite bank of a river, had all been acts of duty.[372] On a number of occasions lists of recommendations in respect of the Indian Mutiny were forwarded from the Horse Guards to the War Office with expressions of doubt by the Duke of Cambridge as to how far some of the cases went beyond the line of duty;[373] as, for example in the case of Lt.Bogle, whose act in leading the way into a loopholed house during the attack on Oonao was 'perhaps no more than duty required',[374] though in each such case he accepted that the names

371   PRO, WO 32/7305
372   PRO, WO 32/7310
373   PRO, WO 32/7335
374   PRO, WO 32/7331

should go forward, since they had in all cases been recommended following examination of their claim to the distinction by boards of officers. Similarly, Mr Pennington, at the WO, noted in connection with the recommendations for the storming of the Taku Forts in China in 1860, 'It was decided on 012/536 [which appears to be no longer extant] not to entertain certain claims to the Victoria Cross sent here by Sir Hope Grant from China, on the ground that what had been done in each case appears to have been done in the course of duty, and that the persons recommended would be otherwise rewarded'.[375] The official policy of the time was very clearly stated by Sir Edward Lugard in a letter to the Military Secretary at the Horse Guards on the 17 Jan 1861: 'Sir Hugh Rose [the CinC in India] considers that, as the Victoria Cross has been granted in India for an act of duty very bravely performed, Captain Dartnoll is fully entitled to it. With reference to this statement, I am directed to request you will observe to His Royal Highness that if Captain Dartnell simply discharged his duty on the occasion in question, however gallantly he may have done so, it appears to the Secretary of State that his claim to this high distinction is not established. An act of duty, bravely performed should not, in the Secretary of State's opinion, be held of itself as a sufficient qualification for the Victoria Cross'.[376] Nor was this opinion confined to officialdom, for the file on the award of the VC to Lt Dick-Cunyngham, decorated for exposing himself to enemy fire in order to rally a wavering attack at the Sherpur Pass in Afghanistan on 13 Dec 1879, contains an anonymous letter, signed 'A Witness of What Happened', reading 'If Lieut. M. Dick-Cunyngham, 92nd Regt. is recommended for the Victoria Cross for doing what any officer would have done in like circumstances then the Cross is not worth striving for. Ask for the opinion of his brother officers'.[377]

The first sign of an alteration in the official attitude would seem to have been shown in the remarks made by the Duke of Cambridge, as conveyed by Gen Dillon, the AMS, to the PUS on 16 Jan 1880, regarding the case of Capt E.H. Sartorius, who had shown marked gallantry in leading a very small body of men against a force of Afghans, of unknown strength, who were occupying an almost inaccessible position, at the top of a precipitous hill at Shahjui, on 24 Oct 1879. The Duke of Cambridge, while doubting whether the case came within the strict definition of the statute, forwarded it for consideration, with the

375   PRO, WO 32/7356
376   VCR, i pp316/7
377   PRO, WO 32/7393

added suggestion that it might be desirable to amend the VC Warrant in order to admit marked gallantry in the performance of an act of duty.[378] This represented a fairly radical departure from previous thinking on the subject, and one can only speculate as to what had led Cambridge to take this new view. However, the moment was not altogether unpropitious for re-examining official policy, for there had only recently occurred a complete change at the head of the civil side of the WO, Ralph Thompson, formerly Assistant Under Secretary, succeeding the Hon J.C.W. Vivian as PUS in 1880, the new AUS being Col Deedes, whose name had first appeared listed among WO staff in *Whitaker's Almanack* for 1879, when he appeared as Private Secretary to the S of S. The more active part in discussing a possible alteration to the Warrant seems to have been taken by Deedes. On 19 Mar 1880, he wrote to the Queen's secretary, Sir Henry Ponsonby: 'Knowing the great interest Her Majesty takes in the Order of the Victoria Cross, Col Stanley [at that time S of S for War] would not take into official consideration any suggestion for altering the wording of the Statutes of the order, without first ascertaining HM's wishes on the subject.

'Should HM not object Col Stanley wd. be inclined to alter the terms of the Statutes so as to admit such a case as I send herewith. [Probably that of Capt Sartorius, though the papers referred to are not now with the letter.] Hitherto, Para: *Fifthly,* wh. I have underlined ["performed some signal act of valour or devotion to their country"] has governed the grant of the VC and it has been read as not properly admitting those who altho' they had behaved with conspicuous courage, had been only *performing their duty.* The underlined portion of the *Preamble* however appears to have contemplated going beyond the above reading of Para 5 ["rewarding individual instances of merit and valour"]. There can be no doubt that the Statutes have been stretched more than once, and it is a question whether it wd. not be better to enlarge them so as advisedly to admit cases where men "in performance of their duty" have signally distinguished themselves. Will you ascertain Her Majesty's pleasure. Please return enclosures.'[379]

To this letter Ponsonby replied from Windsor Castle on 22 Mar, 'The Queen approves of an amendment being introduced into the Statute of the Victoria Cross in the sense you propose, but would like to see what it is before it is officially submitted'.[380] A pause then occurs in the discussions, during which Deedes was presumably thinking out

378   PRO, WO 32/7391
379   Royal Archives, E/25, 51
380   PRO, WO 32/7394

the exact form his proposed amendment was to take. On 16 Apr Deedes was in a position to address a minute on the subject to the S of S, who was now apparently brought into the discussion for the first time. In this he suggested the addition to the Warrant of the words 'or shall have displayed marked gallantry in the performance of their duty'. 'This is admittedly *extending* the order,' he wrote, 'and wd. appear to be at variance with yr. minute of 24 Nov. '79 on 3200/174 but then if "performance of duty" were *substituted* for the present wording, while preventing men going out of their way to obtain the coveted distinction it would prevent it being conferred for these rare cases but the most daring of all which occasionally happen when a man at great personal risk performs some really gallant act such as Cavanagh [sic] did at Lucknow which is distinctly outside the performance of his duty. I think on the whole therefore that the present suggestion is the best and submit it for your approval', to which Col Stanley replied 'The Queen should see first, but I quite agree'.[381]

On 23 Apr Deedes wrote once more to Ponsonby: 'In accordance with the instructions conveyed in yr. note to me of 22 March, I send for submission to Her Majesty the proposed alteration, in the Statutes of the Victoria Cross — It is proposed to *add* the words in Para *Fifthly* "or shall have displayed marked gallantry in the performance of their duty" — The following minute to the Secy of State will perhaps best explain the reasons that prompted this addition so I give it verbatim. [Here follows substantially the text of Deedes' minute of the 16th, which has just been quoted.] To this Col Stanley said "I quite agree" and has desired me to submit for HMs approval.'[382]

This must, incidentally, have been one of Stanley's last official acts as S of S, for it was in this same month that Disraeli's government was defeated at the General Election, with the consequent formation of Gladstone's second administration, and his supersession at the WO by Mr Childers. On 25 Apr Ponsonby replied to Deedes 'The Queen approves of the proposed alteration as marked by you on the enclosed papers'[383] and it was at this point [somewhat reversing the sequence that might have been expected] that drafts of a new warrant began to be prepared and circulated for departmental comment, and in the course of these discussions what was under consideration changed into a general revision of the entire Warrant.

The first draft of a new warrant was available for circulation in May,

381   PRO, WO 32/7391
382   Royal Archives, E/25, 61
383   PRO, WO 32/7394

this being sent to Sir Albert Woods, Garter King of Arms [who, it was mentioned in the related correspondence, had been concerned in drawing up the Warrant of 1856], and to the Duke of Cambridge. It was from this quarter that came the suggestion which was to add much to the elaboration of the document, that it would be better to recite the full regulations and amending Warrants, omitting, however, reference to 'acts of conspicuous courage and bravery in cases of extreme danger such as the occurrence of a fire on board ship or of the foundering of a vessel', which they stated to have been, although not acted upon on that occasion, to take account of such cases as the *Sarah Sands*.[384] This, they observed, had constituted a straining of the Statutes; and was now redundant as such cases were met by the Albert Medal – thereby sealing the fate of the Warrant of Aug 1858.[385] Woods and the Duke approved the new proposed qualification of marked gallantry in the performance of duty and thought, with these provisos, that the alterations appeared to meet all requirements.[386]

From this point a full-dress new draft went forward. The early part of this, which was based on the Warrant of 1856 contains little that is remarkable – the Royal Titles in the superscription are amended to bring them up to date [the Queen was now Empress of India], the preamble puts the reference to the 1856 Warrant into the past tense and incorporates, as had been suggested, reference to the subsequent Warrants of 29 Oct 1857, 10 Aug 1858 and 1 Jan 1867, all of which it proceeds to repeal and abrogate, the first four clauses of the 1856 Warrant being then re-enacted. With Clause 5 an entirely new draft is brought forward, in an attempt to combine the terms of the 1856 Warrant with those of 1867 to comprise all Regular and local overseas forces. In its first form this read: 'It is ordained that the Cross shall only be awarded to those Officers or Men of Our Naval and Military Service or Local Forces raised or to be raised in Our Colonies and their dependencies who have served Us in the presence of the enemy; or who may be called upon to serve in co-operation with Our Troops in military operations undertaken for the suppression of rebellion against Our Authority; or for repelling an invasion by a Foreign Enemy and shall have performed some signal act of valour; or devotion to their country, or have displayed marked gallantry in the performance of their duty'.

---

384   See Chapter 13
385   See Appendix VI
386   PRO, WO 32/7394 and for all that follows, except where otherwise indicated.

This draft clause was in its turn redrafted, but without removing its main innovation. The revised form read: 'Fifthly. It is ordained that the Cross shall be awarded for the performance of some signal act of valour or devotion to their country, or for the display of marked gallantry in the performance of their duty in the presence of the enemy when engaged against a Foreign Enemy or in the suppression of rebellion against Our authority by:-

    (a)   Officers or Men of Our Naval and Military Service and of Our Indian Naval and Military Service. [The second "Naval and" have in fact been deleted, and a marginal note made, "Query. Is there an Indian *Naval* Service? There was, I think, in 1857, but IO should be asked."]

    (b)   Officers or Men of Our Auxiliary and Reserve Forces (Naval and Military).

    (c)   Officers or Men of Local Forces raised or to be raised in Our Colonies and their Dependencies.'

This was obviously an improvement in drafting, as it divided the subject matter into two logical halves; first, it now stated what conduct was required to earn the VC and then those bodies of men to whom the Cross was open were tabulated. Here what might have been an oversight in the first version was corrected, in that a specific reference was made to the Indian forces, which had originally been distinct as the forces of the East India Company, and were still arguably an entity requiring a separate reference as not part of the British Army. Of greater importance, however, was the new section (b) above; that these forces would have to be brought within the scope of the VC had been pointed out by the Duke of Cambridge at the time the 1867 Warrant was under discussion[387] but this was the first time anything had been done to implement this.

The first draft then proceeded to re-enact Clauses 6 to 11 of the 1856 Warrant, but an amendment was made to Clause 12, so that recommendations would now be submitted to the Queen 'by the Officer Commanding in Chief of Our Army, with the approval of Our Secretary of State for War' which took cognisance of a change of internal procedure which was currently under discussion, and which relates to the fact that Cardwell's army reforms of ten years previously had ended the old dualism of military administration divided between the Horse Guards and the WO, thus making the CinC one of the subordinate heads under S of S. The remaining clauses were also

387   See p153

re-enacted, though in a further revision the references to claimants to the VC were deleted from Clauses 8 and 12 — thus far had opinion changed from the original views of Prince Albert,[388] though his faith in the virtue of the award going to those who claimed it was by common consent misplaced, and indeed, when the New Zealand Government had [somewhat improperly] created their own award of the New Zealand Cross in 1870, their Warrant had expressly forbidden claims by the individuals concerned.[389]

The draft also contained an entirely new additional Clause at the end. This read as follows:- 'Lastly: It is ordained that nothing herein contained shall be deemed or construed to annul or abate the rights and privileges of any person on whom We have been pleased to confer the decoration of the Victoria Cross (save and except those whose names have been erased under the above recited Regulations). All persons therefore who are now entitled to wear this honorable distinction, We hereby declare shall continue to hold the same in as full and ample a measure as they possessed the same antecedently to the enactment of these present Rules and Ordinances'.

This may probably be read as a note of caution. No attempt had previously been made to recast the entire Warrant, and this clause was probably envisaged as a safeguard to stop any legal argument as to how the replacement of the old Warrant by a new one might have prejudiced those awarded their Crosses under the old document. On 10 Dec the draft was ready for submission to the Admiralty to invite their Lordships' comments thereon. In the covering letter that went with it its main significance was clearly indicated as lying in 'including therein cases in which "marked gallantry" has been displayed "in the performance of duty", the words of the existing Warrant which required the performance of "some signal act of valour or devotion to their country" having been interpreted as excluding such cases', and 'in rendering Officers and men of the Auxiliary and reserve forces eligible for the distinction', and also 'that advantage has been taken of the opportunity thus afforded to review the warrant generally, by including in it the modifications which have been introduced by warrants issued since the decoration was instituted'.

The only observation which the Admiralty wished to make on the new text was to suggest the addition to the fourteenth Clause 'such pension to be in addition to any other pension or pensions which they

388 See Appendix II
389 *Medals and Decorations of the British Army and Navy,* Vol ii, p390

may be receiving or entitled to, from any other source whatever'. Apart from this, they indicated in their reply of 29 Dec, they approved the new proposals. The first reaction to this suggestion within the WO was a minute of 31 Dec 'If a man holding a VC pension were to get his commission would not the pension cease? But when placed on half pay do you consider the insertion of the words would give rise to a claim to revert to such VC pension?' It is not quite clear to whom this query was addressed, but whoever it was shared the questioner's doubts, for a reply to this minute, dated 4 Jan 1881, read 'The VC annuity ceases entirely from the date on which a grantee becomes a commd. officer and the proposed words would undoubtedly give rise to claims which could not be allowed'.

All these papers went before the Permanent Secretary on 5 Jan, with a note, presumably written by Col Deedes, 'I do not see the necessity for the addition as the pensioner would receive the pension in addition to any other in the same way that he can now receive pension for wounds or meritorious service'. And in putting this before the S of S Mr Thompson added, 'I agree. The words proposed seem to be· unnecessary and might lead to complication in the event of the holder being commissioned'. In the face of this unanimity it is hardly surprising that Childers accepted the advice of his officials, and the papers were returned by him, marked 'Apd. Let the Admiralty know the reason'.

Only a few days were now to elapse before, as was usual, the first unofficial submission was made of the proposed new Warrant to the Queen. But on Jan 12 the first warning light appeared. On that day Ponsonby wrote to Childers, this time from Osborne: 'The Queen will keep for the present the recommendations regarding the Victoria Cross so that she may give them full consideration'. The exact sequence of the following documents is a little obscure, but is probably best explained by assuming a missing letter from Ponsonby, indicating that the Queen could not approve the new Warrant, as upsetting too much of the old, and reading the following undated document, which is also unsigned, as the draft of a letter sent by Thompson to Ponsonby in reply. This reads:- 'I have been carefully working over the V.C.W. to see if I could suggest some words which would remove our difficulties of interpretation without opening the door wider than it is.

'I find a curious discrepancy in the W[arran]t as to the qualifications for the decoration. In the preamble it is described as "bravery in action before an enemy". In the para. headed "fifthly" it is described as having performed "some signal act of valour or devotion to their country". In the next para ("sixthly") it is described as "conspicuous bravery" and again in para headed "15thly" it is described as "a gallant and daring act".

'This I think shows the necessity for some revision of the wording and what I would suggest is a combination of the definition in the 5th and 6th paras and that the qualification should be "conspicuous bravery or devotion to their country in the presence of the enemy".

'If you agree in this and will kindly let me know whether H.M. would be likely to approve of such an alteration throughout the Wt. I will get Mr. C. to forward it in proper form.'

The next certainly dated document in the correspondence, from Ponsonby at Osborne, on 8 Apr 1881, which makes the Queen's position very [and most interestingly] clear, would seem to fall into place as the reply to this. It read as follows:- 'We are engaged in the difficult task of making regulations for the purpose of rewarding those who break regulations.

'The original Statutes were drawn up under the supervision of the Prince Consort and The Queen's [wish] is that these should remain as they are with all their imperfections — for under them every sort of person has been rewarded and plenty of loopholes existed through which doubtful cases were lugged in.

'But as Mr Childers earnestly pressed her to some alterations The Queen consented to do so as long as it did not enlarge the order which she thought was already too large.

'The discrepancies you mention are glaring — and I think the amendments in the sense you suggest would meet with the Queen's approval.'

Presumably the PUS communicated his partial success to the S of S, and the following letter was sent in answer on 10 Apr:- 'My dear Thompson, We must hope for the best about "Nemesis". I think your proposal about the V.C. will be the best, although I always prefer consolidation to amendment. Perhaps you had better send it privately to Sir H. Ponsonby, and if he sees no difficulty I write [? will] formally submit it to H.M. ..... Yours sincerely, Hugh M. Childers'.

Evidently Mr Thompson followed this advice, for on 14 Apr Sir Henry Ponsonby wrote, presumably to Thompson, though the letter is only addressed 'Dear Sir' this time from Buckingham Palace, 'I think your proposal will solve the difficulties and that the Queen will approve of this additional Statute. HM's chief desire is to prevent the order being too common. And this will, I think meet all that is required. Many thanks to you.' The Warrant itself was signed by the Queen on 23rd of the same month.[387a]

What had been saved of that proposed originally? In form very little, but that little did embody two important points, the redefinition of the qualification for the VC, and its extension to the Reserve and Auxiliary Forces. From the course of the discussion that has been traced out it is apparent that two common readings of this Warrant are incorrect; firstly, it was not designed to simplify difficulties of interpretation of the conditions of award as amended by the various Warrants which had been issued since 1856, but as the unsigned draft letter which has been attributed to Thompson makes clear, to remove the inconsistencies of language contained in the 1856 Warrant itself; secondly, it was not directed to the revocation of the Warrant of Aug 1858, whose days, as the remarks of the CinC and Garter King of Arms prove, were clearly numbered from the time of the institution of the Albert Medal in 1866.

As will be observed, one of the most revolutionary proposals of the original draft, that which made acts of duty eligible for the Cross, does not appear in the new Warrant, nor would the new definition appear any more favourable to this circumstance than that of the 1856 Warrant. The truth, however, was very strange, for with one accord the doctrine was adopted that the new Warrant did do just this, difficult as it appears to square this interpretation with the governing instrument.

On 2 May 1881, just a fortnight after the new Warrant had been signed, Deedes brought forward the case of Capt Sartorius once more, submitting that it came within the new statute and that Sartorius was now eligible for the VC. The remarkable feature of this contention was that there was nothing in the Warrant upon which it could be based, following the abandonment of the original draft, which certainly had contained such a provision. Perhaps even more remarkable is that it was accepted – Deedes' submission was forwarded to Childers on 6 May, with a recommendation for his approval, which he gave on the 9th, a memorandum was laid before the Queen for her approval on the 12th, and the award gazetted on 17 May 1881. That this was not an isolated decision was shown in 1892 when recommendations were under consideration for the operations in the Hunza and Nagar country on the North West Frontier in Dec 1891.[388a] At the storming of the Nilt Fort Capt Aylmer and Lts Boisragon and Badcock had all distinguished themselves, but whilst the VC was sought for the first two [and

387a See Appendix IX
388a PRO, WO 32/7416

eventually granted them] the AMS, India, thought that Badcock's case would be met by the DSO [which is what he eventually received] since he had merely led troops to their support. However, the Duke of Cambridge thought that Badcock's conduct after he was wounded constituted an equal claim to the Cross, and the matter received some consideration. What is interesting is the view of the AG, at that time Sir Redvers Buller; although he saw no positive objection 'I doubt that he should get it because I have always conceived that the decoration of the Victoria Cross was intended to commemorate the performance of an action involving distinct military initiative outside the path of regular duty'. This would have contradicted the whole policy which had been followed since the signing of the new Warrant, and it is interesting to observe that the WO file contains a note citing the 1881 Warrant in refutation of Buller's view. So, whatever was in the Warrant, there was no doubt as to what was being read in to it. In fact, the words 'extreme devotion to duty in the presence of the enemy', the nearest form to the lost term of 1881 only appear in a VC Warrant in 1920.[389a]

There was, of course, one vital distinction still preserved when the idea of accepting acts of duty as eligible for the award of the Cross was adopted, that the person concerned could be regarded as a free agent. Thus, the award of the VC to Sgt Robert Scott, for his part in throwing time-fuse shells as hand grenades over a line of barricades, from which the enemy were directing a heavy fire at the attack on Moirosi's Mountain in South Africa in Apr 1879 was at first refused, until it was established that he had acted as a volunteer and not under orders in doing this.[390] This was, of course, before the institution of the new Warrant which was read as covering acts of duty, but the same reasoning was clearly at work in the rejection of the recommendation of VCs for Lt E.G. Earle, on the grounds that his act was that of a subordinate officer under orders, and who received a DSO, and Sgt-Maj Jillings, who since he was serving as the observer in his aircraft it was 'not considered that he was a sufficiently free agent for it to be established that... he was acting on his own initiative'; having been commissioned whilst his case was under consideration Jillings ended up with a Military Cross. Both of these examples are taken from the initial set of recommendations for the VC made by Sir John French from France in 1914.[391]

There was, however, one field of activity in which the conception of the act of duty being a bar to the VC lingered rather longer. The

389a See Appendix XII
390   PRO, WO 32/7408
391   PRO, WO 32/4993

circumstances where this applied may be seen in the remarks addressed
by the AMS to the AG, Sir Evelyn Wood, on 14 Jan 1901, apropos the
conduct of Lt Douglas at Magersfontein. 'It appears to me,' he wrote,
'that if this decision be accepted as a precedent, to assert that a gallant
act such as here described, i.e. succouring the wounded, if performed
by any officer, N.C. Officer or private in the Army may be awarded the
VC but if a similar act of gallantry be performed by a Medical Officer it
is to be regarded as a simple act of duty. I submit that such a decision is
not in conformity with the spirit underlying the creation of the
Decoration of the VC and it is a grievous injury to the R.A.M.Corps.

'It must appear from the dispatch that Lt Douglas was not merely
accompanying the regiment to which he was attached but advanced
alone through a severe fire to render immediate assistance to those who
required it. It was for precisely similar acts that the VC has previously
been conferred on Medical Officers.'

Whoever's views the AMS was combatting, his opinion seems to have
generally prevailed at the WO, for two days later Sir Evelyn Wood
referred the matter to the MS, in the following terms: 'Will you please
consider this point and speak to the Commander in Chief; it is not one
I think for the Adjutant General to deal with. I venture, however, to
suggest that while so far as I understand the reports further information
would be essential before the Queen could be asked to give the Victoria
Cross to Mr Douglas — yet it does appear that he was doing a very
brave act, and not within the scope of his duty. I imagine that a Doctor's
duty in action is to attend the wounded at the Dressing Station and I
gather that at Magersfontein this Officer went forward either into or in
advance of the firing line and there attended to save wounded.'

These papers did not elicit any comment from the CinC, Lord
Roberts, for some few weeks, but on 8 Mar 1901 he commented, 'I
agree with the AG and consider that Lt-Gen Lord Methuen's strong
recommendation in favour of Lt Douglas being given the VC should
be accepted'. The papers were endorsed, 'Submit to S of S' on the
following day, and on the 11th the S of S added his initials and 'I
entirely agree'. The recommendation was submitted to King Edward VII
and approved by him later that month, the award being gazetted on
29 Mar 1901.[392]

Exactly the same ground was traversed in the case of Surgeon-Capt
Arthur Martin-Leake, later to become the first recipient of a bar to the
VC. The recommendation was forwarded by the Inspector General of

392   PRO, WO 32/7953

the South African Constabulary to the AG as possibly deserving of the VC on 3 Mar 1902. The opinion of the Principal Medical Officer in South Africa was sought on the point as to whether Martin-Leake was doing anything more than his duty, and his reply may be regarded as masterly. Martin-Leake had, he considered, done well, though he trusted the majority of medical officers would have done the same had they had the opportunity; Martin-Leake had had the chance of distinguishing himself and took it but could certainly have been more careful of his own safety without incurring censure. But the question ' "Was he doing any more than his duty" would exclude every one from the VC for it is every one's duty to do his very best.' Despite this admirable reply the recommendation was still forwarded by Lord Kitchener as one for the DSO rather than the VC, as he still felt Martin-Leake was only carrying out his manifest duty, and this point received a good deal of discussion in the WO papers, with especial reference to the 1881 Warrant. In the course of these it clearly emerged that in the case of Capt Schofield, who eventually received the VC for his part in the attempt to save the guns at Colenso, which had cost Lord Roberts' son his life, the same objections of the act being one of duty had been raised by Gen Buller; that the terms of the April 1881 Warrant had been pointed out to him, but that he had still objected to any such recommendation for Schofield, and that it had only been decided by the CinC and S of S after reference to South Africa, and over the head of Buller, that Schofield should be so recommended. In fact, Lord Roberts' submission to the S of S, a month after Kitchener's recommendation, was for Martin-Leake to receive the DSO only, and it was Brodrick's reply on 30 Apr 'This would almost have seemed to me a case for VC' that finally settled the matter. Roberts thereupon instructed the MS to prepare a submission to the King for a VC, which was made on 8 May and the actual award gazetted on 13 May 1902.[393]

Perhaps the main importance of this last episode lies in the phrase which had come from South Africa 'It is every one's duty to do his very best'. With this corollary to the Warrant of Apr 1881 it would be difficult in future for anyone to debar a soldier from the highest reward for the highest courage, as Gen Buller had attempted to do, on account of the act being one of duty — for if one had a duty to do one's best, how could any act of courage not be regarded as an act of duty?

393   PRO, WO 32/4990

Chapter 16

Warrants from 1918 to the Present Day

IN JUST OVER FOUR years from 1914 to 1918 more Victoria Crosses [582] were awarded than in the whole of the previous fifty-eight years of the Cross's existence [522], and much had been done which, whilst it would have required a very pedantic mind to argue that the spirit of the 1856 Warrant had been betrayed, had involved actions not within its express terms. This has already been demonstrated as regards post-humous awards, and in the strict application of the rules for selection of recipients by ballot. There was, too, an outstanding doubt regarding the eligibility of members of the Merchant Navy, so it can hardly have come as any surprise that the suggestion should have come from the Admiralty of the desirability of a committee to consider the amendment of the Victoria Cross Warrants.[394] In referring this matter to the Permanent Under Secretary, Sir R.H. Brade, on 23 Jul 1918, the Deputy Military Secretary pointed out that the control of the VC, and the preparation of its statutes, was vested in the Secretary of State for War; he also implied that something of this nature was already under consideration. To this Brade replied on 29th that he would submit a recommendation at once to the King that a committee should be formed, to hear the views of all interested departments and co-ordinate their views before drafting new statutes; this would both meet the view of the Admiralty and also preserve the initiative in such matters of the WO. 'The original statutes were, as you know, framed by the S. of S. for War and First Lord in conjunction with the Prince Consort. Co-operation from the earliest will be expected.'

On 1 Aug 1918 Col Graham wrote to Sir Frederick Ponsonby, the Keeper of the Privy Purse, and son of the Sir Henry Ponsonby whom we met in the last chapter. He indicated that the time seemed appropriate for the redrafting of the VC Warrants, and asked that it might be submitted for King George V's consideration whether a committee

---

394   PRO, WO 32/3443, and for the whole of this section.

might be set up for this purpose. Sir Frederick replied on 3rd to say that the King had been much interested to hear about the many Warrants, approved of all these being embodied in a new Warrant, and thought a meeting of the government offices concerned with the WO would be a good idea. Of the points which might engage the attention of this committee, the King felt that the one of the eligibility of women should be discussed privately; they might perform gallant services as car-drivers or as nurses, but were not eligible under the statutes. The fact of their being eligible might be resented in the Army, so it would be best to go carefully into the matter before any decision was arrived at, though if civilians were made eligible the question why women should not be included might be difficult to answer. A press release could notify the extension of the award to the Royal Air Force, and the use of the red ribbon for all services.

With this evidence of royal approval the proposed interdepartmental committee was set up, the chairman being Sir Frederick Ponsonby, who thus signified and implemented the royal interest in the subject, and a press release was issued to announce the setting up and purpose of the committee on 7 Aug 1918. Its terms of reference, which were presumably drawn up by Brade and Graham, the DMS, in conjunction with Ponsonby, were as follows:- 'To consider and to advise His Majesty through the Secretary of State for War as to:-

(a)   What amendments to the Victoria Cross Warrant of 29 January 1856 are necessary to give effect to the decision to extend the decoration to the Royal Air Force.

(b)   What variations are recommended in respect of clauses vii, viii, and xii, respectively, in order to render the application of these clauses more in keeping with the requirements of modern warfare.

(c)   What amplification, if any, is necessary to facilitate the interpretation of clause xiii.

(d)   A draft warrant to consolidate and embody in the original Warrant of 29 January 1856 the following supplementary warrants

    (i)   1 Jan 1867 – Extension of the VC to certain Local Forces in New Zealand.

    (ii)   23 Apr 1881 – Definition of the service qualifying for award, and the extension of award to Auxiliary and reserve Forces.

    (iii)   6 Aug 1881 – Extension of the VC to members of the Indian Ecclesiastical Establishment.

     (iv)   21 Oct 1911 – Extension of the VC to the Indian Army.

     (v)   1 Nov 1858 – A special warrant (not published) extending the VC to certain civilian Volunteers who served under Military Commanders during the Indian Mutiny.

(e)   The eligibility for the VC of Indian Imperial Service Troops and certain Levies who serve side by side with Imperial Troops.

(f)   A new clause to support posthumous award of the VC as the existing Warrant does not legislate for such awards.

(g)   The advisability or otherwise of extending, in certain circumstances the award to women and to civilians.'

Thus was finally brought about what Mr Childers, at the WO, had wished for thirty-seven years previously, and which he had then failed to effect, a comprehensive review of the Warrant as a whole, instead of an attempt to patch. He had, of course, been at a disadvantage, in that he had run into Queen Victoria's objection to any tampering with something she could regard as a memorial to the Prince Consort but now, with this obstacle removed, a very creditable attempt was being made to look at all the problems as a whole.

One of the earliest moves by the WO was to invite the views of the other interested departments on the question of extending the VC to women. The India Office had no objection provided the standard of merit was not lowered; the Colonial Office said much the same, adding that it thought it would be in accord with public opinion to make women eligible; the Home Office [the only occasion on which they were consulted in this connection] commented that the Albert and Edward medals could go to women, and that this was as far as their interest in decorations went; the Air Ministry thought it only logical to include women, and also civilians, subject to a precise definition of eligibility. The only dissenting voice came from Rear-Admiral Everett, Naval Secretary at the Admiralty and, for its true flavour of the real old sea dog, his letter deserves quoting in full:-

'My Dear General,

At first blink, it seems logically indefensible to debar the fair sex from being awarded the VC, provided of course they *"have performed some signal act of valour or devotion to their country"*.

But there are other considerations, both concrete and abstract, which, it is thought, render the idea impracticable, although it is certainly quite possible that a woman could under certain conceivable conditions earn one.

It must be fully realized that the standard of valour and devotion to duty for the Victoria Cross is now very much higher than it was in the earlier years of its introduction. In fact it may be said that the standard now required for the award of a VC is far, far higher than the actual words express.

Literally the Victoria Cross could be awarded for any signal act of valour and devotion to duty, and if women are to be eligible, will not the ordinary gallantry of man render his judgment lenient; will he not be soft-hearted towards the woman (marriage proves this) and give her the benefit of the loosest interpretation of a female act of valour or devotion to duty; will he not be inclined to say "By Jove (Mars or Venus), for a woman that was a splendid deed", and assess her award by virtue of being influenced by her sex? Will not, therefore, the traditional interpretation of a signal act of valour and devotion to duty be elastically applied to the so-called frail sex?

I believe these are practicable considerations which must be taken into serious consideration.

Again, let us suppose that women are eligible, let us hypothecate a retreat where some bloody-minded virago WAAC is overtaken by a Hun, might she not be the more induced to take up a bundook and battle with a Hun; might she not be all the more tempted to take some very unladylike action or conduct herself in such an unseemly manner from the universal standard expected of the fair sex that the enemy would proclaim all women combatants and shoot them at sight?

To my mind, it may be a narrow masculine one, it would be a dangerous move to include females into the VC area. There are enough bickerings in the masculine line as to whether this man or that should or should not have been awarded a VC, but if the hysterical female world is to be allowed in, God help the poor devils who have to make decisions.

Until the time comes when men and women are treated alike, when chivalry is dead and buried, when the natures of men and women are identical (which, thank God, is a natural impossibility) then, and not till then, will it be wise to artificially place women on the same rude footing as men.

Them's my sentiments, but what you want is the opinion of the official Admiralty. That I will obtain as soon as possible and let you know.

I merely send this hot air in case it contains any sense which may be of use to you.

Yours sincerely, A.F. Everett.'

On 24 Aug 1918 Mr R.U. Morgan of the WO was appointed to act as secretary of the committee, which held its first meeting on 30th of that month. Those present on that occasion were, [in addition to Sir Frederick Ponsonby in the Chair and the Secretary], Col Graham representing the WO, Rear-Admiral Everett representing the Admiralty, Col R.H. More for the Air Ministry, Col S.D. Gordon for the India Office and both Lt-Col A.E. Beattie and Mr H.C.M. Lambert on behalf of the Colonial Office. We are singularly well informed of the proceedings of this committee, for the full transcript of the shorthand record of its two meetings is preserved in the PRO, even to the extent of showing which unfamiliar proper names defeated the shorthand writers, as, for example, that of the Q Ship HMS *Pargust*, which emerged as *'Parkhurst'*, and that of the South African VC Major Phipps-Hornby, who turned into 'Fitz Hornby'.

One of the first questions to be discussed was the basic strategy of defining eligibility. The Chairman at first suggested that the three services should be kept in three separate paragraphs, but against this Col Graham urged the advantage of laying down at the outset what the decoration was for and then to get all the services in one paragraph, a view which was endorsed by Everett and Gordon. Admiral Everett also stressed the need for stiffening the definition of the qualification for the Cross, a view that was generally shared. As Graham pointed out, this was needed to prevent what he referred to as 'The VC Committee of each department' taking an independent view of the standard required. He added that 'You cannot compare the VC in this war with any previous war because people are getting the MM now for what would have won the VC in the South African War'. Ponsonby now brought the discussion back to the point which had originated his suggestion of separate paragraphs for each service, namely the question of how to fit the RAF into the provision for immediate awards under the eye of the commander. However, it now emerged that the Admiralty would be happy to see this provision dropped, while Graham stated [with distinctly dubious accuracy] that the Army had never made use of it. The suggestion then emerged that the seventh, eighth and twelfth clauses of the Warrant, which dealt very largely with this subject, might be telescoped into one and the whole of this provision simplified. This raised the question of the interpretation of the phrase 'such description and attestation of the act as [the officer commanding] shall think requisite', and revealed an interesting divergence of departmental practice; Col Graham stated that two witnesses were required by the Army, this being their private interpretation of the demand for 'conclusive proof', which was 'a domestic arrangement on the part of the Field Marshal in France', whereas the Admiralty had never thought previously of such emphasis being placed on the word 'conclusive', and had no such rule.

From here the discussion moved on to the question of the selection of recipients by ballot, which has already been dealt with[395] and then to that of the general consolidation into one document of all those forces who had been made eligible by Warrants subsequent to that of 1856. One suggestion that was made was that the whole matter could be simplified by stating who was ineligible, but this was not pursued. Lambert, for the Colonial Office, had a point to make here, as he wished to see included Colonial troops fighting on their own, and not alongside Imperial forces. Graham stated, again on somewhat dubious grounds, that members of the King's African Rifles and Frontier Force Rifles had not been regarded as eligible until Indian native troops had been brought in, though no case had in fact arisen for consideration. He also stated that a WO letter of 21 Mar 1916 had told the Colonial Office that it had been decided that the 1867 Warrant covered all Dominion and Colonial forces, but Lambert objected that the Warrant did not so read. This led to the Admiralty raising the question of members of the Merchant Navy, which has also already received attention.[396]

Another point to be raised was the question of the unpublished Warrant of 1858, for deeds not in the presence of the enemy. That it was undesirable to have such a provision was agreed, the only doubt, principally arising from the fact that it had never been published, was whether it required any explicit cancellation. The general opinion was, however, that so long as it clearly was regarded as cancelled, there was no need to take any specific step.

The discussion then passed on to the question of eligibility for women. Ponsonby was opposed to this, as this would mean they would have to be considered as combatants, which might give the Germans justification for shooting them, whereas they could never be in a position to fight in any conditions [which echoed some of the points in Admiral Everett's letter]. Col More pointed out that doctors and chaplains received the Cross although they were non-combatants, to which Everett objected that it was their business to go into the firing line and be in the fight and it was not the business of women to do so; when Gordon remarked 'They may be there helping', Everett's final retort was 'They ought to clear out', but it was plain from the generality

395 See Chapter 10
396 See Chapter 12

of departmental views that he was unsupported. Most probably agreed with Graham's view that the circumstances were unlikely in which a case would arise, but that they should nonetheless be included in the Warrant. A suggestion was made that a simple reference to eligibility to 'civilians of both sexes' might be all that was required, but it was pointed out that this by itself would rule out nurses. There was some discussion also on whether the reference to the eligibility of women should be in the preamble of the Warrant or in the statutes themselves. It was agreed that any reference to civilians should take up the limitation to those serving under authority, and reference was made to the wording to this effect in the 1858 Warrant.

From here consideration passed to the question of posthumous awards, a subject which has already been discussed,[397] but which showed a general agreement that these should be authorised by the Warrant, despite the illogicality that this was the only award for which it would be permissible. Somewhat remarkable, however, was Ponsonby's assertion in the course of the discussion that 'No one can get the VC when he gets killed during the action in which he earns the decoration', since this view was at least sixteen years out of date, and had been contradicted many times since the outbreak of the Great War.

One point that appears to have been accepted without any debate was that in future the Cross should be worn with a red ribbon by all services, instead of red for the Army and blue for the Navy. The meeting adjourned, leaving Mr Morgan to draw up and circulate a revised Warrant in the light of what had been said.

The exact date upon which Morgan produced his draft is not recorded, but a number of drafting comments were made by the DAMS on 8 Oct. One of these was to object to the reference to claimants 'as no individual can claim a decoration', a remark which finally demolished one of the most strongly urged contentions of Prince Albert in 1854. He also pointed out that reference to 'Matrons and Sisters' in respect of the eligibility of the nursing services was too narrow, and for the term 'Native Officer' which Morgan had employed should be substituted 'Indian Officer'. It was at this point too that the Admiralty first raised their suggestions on the inclusion of a reference to participation in a VC ballot in a man's record, and on a new sliding scale for the number of Crosses to be so distributed.

The Committee held its second meeting on 12 Nov 1918. The only change in those present was that this time the WO representative was

397   See Chapter 8

Lt-Col Lord H. Montagu-Douglas-Scott, and that for the Admiralty, Commodore Bentinck. The basic aim on this occasion was to consider any further amendments or additions that might be desirable in the draft Warrant that Morgan had circulated. The first suggestion [from the Admiralty] was that the Warrant should include instructions about the wearing of a replica on the ribbon; at the time it was generally agreed that this was not a matter for the Warrant, though it did in fact appear in the final version. A reordering of the wording of Clause 1, which described the Cross, a new wording which tightened up the description of the requirements for the award of the Cross, and the inclusion of a clause permitting the posthumous award of the Cross were all rapidly agreed. On the sixth clause, a new and more comprehensive definition of the forces eligible for the award, the Colonial Office representatives pointed out the necessity of including a reference to the marine services of the Dominions, Colonies, Dependencies and Protectorates, which had been overlooked. One clause which did cause discussion was that regarding the number of Crosses to be awarded by ballot, according to the size of the unit involved, a matter which was finally settled on the terms suggested by the Secretary. One suggestion was adopted in the discussion which did not survive into the Warrant as published, namely that this should include a reference to the presentation of Crosses to next of kin of deceased recipients. The draft clause referring to native officers was generally disliked, as it was felt by no means clear what the term meant. The intention was, apparently, to cover native levies, but the Colonial Office in particular was against the wording proposed. Nice points of status were also raised in connection with Naval warrant officers and Viceroy commissioned officers in India, for each of which the Secretary undertook to redraft the proposed clauses. The draft of the clause on expulsion for misconduct was amended to include women as well as men, and at this point the question was raised as to whether desertion was included in this; Sir Frederick Ponsonby thought it was not. The only other question to be raised was whether, from the point of view of the special pension, nurses were regarded as of officer status, but the point was left somewhat unsettled. This concluded the second meeting of the Committee, and it was left to Mr Morgan to produce a Warrant to incorporate all the points that had been raised.

On 23 Jan 1919 Ponsonby wrote to Morgan to say that he had consulted the Central Chancery of the Orders of Knighthood on the point raised by the Admiralty regarding reference to the wearing of the replica on the VC ribbon, and that they had advised it should be included in the Warrant, as being more a question of insignia, so the point went in to the draft.

The exact date upon which Morgan finished his work does not appear, but it must have been within the next three or four weeks that the text of the new Warrant[398] went before the King. On 7 Mar 1919 Lord Stamfordham, the King's Private Secretary wrote to Winston Churchill, the S of S for War, 'As I mentioned to you in conversation, The King was averse to the inclusion of women and civilians among those eligible for the Victoria Cross. I explained to His Majesty the points which you raised in favour of allowing the terms of the Warrant to remain as recommended by the Army Council. The King has, therefore, signed the Warrant, but His Majesty hopes that its publication may be deferred until we are no longer in a state of war. This would ensure no question of making the Warrant retrospective'. To this Mr Churchill replied on 12th that he was happy to agree. The new Warrant thus went into cold storage, and remained there until Sir Herbert Creedy who was PS to the S of S, wrote to Ponsonby on 17 May 1920, 'I am given to understand that you see no reason for further delay and if so perhaps you would be good enough to take steps to ascertain His Majesty's pleasure as to whether the present is an opportune time for publication'. In the time that had elapsed all the remaining VC awards in respect of the Great War had been gazetted [the last – that to CSM Evans – on 20 Jan 1920], and a short Act of Parliament had been passed giving a legal date for the end of hostilities. On 22 May A.H.L. Hardinge replied, 'I am desired to inform you that the King has now given his approval to the publication of the new Victoria Cross warrant', and the date of this letter was in fact the date inserted on the Warrant as the date upon which the King had given his signature.

It may seem ironic that so carefully thought out a document as this new Warrant should have had so short an operative life, as it was in its turn abrogated and replaced by another Warrant in 1931, so that only four VCs – those to Capts H.J. Andrews and G.S. Henderson, Lt W.D. Kenny and Sepoy Ishar Singh – were ever awarded under its authority. The reason for this short life was the precedent that the 1920 Warrant had itself created, that all alteration to the terms of the Warrant should be by means of complete repeal and re-enactment of all previous clauses which were to remain unamended, rather than by the patchwork method of supplementary warrants of the period up to 1911, a precedent which was again to be followed in 1961.

398   See Appendix XII

The first point to arise requiring an amendment of the Warrant was contained in a letter from the Central Chancery of the Orders of Knighthood to the WO on 18 Dec 1923, stating that the King had been graciously pleased to direct that a standard size should be laid down for a miniature VC, and that a sealed pattern should be kept in the Central Chancery for all future badges of this nature. The Central Chancery therefore requested the WO to make the necessary insertion in the VC Warrant to cover this matter.[399] These papers appear to have been filed away at the WO for action at an appropriate time.

A further point arose with the report of the Interdepartmental Rewards Committee on the question of forfeiture and restoration of medals and decorations, which had recommended that whilst the offences entailing such forfeiture should be laid down, they should not be detailed in the Warrants themselves, which had a very direct bearing on the twelfth clause of the 1920 Warrant.[400] It was at this time that discussion of amendment seems actually to have started in the WO, though after an initial round of consideration in Jan 1927, the matter seems to have gone into abeyance until May 1929, when the Admiralty raised the point that the tenth clause also required amendment to exclude warrant officers in the Royal Marines from the £10 pension, as in the Admiralty's view they were analogous with Naval warrant officers.

At this time there were obviously enough matters for consideration to make the project of a full revision of the Warrant worth embarking on. A constitutional point was raised by the Government of Australia with the Dominions Office, as to the wording of the proposed new clause on deprivation of the Cross, which was to be on a recommendation by the First Lord of the Admiralty or of one of the principal Secretaries of State. The point raised here was that, though such a recommendation might go through these, in the case of the forces of the Dominions, it would not be within their competence to make such a recommendation upon them, a point which was met by amending the text to read 'by or through the First Lord [etc]...'. A.G.4 (Medals), at the War Office, suggested that a reference should be made to the VC ribbon being 1½ inches wide, as was done in the Warrant for the MC, a point which was accepted, and proposed that the new Clause 13 – the one which had occasioned comment from the Australian Government – should contain a definite reference to the S of S for War and for Air. This had an initially favourable response [there is a marginal note '? yes' against

399   PRO, WO 32/3442 for all matters relating to the 1931 Warrant.
400   See Chapter 7

it] but nothing finally came of it, presumably as the Australian comment had shown that there might be circumstances in which other Ss of S, such as the Dominions Secretary, might need to be involved.

Beyond these points all the revisions found to be necessary in the text were essentially matters of dotting Mr Morgan's 'i's and crossing his 't's. 'Secretaries of State' became 'Principal Secretaries of State', the 'Royal Sign Manual' ceased to be 'Royal', all the numbering of clauses was put into italics, and a considerable number of capital letters were altered to lower case, and *vice versa.* The new Warrant, incorporating these amendments was signed by King George V on 5 Feb 1931.[401] The main points at which it differed from the old text were, naturally, a reference in the new preamble to the repeal of the 1920 Warrant, a new twelfth clause meeting the Central Chancery's request for a stipulation on the miniature VC, a new thirteenth and fourteenth clause to replace the old twelfth clause on forfeiture of the Cross for misconduct, to meet the recommendations of the Interdepartmental Committee, and an entirely new final clause reserving to the Crown the powers of altering the new Warrant, the only surprising thing about which is that no such provision had previously been included.

The Warrant of 1931 was to remain the basic document for another thirty years, but during that period a number of amending warrants were signed in order to meet various changes in circumstance. Thus, on 9 May 1938, an amending Warrant was published to bring within the terms of award the forces of Burma which, since 1 Apr 1937, had ceased to be part of India, and so now required to be individually listed among those eligible for the VC.[402] In exactly the same way a further amendment was required with the creation of a new grade of Warrant Officer [WO.III], in the British Army, since the 1931 Warrant only specified as eligible Warrant Officers Grades I and II, which was dealt with by another Royal Warrant of 21 Aug 1939.[403] Similarly, the creation of an Indian Air Force also required mention of its personnel to be made among those listed as eligible, and this was done by a further amending Warrant of 25 Jan 1941.[404] The final amendment to be made to the Warrant of 1931 dates from 31 Dec 1942,[405] and was a rather more comprehensive piece of work. Its origin is traceable to a letter sent to Sir James Grigg, PUS at the WO by Sir Robert Knox,

401　See Appendix XIII
402　See Appendix XIV
403　See Appendix XV
404　See Appendix XVI
405　See Appendix XVII

Secretary of the Committee on the Grant of Honours, Decorations and Medals in Time of War, on 18 Oct 1941.[406]

'The War Office will, I expect, now wish to prepare an amending Warrant for the Victoria Cross', he wrote. 'The necessary changes appear to be:-

1. *Women's Services*

   Inclusion of the ATS [Auxiliary Territorial Service] and the WAAF [Women's Auxiliary Air Force].

   Women commissioned and serving with the RAMC and the Medical Branch of the RAF appear to be provided for satisfactorily in the existing warrant.

2. *Royal Indian Navy*

   As part of the 7th Clause [sic − clearly 6th is intended] of the Warrant is to be amended it may be desirable to consider the substitution of this description for our "Indian Marine Service" in Clause 6(ii).

3. *Indian Air Force and Indian Air Force Volunteer Reserve*

   The Air Ministry state that the Viceroy has recently raised the question of making the IAFVR eligible for the Victoria Cross. Members of the IAF itself do not appear to be eligible. (See Clause 6(4)).

4. *Sudan Defence Force.* Should perhaps be included.

   The Air Ministry have kindly submitted the following rough re-draft of Clause 6 and proposed amendment for Clause 9 to show the type of draft they think might be used.

   CLAUSE 6. *Delete* this clause and *substitute:-*

   "Sixthly. It is ordained that the persons eligible for the Decoration of the Cross shall be

   (1) Persons of any rank in the Naval, Military or Air Forces of Our United Kingdom of Great Britain and Northern Ireland, of India, of Burma, of Our Colonies, and of Territories under Our Suzerainty, Protection or Jurisdiction, including the Home Guard and in India members of Frontier Corps and Military Police and members of Indian States' Forces and in Burma members of the Burma Frontier Force and Military Police, and including also the military Nursing Services and the Women's Auxiliary Services.

   (2) Persons of any rank in the Naval, Military or Air Forces

---

406 PRO, WO 32/9954 for this letter and all other matters relating to this Warrant.

belonging to any other part of Our Dominions, Our Government whereof has signified its desire that the Cross should be awarded under the provisions of this Our Warrant, and any Territory being administered by Us in such Government.

(3)   Civilians of either sex serving regularly or temporarily under the orders, direction or supervision of any of the above named forces."

CLAUSE 9. After sub-clause (e) *insert* new clause:-

"The foregoing references to male members of the Forces include equivalent ranks of the Women's Auxiliary Services".

The above is adapted to some extent from the terms of the George Cross Warrant, constructed here, which was agreed by all Departments. I enclose a copy. The various Departments concerned will no doubt be glad to see the new draft of the Victoria Cross Warrant in terms which the War Office recommend.'

It is interesting to note how much, on this occasion, the initiative for the new Warrant had passed outside the WO. With the setting up of a committee to deal with the granting of honours in time of war it was obvious that the WO role would be lessened to some extent, and it was hardly surprising that such a body should collect views from other departments, but it is noteworthy how ready these other departments were to bring forward their opinions and, in particular, the extent to which the Air Ministry were expressing these not merely on what might be regarded as departmental concerns, but on the structure of the Warrant as a whole. However, so far as India was concerned, Knox's expression of view of 18 Oct was to prove premature; on 24th he had to inform Grigg that the India Office had further points to raise regarding the RINVR, pensions for the RIN and a wording to include the Burma Volunteer Air Force. On all of these he hoped to have a note from the India Office within a fortnight, but, in fact, it was only on 20 Dec that the India Office were able to forward the Viceroy's telegram of 17th on the subject of amendments to the Warrant, which, as they themselves said, they had obtained from him after much delay. A certain exasperation may be detected in their comment on this telegram: 'The only point that needs any explanation is the revision India wishes to make in "eleventhly". This is due to the fact that up to date India has forgotten to include the Royal Indian Navy for monetary awards and now proposes to do so'.

The Viceroy's telegram had spelled out in great detail the financial provisions that were proposed for inclusion in the Warrant, and on

30 Jan 1942 the India Office stated that this redrafting was considered necessary to bring the clause into accordance with the Government of India and Government of Burma Acts of 1935. However, on 25th March the India Office put forward a much less specific alternative wording for this clause, and it was this form that was finally adopted in the new Warrant.

It is somewhat curious to note that it was only after matters had been settled with the India Office that the WO sought to discuss Knox's fourth point, regarding the Sudan Defence Force, with the FO, the amended text of the sixth clause being sent for their views on 1 Apr. Their reply was made, after consultation with their Legal Adviser, on 11th. The FO view was that the Sudan could be said to be under the Sovereign's jurisdiction, but that a condominium was really *sui generis,* so it would be best either to mention it by name after the reference to Burma or, since there was another condominium [the New Hebrides], to add after the words 'protection or jurisdiction' 'or under the jurisdiction jointly with another power'.

It was only after all this preliminary work had been done that an Interdepartmental Committee was summoned to meet on 7 May under the chairmanship of Lord Croft, one of the Joint Parliamentary Under Secretaries of State for War. One of the first points to engage attention was the application of the phrase 'under Our suzerainty' to the local forces of Malaya and the territories of Aden and Zanzibar. Here the difficulty of devising a suitable wording was found so great that the Committee agreed that note should simply be made of the problem and a recommendation made that any case arising be dealt with under the final [dispensing] clause of the Warrant. A particularisation of the Ulster Home Guard in the draft was agreed should be dropped and covered by the phrase 'Home Guard or any lawfully constituted force corresponding thereto'. Gen Floyer-Acland, the MS, who attended this meeting, sought at one stage to achieve comprehensiveness by simplifying eligibility to 'persons serving in any authorised force under a British commander', but to this it was objected that this would make Allied servicemen eligible, and when his WO colleague Mr H.E. Smith suggested 'any armed service of the Crown serving under a British Commander' this succumbed to the objection that such wording would render ineligible any British serviceman serving under an allied commander. Mr White, the Air Ministry representative, pointed out that the proposed amendment which had originated in his department was substantially in the terms of the GC Warrant, and he foresaw difficulties if the

Services were specified in the GC Warrant but not in that for the VC, and the amendment as originally drafted was accepted. The reference to the VC being available to such Dominions as desired it, was similarly one taken from the GC Warrant and, whilst it was felt a little late in the history of the VC to ask Dominion governments if they wished to participate in its award, it was agreed to refer the point to them. Some doubt was also expressed as to the correctness of the reference to '*Our* Merchant Navy' but this the Committee decided to accept. A more substantial point regarding the Merchant Navy was raised by Mr White [here again showing Air Ministry concern outside its departmental brief] who reported that the Committee on the Grant of Honours, Decorations and Medals in Time of War had recommended that military honours should not be introduced in place of civilian ones for the Merchant Navy. The general feeling of the Interdepartmental Committee was clearly that, except when the Merchant Navy was acting in collaboration with the Royal Navy, as at Dunkirk, this should be the practice, though as White pointed out, the draft they then had before them would not so limit it. It was eventually agreed to ask the Admiralty to reconsider this point. One further amendment was suggested, to remove the reference to political officers as out of date, but this was negatived when it was pointed out that cases could still arise where these were involved. All other points in the proposed amendments were then agreed without discussion.

Subsequent to this meeting, the Dominions Office, who had not been represented, pointed out that an amendment was required to meet the constitutional position of the Dominions. As a result of this further amendment, a proposed paragraph 6(2), which would have dealt with the availability of the Cross to those Dominions that requested it disappeared as a separate sub-paragraph, both this and the Dominions Office point being dealt with in an amended version of 6(1). The Admiralty also indicated that, despite the inconsistency with the decision of the Committee on the Grant of Honours, Decorations and Medals in Time of War, they wished to have the eligibility of the Merchant Navy preserved in the Warrant. Here, however, a delay arose, for at this point the Minister of War Transport raised the question of his joint responsibility with the Admiralty for military awards to the Merchant Navy. This, no doubt, explains why it was not until Nov 1942 that the Committee on the Grant of Honours reported to the King on the subject of amending the VC Warrant.

It was, perhaps, fortunate, that in this case the preparation of the new Warrant had not been left solely to the WO, for matters had been

WARRANTS FROM 1918 TO THE PRESENT DAY   185

raised with this Committee of which the WO had been unaware, and a new section had been added to the Warrant to meet these. The point at issue was that of direct submission of recommendations from Dominion governments to the Sovereign. This had originally been requested by South Africa, and had been conceded in the case of other decorations, whilst the Dominion of Canada had already made a direct submission in the case of a naval officer, though this had been turned down as not of the required standard anyway. The new Clause 8, which dealt with this point, must therefore be regarded as the handiwork of this Committee and not of the WO. It is of interest to note, however, that though this right was conceded to Dominions governments in 1942 it does not appear to have been exercised by either Australia or New Zealand. The Committee itself, of course, had no S of S to lay any amending Warrant before the King, so, although it was not fully the document of the WO, it was by the S of S for War, that it was presented to King George VI for signature on the last day of 1942.

At first glance it may appear that this succession of amendments to deal with the coming into existence of new forces which had to have their eligibility written into the Warrant represents no change from the policy of the 19th century. But in fact this was not the case; in the 19th century such warrants were almost entirely drawn up as the result of the need arising to confer the Cross on someone belonging to a force that had not been listed in the Warrant. The 20th century showed itself more prescient; the creation of a new force was of itself taken as the signal to prepare a new Warrant so that, should the need arise, the VC would already be available to its members; in fact, in most of the cases covered by these amending Warrants the circumstances never did arise and the powers granted by them have remained unexercised.

All of the 1931 Warrant and its amendments have now been swept away by a new Warrant, dating from 30 Sept 1961.[407] This was drawn up principally to account for changes in the constitutional position of the Commonwealth, and of the alterations in the financial provision for VC recipients which had taken place in 1959.[407a] It was again the result of an interdepartmental committee, attended, it is understood, by representatives of all interested departments, under the chairmanship of Sir Norman Brook, the Permanent Secretary at the Treasury, but the draft which was accepted may be taken as having been almost entirely the work of the WO.

407   See Appendix XVIII
407a   See pp195/8

Chapter 17

Financial and Legal Aspects

THE ORIGINAL provision for financial reward to the winner of the
Victoria Cross was £10, so long as he was not a commissioned officer.
The adequacy of this amount was first officially called into question in
connection with Piper Findlater's somewhat unconventional attempt to
gain a livelihood following his winning the VC at Dargai on 20 Oct
1897, and discharge from the service consequent on the wounds he then
received. The award was gazetted on 20 May 1898, and a parliamentary
question on 13 Jun showed what had then followed. Dr Farquharson,
the Member for Aberdeenshire West, asked 'Whether the Military
authorities recently stopped Piper Findlater's engagement at the
Alhambra Music Hall, and forbade the Officers and pipers of the
Aberdeen Depot to patronise his performance there; and whether there
is any precedent for this official interference with the free action of a
discharged soldier?' Mr Pirie, the Member for Aberdeen North, added a
further question which widened the scope of the matter into the
general one of the financial reward for VC winners. His question was
'Whether Piper Findlater VC has been offered a post as compensation
for forgoing a means of gaining his living, a means which was undesirable
from a military point of view; and if so, what is the nature of that post
and its emoluments; and whether, arising out of this case, and the
possibilities that might arise from similar cases in the future, the
Government could see their way to bestow a better pension than the
existing one of £10 per annum on soldiers who receive the highest mark
of distinction which can be bestowed by their Sovereign, more especially
in view of the fact that several VC men are known to have lately ended
their days either in a workhouse or in great destitution?' Evidently the
Findlater scandal had caused some quick action by the WO for, when
Mr Brodrick, then US of S for War, rose to reply, he had something
concrete to announce. He first dealt with the particular incident from
which the questions had arisen. 'The circumstances of this case are as
follows: Piper Findlater received the Victoria Cross from Her Majesty's

hands on 14 May 1898 [sic. The evidence appears to be conclusive that Findlater actually did receive his Cross six days before it was gazetted], and was advertised shortly afterwards to appear at a music-hall. The military authorities requested that this appearance should not take place, it being repugnant to military feeling that an exhibition should be made at a music-hall of a soldier who had been so recently decorated by the Queen. For the same reason they forbade the attendance of the officers and pipers of the Aberdeen Depot at his appearance at Aberdeen. There are no precedents for such an exhibition. Piper Findlater's financial position is as follows: He receives £10 a year with the Victoria Cross; he also has a pension of 2s. a day, or £36.10s. a year, for his wound and gallant service, and I understand he has had an offer from the highest quarter of a permanent post with a residence, though I am not aware of the precise conditions and emoluments. An ample provision for a man in his position has thus been secured him.' Brodrick then went on to make an announcement on the general issue, and the fact that he was in a position to do this within less than a month after the whole matter had started indicates how rapidly the point at issue had been dealt with. 'In reference, however, to soldiers earning the Victoria Cross, who, from old age, or infirmity not due to their own fault, may be in poor circumstances and unable to earn a living, it has been decided that at the Secretary of State's discretion the sum of £50 a year may be granted by way of pension in lieu of the £10 which has accompanied the Victoria Cross since its institution.'[408]

Though Mr Pirie's interest in the subject clearly arose from the particular case of Piper Findlater, he was evidently interested in the wider implications for, having got the announcement of a concession from the WO, he returned to the question a fortnight later to press the Admiralty in the same direction. On 27 Jun he asked the First Lord of the Admiralty, Mr Goschen, 'Whether he is prepared to grant to sailors if in destitute circumstances and unable to work, and who may have been awarded the Victoria Cross, the same consideration of their cases as has recently been accorded to soldiers; and if so, whether the pension of £50 a year, though not retrospective, will be awarded irrespectively of the date on which the VC was given?' To this Goschen replied 'The case of seamen of the Navy who have been awarded the Victoria Cross will be dealt with in the same spirit as in the recent announcement with regard to the Army, though the conditions are naturally different'.[409]

408   *Hansard,* 4th Series, lix, cols 34/6
409   *ibid,* lx, cols 220/1

When the papers were going through the WO before Brodrick made his announcement the point was established that the £50 should be at the S of S's discretion, and Treasury agreement that they would not require to be consulted was in fact given on 11 Jun 1898,[410] which suggests by how narrow a margin of time Brodrick had been able to make his announcement on the 13th. In fact, there is evidence in the VCR of this discretionary power being used quite flexibly, additional pensions being granted of various amounts and the amounts changing, being either increased or decreased from time to time as, presumably, the circumstances of the beneficiaries altered. The £50 was clearly regarded as a maximum figure and the S of S's discretion was taken as allowing him to fix any amount within that figure, and for any duration he pleased. However, it is clear that some embarrassment was caused at the WO when Mr Gifford, Principal Clerk at the Admiralty, wrote to ask on 15 Jan 1901 what were the WO views in respect to the principle which ought to govern the increase of the VC Annuity. The real question seemed to him to be what were 'poor circumstances', the phrase which had been used in the 1898 announcement. War Office department F7 pointed out in a minute on 11 Feb that these words did not appear in Article 1249 of the Royal Warrant which governed the pension. They were of opinion that it was the original intention to make up the *total income* of the VC annuitant to £50 a year, but as Article 1249 was worded the total pension from public funds could be increased to that amount at the discretion of the S of S. The Assistant Accountant General informed Gifford that the WO had never yet had to consider the point raised by him, but that if they had they would have endeavoured to deal with it as liberally as possible. There was evidently some apprehension about placing this view too formally on record, for the department concerned was informed 'This is a semi-official letter and it would be best to let it remain so. Please cancel registry and keep this in the Branch as a Departmental paper'.[411]

Despite the intentions of this new financial provision, it does not seem that all cases of financial want among ranker recipients of the Cross were met, for in Jan 1904 a winner from the Afghan Campaign of 1880 had to be informed that there were no funds from which the sum of £60 he had sought in an appeal to Lord Roberts for the recovery of his VC and medals, could be advanced,[412] and in at least one case of a

410   PRO, WO 32/7428
411   VCR, iii p402
412   *ibid*, p113

VC forfeiture, a few years after this, the recipient stated that his theft had been committed on account of the distressed situation of his wife and family.[413]

One confusion that arose in connection with the VC Annuity was the introduction of a special pension of sixpence a day for gallant conduct. This was primarily associated with the Distinguished Conduct Medal, though even here the Treasury appear to have ruled against its being awarded in every case.[414] However, if some Medallists received it the argument for all VC men [who must, axiomatically, have shown even greater gallantry] receiving it seemed irrefutable. The question as to whether any man could receive this in addition to the VC annuity produced some very involved discussions with the Treasury, who clearly objected to anyone getting two pensions on the same account. The case of Piper Findlater apparently brought this topic to a head when, on 29 Jun 1898 it was agreed that he should have this sixpence and, in immediate consequence, it was ruled that all VC men were to have it.[415]

A somewhat curious interdepartmental wrangle was to arise during the First World War over the question of responsibility for the payment of the VC annuity to colonial recipients. This was triggered off by a letter from Pte Keyzor, of the Australian Imperial Force, who wrote to the MS on 12 Jul 1916, to enquire when he could expect to receive the £10 annuity in respect of the VC he had been awarded on 15 Oct 1915, for his bravery in Gallipoli on the preceding 7 Aug. The WO reaction to this enquiry was to send a letter to the Australian High Commissioner to the effect that all charges arising out of the Australian Imperial Force were to be borne by the Commonwealth Government. The matter did not end here, however, for on 12 Aug Bonar Law, as Colonial Secretary, wrote that he did not understand the WO's action 'the liability being in his opinion clearly one for discharge by the Exchequer. Provision has been made for the grant of the annuity in the case of the VC and of the gratuity in the case of the DCM by the Royal Warrants which established these decorations and it is not possible now to dissociate the pecuniary awards from the decorations themselves..... Nothing should be done which would prejudice the Imperial character of these decorations'. To this the WO produced the somewhat sophist reply that 'only the honour has been granted, and the question is whether any pecuniary award is to follow, and if so, who is to pay it?' The

413   *ibid*, p479
414   PRO, WO 32/7434
415   VCR, ii p396

point was also made that the Imperial character of the award might be more truly preserved by the Dominion government giving the pecuniary award. It did, however, have an objection of greater weight in connection with the DCM and on 26 Aug the Colonial Office conceded that the WO was only acting under the Pay Warrants in this respect, and these did not apply to the Dominions. So, when the WO initially gave way to Bonar Law it was only to seek Treasury permission for payment of the VC annuity to Colonial troops. But this was not enough for him; on 25 Oct he took the matter of the DCM gratuity to Lloyd George himself and, a month later the WO was seeking Treasury approval to it making these payments also.[416]

The next occasion upon which the question of the amount of the pension was raised was in 1920, in a letter sent from the Admiralty to the Army Council, on 3 Jul, to inform them that the Lords Commissioners had under consideration the question of (1) an award to a dependant widow or mother of a member of the forces who might have been awarded the VC who died shortly after receiving the annuity, if such dependents were in indigent circumstances; (2) in view of the fall in purchasing power of money, revising the financial provisions to £20 for the normal annuity, £10 for a bar, and supplementation of up to £75 in necessitous cases; (3) bringing the dependant relatives of case (1) within the scope of the proposed £75 indigency provision. Col Graham, the DMS, in seeking the views of the Finance Branch, thought that, since the VC was on a pinnacle, any request for parallel treatment for other awards could be stifled, but feared any move would lay the way open to claims from all the officer recipients who received no financial benefit. Mr Ashley, giving the financial view, was in favour of keeping the monetary award at a token amount of £10; were this increased to £20 it would look like a real pension, and they would be faced with the question as to how men could be expected to live on it. He thought that giving pensions to widows or mothers would be a dangerous precedent; even were the VC on a pinnacle, raising its financial benefit would certainly produce other claims, and officer recipients would certainly raise the issue of their having been penalised by accepting their commissions. In general he went along with Graham in not wanting to make the Cross pecuniarly valuable. Much the same views were given by the MS, Sir Philip Chetwode, and the AG, and with these comments the papers came before the S of S, Winston Churchill. On 16 Jul he gave his opinion 'I think we should support Admiralty.

Nothing does more harm to the service [than to] have men with VC in dire poverty. Of course it should apply to officers too'. The WO's official line therefore became that they would support the Admiralty's line in general, as a matter of public policy, but it was to be understood that the VC stood alone in such matters, and that they did not favour the Admiralty's proposals in regard to widows and mothers. A letter to this effect was sent to the Admiralty on 23 Aug, in which the inclusion of officers within the new proposals was explicity mentioned.

On 18 Aug a pensions Warrant was issued under which pensioners whose awards had commenced before 4 Aug 1914, were resident in the British Isles and aged over sixty or infirm, were granted pension increases of 50 per cent if their total pension were less than £50; 40 per cent if between £50 and £100 for single men or £130 for married men; 30 per cent if up to £150 for single men or £200 for married men. Since the VC pension was mentioned in this Warrant, Graham raised the query as to whether this did not more than meet the Admiralty's case; he received no answer, but since the original proposals were still being proceeded with it is evident that the effect of this pension Warrant was not so regarded.

An enquiry from a new source arose on 2 Oct, when Lord Stamford-ham, the King's PS, forwarded to the WO a copy of a letter he had received from Sgt Hampton, a Boer War VC, seeking to draw the attention of the King to the fact that while all other pensions had increased, that for the VC had not. In forwarding the letter, Stamford-ham commented that there did indeed seem to be something in the contention. Sir Henry Creedy replied on 6th that the WO had supported an Admiralty proposal to this effect, but that nothing had yet come of it. In fact it was only on 19 Nov that the Admiralty wrote to state that they were glad to note the support the Army Council were prepared to give their proposals, and agreed not to press those parts that the WO did not support. It had been pointed out to the Admiralty that the great majority of cases involved were in fact Army ones, so they now agreed that the initiative in altering the Warrant would be more appropriately taken by the WO. The Admiralty also stated that they had forwarded copies of the correspondence to the Air Ministry to obtain their concurrence. On 27 Nov Mr Ashley suggested the line they should go forward on was the £20 basic annuity, £10 bar annuity, £75 in cases of indigency, but no annuity for officers, who would, however, be eligible for the indigency pension, which was agreed by Gen Godley, now MS, on 30th. This dropping of the annuity provisions for officers was apparently strengthened when the Air Ministry's letter of 3 Dec came to hand, since the only point at which they differed from the proposals communicated to them by the Admiralty was in wishing to see officers excluded from the financial provisions. It was on the basis suggested by Ashley that the WO sought Treasury sanction for amendment to the Warrant on 6 Dec 1920. In making this request it was stated that there were two hundred and seventy soldiers then in receipt of the £10 annuity, plus eight being paid from Indian funds, and eight in receipt of higher amounts of from £20 to £50, so that the estimated total cost of the proposal was not more than £3,000.[417] The Treasury's reply was, however, that 'the matter should be deferred for consideration in more favourable financial circumstances'. It was again considered in 1930 [presumably in connection with the redrafting of the Warrant at that time] but the S of S for War then decided that it could not be pursued.[418]

By the original terms of the Warrant, it was only the non-commissioned recipient who received any special pension in respect of the Cross. A question not clearly settled in the Warrant itself was what should be done in the case of a man who had won the VC in the ranks and was subsequently commissioned. However, there can be no doubt as to what official practice was in this respect, no matter how insecurely founded this might be; it was that, on being commissioned, the recipient of the VC lost his pension. When the revision of the Warrant was under discussion in 1880 the Admiralty suggested that an addition should be made to the rule dealing with the pension 'Such pension to be in addition to any other pension or pensions which they may be receiving or entitled to, from any source whatever'. In the discussion that took place on this suggestion at the WO, the departmental policy was fully displayed, for the first reaction was a minute in the following terms:

'If a man holding a VC pension were to get a commission would not the pension cease?

But when placed on half pay do you consider the insertion of the words would give rise to a claim to revert to such VC pension?'

The source of this WO minute is not quite clear, nor is that of its reply, but evidently both writers were in agreement, for the reply was 'The VC annuity ceases entirely from the date on which a grantee becomes a commissioned officer and the words proposed would undoubtedly give rise to claims which could not be allowed'.

From here the matter was sent forward to the PUS, with a further

417   PRO, WO 32/9394
418   PRO, WO 32/9408

note, 'I do not see the necessity for the addition as the pensioner would receive the pension in addition to any other in the same way that he can now receive pension for wounds or meritorious service'.

The matter finally went before the S of S, with the PUS's comment 'I agree. The words proposed seem to be unnecessary and might lead to complications in the event of the holder being commissioned'. In view of this unanimity of advice it was hardly surprising that the S of S's reply was 'Apd. Let the Admiralty know the reason'.[419] Evidently, the department was agreed at all levels at that time, that the VC annuity ceased on the commissioning of the holder.

This remained the situation for a further ten years until on 27 Oct 1890 the GOC Aldershot submitted an application recommending that Quartermaster and Honorary Lt W.T. Marshall, who had won his VC as a Quartermaster-Sergeant six years previously, might be allowed to retain the VC annuity he had held before his promotion to a commission. On 6 Nov Gen Harman, the MS, wrote to the Financial Secretary, in total contrast to the views of ten years previously 'This meritorious soldier having been commissioned subsequent to gaining the VC and consequent pension of £10 per annum, I cannot conceive that it was ever intended that such promotion should involve deprivation of this life pension. If this is not covered by the Warrant I think it might be. Will you please consider the question.' The intervening stages of the discussion do not seem to have survived in this instance, but it was finally decided by the S of S, Stanhope, that these pensions were to be retained by VC holders on promotion to commission, as from 1 Apr 1890. There were five beneficiaries of the change, the most senior of whom in rank was honorary Maj-Gen Luke O'Connor, who had earned his Cross as a Sergeant, but had been commissioned on the occasion of his exploit at the battle of the Alma. He had, in fact, already received his commission by the time his award was gazetted and had therefore never previously actually received the ranker pension, so the fact that he was a beneficiary under the new ruling shows that it was liberally interpreted. The others, like Marshall, who was of course included, were all Quartermasters. They were John Berryman, who had won his Cross as a Troop Sergeant-Major at Balaclava, and was now an honorary Major; A. Boulger, a Lance/Corporal from the Indian Mutiny, and now honorary Lieutenant-Colonel and H. McDonald, a Crimean Colour-Sergeant, who was now an honorary Captain.[420] Consideration

419 PRO, WO 32/7394 for the whole of this episode.
420 VCR, ii p349

was given to an amendment to the Warrant to cover the new policy but this was finally decided not to be necessary.[421] The precedent laid down in the case of O'Connor was followed, in the case of William Robertson, who was awarded the VC for his conduct at the Battle of Elandslaagte, on 21 Oct 1899, when he was a Sergeant-Major, but only had his award gazetted on 20 Jul following, having been promoted to the rank of Quartermaster and Honorary Lieutenant on the intervening 12 May. The query was raised in the WO as to whether Stanhope's ruling did cover such a case [that of O'Connor does not seem to have been noticed] though it was suggested that as the pension started from the date of the act of bravery, even though it could not, of course, be paid prior to the award of the Cross being gazetted, Robertson was in receipt of the pension prior to his being commissioned. This view was accepted both by the MS, Gen Grove, and the Accountant-General, in their comments of 28 and 29 Aug that year.[422]

The only point which remained open to discussion in this connection was the extension of the annuity to all ranks. Col Maude, VC, commented in his *Memories of the Mutiny* in 1894 'There seems no good reason why officers should not receive the same monetary allowance which non-commissioned officers and soldiers in the ranks are paid when they get the Cross. The Germans do, and it is ridiculous, nowadays, to pretend that "money is no object" to a British officer; especially when we have the brilliant example of our only General (but one) receiving £30,000 for a six-weeks' campaign! No retired officer ever dreams of wearing the bit of bronze; and, if he live abroad, it is necessary for him to post a half-yearly certificate of existence, in order to retain his name on the list. One is tempted to ask: *"Cui bono?".*'[423] The general point regarding the need of money by retired officers was evidently no academic one, for in June 1897 it was placed on record arising out of the case of Dr Douglas, who had won his Cross in the Andamans thirty years previously, that a sold VC could not be replaced, and that the C in C much regretted that an officer should sell such an honourable distinction.[424] Nor, evidently, was Col Maude disinterested himself in the financial question, for the same papers on Douglas also refer to Maude's own application for the loan of a Cross to replace the one he himself had sold, and he had to be told, on 30 Sep 1898 that the

421   PRO, WO 32/7415
422   PRO, WO 32/7900
423   *Memories of the Mutiny,* ii p332
424   VCR, ii p386

new £50 provision, which had been announced in connection with Piper Findlater, and for which he had applied, did not apply in his case.[425] Curiously enough, it was in respect of this special annuity that the principle of extension to officers was first conceded. On the Admiralty raising the question of improving the annuities in 1920, the WO reply indicated that the Army Council would favour the new proposals applying to officers also[426] and what emerged, in the new regulations, was an annuity of an amount that should not exceed, in total with other non-contributory public pension, the sum of £75 a year, for holders of the VC who were unable through age or infirmity to earn a livelihood, and for this both officers and other ranks were eligible, though to the basic £10 pension plus sixpence a day gallantry money only men below commissioned rank remained entitled.[427] The terms of the Royal Warrant of 18 Aug 1920, already referred to, allowed additions to those who were over sixty, or invalided from the army, or were permanently incapacitated, and in 1958 it was estimated that the great majority of annuitants were receiving such increases which, on average, nearly doubled the basic £10 a year.[428]

The logical further step of bringing all ranks within the scope of that part of the pension paid without any test of ability to earn a livelihood arose out of a general campaign for an increase in the VC pension, the first step in which may be identified in the Parliamentary question tabled by Mr McKibbin to the Chancellor of the Exchequer, as to what sum would be required to provide the equivalent of the £10 instituted in 1856 at the present day. This question received a written answer from the Prime Minister, Sir Anthony Eden, on 21 May 1957, and contained a quite inexplicable reference to the £10 annuity, which had, of course, figured in the 1856 Warrant as having been authorised in 1878.[429] The next move was a parliamentary question put down by Mr Simmons, himself a disabled veteran of the 1914-18 War, which sought both the extension of the pension to officers as well as rankers, and, 'as the present gratuity of £10 per annum inadequately expresses the nation's gratitude to those whose courage won them the Victoria Cross', that the amount should be substantially increased. The PM's reply, on 14 Nov 1957, was, frankly, unsympathetic. After referring to

425   *ibid*, p394
426   VCR, iii p342
427   Information given in *Hansard*, 5th Series, 508, Written Answers, col 52
428   *ibid*, 595, Written Answers, cols 49/50
429   *ibid*, 570, Written Answers, cols 6/7

the answer previously given to McKibbin, and pointing out the various ways outside the VC pension in which needy ex-soldiers could be assisted, he concluded 'It is not proposed to make any change at the present time', an attitude he maintained despite the reference by Mr Simmons to the case of an ex-officer who had won the VC and been wounded at Gallipoli, and who now, at the age of 81, had to appeal for the loan of £100 in order to enable himself and his 77-year-old wife to live.[430]

A twelvemonth later a written reply to a question put down by Sir John Smyth, himself a VC of the First World War, and at that time chairman of the then Victoria Cross Association, elicited the information that at that time ten ex-soldiers were in receipt of the full £75 annuity, and 125 of lesser amounts.[431] However, the next occasion upon which the matter came up on the floor of the House of Commons was on 24 Jan 1959, when Mr Shinwell made something of a scene over the case of a holder of the VC who was an old-age-pensioner, whose total income from all sources was £5.4s. a week, and was precluded, under the terms of the Royal Warrant from benefitting from the £75 annuity, which he described as disgraceful. Mr Soames, replying to the question as S of S for War, rehearsed the usual arguments regarding the limitation imposed by the Warrant on the *total* amount payable by way of non-contributory pension from public funds, to the evident dissatisfaction of Mr Shinwell, but when Mr Turton suggested that, since Parliament had been increasingly generous in the matter of disability pensions since 1950, when the terms of the Pension Warrant in question had been drawn up, it might well be time to look at the whole question again, he agreed and made the statement, which appears to be utterly unsubstantiated by the record, 'The Prime Minister referred to this very point in answer to a Question on 14 Nov 1957'.[432] This seems, however, to be the first clear indication of official sympathy with the demand that was being mounted.

A week later Mr Simmons returned to the subject, with a question addressed to the Prime Minister, who was now Mr Macmillan, 'If he will now reconsider the position of holders of the Victoria Cross who find themselves in needy circumstances by entirely disregarding war disability pensions in the determination of means'. As he pointed out in a supplementary question, such pensions were disregarded for Public

430   *ibid,* 577, cols 1142/3
431   *ibid,* 596, Written Answers, col 36
432   *ibid,* 607, cols 1196/7

Assistance, and it was highly invidious that holders of the VC should be placed in a worse position than recipients of National Assistance. Mr Macmillan's reply, given on 30 Jun, was distinctly encouraging: 'This is a matter which, as the House knows, has often been raised in the past; but I am quite prepared to look at it again..... The details are rather complicated, but I will do my best to look into the matter and to see if a solution can be found'.[433]

A fortnight later, in answer to a further question from Mr Shinwell, as to the progress being made in the matter, Mr Macmillan stated that he was discussing the matter with the departments involved, made it clear that he was looking into the matter personally, and added that Sir John Smyth was a party to the discussions.[434] The awaited announcement came on 28 Jul. 'We propose,' the Prime Minister stated, 'to replace these arrangements by new ones, under which all holders of the Victoria Cross for whom the United Kingdom Government are responsible, both officers and other ranks, will be paid on annuity of £100 irrespective of need or any other conditions. This, like the existing payments, will not be taxable..... One of the difficulties is that we can do all this by Royal Warrant but the question of assistance from the National Assistance Board has been raised. We cannot alter that except by Act of Parliament, but the Chairman of the Board has assured me that he has given instructions that any case of a holder of the Victoria Cross applying for National Assistance shall be referred to headquarters, and, as the House knows, the Board has certain discretionary powers which can be exercised in individual cases and I shall therefore be greatly surprised if any difficulty of this kind arises'.[435]

This announcement was the main matter which required to be written into the terms of the Warrant. This was dealt with by drawing up an entirely new document, repealing all the old terms and re-enacting such of these as were still relevant, together with the new terms in a new Warrant, this being signed on 30 Sep 1961.[436] Under this the new pension became operative from 1 Aug 1959, which was obviously tied to the date of the House of Commons announcement. The only feature that is a little curious was the disappearance of the provision of an additional pension for the possession of a bar. Since all recipients of bars had, in fact, been officers such additional pension had never been

433   *ibid*, 608, cols 246/7
434   *ibid*, 609, col 211
435   *ibid*, 610, cols 314/6
436   See Appendix XVIII

paid; perhaps it was felt that to present such recipients with a double pension where they had previously received nothing would have seemed over generous.

There is evidence that, prior to the signature of the 1961 Warrant it had been the practice in the case of posthumous awards for £50 to be credited to the estate of the recipient[437] but no information has been forthcoming of the authority for this, the date from which it operated, or whether any alteration took place following the revised financial provisions of the new Warrant.

As has already appeared, the sale of his Cross by a recipient was, not surprisingly, looked on with disfavour by the authorities. For a serving soldier to do this was clearly an offence under the Army Acts, but such legislation could not, obviously be invoked against a recipient while he was not actually serving[438] and, equally, it was ruled in 1899 that unless the recipient was under the Army Acts at the relevant time, no action could be taken against anyone who tried to induce a soldier to sell his VC.[439] Quite clearly the WO had little control over the physical possession of VCs when the recipient was no longer serving or had died. Thus it was noted in October 1899, 'This Department has no power to prevent the sale of the VC (and Crimea Medal) belonging to the late Sgt Cambridge RA'.[440] Similarly, when the son of James Thompson wrote to the WO to report the death of his father on 5 Dec 1891, there can be no doubt what reply was given to him, even though this does not seem to be on record, regarding his enquiry as to whether he could claim the VC and medals which his father had sold, and to whether he would have to pay for them.[441] The sale of VCs was, however, always a matter of interest to the WO, sometimes, indeed, with curious results. For example, when the proposed sale of what was alleged to be the Cross won by Pte Flawn in the Basuto War of 1880 was announced in August 1904, Flawn was able to prove that he had never parted with his Cross and, on examination, Hancocks did not think that the specimen being offered for sale had been engraved or manufactured by them.[442] It was at much the same time that a Cross claiming to be that awarded to Pte Timothy O'Hea appeared on the market, being offered for sale at Debenham's in August 1900. Six

437   *List of the Recipients of the VC,* The WO, (M.S.3) Jan 1953, p25
438   See Chapter 7
439   VCR, ii p405
440   *ibid*
441   *ibid,* p357
442   *ibid,* p216

years later another Cross was produced by Mr E. Du Farr, President of the New South Wales Art Gallery, which he stated had been handed to him by his brother-in-law, to whom O'Hea had handed it before he left for an expedition into the Australian bush from which he never returned. This second Cross was examined by Hancocks in 1907, and stated as in their belief genuine but, without having both Crosses before them this could hardly be regarded as final judgement. The actual comparison did not take place until April 1953, at which time the Australian Cross had returned to this country to be presented to the Rifle Brigade in 1951; the Debenham's Cross, which was believed to have come from a Mr Phillips in London, had been bought by Spink's on behalf of a client believed to be the American collector, Mr Sanford Saltus, who had left his collection to the American Numismatic Society, in whose ownership it now was. As a result of this comparison the Rifle Brigade's specimen was finally declared genuine, one point in its favour being that it bore the correct date of 9th June, 1866, whereas the date on the other specimen was the 19th.[443] This error may give a clue as to when the spurious Cross was manufactured. The date of O'Hea's exploit is not uncommonly given as the 19th, but the *London Gazette* gives this quite unambiguously as the 9th; however, the earliest source in which the mistake occurs would appear to be the first edition of D.H. Parry's book on the VC, which appeared in 1895, under the title *Britain's Roll of Glory* [the title changed in later editions to *The VC, Its Heroes and their Valour*].

It was hardly surprising that after the events of 1900 and 1904 in connection with fraudulent VCs, that the WO should have written to Hancocks on 14 Sep 1906: 'In view of the recent sales of Victoria Crosses it seems very desirable that there should be some private mark on such decorations so that genuine Crosses may be distinguished from spurious imitations, and I am therefore to enquire whether it would be possible for you in making the Crosses to place on them such a private and inconspicuous mark as would not be likely to be imitated.

I shall be glad to be favoured with your observations or other suggestions at your early convenience'.[444]

It appears that Hancocks proceeded in this matter with extreme circumspection, for the only reply to this letter on record is a note by the AMS, Crawford [who had signed the letter to them] dated 23 Mar 1907, 'Messrs. Hancocks telephoned today that they now mark all VCs issued by them which will enable them to identify a genuine or spurious

443   *ibid,* insert at p73
444   VCR, iii p158

one at once. This was done in the case of the six posthumous VCs lately issued'.[445] From this it would appear that the nature of the marks being used were kept so private to Hancocks that even the WO were not informed of their precise nature.

One case in which action was taken in connection with the possession of a VC after the decease of the recipient related to Lt R.H.M. Aitken. His recommendation was one of a number of late submissions from the CinC India in respect of the Indian Mutiny, which reached the WO on 1 Apr 1863, was submitted to Queen Victoria for approval on 13th of that month and was gazetted on 17th. According to the file the Cross was presented to him in May 1865, at Lucknow, on the spot where the acts for which it was bestowed had been performed.[446]

However, this did not tell the full story of the presentation, for the circumstances of what actually happened at Lucknow appear to be those described by Gen Adye, though he does not actually name Aitken in his account:

'On arrival at Meerut I found that Sir Hugh Rose had seriously injured himself, having broken several ribs by a fall out hunting, so that for the time our movements were at a standstill. However, early in 1865, as soon as he had recovered, the headquarters staff continued their tour, and arrived at Lucknow, where a somewhat amusing incident occurred. During the Mutiny, an officer had gained the Victoria Cross for gallant conduct in the residency, but owing to some delay had not actually received the decoration; and the Commander-in-Chief was therefore glad of the opportunity of presenting it to him on the very spot where he gained it. A general parade was ordered, the troops to be formed up round the ruins of the Residency; and all the civilians and ladies of Lucknow were invited to be present. On the morning, when the hour of parade was at hand, the staff assembled in readiness in a bungalow, and it was understood that the Commander-in-Chief was preparing an appropriate speech for the occasion. Search was made for the box containing the Victoria Cross, but it was nowhere to be found, and after anxious hurried inquiry we discovered that by some mistake it had been left behind at Simla in the Himalayas. This was awkward, especially as Sir Hugh would naturally be annoyed at so unfortunate an error. The suggestion was made that some officer of the garrison should be asked to lend his for the occasion; but that also failed, no officer nearer than Cawnpore (fifty miles off) having gained one. There was no

445   PRO, WO 32/7505, see also reference in Chapter 8
446   PRO, WO 32/7363

time to be lost, and at length Colonel Donald Stewart [later Field-Marshal Sir Donald Stewart], the Deputy Adjutant General, volunteered to inform the Commander-in-Chief; an offer which was at once accepted. Stewart on entering the room found Sir Hugh engaged in considering his speech, and then cautiously and gently announced that a slight mistake had occurred, and that the Victoria Cross had been left behind. The Commander-in-Chief, as anticipated, was angry, and complained that he had been treated with neglect. However, after he had cooled down, Donald Stewart said that in his opinion the difficulty could readily be got over; and, taking the cross of the Companionship of the Bath from his breast, suggested that it should be presented to the officer on parade, in lieu temporarily of the other; pointing out that the troops and the assembled company would not be near enough to distinguish the difference. Sir Hugh at once took in the situation, accepted the compromise, and acted accordingly. The decoration was presented, the Commander-in-Chief made an appropriate speech, and the demonstration altogether was a success. My remark to the officer afterwards was that as the Queen had given him the Victoria Cross, and the Commander-in-Chief the Bath, I thought he was entitled to wear both for the future. There was a ball in the evening in honour of the occasion, and in default of a real cross he had to wear a painted leather imitation one.'[447]

However, it appears that it was not merely a question of the Cross having been left behind at Simla, for on 20 Nov 1865 Lord Hartington, the S of S for War, wrote to the CinC, East Indies, stating that a duplicate VC would be supplied at Maj Aitken's expense, to replace one lost,[448] which letter was followed by a further one on 5 Apr 1866, saying that since the VC in question had been lost before he received it, Aitken would be relieved of the cost of its replacement.[449] Obviously the Cross originally sent out for him had disappeared completely.

Aitken died as a Colonel in 1887, and the next development in the story was not to take place until 1900, when his widow wrote to the WO. Her late husband's VC was in her possession, but one claiming to be it was being offered for sale at an auction; she therefore demanded that the WO should take action to recover the duplicate. The papers in the WO file recapitulate the story that has already been related; that Aitken's original Cross had been sent out to India, and that it had there

---

447   Gen Sir John Adye, *Recollections of a Military Life,* pp 226/8. I am indebted to Canon Lummis for this reference.
448   VCR, ii pp48/50
449   *ibid,* p61

been lost or mislaid, varying the account of the Lucknow presentation, however, in saying that Aitken had actually been decorated with a paper substitute, and that a replacement Cross had been sent out subsequently, which had never been out of the family. The Cross now being brought forward was being sold at the order of Mrs Judge, widow of Maj Judge, 2nd (PWO) Gurkhas, who claimed that this, clearly the original Cross that Aitken had never received, was her own property, having been purchased by her husband in Simla in 1894. She was, however, directed by the WO, at the instance of Mrs Aitken, to surrender it, which she did, though indicating, in her letter to the WO of 3 Jul 1900, with how much regret she did this, as she still considered it hers by right.[450]

This was not quite the end of the story, however, for Mrs Judge then attempted to obtain from the WO reimbursement of the £35.10.0. her husband had originally paid for the Cross. This was refused, on the grounds that, as the Cross had never reached its recipient, it remained the property of the Crown, and that it had been disposed of to her husband by someone who had no right to it.[451] The source from which Maj Judge bought this VC does not appear in the papers. The WO did consult the Treasury Solicitor as to whether any action could be taken over the original sale, but he advised that this was impossible, basing this opinion on the legal doctrine of 'marché ouvert'.[452]

The concern of the WO over men disposing of their Crosses has already been indicated. An attempt to assert control over this was made in 1903, following an enquiry from a Birmingham dealer as to whether he would be in order in purchasing one. On 21 Apr the AMS referred to the AG for consideration that a discharged man could legally sell his Cross and that the buyer was not liable to any penalty under the Army Act, although in his opinion such sales should be prevented if possible. The reply given by the AAG on 23rd was, 'We cannot prevent it without interfering with the liberty of the subject'. At this point Lord Roberts as CinC suggested that a man who disposed of his Cross should lose his pension. This suggestion was referred to the Deputy Judge Advocate General who pointed out that this would require a new VC Warrant, and feared that such a restriction would simply raise the price of VCs and make the temptation to sell all the greater. On 26 May, Brodrick approved the preparation of a new Warrant and such

450   PRO, WO 32/7442
451   PRO, WO 32/7441
452   PRO, WO 32/7439

a document was in fact drafted. Brade, the PUS clearly did not like the new move and pointed out that it was against principle to make laws of general application on individual cases [though the history of the VC Warrants was full of cases where this had been done], and also to make ones of which enforcement was doubtful; even if a case did come to notice of a VC having left the recipient's possession, the man could simply claim he had lost it or allege it had been stolen. To this Lord Roberts conceded a good deal of force, but thought [on 20 June] that the point could simply be met by the man not getting his £10 unless he produced his Cross. Brodrick indicated [on 24th] that he hardly agreed with his PUS, since the £10 pension was only during pleasure, and what had been given could be withdrawn. Roberts, in a further note, admitted the difficulties of implementation, and seemed to be weakening in his support. It was, however pointed out to Brodrick that the Warrant did not support his view of the enjoyment of the pension during pleasure, and that he could only achieve the end in view if the new Warrant was made retrospective. It seems that at this point Brodrick realised that the objective would not be achieved and his final note in the papers, dated 15 Jul 1903, was 'Leave alone'.[453] No subsequent attempt seems ever to have been made to prevent in this way holders of the Victoria Cross from disposing of their decorations.

453   PRO, WO 32/7487

Chapter 18

The Mechanics of Award and Issue

THE OFFICIAL PATH taken by a recommendation for the conferment of a Victoria Cross in its early days can be described quite simply. The recommendation would start with the man's immediate commander, or the man would submit his claim for the decoration to him, and would thence progress up the chain of military hierarchy until it reached the local Commander-in-Chief. He would then submit the case to a board of officers, and in the event of a favourable report by them, would forward the recommendation with the endorsement it had received at each level to the Horse Guards. This would then be forwarded to the War Office, with the view of the Duke of Cambridge as CinC of the British Army, giving his opinion from the military point of view. The key person in the WO was Mr Pennington, who would now give his opinion on the compatibility of the recommendation with the terms of the Warrant [of which the civil, and not the military, administration was the interpreter] to the Permanent Under Secretary, who would lay the papers before the political head, the Secretary of State for War. It was the latter's decision as to whether or not the case should be laid before the Queen for her approval, though there seems to be no case where a S of S has not followed the advice of his PUS. Once this decision had been given a formal submission was prepared in the WO to be laid before the Queen, who approved it with her signature. On their return from the Queen the papers went again to Pennington whose next duty was to prepare statements for insertion in the *London Gazette* and record in the Victoria Cross Registry; here a slight saving of labour was effected, as the Registry record will be frequently found to consist of a copy of the *Gazette* proof pasted in the Register. At the same time he would also, in the case of a ranker, notify what he simply addressed as 'C', that a payment of £10 per annum to the man in question was to commence from the date upon which the exploit had been performed. On the return of the papers from the Registry he would then draw the required Cross from the stock of unnamed VCs, which were held in the office under his keeping,[454] send this with the necessary instructions to Hancocks for engraving and, on its return, arrange for its transmission either to the Queen or to the local General Officer Commanding for presentation.

This was the broad outline. However, in practice matters did not always follow the routine so smoothly, even though it was always the effort of the WO [or perhaps one can say Mr Pennington] that it should be adhered to. One of the complications was that the first time the system was really operated [for the selection of recipients after the Crimean War was clearly a different matter from conferring awards while a campaign was actually in progress] was during the Indian Mutiny. Here there was a very particular complication, in the existence of two distinct authorities in the country – that of the British Army, and of the East India Company. On 22 Aug 1857 the Governor-General of India forwarded to his Court of Directors Gen Havelock's telegram of 18th of that month and extracts of his dispatches, recommending the award of the VC to Lt Crowe, his own son Lt Havelock, Pte Hancock and Pte Purcell. These documents the India Board forwarded to Lord Panmure on 28 Nov 1857, to whom they were submitted for consideration and decision by Sir Henry Storks, the PUS, on 7 Dec 1857. Panmure's reply on the 9th was 'I presume that this is the first intimation we have had from the India Board of these recommendations. They should be sent to CinC in order that he may give an opinion. The recommendation should have been made through the CinC in India and must be so done in future – but I think we may overlook the irregularity. It seems to me that Havelock's recommendation serves my purpose. I am not quite so sure of those by Sir H. Barnard but would like to have the CinC's opinion'. A letter was duly sent to the President of the Board of Control pointing out the irregularity of this submission, but all the four men in question were duly gazetted for the VC on 15 Jan 1858.[455]

The letter to the Board of Control does not seem to have achieved its purpose in making the Board adhere to the WO's conception of the appropriate channels, for on 16 Aug 1858, Pennington, the stickler for routine, observed to Storks, 'I cannot help thinking that there is some inconvenience in the practice which the India Board has lately adopted of forwarding claims for the Victoria Cross received from India to the Horse Guards in the first instance, instead of to the Secretary of State.

454   PRO, WO 32/7377
455   PRO, WO 32/7309

I do not see why the practice first adopted should not be continued of sending these claims direct to the Secretary of State, who usually calls for the opinion of the General Commanding-in-Chief, and is guided by that opinion..... The result of the present practice seems to be that the Horse Guards avoid giving a decisive opinion in any case and throw the responsibility of the decision on the Secretary of State'.[456] However, no notice seems to have been taken of this particular objection.

To make the subject of recommendations from India at this time still more confusing the two authorities, namely the CinC of the British troops in India and the Governor-General in Council, were not operating in exclusively distinct spheres of responsibility. Thus, of a list of thirty-one names submitted from the Governor-General in Council in May 1858, Pennington had to report that twenty-four had already been the subject of action by the CinC India, who had already provisionally conferred the Cross upon them, as he was entitled to do under the Seventh Clause of the Warrant and, indeed, nine of these provisional awards were already in the process of being confirmed.[457] The fact that so many of the Mutiny awards were provisionally conferred by the commander on the spot was a further element of confusion; clearly, on occasions, Pennington found it difficult to decide whether the papers coming into the WO represented provisional awards for confirmation by the Queen, or recommended grants for her approval. There was at least one list of nine names forwarded by the Horse Guards to the WO on 30 Nov 1858, as for confirmation, which bears Pennington's marginal note, 'for approval, not for confirmation. The Cross does not appear to have been conferred on the spot, as in the letter of yesterday'.[458] However, on 11 Dec the Horse Guards forwarded a further list of names, eight of which were described as for confirmation, and four for approval, so that is apparent that usually the two differing circumstances were observably distinct.[459] The letter to which Pennington referred on receipt of the Horse Guards letter of 30 Nov had, in fact, contained twenty-four names for confirmation, but the only matter Pennington had found for comment among these was that one of those so distinguished had died before his name was submitted for confirmation.[460] It is, perhaps, worthy of comment that, although some of these awards when published in the *London*

456   PRO, WO 32/7316
457   PRO, WO 32/7317
458   PRO, WO 32/7319
459   PRO, WO 32/7320
460   PRO, WO 32/7318

Gazette were stated to be in confirmation of provisional awards made by the General Officer Commanding in the Field, in by no means all such cases was this indicated.

Freely as the power conferred on General Officers commanding in the Field by the Seventh Clause of the Warrant had been exercised during the Indian Mutiny it did not survive this campaign. The change of approach is illustrated by the remarks of Gen Sir Hope Grant, in 1861, in reference to his recommendations for the men who had served under him in the Second China War the year before, 'To two of these, Ensign Chaplin and Pte Lane I made a promise at the time that I would recommend them for this distinction [the Victoria Cross], and in doing so I did not avail myself of the power conferred by that clause of the Royal Warrant which allows the Commander of the Forces to confer the Victoria Cross on the spot for actions performed under his observation, and which power has been exercised by various General Officers, but I cannot but feel that my promise so given was almost tantamount to a provisional bestowal of that distinction'.[461] It might possibly be thought that the discontinuance of such provisional conferments of the VC [which the Warrant confined to acts performed under the eye of the Commander] was due to the growing distance which was developing between the general at headquarters and the troops in the front line, but this was clearly not the case for had conferment on the spot still been in vogue a case for its exercise would have been that of L/Cpl G. Sellar in Afghanistan in 1879. Gen Roberts, at that time Officer Commanding in East Afghanistan, was able to write to the MS at the WO, 'From my own position in Sherpur, I observed through my telescope, the markedly forward conduct of an individual soldier, who from the first was conspicuous in leading the way. The following day I desired Lt-Col Brownlow commanding the Regiment to identify the man if possible. He did so at once, and found out that it was L/Cpl Sellar who I visited shortly afterwards in hospital where he was lying badly wounded, and whom I assured there and then that I would bring his gallant conduct to the notice of the Field-Marshal Commanding in Chief'. As Col Brownlow observed to the MS 'a more distinctly substantiated act of gallantry has not been reported from Afghanistan'.[462]

Even without the involvement of such autonomous bodies as the Indian Board of Control, irregularities in the submission of claims and

461   PRO, WO 32/7356
462   PRO, WO 32/7401

recommendations for the VC through the appropriate chain of command still took place though, usually, such moves were heavily frowned upon by the WO and Horse Guards. In Dec 1858, a letter was received at the Horse Guards from Surgeon Thomas Carey of the 64th Regt, regarding a petition which had been forwarded from the private soldiers of that Regiment, recommending the writer of the letter for the VC for his services in the field and in saving the life of one of them. He was, however, informed that his letter failed to establish his claim, 'The recommendation of any individual for the VC by the soldiers of a regiment without the sanction of the Commanding Officer is in itself a great irregularity, and one which it was your duty to have repressed instead of founding a claim upon it in direct opposition to your commanding officer's opinions'.[463] Usually, however, the irregularity was not of such a 'grass-roots' nature as this. On 1 Jan 1858 Sir Colin Campbell forwarded a General Order published by Maj-Gen Wilson, commanding the Delhi Field Force, in which provisional awards of the VC were made to Bugler Hawthorne and Sgt J. Smith, to the WO. The WO's response to this, whilst confirming the awards, was to inform Sir Colin on 17 Mar that these awards were irregular in not having been submitted through him, so that Gen Wilson might have had the benefit of his advice before submitting them and that it was convenient to the interests of the Public Service that recommendations should always be received through him, so that delay might be obviated through the need arising to refer such back to him for observation. Curiously enough, Pennington had originally raised objection to the submissions on a different score; in his view the General Order was in accordance with the terms of the Warrant, but that the irregularity lay in an officer subordinate to the chief officer in command addressing himself direct to the S of S.[464]

The elected recipients of the VC in respect of the action of the 8th Hussars at Gwalior were provisionally awarded the Cross by Sir Hugh Rose, and notification submitted by him for confirmation direct to the WO in January 1859. In this case Gen Peel, at that time S of S, consented to waive the rule that transmission should be through the CinC India for, obviously, there was little useful comment he could make in the case of conferment by election. However, the papers contain a note by Pennington suggesting that, despite this case being conceded as an exception, Lord Clyde should be informed that the

463   PRO, WO 98/2
464   PRO, WO 32/7311

Government considered adherence to the rule desirable during the operations in India.[465] In the following October the CO of the 32nd Regt, which had now returned to England from India, submitted a roll of one officer and eleven NCOs and men for the award of the VC, of whom three eventually received it. On 3 Nov Pennington pointed out to Sir Edward Lugard that none of these recommendations had gone through the CinC in India, and he saw no reason to make any exception in this case, particularly since it would constitute an inconvenient precedent if commanding officers were allowed to bypass the CinC. Lugard, in bringing this matter to the attention of the S of S, Sidney Herbert, indicated that he agreed in general with the point raised by Pennington, but thought that since the regiment was now home, and all the parties concerned and evidence was in this country, there was not much advantage in referring the matter back to Lord Clyde, who would have no more information available, and had not even held the command at the relevant time. On these grounds Herbert allowed the recommend-ations to go direct to the Queen, but a letter went to the Horse Guards nontheless to say that in any other circumstances reference to Lord Clyde would not be dispensed with.[466] Such bypassing was not only a feature of the Mutiny, for as late as 1901 there is reference to the impropriety of a recommendation which had [in somewhat unexpected language for a Government department at that date] 'practically given the GOC, S Africa the go-by'.[467]

The question as to what were the correct official channels was sometimes a little difficult. The WO was clearly somewhat puzzled as to how Gen Outram came to be recommending Commander Rennie of the Indian Navy for his services in the Persian War of 1856, and equally to whom this recommendation should be referred. Pennington came to the conclusion that Outram had acted as the commander of the expedition, and therefore sought to refer the matter to the CinC, as Outram's superior. Sir Henry Storks, Pennington's chief, thought this rather an anomaly, and the matter was finally referred to the Admiralty, who, however, found Rennie's service to have been no more than an act of duty.[468]

The case of Pte Hodge of the West India Regiment, was at first considered irregular, since it was submitted by Col D'Arcy, the Admin-

---

465   PRO, WO 32/7321
466   PRO, WO 32/7336
467   VCR, iii p23
468   PRO, WO 32/7310

istrator of the Gambia, direct to the Horse Guards without going through the Colonel of the Regiment in Gambia. General Peel, before whom the papers came as S of S, agreed to submit the recommendation on this basis, however, since D'Arcy was in command of the force engaged [two companies of the West India Regiment and a hundred Gambia Volunteers], as the officers of the support group could not see what occurred for smoke, the other officers of the storming party were killed and D'Arcy was the only one left to testify to Hodge's conduct.[469]

Something of an irregularity was also permitted in the case of the Rorke's Drift VCs. The original recommendations for the awards of the VC were submitted by Lt Bromhead, and contained the names of the six men from his company of the 24th Foot, Cpl Allen, Ptes Hook, Hitch, Williams and the two Ptes Jones. These recommendations were forwarded by Bromhead's commanding officer on 15 Feb 1879, without addition and it was when this document came before Lord Chelmsford to forward to the Horse Guards that he personally added to it the names of Lts Chard and Bromhead without, it appears, any recommendation from the immediate superiors of the two.[470]

A more recent case of an irregular submission concerned the recommendation of Sgt J.D. Hinton for his bravery at Kalami, Greece, in April 1941. Here the recommendation was contained in a letter sent to the WO through the International Red Cross, submitted by Maj G.H. Thomson, the Senior Medical Officer in the British Prisoner of War Hospital at Kalami, where Hinton was at that time a captive, and followed a deputation of ten captive officers to Thomson, urging him to make the submission. The irregularity of this submission was noted by the WO at the time, but condoned as it was recognised that no other channel was open to the Major in the circumstances.[471]

One feature of the office procedure maintained for many years was that the only channel of access by which recommendations for the VC could come before the Sovereign was through the S of S for War. Presumably this exclusive prerogative was derived from the Eleventh Clause of the 1856 Warrant, even though the Twelfth Clause appears to put the Lords Commissioners of the Admiralty on an equal footing in certain cases. However, whatever might be read into the Warrant, the practice was quite definite. On the occasion of the submission of the first list of names for the VC, the Admiralty sent to the WO on 13 Feb

469   PRO, WO 32/7371
470   PRO, WO 32/7390
471   PRO, WO 32/9957

1857 a list of those they wished to recommend, and a letter was sent to them by the WO on 23 Feb to say that their list had been approved.[472] A similar approach by the Admiralty can be found among the WO papers for each recommendation of a naval VC up to and including that to Capt A.K. Wilson in 1884; there is, however, no trace of any such approach in subsequent cases, the next one being that to Surgeon W.J. Maillard in 1898, so one may conclude that the right of direct access to the Sovereign by the First Lord of the Admiralty had been conceded on some occasion between these two dates. This concession to the Admiralty was exceptional. Such cases as merited the award of the VC in the course of the Mashona rebellion of 1896 were, on being brought to the notice of the Colonial Office [whose concern the rising was], referred by them to the WO, who also, on this occasion, had to deal with recommendations from the Board of Directors of the Rhodesia Company.[473] Equally, when the person being recommended was a member of the Indian Army, for whom the appropriate channel was obviously the India Office, such recommendations were submitted to the WO for their approval, and were not submitted to the Sovereign by the S of S for India. In cases where forces of the two armies were serving alongside each other, however, the same exclusiveness worked in both directions. Thus, when the papers relating to the action at Deh Khoja, in Afghanistan, on 16 Aug 1880, were before the WO, Col Brownlow, the AMS for Indian Affairs commented to the MS, 'I am of opinion that Pte Thomas Ashford, 7 Royal Fusiliers has well earned the Victoria Cross. It appears to me that Lieutenant Chase is equally entitled to it but being an Indian officer the recommendation will perhaps come in due time through the IO' [India Office], as indeed it did, both being recommended to the Queen on 29 Sep 1881, and gazetted on 7 Oct.[474]

Cardwell's reorganisation of the WO in 1870, by which the Horse Guards and the CinC ceased to be independent authorities, made less difference to the routine of VC submissions than might be expected, though the unification of the clerical work within one department may well have met with the approval of Pennington, who had had occasion to point out blunders committed by the Horse Guards in their paper work, 'and these not the first', as long ago as November 1857.[475] The Duke of

472   PRO, WO 32/7302
473   PRO, WO 32/7419
474   PRO, WO 32/7400
475   PRO, WO 32/7306

Cambridge remained as the fount of military opinion, and his views had still to be sought as those of a vitally concerned departmental head, with the MS as his official mouthpiece, to whom the PUS addressed the requests for military opinion on behalf of the civil head of the department, the S of S for War. Probably of more immediate significance to those working in the WO must have been the retirement of Pennington himself, who seems clearly to have been a representative of the older establishment of Civil Servants. This event cannot be exactly dated, but the last recommendation for the VC with which he dealt was that to Capt G.N. Channer, gazetted on 14 Apr 1876, and the first with which he certainly did not was that to Capt John Cook, gazetted on 18 Mar 1879. His duties of advising the PUS on the eligibility of the cases recommended under the terms of the Warrant henceforth devolved on the newly revived post of Assistant Under Secretary of State, which had been in abeyance from 1871 to 1877. Col Deedes, who assumed this office in 1879, was the first holder of it to be unmistakeably carrying out Mr Pennington's former function. A fairly typical example of his role is to be found in the recommendations submitted in respect of two Indian Army officers, Capts Hammond and Vousden, in respect of their conduct on the Koh Asmia Heights, near Kabul, on 14 Dec 1879. Here all the papers were forwarded from Simla to the S of S for India on 1 Jun 1880, and from the India Office to the WO on 27 Jul. Here they went first to Cambridge, as CinC, who passed them over to the S of S's department with a pencilled note, signed George, 'Both admirable acts of gallantry, but I don't know if they come within the statutes of the Victoria Cross and yet I should not like to refuse either of them' – a not uncommon line for the Duke to take in his recommendations. In forwarding the papers for the S of S's approval Deedes added the very Pennington-like observation, 'I submit that both these cases come under the new statute "Conspicuous bravery or devotion to their country in the presence of the Enemy" and that Hammond and Vousden are eligible for the VC. I may observe that both would have been so under the old statute in my opinion'.[476] The reference to the old and the new statute [which is that of April 1881, discussed in Chapter 15] no doubt explains the reason why Deedes delayed putting the recommendations before the S of S until May 1881 as, presumably, he wished to have the revised form the Warrant was to take settled before doing this.

At this time also a change of considerably greater significance – at least to the individuals concerned – took place in the procedure for the

476   PRO, WO 32/7396

last stage of the processing of VC recommendations. In a letter of
12 Jan 1880, Sir Henry Ponsonby, presumably writing on the Queen's
instruction, asked the WO if it would be thought undesirable for the
actual submission to the Queen for the approval of the award of a VC
should be made by the CinC instead of by the S of S. Points made in
the discussion of this request were that the statutes were silent on the
mode of submitting names, so that this was purely a departmental
matter. No constitutional question was involved, since submission by
the CinC implied the consent of the S of S, who entrusted certain
matters to the CinC as head of the Military Department. It was also
pointed out that the CinC was in fact already submitting recommendations to the Queen in respect of the DCM so the question could well
be raised why he should not submit for both. Fears were also expressed
that the whole matter might become much more elaborate if certain
suggestions being made in this connection were adopted. It was in this
state of opinion that Ponsonby wrote again on 22 Jan to say that the
Queen's wish would be that the CinC should be responsible.[477]
Presumably no advantage was seen in altering the procedure for a
number of recommendations which were actually in the pipeline, for a
note on the papers states that the award to Capt R.K. Ridgeway,
gazetted on 11 May 1880, was the first to be dealt with under the new
procedure of submission of recommendations by the CinC [who had, of
course, first obtained the approval of the S of S for their submission to
the Queen],[478] whereas two batches of awards under the old procedure
had been gazetted prior to this but subsequent to Ponsonby's second
letter. The only query that this change raises is why the Queen should
have asked for it at that precise moment. One may well suspect that it
was intended as a sop to her cousin, the Duke of Cambridge, whose
authority had been severely curtailed by the reform of the War
Department carried out by Cardwell as Secretary of State, as has
already been mentioned. However, all this had taken place in 1870, ten
years previously, so the question of action in 1880 is something of a
puzzle. The most likely explanation seems to lie in the incidence of
military events. From 1870 to 1878 the number of recommendations
for the VC was very small — seven were awarded in the nine years — so
that the matter may well have lain dormant. In 1879 military activity
flared up in both South Africa and on the Indian frontier, producing no
fewer than twenty-six new awards, so that it was an aspect of the

477   PRO, WO 32/7392
478   PRO, WO 32/7395

duties of the S of S that would have been brought very much to the Queen's notice. In January 1880 more news of military operations was clearly to come — indeed, on the very day that Ponsonby wrote his first letter, a leader in *The Times* had referred to the country's expectation of news of the operations by Sir Frederick Roberts in Afghanistan — so that this may well have been seen as an appropriate moment to get the new procedure agreed to deal with the further recommendations which could be soon expected. The change of organisation at the lower level corresponding to that at the higher level took place shortly afterwards, in September 1880, when what was referred to as 'the VC work' was transferred from the old WO department C2 to the MS's department, where it has remained ever since.[479]

The use of boards of officers to investigate claims to the VC has already been referred to. It is evident from the papers reaching the WO from India during the Mutiny that they were very freely employed. On 25 Jan 1859 Lord Clyde wrote to the Horse Guards from Lucknow, forwarding a copy of the General Order by which he had provisionally conferred the VC on Lt Hackett and Pte Monger, for exploits performed under his personal command but which he had nonetheless had confirmed by a board of officers, and at the same time forwarded five names of men whose exploits had not been performed under his personal command, but who had been recommended on investigation by the board of officers he had appointed. The opinion of such a board was, however, not taken as the final judgement for, when these papers were forwarded from the Horse Guards to the WO on 25 Mar, it was indicated that Cambridge did not consider the evidence sufficient in three of the cases. This meant that there was something of a conflict between the authorities for, as Pennington pointed out, Clyde was presumably satisfied when the board was held, having all the witnesses on call, and might be regarded as the best judge of whether their claims were established. Sir Edward Lugard appears to have read this as a suggestion that the recommendation of the Duke of Cambridge should be dispensed with, which 'I cannot propose' but all Mr Pennington apparently meant was that the Horse Guards should be informed that these three names should not be recommended until the Duke had satisfied himself in the light of fuller information.[480] In fact they never were.

This second use of the board appears to indicate what was Clyde's

479   VCR, iii p162
480   PRO, WO 32/7324

general policy, which seems to have been to make particular use of boards of officers to investigate claims to the VC made by men not under his personal command,[481] whereas the use of one to confirm actions under his personal command seems somewhat unusual. Such investigations were clearly found helpful by Cambridge, as is indicated in his comments on a list of recommendations forwarded to the WO on 17 Oct 1859, containing eight names. Three of these, he thought, clearly came within the Warrant; the remainder he had no hesitation in recommending as very gallant, but was in some doubt as to whether the acts were beyond the line of duty. However, since they were all recommended by a board of officers, he submitted them all for consideration and, in fact, after some deliberation at the WO, a letter was sent to the Horse Guards saying that, since each name had been recommended by a board of officers, all would be submitted to the Queen, all being in fact gazetted on 11 Nov 1859.[482]

Such boards were by no means always held immediately after the exploit they were required to investigate. Thus, after the reason for the delay in bringing forward the claim of Surgeon H.T. Reade had been satisfactorily explained [it was in fact due to the dangerous illness of his CO at the time, and the regiment's subsequent frequent change of COs] the submission of a claim in respect of exploits in September 1857 was allowed to go before a board at the end of 1860, and its recommendation eventually allowed to proceed, even though other claims relating to undoubted acts of bravery, had been ruled out on account of the time that had elapsed since they were performed.[483] Boards could even be held in England, after the regiment concerned had returned from India though, in these cases, where all the evidence was available in England, reference to the CinC India was dispensed with.[484] One somewhat remarkable case where such a board was held in England, on the suggestion of the Duke of Cambridge and with the approval of the S of S for War, at that time Lord Herbert, was that of Pte S. Morley, of the Military Train. Morley, in the words of his CO, 'having made a representation to Brigadier-General Lord Geo. Paget, CB, at his half-yearly inspection of the Battalion at Aldershot considering himself entitled to the Victoria Cross for gallant conduct in the field in India'. The board appointed to consider his application consisted of

481   PRO, WO 32/7343
482   PRO, WO 32/7335
483   PRO, WO 32/7348
484   PRO, WO 32/7346

Lt-Gen Love and Maj-Gens Lord Rokeby and Lawrenson; they found in his favour and his Cross was duly gazetted on 7 Aug 1860.[485]

In the case of the selection of the recipients for the Crimean War a single board was set up to investigate all claims submitted, but those set up on subsequent occasions were strictly for the determination of a specific incident. The exact status of such boards seems to have caused Pennington some concern, for when the Horse Guards informed the WO on 16 Apr 1860 that the name of Pte J. Pearson of the 86th Regt was being recommended by Lt-Gen Love, Maj-Gen Lawrenson and Brig-Gen Russell, being assembled as a Board of General Officers to investigate claims to the VC, Pennington commented to Sir Edward Lugard that this was the first he had heard of any such board, adding that, since the board which had investigated claims in respect of the Crimean War had been set up by order of the S of S for War, the same would appear to be necessary to constitute any further board in this country to investigate outstanding claims. His mind was only set at rest on this point when he established that this board was only to investigate certain claims coming to the notice of the CinC, and not to investigate claims generally.[486]

Subsequent to the Indian Mutiny boards were certainly held at Tientsin in 1861 to investigate the claim to the VC of Hospital Apprentice Fitzgibbon, who eventually received the Cross,[487] in the West Indies in 1862 to investigate the case of Lt Bourke [who did not],[488] in Canada, in respect of the conduct of Pte O'Hea, in 1866 [who did],[489] and one was suggested, though apparently not called on to act, in respect of the non-combatant Crosses awarded in the Andamans in 1867.[490] During the remainder of the nineteenth century their use seems to have lapsed, although one was certainly convened by order of the CO of C Division, South African Constabulary, to enquire into the 'reported gallant behaviour of Captain [Martin-] Leake... on February 6th 1902', which board met at Roodebak on the 12th of that month.[491]

What may be regarded as something of an analogy to this use of boards was evident in the suggestion which appears to have emanated from Lord Stamfordham on the outbreak of the First World War,

485   *ibid*
486   PRO, WO 32/7341
487   PRO, WO 32/7357
488   PRO, WO 32/7372
489   *ibid*
490   PRO, WO 32/7373
491   PRO, WO 32/4990

which was that a joint committee should be set up by the WO and the Admiralty for the examination of recommendations submitted for the award of the VC. On 3 Oct 1914 Gen Codrington, the MS, wrote to Brade, the Secretary at the War Office, 'I put this scheme before the Secretary of State [Lord Kitchener] yesterday. He preferred not to have any joint action with the Navy, and does not think a Committee such as I suggested would serve a useful purpose. But he thought a small committee should consider recommendations for the Victoria Cross'. Brade's reply to this the following day was 'Perhaps the Military Member would suggest the constitution'; to which Codrington offered a composition of himself, as MS, an officer to be nominated by the AG, and Brade as Secretary of the War Office. On being approached the AG suggested the Director of Personal Services, and it was on this basis that the committee was constituted, even though Brade, as a civilian, evidently felt a certain diffidence in taking part. 'So far as the Committees on the VC recommendations are concerned', he wrote on 30 Oct, 'I am ready to help but I don't suppose my services would be of much use.'

The committee was soon at work. On 12 Nov the MS, now Maj-Gen Sir Frederick Robb, wrote to the S of S: 'The Committee have had before them recommendations from Field Marshal Sir John French for the award of the VC to 24 cases, of which 12 are for Officers and 12 are for Warrant Officers, Non Commissioned Officers and Men.

'They have compared these with the Statutes and they submit that the recommendations are in accordance therewith and that those shown on the attached schedule should be laid before the King forthwith.[492]

'The remaining cases they cannot deal with at the moment as further information is received [sic]. They have telegraphed to the Military Secretary at General Headquarters for this information. In one case they have been able to take the evidence of an eye witness of the occurrence and to supplement the somewhat meagre information furnished in the papers. They have also informed the Military Secretary at GHQ that if possible any reports made by eye-witnesses of the acts of gallantry for which the award of the VC is recommended should be forwarded in order that the circumstances may be made clearer than in the brief notes submitted in the recommendations.'

492   The names in this schedule were those of Lt M.J. Dease, Battery Sgt-Maj G.T. Dorrell, Cpl C.E. Garforth, Capt F.O. Grenfell, L/Cpl C.A. Jarvis, Sgt D. Nelson, Capts H.S. Rankin, D. Reynolds and T. Wright, (all gazetted on 16 Nov 1914), Lt J.H.S. Dimmer (gazetted on 19 Nov) and L/Cpl W. Fuller (gazetted on 23 Nov).

The Committee set up in 1914 continued to operate for the remainder of the War, though with one change of composition. On 10 Aug 1916 the MS wrote to the AG and the DCIGS: 'The Director of Personal Services has expressed to me his desire to cease to act on the VC Committee appointed by the late Secretary of State in September 1914 [sic]. If that is carried out I hope the Deputy Chief of the Imperial General Staff will take his place. There is very little to do'. To this the AG agreed that the DCIGS was certainly the person most concerned, and the DCIGS indicated that he had no objection to serving. This appears to be the only alteration to be made in the constitution of the committee during its existence.[493] A very similar committee was constituted for the same purpose during the Second World War, when its membership consisted of the PUS, the CIGS and the MS.[494]

The question of authentication in relation to a recommendation for the VC could take two forms. Usually it was simply a question of authenticating what the person recommended had done but it could also, on occasions, be the action of the CO which required authentication. This latter circumstance could arise in the case of the subsequent death of the commander. This was the case concerning Capt Peel's Naval Brigade in the Indian Mutiny. A number of his recommendations had been incorporated in Lord Clyde's dispatches, following the procedure which had been laid down for all Naval Brigade submissions. However, on 1 Jan 1858, a week after three such recommendations had been published in the *London Gazette*, Commander Young submitted to the WO copies of recommendations made by Peel before his death which included, in addition to these three, the names of himself [as Lieutenant], and the Nova Scotian negro Able Seaman William Hall, claiming in addition that these Crosses had been promised by Peel in the presence of Lord Clyde. In forwarding Young's letter to Storks, Pennington observed that although these awards were recommended by the Admiralty there was nothing to show that Clyde had confirmed Peel's promise, and he therefore suggested reference to Clyde, a course which was agreed by Peel, the S of S for War, on the 14th, and the Admiralty were so informed on 18th. However on the 25th Sir John Pakington, the First Lord, wrote to Gen Peel asking 'whether, in such circumstances, the delay for reference to India is necessary or desirable'. Peel was, evidently prepared to reconsider the matter for, on the

493   PRO, WO 32/4993 for all the above
494   PRO, WO 32/9956

following day, he replied to the First Lord 'If you are satisfied that the omission on his [Clyde's] part..... has been accidental I will submit the names of this Officer and Seaman to the Queen at once, as you wish, and so avoid the delay of a reference to India'. Pakington replied accepting this proposal on the 28th, but the submission had in fact already been prepared on the 26th, the papers being marked by Pennington 'acted on by anticipation', and the two awards were published in the *London Gazette* of 1 Feb.[495]

A somewhat complex issue arose regarding promises in the case of Maj Trevor in the Bhootan expedition of 1865. Trevor maintained that he had been promised this reward by the CinC, Sir William Mansfield, whereas the latter held that the brevet majority conferred on Trevor was in satisfaction of all claims. Trevor applied to Mansfield to reconsider his claim, on the ground that by withholding his support from it Mansfield was implying censure on Trevor's conduct in the field, and upon Mansfield's declining to reconsider, enlisted the support of the Governor-General and a majority of his Council for his view that he had been promised the Cross by the GOC in the presence of other officers. Gen Tombs, the General concerned, was prepared to say positively that he had made such a promise, although the Governor-General's Council was not unanimous as to whether Tombs' language constituted a promise. Maj Trevor was, in fact, awarded the VC when the recommendation was submitted to the Queen by the WO in December 1867, but this was done without Sir William Mansfield's concurrence.[496]

The type of detail which could be inquired into so far as the conduct of the individual recommended was concerned can be illustrated by the discussion which took place at the WO on receipt of the recommendation of Capt F.A. Smith for his conduct in New Zealand on 21 Jun 1864. Pennington drew Lugard's attention to the significant detail: 'Captain Smith, it is stated, having been previously wounded, jumped down or fell into the Rifle Pits, ∴ I presume there will be no objection to submitting these cases to Her Majesty, as recommended'. Lugard, in placing the matter before the S of S, Lord de Grey, on the 14th, spelled out the matter in rather more detail. 'Sergeant Murray's conduct clearly merits the Victoria Cross – but I have some doubts respecting Captain Smith's claim as it is not very clearly shown whether he *jumped* or *fell* into the rifle pit. This discrepancy in the evidence should have been cleared up or explained by Lieutenant-General

495   PRO, WO 32/7322
496   PRO, WO 32/7374

Cameron before he sent forward his recommendations accompanied by the conflicting documents.

'As the Lieutenant-General recommends Captain Smith for the distinction you are justified in presuming that he did satisfy himself on this very important point; and if you approve of Captain Smith's having the Cross I would suggest that this be commented on, and the Lieutenant-General be enjoined in future to clear up any doubtful points before submitting his recommendation'.

Lord de Grey did approve the award, the citation in the *London Gazette* of 4 Nov reading, 'although wounded previously to reaching the rifle-pits, (he) jumped down in them.....' and a letter along the lines suggested was sent to the Horse Guards on 19 Oct.[497]

As an example of the searching enquiries that could be undertaken before a recommendation for the VC was sent forward, the question-naire administered by Buller, as Gen Evelyn Wood's Chief of Staff, to Col Gildea, in respect of the latter's recommendation of Trooper Danaher and L/Cpl Murray, for their conduct at Elandsfontein during the First Boer War, has survived. It reads as follows: '.....

Q1. – How far did they advance under very heavy fire?
A. – About 500 yards.

Q2. – Did they leave a formed body of troops in order to advance and was that body halted or retiring at the time?
A. – Lance Corporal Murray formed one of a body of 12 mounted infantry halted in skirmishing order at large intervals; this body of men were dismounted and under cover. Trooper Danaher of Nourse's Horse formed one of a party of 4 men of that Corps engaged in a similar manner as the Mounted Infantry of 94th Regiment. Lance Corporal Murray and Trooper Danaher advanced from the right of the line of skirmishers.

Q3. – How many of our side were there near to Corporal Murray and Trooper Danaher at this time and how near?
A. – No men were near to Lance Corporal Murray and Trooper Danaher at the time they got up to the wounded. The nearest party of our forces to these men was the one referred to in Answer 1, viz. remaining 11 94th M.I. and 3 Nourse's Horse.

Q4. – How far off were the enemy and how many in number?
A. – The enemy about 60 in number were 600 yards off from the skirmishers and consequently about 100 yards off Corporal Murray and Trooper Danaher when they arrived at the wounded men.

497   PRO, WO 32/7366

Q5. – Did these two men reach Private King, and if so under what conditions did they again leave him?
A. – Both men reached Private King and Lance Corporal Murray was shot while speaking to him and fell by his side. Lance Corporal Murray then told Danaher to go back as he could do no more and could move neither of them.

Q6. – The fire is described as "very heavy"; how many of the enemy were firing and from what distance?
A. – About 60 of the enemy were firing from bushes at a distance of about 100 yards from Private King.

Q7. – Trooper Danaher is described as alone remaining and hard pressed. What is meant by this?
A. – It was meant that the man Danaher was "alone remaining, unwounded and was hard pressed to regain his party" not from being pursued but on account of the heavy fire poured in on him.

These answers have been given by Lt O'Grady, 94th Regiment, who was in command of the MI.'[498]

It is perhaps worth recording that, after all these explanations, the two recommendations for the VC were approved. Searching enquiries of this nature were not unique to this period. When the VC Committee of 1914-18, 'in view of the necessity of maintaining the high standard for which the particular decoration is intended', sought further information prior to placing certain of Sir John French's VC recommendations before the King, the type of question which was asked was, as in the case of L/Cpl Dobson, who left the trenches under heavy fire to bring in wounded, 'What distance did he cover and how many times?'[499]

The question of attestation which arose directly from the wording of the VC Warrant turned on the eighth Clause 'the officer commanding the force in the field..... shall call for such description and attestation of the act as he may think requisite'. This was one of the difficulties foreseen in the case of conferring the VC on Maj R.W. Sartorius, for his ride through Ashanti where, as he was the only European officer participating, it was doubted whether there would be any sufficient testimony to his conduct.[500] It was to regularise the interpretation of this requirement under the Warrant that, as was mentioned at the 1918

498   PRO, WO 32/3418
499   PRO, WO 32/4993
500   PRO, WO 32/7378

interdepartmental committee, it was laid down as a private interpretation — 'a domestic arrangement on the part of the Field Marshal in
France' — that this meant statements by two witnesses.[501] In more
recent days the number of witnesses required appears to have been
increased to three.

There have been a number of curious instances relating to the matter
of witnesses of VC actions in the years since the First World War and,
although official sources are not in all cases available for this period, the
facts in these instances seem to be sufficiently reliably reported to be
accepted. One certainly to be mentioned among these is the posthumous
award of the VC to F/O L.A. Trigg for his exploit in attacking, and
sinking, a surfaced U-boat in August 1943. His own aircraft was shot
down by the U-boat in the course of the attack and there were no
survivors from his crew; a number of survivors from the crew of the
U-boat were, however, picked up, and it was on their statements, as
witnesses, that the award of his Cross was in fact based.[502]

Papers which have become available show a certain analogy in the
case of Sgt J.D. Hinton, in that the chief witness to his exploit, although
on the same side as the sergeant, was similarly at the receiving end of
Hinton's attack. Maj Thomson, by whom Hinton was recommended,
had already been captured by the Germans, and was travelling with
their column advancing on Kalami, which Hinton tried to halt. The
Major had, in consequence, heard Hinton's shout of 'To hell with this;
who'll come with me?' seen him make his rush, and had been able to
recognise him when he treated his wounds as a Medical Officer after
Hinton also had been taken prisoner.[503]

The last VC to be awarded for the Second World War, a posthumous
award to Lt G.A. Cairns, one of the 'Chindits', was not gazetted until
May, 1949, just over five years after the exploit it commemorated. This
was due to the fact that the recommendation had been with Gen
Wingate, who had commanded the 'Chindit' force, at the time he had
been killed in an air crash, all the records perishing with him. When an
attempt was made to revive the recommendation it came to light that
two of the three original witnesses had also been killed since giving
their accounts. The final revival of the recommendation at the end of
1948 was engineered by Cairns' widow, her Member of Parliament, and
Maj Calvert, who had commanded the brigade of which Cairns' unit

501   PRO, WO 32/3443
502   *The Bronze Cross,* pp44, 82
503   PRO, WO 32/9957

formed part, but as official papers for this period are not available, the exact role of the WO in the proceedings cannot at present be ascertained.[504]

The most recent case of all to present a feature of interest in this context is that of Maj P.J. Badcoe, who was awarded the VC, once again posthumously, for his conduct in Vietnam, when serving alongside the Vietnamese in 1967. The particular point here is that, of the three witnesses whose testimony was accepted for the award, two were completely illiterate.[505] This, whilst unusual, is by no means unique; Sgt Leakey was serving with the King's African Rifles at the time that he won his VC, and the witness statements in his WO file, which are accompanied by the appropriate translation, have clearly been taken down as dictated in Swahili, and are signed with the witnesses' thumb-prints. It is interesting to note that, when originally submitted, the VC Committee was divided in its views of Leakey's act, the CIGS and the PUS thinking it of VC standard and the MS not, and that when it was put before King George VI in March, 1942, he agreed with the MS, Gen Floyer-Acland. It was only when the case was resubmitted with what Gen Cunningham described as 'further and important details', three and a half years later, that the King gladly gave his approval.[506]

Reconsideration of cases in which there has been doubt about the appropriate award for the standard of conduct displayed has not been unusual, but the case of CSM Peter Wright of the Coldstream Guards presents some special features. On 27 Jan 1944 Wright was awarded the DCM for his conduct at Salerno. On 19 Jul Lt-Gen Loyd, GOC Brigade of Guards, wrote to the MS pointing out that the original recommendation had been for a VC and that the citation compared very favourably with that of many VCs. In reply Brig Evans wrote for the MS on 22 Jul that when the recommendation had been put to Gen Alexander as CinC 15th Army Group he had amended this to one for a DCM; he had obviously given the matter very careful consideration, so it was not thought advisable to reopen it. In private he added that Gen Alexander had not considered the case quite up to VC standard, and that the alteration was in his own handwriting. However, it was not only Loyd who was interested in this award. King George VI was at that time visiting his troops in Italy and on 25 Jul a secret cypher telegram was received at the WO 'HM spoke to General Alexander and apparently

504   John Frayn Turner, VCs of the Army, 1939-51, London 1962, pp93/5
505   Information given to the author from a private Australian source.
506   PRO, WO 32/9955

expressed his opinion it should have been a VC. Presumably if HM wishes he can cancel General Alexander's award and (grant) a VC. Grateful for confirmation within three days.' When Sir Alan Lascelles, the King's PS, was asked who had enlisted the King's interest in the matter he did not remember any one individual, but many people had expressed the opinion that it should have been a VC. In view of the very recent advice the MS had given to General Loyd that the matter should be left alone the MS found himself in a somewhat embarrassing position but Lascelles, pointing out that the King could only give the VC or DCM on the recommendation of his minister, and that the substitution proposed in the telegram was nonsense, suggested that Gen Alexander could be informed that if he was prepared to revise his previous decision, the usual steps for an award could be taken. This was in fact what happened, Gen Alexander writing very tactfully to the Under Secretary at the WO on 29 Jul, 'I have had reason to reconsider this matter and I hereby resubmit the citation with a recommendation for the award of the Victoria Cross'. The appropriate draft submission, accompanied by a request for the cancellation of the DCM went to Lascelles on 17 Aug, being followed by a formal submission to the King on 18 Aug, and both the award of the VC and the cancellation of Wright's DCM were duly gazetted on 7 Sep 1944.[507]

A question of some administrative significance in the early days of the VC was the date up to which claims in respect of any particular campaign could be accepted. Thus, when on 14 May 1858 the Duke of Cambridge submitted nine recommendations in respect of the Crimean War,[508] the claims of each one having been established by a board of officers on 29 Apr, Pennington thought fit to point out to Storks, on 19 May, that the original call for recommendations had been requested by Lord Panmure on 5 Sep 1856, that the board which was to consider the claims submitted had sat from time to time and considered a great number of submissions, but that more than two years had now elapsed since the signature of a peace treaty terminating the war and that a reasonable time had now been given for the consideration of claims. He therefore suggested that a letter should go to the Horse Guards, saying that whilst the present list would be submitted to the Queen the S of S would be glad to be informed that the examination of such claims

507   PRO, WO 32/11049
508   These were Capt H.C. Elphinstone, Colour-Sgts G. Gardiner, P. Leitch, and H. McDonald, Surgeon J. Mouat, Sgt H. Ramage, and Bt-Maj M. Walker, all of whom were gazetted on 2 Jun 1858, this being the last occasion on which Crimean VCs were gazetted in quantity.

would be concluded at an early period, a suggestion which received the approval of Gen Peel, the S of S for War, on 20th.[509] On 22nd a letter was sent to the Duke of Cambridge, over the signature of Gen Peel, which concluded '..... as more than two years have now elapsed since the ratifications of the Treaty of Peace with Russia were exchanged it appears to me that a reasonable time has been allowed for the consideration of the claims to the Victoria Cross for Acts of Gallantry performed with that Power. I should accordingly be glad to be informed whether it is probable that the examination of claims which my predecessor requested to be made in the letter which he addressed to Your Royal Highness under date the 5th September 1856 will be concluded at an early period'.[510] In his reply of the 24th the Duke agreed that it was desirable to bring the submission of claims to a conclusion, and hoped that there would not be many more. However cases were continually being pressed on him which he felt unable to reject on grounds of lateness if there was an act of gallantry which appeared to entitle those involved to the award; he undertook to be guided by the strict terms of the Warrant in this. The reply sent to this, on 2 Jun, following Pennington's proposal of 26 May, was that the S of S was happy to note the CinC's agreement that such claims should be brought to a conclusion, and the Duke was at the same time informed of the approval of his recommendations for submission to the Queen.[511] Only two more awards of the VC were made for the Crimea, and in both cases the circumstances were a little exceptional. On 12 Jul of that year Sgt-Maj Wooden wrote to Dr Mouat, who had just had the Cross conferred on him, making a claim to have assisted him in the work of succouring the wounded at Balaclava, for which he had received his decoration. This claim Dr Mouat forwarded to the Horse Guards, indicating that he supported it, with the result that the MS wrote to the WO on 4 Oct: 'His Royal Highness feels very unwilling to bring forward any further claim for the Victoria Cross for an Act performed at so distant a period but as the Decoration has been conferred on Dr James Mouat for the part he took in the rescue of Lt. Colonel Morris and Sergeant Major Wooden appears to have acted in a manner very honorable to him on the occasion and by his gallantry been equally instrumental in saving the life of this Officer, His Royal Highness is induced to submit the case.'[512] This late claim was approved, and

509   PRO, WO 32/7308
510   VCR, i pp93/4
511   PRO, WO 32/7308
512   PRO, WO 32/7326

Wooden's VC was gazetted on 26 Oct 1858. What was to be the last award of all was initiated [or rather revived] by a letter to Sir Charles Yorke, the MS at the Horse Guards, from Maj F. Miller on 26 Jan 1859. 'As the Victoria Cross has already been bestowed on an officer for a very similar act (viz. jumping over a wall in face of the enemy to encourage his comrades),' Miller wrote, 'I am induced to hope that His Royal Highness may recommend Her Majesty to confer the same distinction on myself'. In forwarding this letter to the WO, Sir Charles Yorke had an admission to make, 'I have to add', he wrote on 20 Apr 1859, 'that it was evidently intended by the Board by which such cases were investigated in the first instance to recommend that of Maj Miller and His Royal Highness regrets that it has been lost sight of until the present time and can only presume that it was mislaid amongst the mass of correspondence on the subject'. In passing these papers forward to Sir Edward Lugard, Pennington commented that Crimean awards had closed nearly a year ago but, since this case had not been put forward through an oversight no objection should be raised to its submission to the Queen, which was done and Miller's Cross finally gazetted on 6 May 1859.[513] Although this was the last Crimean VC to be awarded, it was not the last to be claimed. Two years later, claims were received from two further applicants in respect of the Crimean War, Barrack Sgt Bacon of Leeds and Pensioner James Aitken of Leith, but as, in the words of the letters which were sent them from the WO on 3 and 7 May 1861, 'the investigation of all claims to this high distinction on the grounds of Acts of gallantry performed during the Crimean War having for some time been brought to a conclusion', they could not be considered.[514] What seems to have been the final Crimean claim, from a Thomas Ewan, was only declined on 27 Nov 1882, and that repeated what he had already been told four years previously.[515]

The question of a time limit for submissions in respect of the Indian Mutiny was similarly exercising minds at the WO in December 1860, at which time recommendations in respect of five men were declined on account of the lateness of the submissions, though in four cases this was satisfactorily explained, the recommendations in respect of Lt-Col S.J. Browne and Col J. Travers going forward early in 1861, and those of Lieutenants Cadell and Thackeray, twelve months later.[516] On this

513   PRO, WO 32/7327
514   VCR, i pp332/4
515   VCR, ii pp306/7
516   PRO, WO 32/7349

occasion it seems that the initiative in setting a time limit was taken by
the Duke of Cambridge, for in a letter of 31 Dec 1860 from the WO to
the Horse Guards it was indicated that the S of S concurred with the
Duke that a time limit for claims should be set in relation to the
Mutiny.[517] However, the Duke seems later to have had second thoughts.
On 13 Feb 1862, Pennington minuted Lugard regarding the time limit
that had been agreed in this connection; Cambridge had therefore
previously declined to consider a number of cases but was now proposing
to set aside this rule, as the rejection of all cases might lead to
disappointment when it was seen that Crosses had been recently given
for acts performed at the same time, though Pennington pointed out
that these others had been conferred some weeks before the rule on
time had been laid down. 'If the rule is not strictly adhered to every
instance of its infringement will be used as an argument for admitting
fresh cases.' Lugard's reaction to this was to ask for lists of the cases
involved and, as a result of examining these, observed to the Secretary
of State, 'It certainly appears that the Indian Service has some grounds
for complaint'. It was as a result of this discussion that the recommendations for Cadell and Thackeray went forward.[518] The list of awards
gazetted on 25 Feb 1862 can also be regarded as a final clearing up of
Mutiny claims then going through the office, arising from this same
examination, in at least one case [that of Conductor Miller, whose
exploit had taken place in October, 1857] the Duke of Cambridge
having previously thought it undesirable to put this forward due to the
time that had elapsed.[519] In another case of delay, that of Capt H.G.
Browne, whose exploit had been performed on 21 Aug 1857, but
which was not brought forward for nearly five years, Pennington agreed
that the delay was unavoidable and should be no obstacle to his case
being submitted, and his Cross was eventually gazetted on 20 Jun
1861.[520] However, in this climate of opinion, a good deal of surprise
must have been caused by the receipt of the report of a board of
enquiry into claims for the Victoria Cross which had met in Calcutta in
the second half of 1862. This now put forward for the award of the
Cross Cpl C. Anderson and Trumpeter T. Monaghan for their conduct
in Oudh on 8 Oct 1858 [to which Pennington raised no objection, since

517   VCR, i p307
518   PRO, WO 32/7349
519   PRO, WO 32/7351. The awards involved were those to Lt C.G. Baker,
      Capt J. Blair, Lt J.C.C. Daunt, Sgt D. Dynon, Maj R.H. Keatinge,
      Midshipman A. Mayo, Conductor J. Miller and Lt W.F.F. Waller.
520   PRO, WO 32/7350

the delay here was stated to be due to the insecurity of postal communications, with the unit on the march and surrounded by the enemy, so that runners were either killed or deserted, and a submission made at the proper time had never got through], and Colour Sgt C. Coghlan, for his conduct at the seige of Delhi in 1857 [which Pennington did not consider satisfactorily explained in regard to delay, but Sir Edward Lugard put forward in consideration of the importance of the service he rendered and on presumption of the pressure of business on the battalion's CO at that time]. It then also recommended Ptes T. Burke, P. Callaghan and T. Catling for their service at Inkerman, Pte W. Sudders for his service at the Redan, and Pte D. Neill for his service at Jhansi. The three cases which could be regarded as exceptional were submitted to the Queen on 31 Oct 1862 and the award of the Cross gazetted on 11 Nov, but a very firm refusal was given to any consideration of the remaining cases.[521] The last claims of all in connection with the Indian Mutiny did not come to hand until December 1863, when a board reported on the claim of Major Bonham, whose claim had been previously declined by Lord Clyde in 1859, on account of the lapse of time in bringing it forward. He had now revived his claim with Clyde's successor, the papers in the meanwhile having been lost in the AG's office in Calcutta. Mr Pennington was clearly most indignant that this claim was being pressed when the Horse Guards had made the point as long ago as 1860 that claims not preferred within a short time of the act should not be countenanced; Lugard agreed that it would be dangerous to reopen such matters at such a distance of time, and Lord de Grey as S of S accepted the advice that this claim should be refused, as also were those of Assistant-Surgeon J. Lumsdaine, Bombay Medical Service, Major J. Edmondstoune, 32nd Regt, and Surgeon H.M. Greenhow, Bengal Medical Service, all on the same grounds.[522]

As well as dealing with the recipients of the VC, the WO had also to handle the preparation and distribution of the actual Crosses. The supply of new Crosses had to be ordered as necessary, two large orders having been placed at the outset, and those not actually required for immediate distribution being held in stock at the WO. On 24 Sep 1857 Sir Henry Storks wrote to Mr Hancock of Bruton Street, who had manufactured all the Crosses required: 'I am directed by Lord Panmure to acquaint you that his Lordship has given direction to the Accountant General of this Office for paying to you the sum of

£346.7.0, being the amount of your account for the preparation of Victoria Crosses, and I am to request you that you will deliver to Mr Pennington of this office the remainder of the Victoria Crosses — 212 in number, in order that they may be kept in store'.[523]

At the foot of this letter is a calculation showing how the figure of 212 had been arrived at:-

	Nos prepared
March 4/56	106
Feby 7/57	200
	306
Issued	94
Remaining	212

An examination of the dates of the notification of awards in the *London Gazette* shows that, by March 1862, the stock of Crosses still in hand would have been reduced to a single figure, nearly half the holding having been bespoken by the gazetting of eight new recipients on 25 Feb. On 5 Mar, therefore, a further order was placed with Hancock, this time signed by Lugard, Sir Henry Storks' successor at the WO: 'I am directed by the Secretary of State for War to desire that you will prepare without delay 25 Victoria Crosses, in Gun Metal, with swivel bar [sic] and riband complete as in the case of those which you made, by the Secretary of State's order, in the years 1856 and 1857.

'Twenty of these Crosses should be fitted with *red* ribands and five with *blue;* and it should be understood that the cost of each Cross is not to exceed the cost of the Crosses which you originally made, viz. 20/- each Cross complete'.[524]

The five awards gazetted on 22 Sep 1864 would have again reduced the total holding to about a dozen, and a further order for twenty-five Crosses was placed with Mr Hancock on 14 Oct 1864, in almost identical terms, except that on this occasion there was no requirement as to the number with red and with blue ribbons [presumably this meant that all were to have red ribbons] and there was an additional sentence, 'Should you require an additional supply of Gun Metal, it will be supplied to you on your stating the quantity required'.[525]

The next order, again for twenty-five Crosses, and in identical terms to that of 1864, followed on 26 Apr 1876.[526] On this occasion,

523   VCR, i p56
524   *ibid,* pp 366/7
525   VCR, ii pp7/8
526   *ibid,* pp158/9

however, it appears that a fresh supply of metal was required, and also that Hancock had sought confirmation regarding the ribbon for each Cross, for on the 8 May, a further letter [this time addressed, not to Mr Hancock, but to Messrs Hancock and Company], was sent, 'In reply to your letter of 27th ultimo, I am directed by the Secretary of War to acquaint you that orders have been given to the Principal Commissariat Officer at Woolwich Arsenal to supply you with 10 lbs of Gun metal [Plate 8] to enable you to make the 25 Victoria Crosses required by this Office. The Crosses should be prepared with red ribbon'.[527]

Supplying the eight VCs gazetted for Rorke's Drift on 2 May 1879, was no doubt the drawing on stocks which prompted the next order, this time for ten Crosses, on 4 Jun 1879, again in identical terms to the letter of 1864, except for the style of the company to whom it was addressed.[528] The next order, this time for twelve Crosses, followed on 5 Jul 1881, again in almost identical terms, though from now on these letters are written in the name of the Field Marshal Commanding in Chief and not of the S of S, which is presumably a reflection of the change of procedure in submitting VC recommendations to the Queen, which took place at the beginning of 1880.[529] A further order, again for twelve Crosses, was placed in terms identical with the 1881 letter, on 18 Mar 1882;[530] this being followed by a note on 23rd, to the Director of Artillery, 'Messrs Hancocks of 38 Bruton Street require 20 lbs of Gun Metal to enable them to comply with the order given on /1234 for making 12 Victoria Crosses. Will you be good enough to give the necessary directions?'.[531] Evidently, on this occasion, the WO had allowed their stock of Crosses to run dangerously low, for on 1 May 1882 a further communication was sent to Hancocks: 'The Military Secretary presents his compliments to Messrs Hancocks and with reference to his letter of 18 March last requests that they will be good enough to state when the Victoria Crosses therein ordered will be prepared, as at least one of them may shortly be required for presentation by Her Majesty'.[532] The next order, again for twelve Crosses, was placed on 14 May 1885, in what was by now the standard form,[533] and yet a further twelve were ordered on 10 Nov 1896.[534] The next

527   *ibid*, pp 159/60
528   *ibid*, p177
529   *ibid*, p257
530   *ibid*, p285
531   *ibid*, p286
532   *ibid*, pp287/8
533   *ibid*, p333
534   *ibid*, p379

order, also for twelve, was placed on 9 Nov 1898[535] and these must have been the stock upon which the WO was working at the time of the outbreak of the South African War. The impact of this increase in military operations is clearly evident in the next order, placed on 26 Jan 1900, which was for twenty-four Crosses. Although the terms in which the order were placed were the standard ones, some urgency had evidently been conveyed with it for, in an acknowledgement dated the 27th, Messrs Hancocks, who said that they thought they had sufficient gun metal, undertook to deliver the Crosses with the least possible delay.[536] In the circumstances of the war this supply was evidently soon exhausted, for a further twelve Crosses had to be ordered on 18 Sep of that year, and on this occasion more gun metal was required, the Director General of Ordnance, being asked to supply Messrs Hancocks with 20 lbs.[537] Nor did this stock of Crosses last long, for yet another twelve had to be ordered on 14 Feb 1901,[538] twelve more on 10 Jun 1901,[539] and yet twelve more on 23 Oct 1901.[540] Another twelve were required on 3 Jul 1902,[541] which must have taken care of the last of the awards of that war. To the outbreak of troubles in Somaliland and the issue of Crosses arising therefrom must be attributed the order for twelve further Crosses on 14 Sep 1902,[542] though it was presumably this actual order which provided the specimens to be issued in 1907, when six Crosses were sent to the relatives of those men whose names had been published over the years as those who would have been recommended for the award of the VC had they survived. This issue was presumably replaced in stock by the order of a further twelve Crosses on 18 Sep 1908, which would have provided the supply from which the first of the 1914-18 awards were to be met.[543]

Beyond this point the ordering of VCs by the WO cannot be traced as the VCR underwent a considerable change in form on the outbreak of the 1914-18 War, and the placing of these orders was among the items of VC correspondence which ceased to be recorded in it from that time. One change in procedure certainly seems to date from the

535   *ibid*, p397
536   *ibid*, p405
537   VCR, iii p12
538   *ibid*, p21
539   *ibid*, p25
540   *ibid*, p31
541   *ibid*, p42
542   *ibid*, p95
543   *ibid*, p182

time of the War, in that at least since 1920, when the present head of the firm entered the business, the stocks of Crosses available for issue have been held by Hancocks, and not by the WO.[544] The most likely explanation for this change would seem to be the greatly increased frequency with which awards of the Cross were being made — 630 in exactly five years, so that there would have been no time for the Cross to be held in stock before it had to be issued. One can imagine that lists of names to be engraved must have reached Hancocks on occasions before they would have had time to produce the necessary Crosses on which to put them. Obviously in such a situation there would be no opportunity to send the Crosses to the WO for keeping prior to naming, and one may suppose that the practice of committing them to the keeping of the WO, once discontinued, was never revived. Certainly, when VCs were awarded in the Second World War the instruction which went to Hancocks from the WO was that one should be engraved 'from the War Office stock'.[545]

The fact that the Crosses which were available for issue were held by the WO meant that whenever one was to be issued it had to be taken from stock and sent to Hancocks to have the particulars engraved upon it, for which service Hancocks rendered an annual account. Soon after the institution of the Cross this matter appears to have led to some acrimony between Mr Hancock and the WO, for on 9 Mar 1859 Sir Edward Lugard, for the WO wrote to Mr Hancock, 'I am directed by the Secretary of State for War to acquaint you that he has instructed the Accountant General of this Department to pay to you the sum of £19.12s., being the amount of your account for 1858 for engraving Victoria Crosses.

'It appears from this account that the amount now charged by you for engraving each Cross exceeds by 1/- the amount previously charged, and the Secretary of State would therefore be glad to be informed on what terms you are prepared to perform this service in future. He has at the same time deemed it proper to call for tenders from other persons of the terms on which they will undertake to engrave these Crosses in future'.[546] Exactly what reply Mr Hancock made to this letter does not appear but, evidently the threat of depriving him of this work [inconvenient though it would undoubtedly have proved for the WO to send the Crosses elsewhere for naming] was sufficient to bring him to

544   I am indebted to Mr G.L. Hancock Dore for this information.
545   See e.g. PRO, WO 32/11048
546   VCR, i p185

heel. On 29 Mar Lugard wrote again: 'Having laid before the Secretary of State for War your letter of the 14th instant I am directed to acquaint you that he considers your explanation as to the charge made by you for engraving the Victoria Crosses to be satisfactory and the work will be continued to you.

'I am to add that direction has been given to the Accountant General of this department for paying to you the sum of £16.11.6, being the amount of your amended account in lieu of the sum previously authorised'.[547]

Not all transactions regarding the cost of engraving are recorded in the VCR, but Mr Hancock's account for engraving VCs for 1860 is entered as being £4.15s.,[548] though exactly how this is to be reconciled with the twenty-seven Crosses awarded in that year is obscure. Some years later an individual account, relating to the supply of a VC for Gunner Harding, RN, gives the cost of engraving as 3/- and 2/6 for a blue ribbon[549] – this latter item presumably arising from the only Crosses available having red ribbons, and half a crown being charged for the supply of a blue ribbon to replace this. This item would seem also to dispose of a legend that the Crosses awarded to civilians were suspended from a white ribbon, since the Crosses so awarded could only have come from the original manufacture in February 1857, when they would have been supplied with a red or blue ribbon. If, therefore, those awarded under the civilian Warrant, promulgated in December 1858, were to have a different ribbon, some of this stock would have had to be re-ribboned, and a charge would have been incurred for this. Had this occurred, one would expect from the Harding analogy that the transaction would have been recorded in the VCR, but this contains no record of any such occurrence. The charge for engraving appears to be confirmed by the account of 13 Nov 1903, which was for the supply of twelve Crosses, and the engraving of three, and amounted to £12.9.0, the cost of the Crosses having been specified in every order as 20/- complete with ribbon and suspender bar.[550]

The engraving instructions were not usually recorded in the VCR, but one case which was may serve an example for all. This, dated 10 Jun 1879, simply read 'Be good enough to have the accompanying

547   *ibid*, p187
548   *ibid*, p332
549   VCR, ii p304
550   VCR, iii p101

Cross engraved as follows:- On the bar — Lieut. Reginald C. Hart, Rl. Eng. : At Back in Centre — 31 Jan 1879.'[551]

On a few occasions some Crosses have been presented to their recipients unnamed. One such example of this took place in connection with the presentation of their Crosses to two of the heroes of Dargai, Piper Findlater and Private Vickery. In both cases unengraved Crosses, which had been specially sent to Netley, were presented by the Queen to the two men at Netley Hospital on 14 May 1898, six days before their Crosses had actually been gazetted, though both had in fact been recommended by the CinC on 11th. These Crosses were then sent back to the WO on 19th to have their particulars engraved on them. In the letter from Hancocks on 21st, acknowledging their receipt they stated 'We have taken the precaution of giving them separately to our engraver so that the one cannot be commenced until the other is finished, thus obviating the possibility of their being changed'. The exact circumstances in which Vickery received back his Cross do not appear to be recorded, but a curious little document in the WO file gives the end of the story for Findlater's Cross. This reads 'Received from Lt Col Ward my Victoria Cross. G. Findlater VC, Agricultural Hall, 26th May, 1898.'[551a]

There have been a number of occasions upon which the particulars engraved on Crosses have had to be altered. The date given by the Horse Guards to the WO for the date of Lt Symons' Crimean exploit had been wrongly stated as 18 Oct 1854, whereas this should have been 6 Jun 1855. This Cross was retrieved by the Horse Guards, who forwarded it to the WO on 10 Feb 1858, whence it was sent to Mr Hancock for alteration, and returned to the Horse Guards on the 19th.[552] Similarly, early in 1882, Gen Dillon, the MS, wrote to the CinC Madras, regarding the VC awarded to Pte Ashford. In the *London Gazette* his Christian name had been given as John, and his Cross so engraved, whereas his name was Thomas. Dillon therefore requested the return of the Cross, so that the inscription could be corrected. However it was not returned; Sir Frederick Roberts writing on 11 Mar 1882 informed him that the Cross had been altered locally in Madras.[553] There was, however, one alteration which the WO declined to make. In 1861 Frederick Humphrey Jones, who had won the VC as Frederick

551   VCR, ii p178
551a   PRO, WO 32/7422
552   PRO, WO 32/7306
553   VCR, ii pp279/80

Whirlpool, addressed a request from Australia to be recorded under his new name. Lugard, however, informed the GOC Melbourne that he was not to have the naming on his medals altered.[554] Similarly, no action seems to have been taken when Samuel Meekosha, a VC of 1916, changed his name by deed poll to Ingham, beyond the fact being noted in the VCR, though he does not appear actually to have requested any alteration in the naming of his Cross.[555]

Not all the Crosses issued by the WO have been distributed to recipients on their gazetting. Over the years there has been a small but steady trickle of issues in different circumstances, usually to replace Crosses that have been in some way or other lost, primarily as the result of theft, though the exact circumstances do not always appear in the records. One such issue on replacement was to George Hinckley, at that time serving as Quarter Master on the *Royalist*, who lost his whilst attending a funeral at Plymouth. The WO informed the Admiralty on 23 Nov 1863 that this Cross would be replaced, subject to the Admiralty being satisfied that the conditions for replacement were complied with, at a charge to Hinckley of £1.4.0.[556] It is a little puzzling to work out how this sum was arrived at — and it remained the standard charge for replacements — since the cost of the Cross complete was £1, and Hancock's charge for engraving was 3/-. Presumably the extra shilling was to cover postage and the office work involved. The next case of loss to occur was that of Lt Aitken, already discussed,[557] though here the unusual details were that the loss occurred before he received it, for which reason he was eventually excused payment for the replacement, and that the original turned up some thirty years later. In 1868 a new Cross was forwarded to the GOC Melbourne, for transmission to Edward McKenna, whose original Cross had been stolen, the usual charge of £1.4.0. being made to him.[558] On 20 Jan 1872 the issue of a replacement Cross to William Sutton, then of the permanent staff of the Antrim Militia, was authorised, Sutton's original Cross being simply described as lost, and the usual charge made.[559] Six years later a new Cross was forwarded to the India Office for transmission to Mr W.F. McDonnell, who was then an officiating additional Judge of the High Court of Calcutta, to replace his stolen original Cross though, curiously,

554   VCR, i pp355/7
555   VCR, iii p234
556   VCR, i pp461/2 and 464/6
557   See pp200/2
558   VCR, ii pp127/9
559   *ibid*, pp134/5

in the WO letter of 4 May 1878, there is no mention of the usual payment being sought.[560] A slightly different circumstance attended the loss by Francis Fitzpatrick, since this was lost in action against the Boers at Bronkers Spruit, for which reason it was replaced in June 1881 at the public expense. Oddly enough, the original Cross was subsequently found, being returned to the MS at the WO on 18 Aug 1881, but it appears that no attempt was made to exchange this for the replacement Cross then in Fitzpatrick's possession.[561] A further Cross replaced as the result of theft was that awarded to W.J. Gordon in 1892.[562] Another slightly unusual case was that of William Bees, to whose Cross, awarded in 1901, a duplicate bar was issued in November 1929.[563] Although the words in the VCR are simply 'duplicate bar' it seems plain that what was meant was the suspender bar; one suspects that what must have led to this request was that the link by which the Cross is secured to the V on the suspender bar had worn through the V, a point at which considerable wear can often be seen in old specimens. The next actual case of theft was the Cross of Frederick Hitch, lost by him whilst he was serving as an attendant at the Royal United Services Institute in February 1901. In this case he appears to have taken no steps to secure its replacement himself, the WO letter indicating willingness to do this only being written in September 1908, in response to a letter from his son. Two unusual details in this case are that the sum Hitch was required to pay was £1.3.0, and that he was asked to sign a declaration that the new Cross would be returned to the WO should the original at any time be recovered, an undertaking that does not seem to have been asked on any similar occasion previously.[564]

A fair number of the Crosses awarded during the 1914-18 War have also been replaced. Two which were won in very close proximity to each other, those of Capts Willis and Forshaw, both harking from Gallipoli, have had to be replaced, Forshaw's on 9 Nov 1929,[565] and that of Willis on 27 Nov 1965.[566] Others lost and replaced were those to the Indian, Lala, on 1 Apr 1924,[567] that to E.J. Mott, on 9 Sep 1937,[568] and that to T.W. Holmes, on 9 Aug 1935, the only one of the cases of this period in which it is stated that replacement was on payment.[569] The only case to date of replacement of a Cross awarded

560   *ibid*, p166
561   *ibid*, p216
562   *ibid*, p362
563   VCR, iii p35
564   *ibid*, p172

565   *ibid*, p227
566   *ibid*, p225
567   *ibid*, p237
568   *ibid*, p249
569   *ibid*, p274

during the Second World War is that to the Indian, Gian Singh, which was stolen between 26 Jun and 23 Sep 1960, and was replaced on payment on 18 Sep 1961.[570]

The question of the replacement of the Cross awarded to a deceased recipient has been raised from time to time. Such a request was made by Mr Tatlock of Glasgow, in 1906. The reply sent by the WO was: 'I am commanded by the Army Council to acknowledge receipt of your letter of the 27th [of March], requesting that the Victoria Cross presented by Her late Majesty to No.3234 Sergeant McKechnie, Scots Fusilier Guards on 28th June, 1857 and which has since been lost may be replaced.

'In reply I am to acquaint you that a Cross presented to a soldier could not be replaced after his death.'[571] This would appear a definite enough ruling, but it does not seem to have been maintained in all cases. On 13 May 1922 a duplicate of the Cross issued to Pte J. McGovern, of the then 1st Bengal European Fusiliers, who seems to have died in 1891, was supplied to the Secretary of the Royal Munster Fusiliers Old Comrades' Association,[572] and on 10 Jun 1938 approval was given for replacement on payment of the Cross awarded to Capt H.M. Clogstoun, who died in 1861, the charge now being £1.13.0, to the Commandant of the Royal Deccan Horse.[573] One other such case was that of the issue of a duplicate of the Cross won by Capt L.G. Hawker, who died in 1916, to his brother on 3 Feb 1960.[574] In this case, the circumstances were exceptional; the family were living in France but fled to England on the fall of France in 1940, leaving all their belongings, including the Cross. On their return they found their possessions had been looted and the Cross among the items that had disappeared. Its loss was therefore regarded as due to enemy action and replacement eventually followed.[575]

There are a few cases where claims for replacement have been refused. In 1898 a claim from Adelaide, South Australia, for the replacement of the Cross won by Pte W. Jones at Rorke's Drift was refused, as the claimant was not the person awarded the Cross.[576] A similar fraudulent attempt to obtain a Cross seems also to be implied by the letter sent

570   VCR, iv p19
571   VCR, iii p127
572   VCR, i p210
573   VCR, iii p351
574   *ibid*, p225
575   I am indebted to Mr Ross McWhirter, Press Officer of the VC and GC Association, for this information.
576   VCR, ii p392

from the WO to an old soldier of the Royal West Kents, living in Sittingbourne, in 1904: 'I am commanded by the Army Council to acknowledge the receipt of your letter of the 15th [of February], stating that you have lost your Victoria Cross, and have offered a reward for its recovery, and in reply I am to acquaint you that there is no record of your having been awarded the Decoration in question.'[577]

A request was made in 1938 by the Royal Deccan Horse for a Cross to be issued in replacement of that awarded posthumously to Ressaidar Badlu Singh in 1918, but this was declined as the original Cross was still in the possession of Singh's son,[578] and on 30 Aug 1939 Maj D.J. McManus, son of the younger brother of the Pte McManus who had won the Cross in the Indian Mutiny, was informed that he could not be issued with a replacement of his uncle's VC as he was not next of kin as laid down in regulations.[579]

There is also a small group of issues of duplicate Crosses arising from a totally different set of circumstances, namely that the Cross which had been prepared was not in the same place as the recipient. One such case was that of Provisional L/Cpl Farmer, who was awarded the Cross for his conduct in the First Boer War in 1881. His award was gazetted on 16 May 1881, and a Cross prepared and sent out on 27th of that month for presentation by the GOC Natal. However Farmer had returned to this country before this could be carried out so a second Cross was prepared for presentation by the Queen, which she did on 2 Aug at Osborne. On 9 Jul the GOC Natal was, in consequence, requested to return the original Cross to the WO, where it arrived on the same day that the second Cross was presented, the returned Cross being kept in the MS's department at the WO.[580] Exactly the same sequence of events took place in connection with the Cross presented to QMS Marshall in 1884, the original Cross having been sent to Egypt,[581] and with that to Lt Colvin in 1898, which had been sent to India.[582] The reverse circumstances took place in connection with the Crosses presented to Lts Bell and English, and Farrier-Maj Hardham, who were each decorated with unnamed Crosses which had been taken with him by the Prince of Wales [later King George V] on 8 Jul 1902

577   VCR, iii p106
578   *ibid*, p351
579   *ibid*, p355
580   VCR, ii p241
581   *ibid*, p322
582   *ibid*, p395

during his visit to South Africa, the original Crosses being returned to the WO in Sep 1902 by, respectively, the Administrator of Western Australia, the GOC South Africa, and the Governor of New Zealand.[583] There seem to have been some other unrecorded cases of duplicate Crosses being prepared because it was noted in Sep 1907 that there were eight duplicate VCs and two forfeited Crosses in the MS branch at the WO, of which the earliest to be received was clearly that of Farmer.[584] What happened to these duplicates eventually is not clear, since they are certainly no longer there, but it seems probable that they were eventually melted down.

A strange tale of duplication surrounds the VC of Capt Charles Upham. So far as it can be disentangled, it appears that a Cross was prepared and sent out to New Zealand in 1941, but before this could be presented Upham had become a POW. On his release in the Spring of 1945 a duplicate VC was prepared, and he received this from King George VI in May 1945, the original Cross being returned from New Zealand to the WO the following month.[585] In September 1945 Upham, who had now returned to New Zealand, was gazetted for a bar to his VC. He seems to have been approached to return his Cross to have a bar added to it but, following a telegram from the Governor-General of New Zealand asking for the bar to be sent out as soon as possible for presentation, the MS department at the WO wrote to the Dominion Office on 18 Oct 1945, 'Rather than await the return of the insignia presented to Captain Upham by His Majesty at Buckingham Palace the enclosed insignia, which is a new one, has been engraved. I am, therefore, to request you will kindly arrange for the Cross already in the possession of Captain Upham to be returned to the War Office'. This new insignia was presented to Upham by the Governor-General in New Zealand, and a Cross without bar returned to London early in April 1946.

When King George VI was informed of the presentation he immediately asked why Upham had been asked to return the Cross that he [the King] had originally presented to him, and which he thought Upham might prefer to keep. Gen Wemyss, the MS, explained to Sir Alan Lascelles, the King's PS, that he had not wished to entrust the manufacture of a bar and the engraving of a second date on the Cross to an overseas firm; the returned Cross was with Hancocks, and was

583   VCR, iii p31
584   *ibid,* p162
585   PRO, WO 32/11643

untouched. On 14 May Lascelles conveyed the King's suggestion that a bar should be fitted to the returned Cross, this sent out to New Zealand, and the Governor-General exchange this for the insignia he had originally presented to Upham, explaining that this was being done at the King's personal direction. Hancocks were thereupon given the necessary instructions, but pointed out that to alter the inscription on the original Cross was not customary, and that they would prefer to put the date upon which the bar was won on the bar itself; the WO agreed that this had been a misunderstanding and that Hancocks should do as they suggested.

A break occurs in the story here, and the papers do not resume until 1957, when in April of that year the then MS, Lt-Gen Stockwell wrote to Upham regarding a VC and bar with Upham's name on them, which he had in his safe. Upham, however, was quite happy with what he had in his possession; when he had originally received the Cross and bar from the Governor-General he had in fact transferred the bar to the original Cross he had received from King George VI, so nothing needed to be done so far as he was concerned. One can only conclude that the Cross Stockwell had was the Governor-General's duplicate, that had been returned from New Zealand, and which everyone had thought was the original, to which Hancocks had added a bar at King George's suggestion, but which had not gone back to New Zealand as had been intended, on the assumption that it was the original. Stockwell at first thought it should be destroyed, but it was eventually returned to Hancocks to have the engraving erased and be returned to stock; as for the bar, Hancocks were left to deal with this as they thought fit.[586]

A very small number of Crosses have been issued in circumstances other than those so far described. On 29 Mar 1862, two VCs were forwarded at the direction of the S of S to the Secretary of the Royal United Services Institute, for the purpose of being placed in the Institute's museum[587] and specimens were sent, in each case on the request of the institutions concerned, to the British Museum, for deposit in the Department of Coins and Medals, in Jul 1892,[588] and to the Royal Mint for its museum in March 1904.[589] Another specimen was supplied to the Indian Military Academy, Dehra Dun, on 10 Jan 1939[590] and, rather surprisingly at this late date, on 5 Jan 1940, one

586   PRO, WO 32/11644
587   VCR, i p369
588   VCR, ii p361
589   VCR, iii p107
590   *ibid*, preliminary un-numbered page at the front of the volume.

was sent to the Librarian at Windsor Castle.[591] Specimens are to be seen in other official collections [there is one in the Imperial War Museum, for example] but no record of such issues seems to have been entered in the VCR from the years immediately after the First World War until 1930. Perhaps in the same light may be regarded the note of 21 Aug 1882, 'A new Victoria Cross was supplied for HRH [the Duke of Cambridge]'s collection, the one hitherto in the collection having been extracted and sent to the deceased soldier's next of kin to whom it belonged'.[592] However, issues of this nature have always been extremely sparing, and on 17 Jul 1896, Col F.W. Leckie was informed by the AMS that the VC could not be supplied by the WO on payment.[593]

591   *ibid.* This is in all probability the specimen shown in Plate 2(c).
592   VCR, ii p304
593   *ibid,* p378

Chapter 19

Difficult Cases

CASES DISCUSSED so far in this book indicate the development of particular themes in dealing with the award of the Victoria Cross. Occasionally a point of substance has been raised regarding its bestowal only in a single instance, so that there is no development to be traced. Nonetheless, these cases provide matter of considerable interest in the study of how the award of the Cross has been administered and so, for convenience, these three or four such cases are grouped together for discussion in this chapter.

The first is that of Maj R.W. Sartorius, brother of the E.H. Sartorius, whom we met in chapter 15, in connection with the award of the Cross for a gallantly performed act of duty. Major R.W. Sartorius's conduct was brought to notice by the Colonial Office in a letter to the War Office on 11 Jul 1874,[594] following his very gallant ride through the heart of the Ashanti Kingdom with a party of only some twenty men, which had brought him into Sir Garnet Wolseley's camp outside Coomassie just at the psychological moment to induce the King of Ashanti to come to terms. It was plainly his conduct in the course of this exploit that made the Colonial Secretary, Lord Carnarvon, desire to seek a VC for him, but he was equally conscious of difficulties that might arise in this particular instance. As the Colonial Office's letter said, the Colonial Secretary had been led to understand that the circumstances might not fall within the terms of the Warrant, and objections were also foreseen in that Maj Sartorius had held the chief command and had been unaccompanied by any other European, so that no adequate testimony might be held to be available as to his conduct. If, therefore, the general valour of undertaking the expedition was not acceptable, a case would be made in respect of a separate act of valour performed when he was still under the direct orders of Sir John Glover, who was in command of the naval expedition endeavouring to reach

594   PRO, WO 32/7378

Coomassie along the River Volta. Evidence of such an act could be produced, and Carnarvon hoped that this might materially strengthen Sartorius's claim to the Cross.

Mr Pennington's comment on this letter, which he gave to Mr Vivian, the PUS at this time, on 14 Jul, was typically cautious. It was, he said, the first he had heard of the case, and his reaction was to ask for the evidence which was stated to be available and judge on this. It would need a special Warrant from the Crown as the act had not been performed under the purview of the General commanding though, he added, there were precedents for this when the act was a good one but outside the terms of the Warrant, the cases of Heaphy and Kavanagh being examples. Vivian followed Pennington's advice, and the reply he suggested to the S of S was that the WO would be glad to have evidence and would reserve judgment until they had seen this.

Such a letter was evidently sent to the Colonial Office, for on 5 Sept a reply was sent by them, detailing the act of Maj Sartorius in removing to cover, under heavy fire, a Hausa NCO at the attack on Abogoo on 17 Jan 1874, before his ride had been undertaken. Pennington evidently welcomed this evidence as putting the matter on much surer ground than the ride, with its difficulties of fitting within the Warrant, and in summarising the new submission on 12 Sep stressed that there was now a personal act of gallantry for consideration, thus obviating the need of going into the matter of the ride. At this point it was time to obtain the view of the Horse Guards and this was contained in a letter from the AMS to Mr Vivian on 28 Sep. The Duke of Cambridge suggested that the Cross be conferred under the terms of the Warrant for the action at Abogoo, but would like the citation also to cover the ride to Coomassie, which made it fairly apparent what in his opinion had really earned the decoration. However on 20 Oct Gathorne Hardy, the S of S for War, ruled that it should only be recommended on the ground of the specific individual act. It was submitted to the Queen on this basis on the same day and this was the deed cited when the award of the VC was announced in the *London Gazette* of 27 Oct 1874.

The influence of Pennington, desiring to have the case brought within the specific terms of the Warrant, and avoiding hypothetical discussion of matters outside what was clearly laid down [a not uncommon trait in the Civil Service of this period] is clearly apparent in the conclusion of this story. Equally it seems clear that Lord Carnarvon had expected this type of reaction and had, from the outset, shown himself willing to put forward his recommendation in the terms most likely to avoid the obstacles he might otherwise encounter. Had he insisted that Sartorius's claim should be founded exclusively on the ride through Ashanti it is interesting to speculate what might have followed. However, it does seem reasonable to believe that it was the ride that brought the Major's conduct to notice, and certainly Sartorius himself thought this was really what he had received his Cross for,[595] that he would have been unlikely to have received the reward simply for his deed at Abogoo, and that this was very largely made use of as an excuse to bestow an award that had really been earned on another occasion, but for which there were difficulties in the way of bestowing it.

A second case meriting special consideration was that of the award of the VC to Surgeon J.F. McCrea, for his gallantry in an action against the Basutos on 14 Jan 1881, at Tweefontein, in South Africa. Here the point of substance was a political one, as the letter from the WO on 2 Jun 1881 to the Colonial Office, from whence the recommendation of McCrea's name had been forwarded, makes abundantly clear. 'I am to acquaint you', this ran, 'for the information of the Secretary of State for the Colonies, that he has under consideration your letters of 16th March and 26th April last..... recommending Surgeon J.F. McCrea.... Before, however, deciding upon this recommendation Mr Childers [the S of S for War] desires to request that you will call the attention of Lord Kimberley [the Colonial Secretary] to the fact that this act of gallantry was performed by an officer in the Colonial Forces during hostilities which were not approved by HM Government, and he would be glad to be informed whether, under the circumstances, His Lordship considers that Her Majesty should be advised to reward services so rendered.'[596]

The Colonial Office replied to this letter on 16 Jun: 'Lord Kimberley is of opinion that the fact that the policy of the Cape Government which led to the hostilities during which the act of gallantry was performed was not approved by Her Majesty's Government should not prevent Surgeon McCrea's claim from being considered on its merits'. This view was accepted by the WO, the award of the Cross being recommended to the Queen on 22 Jun, and gazetted on 28th of that month.

The fact that such an important issue of principle, that the rewarding of gallant conduct could proceed independently of any political

---

595 See 'The VC and His Dog' by Maj Eric Hebden, in the *Daily Telegraph* of 2 Nov 1967, quoting Sartorius's own papers on the subject.

596 PRO, WO 32/7403 for this letter and its reply.

consideration of the military operations in which it occurred, should have been settled with so little discussion, virtually on the simple fiat of the Colonial Secretary, is somewhat remarkable. Nor is this a purely academic point. It is, of course, impossible to go behind the scenes in relation to confidential official discussions of recent events, but rumours have reached the author from what he believes to be a well-informed source that political questions relating to the award of British decorations to Australian servicemen in Vietnam, fighting a campaign in which Britain was clearly not involved, reached a very critical point, with the British Government in 1963 declining to countenance any such awards, and the Australian authorities contemplating instituting a set of Australian awards which would parallel the British ones, yet be their own and awardable without reference to the British authorities. So there might have been an independent Australian Victoria Cross, Distinguished Service Order, Military Cross, etc, and there seems every reason to suppose that the fact this situation did not come about, and that British decorations, including the VC, were awarded in Vietnam, may owe a good deal to the precedent established in the case of Surgeon McCrea nearly ninety years previously. It is true that, at the time of the announcement of the award of the VC to Major P.J. Badcoe for bravery against the Viet Cong, a Ministry of Defence spokesman was quoted in the press as saying that there was 'nothing out of place' in such an award being made; 'The award is given for gallantry. It is as simple as that. It is open to British and Commonwealth citizens who show this kind of gallantry and has nothing to do with politics'. However, if there is one conclusion that the author would hope this work has demonstrated it is that things are rarely 'as simple as that' in the case of VC awards, and that the very denial, through its being made, is really more of an admission. Certainly, though, if politics can be finally left out of account, the precedent of 1881 lies at the root of the matter.

The third case takes us to the exploit of Capt J.R. Beech at Tokar, in the Sudan. The first intimation of what was involved here came in a Parliamentary Question tabled by Mr Labouchere for answer in the House of Commons on 9 Mar 1891: 'Whether an officer of Her Majesty's service had been recommended for the Victoria Cross on account of his conduct at the recent engagement between the Egyptian Forces and the Forces of the Mahdi at Tokar, and if so whether there is any instance of an officer in Her Majesty's service being recommended for the Victoria Cross on account of conduct in an engagement between the forces of

two powers with neither of which this country is at war?'[597]
Gen Harman, the MS, gave as his view on this, on the 7 Mar: 'No officer
has been recommended to the CinC for the VC on account of services at
Tokar. The VC has been awarded to an officer for service when he was
engaged in Basutoland [presumably he had McCrea in mind]. The VC
has never been bestowed except under the provisions of the VC
Warrant',[598] and the first sentence of this statement formed the reply
given by Edward Stanhope, the S of S for War, to Mr Labouchere
two days later. However, Labouchere was not misinformed — in fact he
was very well informed; so much so, indeed, that his question was
premature and his information ahead of that of the WO. For, on the
same day that his question was answered a recommendation was sent
forward by the Sirdar [the British officer commanding the Egyptian
Army] through the GOC British forces in Egypt, in respect of Capt
Beech, who was serving with the Egyptian Army, for his gallant conduct
on 19 Feb at the action of Tokar.[599] The political situation so far as
the presence of British troops in Egypt at this time was concerned, was
indeed complicated. Since the events of the time of Arabi Pasha in 1882
a British Army of Occupation had been maintained in Egypt proper, in
order to guarantee the bondholders of the Egyptian Debt; the finances
of Egypt, which were then of international concern, being of especial
interest to Great Britain as the result of Disraeli's purchase of the Suez
Canal Shares in 1875. Alongside this force stood the independent native
Egyptian Army which, like most of the country's institutions at that
time, had at its head and throughout its organisation a number of
British subjects, whose prime purpose was to run the body as an efficient
Egyptian organisation. To the south of Egypt proper existed the
territory of the Sudan, from whose control it had been wrested by the
Mahdi and, following the failure of the expedition to relieve General
Gordon, matters in this quarter had been regarded as falling entirely
within the scope of the Egyptian Army. As Lord Cromer, who virtually
ruled Egypt as British Consul General in the country from 1883 to 1907,
described the situation 'Although British military aid to a very limited
extent was subsequently on one or two occasions afforded to the
Egyptian Government, it may be said that from the battle of Ginniss
(December 30, 1885) the defence of Egypt against the Dervishes

597   *Hansard,* 3rd Series, cccli, col 476
598   VCR, ii p350
599   *ibid,* p351

practically devolved on the Egyptian army. That army was now officered by a well-selected body of Englishmen'.[600]

It was one of this body of Englishmen who had now distinguished himself. The papers from Egypt were sent to the MS at the WO, Gen Harman, and the whole complicated issue was gone into. The difficulty appeared to be that Clause 5 of the Warrant laid down that those eligible for the Cross 'shall *have served Us* in the presence of the Enemy', which appeared to be a bar in the present case, but it had been awarded [as has just been shown] in operations of which the Home Government disapproved, in which cases the action could hardly be said to be in the service of Her Majesty. Then, too, officers of the Egyptian army had been granted the DSO for operations in which no British troops were engaged. Also, while British forces remained in Egypt, they might be called upon at any time to assist the Egyptian army in repelling Dervish raids and it was submitted that officers of the British Army seconded for service with the Egyptians might be regarded as serving the Queen whilst so engaged.[601] On 17 Mar a minute sought the opinion of Mr Ralph Thompson, the PUS; he thought it very doubtful whether Imperial awards should be given to officers of the Egyptian Army for operations which are not conducted jointly with British troops, but asked the AG, Sir Redvers Buller, to look at the case. The next day the latter gave his opinion, 'On its merits I think Capt Beech's action [he had saved the life of an Egyptian officer with great gallantry when the latter was surrounded by Dervishes] would qualify him for the VC if it can be given, but I am disposed to think that the VC ought not to be given for an action in which Egyptian Troops alone were engaged. Some Khedival order would appear more suitable'. On the 19th Stanhope the S of S gave his ruling: 'As I understand that the AG is of opinion that this reward should not be given for an action in which Egyptian troops alone were engaged, I express my concurrence with that view, though the service performed was indubitably a gallant one'.

Curiously enough, the papers seem to have bypassed at this stage the Duke of Cambridge. On 1 Apr, Harman wrote to Thompson, 'HRH has now seen this recommendation that Captain J.R. Beech, CMG, 20th Hussars, should be awarded the VC for his conspicuous gallantry at the action of Tokar. HRH considers this one of the most deserving cases for this honourable distinction that has ever been brought to his notice

600   Lord Cromer, *Modern Egypt,* ii p60
601   All these arguments are to be found in PRO, WO 32/7414

and as this was an individual act on the part of a British officer he considers that the fact of his having been at the time lent for service to HH the Khedive and performing service with Egyptian Troops only, should not be a bar to his receiving this coveted award, as the gallantry was personal and independent of the general operations that were directed under the orders of the Khedive.

'In regard to any other decoration that may have been deserved by British officers serving with the Egyptian Army at the operations against Tokar, HRH considers that they may well be limited to those HH the Khedive may be pleased to award.'[602]

In these circumstances the only possible way of proceeding was to consider the Duke of Cambridge's remarks as an appeal against the S of S's decision, and the papers were resubmitted to him on this basis. On 1 May Stanhope gave his final verdict: 'After much consideration and some consultation with my colleagues I have reluctantly come to the conclusion that this cannot be granted. I am sorry to have to refuse it after the warm terms in which it is recommended by HRH but I cannot distinguish it from other decorations sufficiently to say that it ought to be given for a service performed with the Egyptian Army in an operation in which British troops were not engaged'.[603] This decision was conveyed to the GOC in Egypt by Gen Harman in a letter dated 4 Jun 1891: 'Sir, I am directed by HRH the CinC to acknowledge the receipt of your letter of the 9th March 1891, forwarding for favourable consideration the recommendation of the Sirdar of the Egyptian Army that the services of Captain J.R. Beech, CMG, 20th Hussars (attached to the Egyptian Army) rendered at the action of Tokar should be rewarded with the decoration of the Victoria Cross.

'In reply, I am to acquaint you that HRH fully recognises the great gallantry displayed by Captain Beech, and through which the life of Millazim Awal Ali eff Kamil of the Egyptian Army was saved.

'The character of Captain Beech's action was such as in the opinion of HRH to qualify him for the distinction for which he has been recommended, and could such decoration be awarded for it, and it is therefore, with extreme regret that HRH is obliged to acquaint you that it has been decided that the decoration of the VC cannot be awarded for a service performed with the Egyptian Army in an operation in which no British Troops were engaged.

'HRH is, however, much gratified to have been able to mark his high

602   VCR, ii pp351/2 for all the above-mentioned documents
603   PRO, WO 32/7414

appreciation of Captain Beech's distinguished service by recommending
him for the Distinguished Service Order, which HM has been graciously
pleased to confer upon him.'[604]

Perhaps the most remarkable feature of this case is the concluding
sentence of this letter. The logic of the objections to the award of the
VC in the particular circumstance of service with the Egyptian Army
may be conceded, but this would appear to be an objection, not to the
conferment of this particular decoration, but to *any* British decoration
in these circumstances, and Buller's suggestion of a Khedival award
seems far and away the most reasonable. Yet, having built up the case
in logic that they had, the WO then allowed the whole of the argument
to be destroyed, by the granting of another British award, the DSO!

The confusion on this point is still further deepened by the events of
eight years later when, following the battle of Omdurman and fall of
Khartoum, a force under Col Parsons but evidently, from contemporary
accounts, consisting entirely of Egyptian Army units,[605] completed the
expulsion of the Dervish forces from Gedarif Province by the capture
of its capital after a fierce engagement on 22 Sep 1898. During this
action Capt the Hon A.G.A. Hore-Ruthven, in command of the Camel
Corps detachment, saved the life of an Egyptian officer, who was lying
in the path of the advancing Dervishes, and was recommended for the
VC, the recommendation having been passed from the AG of the
Egyptian Army to the Chief Staff Officer of the British Army of
Occupation in Egypt, who forwarded it to the WO in January 1899.[606]
When the papers went before the S of S, at this time the Marquess of
Lansdowne, it was pointed out that Hore-Ruthven was not serving in
his capacity of Captain in the 3rd (Militia) Battalion of the Highland
Light Infantry, but as an officer in the Egyptian Army, and it was a
matter for determination whether his case was within the scope of the
Warrant. Despite this note, however, and the previous case of Capt
Beech, Lord Lansdowne seems to have had no hesitation in giving his
approval to the submission, which he did on 18 Feb, four days after the
papers had been sent forward, and without any comment whatsoever.
It has often been stated that Hore-Ruthven was the first Militia Officer
to win the Cross under the Warrant of April 1881 and, indeed, this
statement was made at one stage as the papers were going through the
WO, but this was far from the truth and speedily corrected. In fact, he

604   VCR, ii pp355/6
605   See *The Times* of 26 Sep 1898
606   PRO, WO 32/7425 for the whole of this paragraph

had applied for leave of absence in order to miss the annual training of his unit and proceed to Egypt as an entirely personal move; but this application had apparently miscarried and he had accordingly been recorded as absent without leave from annual training, and was due to be gazetted out of his regiment on this account unless he resigned his commission. As a result of his conduct at Gedarif it was decided to excuse his absence from training, but it is quite clear that in no sense could he be considered as serving with his battalion whilst in the Sudan.

The reason for this change in policy since 1891 can only be guessed at, since there is no evidence of the sort of discussion to be expected if such a change was made consciously. Yet the root question in the matter had been pointed out to Lansdowne, so he had not given his approval in ignorance. Lansdowne may well have been disposed to regard the action at Gedarif as forming part of what was an essentially British campaign, for the reconquest of the Sudan and so, in a very different light from what at Tokar had been more in the nature of a defensive frontier engagement and, as Cromer had pointed out, the maintenance of this frontier prior to the reconquest had been definitely regarded as a purely Egyptian concern. The basis upon which the 1898 expedition had been undertaken was made perfectly clear in the letter Lord Salisbury, the Prime Minister, had written to Cromer on 2 Aug 1898, when Omdurman still lay ahead, but the impending British control of the Sudan was clearly forseeable. 'You will, however, explain to the Khedive and to his ministers that the procedure I have indicated is intended to emphasize the fact that Her Majesty's Government consider that they have a predominant voice in all matters connected with the Sudan, and that they expect that any advice which they may think fit to tender to the Egyptian Government in respect to Sudan affairs, will be followed.'[607] Cromer himself summarized the political situation in connection with these operations as follows. 'It is true that the Egyptian Treasury had borne the greater portion of its cost, and that Egyptian troops, officered, however, by Englishmen, had taken a very honourable part in the campaign. But, alike during the period of the preparation and of the execution of the policy, the guiding hand had been that of England..... [though] the campaign had throughout been carried out in the name of the Khedive.'[608] So there was every reason for Lansdowne

607   Gooch, Temperley and Penson, *British Documents on the Origins of the War,*
         1898-1914, London 1927, i, p159
608   *Modern Egypt,* ii p113. The politics of the 1898 expedition are dealt with in
         Chapter 33 of this work generally.

to regard the campaign as a whole as a British exploit, and the fact that only Egyptian units were present on the particular occasion as no bar to the award of the Cross. However, an additional factor almost certainly lies in the changed personnel involved at the WO. Lansdowne's predecessor, Stanhope, would clearly have liked to have allowed Beech's recommendation for the VC to go forward, and might indeed have done so if he had not been so strongly advised against, the chief quarter from which this advice had come being the AG, Sir Redvers Buller. It must have made a considerable difference to Lansdowne's position that Buller no longer occupied this post, so that the balance of opinion by which he would have been advised was clearly very different from what it had been on the earlier occasion.

Chapter 20

Views on the Cross and Standards for Award

IT WAS STRESSED at the outset of this work that, at its institution, the Victoria Cross represented a personal reward for an individual act of valour, available regardless of rank or any extraneous circumstance. This implies that there was another view of the acts for which it was awarded, but what this other view comprised has not been examined. One indication of its nature has already been given[609] by the view attributed to Lord Clyde that it was unnecessary in the British Army, whose soldiers, he thought, required restraining rather than egging on to brave deeds. Much the same view was being expressed by the Duke of Cambridge in the case of the recommendation of the award of the Cross to Lt J.A. Tytler; this, he explained, he forwarded to the War Office in view of its being strongly recommended by the Commander in Chief in India, 'who, it is to be presumed, has satisfied himself as to the case and that the circumstances at the moment required such an example to be set by the Officer in question; otherwise the act of an Officer dashing on horseback ahead of all the Troops and alone up to the Enemy's Guns, though it may be admired for its gallantry can scarcely, in His Royal Highness's opinion, be approved'.[610] Here one is getting a little closer to a full statement of the very real professional criticism that the VC did provoke among the military men of the day. Curiously enough, on the evening of the very day that the Duke of Cambridge was penning these words, 30 Jul 1858, a debate was to take place in the House of Commons in which the view was fully displayed.[611] It was not, as might be supposed, simply a wish to discourage foolhardiness, though this came into it. As Lord Elcho said, 'Under the terms on which the

609   See p104
610   PRO, WO 32/7314
611   *Hansard,* 3rd Series, CLI, cols 2360/7

order was instituted such a man as Sir John Inglis, for example, would not be entitled to the Victoria Cross, but any bombardier under him would, who took up a live shell and threw it away, not, it might be, knowing the danger to which he was exposing himself. In point of fact,' he went on, 'the Victoria Cross had a direct tendency to induce young men in the army to do things – gallant they might be, but still rash and *contrary to discipline* – in the hope of obtaining the reward and honour which it conferred'. This, then, was the real substance of the criticism, that the man stepping out of line to perform the sort of act for which the Cross was being awarded was breaking the strict military discipline which the professionals at that time conceived [despite the evidence of the failures produced when it had been applied in the Crimea, and the numerous occasions upon which its absence was then saving the situation in the Indian Mutiny] as the strength of the Army. Gen Codrington, who followed Lord Elcho in the debate, quoted [though not with full approval], the Duke of Cambridge's immediate predecessor as CinC to this effect: 'Lord Hardinge said that the great object in the English army should be to preserve the correct formation of regiments and brigades in line, and not to encourage officers to step out of the line and mar its completeness for the purpose of signalizing themselves by some special action of gallantry; and an order of this sort which was given for such actions might have its inconveniences'. Sir William Fraser spoke to the same effect. He 'feared the institution of the Victoria Cross might have a slightly detrimental effect on the service. The great principle advocated by the late Duke of Wellington for the English army, which, he said, would have gone anywhere and done anything, was the principle of duty. Of all the dispatches written by that great man there was not one in which the word "glory" did occur, or in which the word "duty" did not occur. Such was the mode of modern warfare that it was next to impossible for an officer of any rank to obtain the honour of the Victoria Cross, and he doubted whether its being attainable by subalterns, corporals and men of the line would not lead them to neglect duty in the pursuit of glory'.

However, such views clearly represented a dying creed. The mere institution of the Cross itself shows this, and this is further emphasised by the resistance that was long expressed to the award of the Cross for anything which could be considered an act of duty.[612] In fact, had the two concepts been taken to their logical extreme, no cases could have arisen for the award of the VC, since on the one hand a soldier would

612   See Chapter 15

be precluded from doing anything which lay outside his duty, as this disrupted the strict rule of discipline, whilst on the other no act of duty, no matter how gallantly performed, was held to qualify for the Cross. But, of course, the matter was never argued to these lengths of logic, as will be apparent from the fact that Cambridge himself can be cited as a proponent of both of these doctrines. The general tenor of opinion was, increasingly, that individual acts of gallantry were to be applauded and rewarded, but the older attitude lingered on for some time. In 1879 a newspaper comment on the fighting at Kabul observed 'Perhaps a too great eagerness to win the Victoria Cross may have had some share in bringing about this regrettable loss among the commissioned ranks. To "go in for the Cross" now forms the chief opening for personal distinction in the case of regimental officers, as official despatches generally confine their praises and recommendations for promotion to staff officers',[613] which represents a not dissimilar train of thought from that of the Commons debate of 1858. Similarly the assertion that Capt Duck, of the Veterinary Corps was recommended for the VC by Col Buller for his gallantry in action during the retreat following the disastrous defeat at the Zlobane Mountain in March 1879, when taking a dead man's rifle he volunteered his services with the rear guard and rendered excellent service at a most critical moment, only to have his name struck out by the Supreme Commander on the grounds that he had no right to be there,[614] if well-founded, also seems to echo the emphasis on the maintenance of strict discipline voiced by the speakers in that same debate.

For those who accepted the thinking that had led to the institution of the Cross, a quite different issue arose to exercise their minds. This was that the new award might be cheapened. This fear seems to have been very present with Sir Edward Lugard, the PUS at the time of the disturbances in New Zealand in the 1860s. When the award of the Cross to Leading Seamen Odgers was cited by the CO of the 65th Regt as grounds for conferring the decoration on L/Cpl Ficrook 'as being the first man who entered the far more stubbornly defended position of Mahoetahi', Lugard's comment to the S of S, Lord Herbert, who concurred with it, was 'I do not see sufficient grounds for granting the distinction − indeed the practice of giving it on every petty occasion *lowers the character* of the decoration'.[615] This view was

613   *The Globe*, 15 Dec 1879
614   Maj-Gen Sir Frederick Smith, *A History of the Royal Army Veterinary Corps, 1796-1919*, London 1927, p198
615   PRO, WO 32/7354

expressed in February 1861; three years later, in putting forward five further VC recommendations, again arising from events in New Zealand, Lugard's note to the new S of S, Lord de Grey, in August 1864, read 'Approve? According to precedent these Offrs. and men are entitled to the Cross — but I regret to say it is losing its value in the Army, being looked upon in the light of a medal from the R. Humane Society, instead of a reward for heroic bravery, in leading a forlorn hope, or other daring act, leading to important Military results'.[616] It may be of some interest to mention that the recommendations in question were in respect of Lt Pickard, Assistant Surgeon Temple, Ensign Down, Drummer Stagpoole and Assistant Surgeon Manley, and all did in fact receive the Cross. In the following March he was expressing very similar views to Lord de Grey on the case of Maj Heaphy, 'The Victoria Cross, I regret to say, is not what it was originally intended to be, owing to the extraordinary recommendations made by the Horse Guards for it in cases where a Humane Society Medal would have been appropriate...'[617]

It may be objected that all this evidence relates exclusively to the operations in New Zealand which were, it is true, on quite a small scale, and that Lugard's concern was something of a special case, arising from a reluctance on his part to accept this particular campaign as one of sufficient military significance to justify the grant of the Cross in connection with it. That there is something in such a view may be conceded, but it was by no means the only instance in which such views were expressed. Some fifteen years later the awards of the Zulu War drew a press comment, 'Beyond all question the Cross will be cheapened if it is to be conferred upon every man who puts his powers of physical endurance to their proper use, and carries through the particular service mainly by the natural conduct of a well-balanced act..... It must be confessed that the military authorities in Pall Mall have shown a lavish prodigality in the distribution of the Victoria Cross which would probably startle their contemporaries in Berlin..... We say there is a chance of the Victoria Cross being cheapened by a too friendly eagerness in Pall Mall to recognise acts of equivocal valour'.[618] Less than two months after this was published the Duke of Cambridge commented, when the recommendation came before him, for the award of the VC to Acting Assistant Commissary Dalton for his conduct at

616   PRO, WO 32/7367
617   PRO, WO 32/7370
618   *The Broad Arrow,* 23 Aug 1879. The reference to Berlin is an allusion to the Iron Cross, which at that time was awarded with proverbial sparingness.

Rorke's Drift, 'We are giving the VC very freely, I think'[619] – though it is perhaps only fair to the Duke to mention that this was the tenth recommendation to come before him for this exploit, and that the total number of VCs bestowed on that occasion – eleven – on a force whose effective strength was probably of the order of a hundred [the exact figure is very variously quoted], does represent the most lavish distribution ever, even though posterity's judgement of the defence of Rorke's Drift has tended to vindicate this generosity. At the time when the drafting of the Warrant of April 1881 was under discussion, Queen Victoria had also expressed her concern lest the award might become too common,[620] so Lugard's opinion was evidently fairly widespread.

An instance in which a desire to maintain standards in a somewhat different sense could have impeded a recommendation for the VC is to be found in the case of Colour-Sgt Booth, concerning his conduct on the occasion of the Zulu attack on the Imtombi River on 12 Mar 1879. This matter was brought to notice as the result of three of the survivors of the action forwarding their testimony to Lord Wolseley, the GOC, 'to be of service to Colour-Sergeant Booth', on 20 Dec of that year. This was followed by a recommendation from Booth's CO, Col Tucker, for a DCM, evidently as the result of an enquiry from Wolseley regarding the testimony he had received. Tucker explained his reason for not previously having brought the matter to notice was that to do so would have entailed bringing to light the 'far different conduct of Lt Harward', Booth's exploit having lain very largely in rallying the men of the detachment under Harwood's command after the Lieut had left it. These papers were all forwarded by Wolseley to the WO on 26 Dec 1879, with his own opinion that a VC had been earned. A recommendation to this effect was submitted to the Queen on 20 Feb 1880 and the award of the VC gazetted on 24th, but it is interesting to note that the wording of the published citation makes no reference whatever to the dereliction of duty by Lt Harward which had been the occasion for Colour-Sgt Booth to earn his award in rallying the detachment.[621]

Some concern was evidently caused at the WO by a letter which appeared, over the signature 'Vetus', in *The Times* of 5 Nov 1891, in the course of which appeared the statement 'Writing two years ago, he [Lord Wolseley] alludes to the many who obtain it [the Victoria Cross]

619   PRO, WO 32/7386
620   See p165
621   PRO, WO 32/7388

by asking for it, and by enlarging upon their own deeds of heroism in order to get it'. Evidently this was regarded as a very deep slight on the now accepted standards for the VC, and Gen Harman, the MS, wrote to the PUS on 1 Dec, 'I can find nothing to in any way justify the statement made in enclosed extract of letter signed "Vetus". HRH believed them to be entirely unwarranted. As Lord Wolseley is referred to would the Sec of State wish the question passed to him'.[622] However, this last suggestion does not seem to have been adopted – at any rate no comment by Wolseley on the allegation appears to survive.

The reaction to the letter in *The Times* in 1891 indicates that the standard of conduct for the VC had now been fully established. In fact, there is some evidence from the South African War that COs had become too reluctant to put forward recommendations. A report which appeared in *The Times* of 7 Jan 1901 led Brodrick, the S of S for War, to ask Sir Ian Hamilton why no recommendation had been received in respect of the conduct of Lt Masterson, which had been described in the newspaper account. To this Sir Ian replied, 'It is quite true that Lt Masterson performed the gallant feat of arms described in *The Times* of 7th January. The incident would most certainly have been informally brought to Sir George White's notice, but I should not be surprised to learn that no formal recommendation for special reward had been put forward. My reason for saying this is that I remember Col Park of the Devons was always over-modest in making recommendations and that after Elandslaagte I had to return him his report in order that names might be added, so as to bring his mentions up to something approaching the standard set by other corps'.[623] Sir Ian went on to suggest that this might be a case for the VC, and the letter went to the CinC with Brodrick's endorsement to the same effect. In fact Sir Ian's explanation regarding Col Park was not the true one, for two months later a letter reached the Brigade Major at Lydenburg, enquiring as to the fate of the recommendation Park had submitted via Sir Ian, and it was confirmed that Sir George White had received it. Sir Ian had later to admit, in a further letter to Brodrick, that he had received and endorsed a letter to this effect, but the matter had gone no further, because it had not been followed up by a formal recommendation [apparently he did not regard Park's letter in this light] and 'It was not the business of the Natal Army HQ to worry over the matter'. Masterson's VC was finally gazetted on 4 Jun 1901.

622   VCR, ii p356
623   PRO, WO 32/7462

Certainly, the South African War had a good deal to do with establishing the exalted standards of the VC. To some extent the standards that were now being required were even over-strict. In the case of Capt Schofield, one of those to show marked gallantry in saving the guns at Colenso, Gen Buller wrote, on 16 Dec 1899, 'I have differentiated in my recommendations because I thought that a recommendation for the VC required proof of initiative, something more in fact than mere obedience to orders and for this reason I have not recommended Captain Schofield, Royal Artillery, who was acting under orders, though I desire to record his conduct as most gallant',[624] this incidentally, occurring in the latter in which he did recommend Roberts, Congreve, Nurse and Reed for the Cross. A reply went from the MS to Gen Buller on 31 Jan, pointing out that the Warrant of April 1881 was held to permit its award, for marked gallantry in the performance of duty. 'In these circumstances' the letter continued, 'I am to suggest that it is for your consideration whether you are now in a position to recommend Captain H.N. Schofield for the grant of the VC.' Despite this pretty clear indication of the WO view of the matter, Buller did not feel he could change his view. Lord Roberts was strongly of the opinion that Schofield merited the award, and matters were even taken to the length of obtaining the view of Capt Congreve, one of those who had obtained the VC on that occasion; his view being that if anyone had earned the Cross, then Schofield certainly had, and that if it was a matter of acting under orders, then so equally were Lt Roberts and himself. The matter was only brought to a conclusion when the question of Colenso awards was reopened in April 1901 with the release of Pte Ravenhill from captivity as a POW, and the subsequent bringing to notice of his conduct at Colenso, which was also considered worthy of the VC. On receiving these papers Brodrick noted them, 'If another VC is given for Colenso ought not Capt Schofield to receive it?' and Lord Roberts, now CinC replied, 'I think that Pte Ravenhill and Captain Schofield should both get the VC for their actions in endeavouring to save the guns at Colenso. I was reading Sir Redvers Buller's dispatch again the other day and intended to bring Major Schofield's conduct to your notice'.[625] It was on the action of these two, more or less over the head of Gen Buller, that Schofield did finally receive his VC.

---

624 PRO, WO 32/7470 and for the remainder of this paragraph except where otherwise indicated.

625 PRO, WO 32/7469

On the other hand, the South African War was not without its imputation, at a high level, of something akin to favouritism in the selection of those to be recommended. Following the battle of Elandslaagte, which had been very much the affair of the 2nd Bn The Gordon Highlanders, Gen Sir George White, himself a former Gordon Highlander, forwarded nine recommendations for the VC, five of which were from this battalion. General Buller, through whom the recommendations passed as GOC, Natal, made the somewhat derogatory comment, 'I am constrained to remark that I fail to understand the principle upon which Sir G. White has based his selections for the Victoria Cross unless it is that the fact of being in a certain regiment raises a special claim'. Lord Robert's rebuttal of this insinuation − 'I cannot agree with Sir Redvers Buller in thinking that the Gordon Highlanders have been unduly favoured in the nominations put forward..... Whatever names may have been submitted to him by Sir George White for the Victoria Cross I feel confident that the respective claim of each officer and man was carefully and impartially considered, and that his selection was in no way influenced by his former association with the Gordon Highlanders' − whilst being in so many words a tribute to Sir George was also, by implication a testimony to the esteem of the Cross.[626]

Some suggestion of favouritism may possibly be read into Lord Roberts' comments on the recommendations submitted for the VC in respect of Lts Bell and English, and Farrier-Maj Hardham, for whom Gen Hamilton had suggested DSOs and a DCM, on the grounds that he scarcely thought them VC cases, although the favouritism he inclined to was defensible. His comment on these cases was 'I would give the VC as recommended by Lord Kitchener. He is not likely to do this unless he was satisfied that it was deserved. Moreover it seems to me desirable to show the Colonials that we appreciate their gallantry [Bell was from Australia and Hardham from New Zealand] and their coming forward to help us. We may require them to do so again perhaps ere long'.[627]

An example of strictness in interpretation of the terms of the Warrant is to be found in the case of the recommendation of the award of the Cross to Trooper Henderson of the Buluwayo Field Force, submitted by the Colonial Office [and also by the Rhodesia Chartered Company] in 1897. Henderson's exploit consisted in bringing a wounded companion to safety through thirty-five miles of country full of armed natives, following the ambush of a party of troops by these natives. On

626   PRO, WO 32/7899
627   PRO, WO 32/7464

10 Mar 1897 the query was raised in a letter from the WO to the Colonial Office as to whether Henderson had actually shown bravery under fire — 'the statement that the return journey was mostly affected by night would seem to point to the endeavour having been to avoid the enemy as much as possible..... [in which circumstances] it would not..... come within those actions which can be rewarded with the decoration'.[628] However, the Colonial Office was evidently able to deal with this objection to the satisfaction of the WO, for the award of the VC to Trooper Henderson was duly gazetted on 7 May 1897, the citation containing the statement that 'they had, therefore, to proceed principally by night, hiding in the bush in the daytime'.

It is in the light of such cases as these that can be seen the justification for Admiral Everett's remark in his letter of 7 Aug 1918, already quoted,[629] 'the standard of valour and devotion to duty for the Victoria Cross is now very much higher than it was in the earlier years of its introduction. In fact, it may be said that the standard now required for the award of a VC is far, far, higher than the actual words [of the Warrant] express'. However, in the view of Col Graham, the DMS at the WO at this time, the final elevation of standards was only to be attributed to the Great War; 'You cannot compare the VC in this war with any previous war, because people are getting the MM now for what would have won the VC in the South African War'.[630] Graham's imperfections as an interpreter of the past records of his department have already been pointed out,[631] and his actual words here no doubt contain a substantial element of exaggeration. Nevertheless, as testimony to the fact that a considerable raising of requirements had taken place, they may be accepted. The reference to the Military Medal is significant; formerly there had been only two grades of award for gallantry; the VC as the superior, and the DSO and DCM (or CGM for the Navy) as the inferior. With the introduction of a third grade (MC, MM, DSC, DSM) inferior to both, some tendency to elevate the standards of both the superior grades was to be expected. Similarly, even though, as the cases of its award quoted in this book have shown, the award of the DSO was often in circumstances somewhat distinct from those of the VC, its institution in 1886 must have contributed to the upgrading of the requirements for the Cross. However, due to the fact that for most of

628 VCR, ii pp381/3
629 See pp172/3
630 See p174
631 See Chapter 16

the first thirty years of its existence citations for the award of the DSO simply took the form, 'For services in such and such operations', it is difficult to compare the circumstances in which the two decorations were awarded in any great detail.

Comment has frequently been made on the strong humanitarian element in awards of the Cross, with reference to the number of citations in which the recipient's exploit has involved bringing succour to the wounded. On examination, however, official thinking on such exploits proves to have been somewhat complex. The first comment of interest in this connection arose in the case of Lord William Beresford, who was recommended for the Cross [which he received] for turning to assist Sgt Fitzmaurice, whose horse had fallen with him, during the retirement of a reconnoitring party which was closely beset by hostile Zulus. When the papers came before Col Evelyn Wood, as column commander, he forwarded these to Lord Chelmsford with the comment 'Staying near the enemy to help a wounded man in Europe and in Zululand presents all the difference of a captivity more or less irksome in the one case and in the other the almost certainty of painful death, accompanied by atrocious mutilations',[632] from which one may conclude that succouring the wounded, of itself, and not involving exceptional risk, would not have commended itself to Wood as a ground for recommendation. On the other hand it could be, and was, argued that to save wounded men from falling into the hands of a barbaric enemy was an act of duty. When, following the Mohmand operations on the North West Frontier in 1908, VC recommendations were submitted in respect of Lt G.F. Waterworth, 2/Lt W. Platt and Pte H. Lloyd, together with DCM recommendations for five other rankers, all for their part in bringing in wounded in a rearguard action, the CGS objected that bringing in the wounded was a matter of obligation on the Frontier, and that doing one's plain duty in this fashion was hardly a special act of valour or devotion in the terms of the Warrant. This view prevailed and both officers who, it was conceded, had acted well, were granted the DSO, and all six rankers received the DCM.[633]

A slightly different demur was voiced by Lord Kitchener in forwarding a list of recommendations, one only of which he himself supported, though one other was selected by Brodrick and Roberts as worthy of the Cross. In his accompanying letter of 26 Jun 1901 he wrote, 'I think that some steps should be taken to discourage recommendations for the

632   PRO, WO 32/7382
633   PRO, WO 32/7506

Victoria Cross in civilised warfare in cases of mere bringing in of wounded and dismounted men. The case of Lt Price, herewith forwarded, well exemplifies my point; his efforts to bring in Lt Delmahay and Pte Sheddon resulted in the former being again wounded and the latter killed'.[634] Lt Price, incidentally, did not receive the VC, though he is presumably the same man as the Capt B.G. Price on whom a DSO was conferred ten days after the announcement of the award of the VC to Lt Dugdale and Sgt Traynor, whose names had figured in the list.

Evidently Kitchener was not alone in his view, for on 3 Sep 1902 Sir Ian Hamilton noted, in forwarding the recommendation for the award of the VC to Pte William House [which he received], 'I have usually objected to VCs being awarded for "rescuing" wounded men in civilised war when (if they lay quite still) they were probably safer than being rescued. But the particular coolness of this man as evinced by his warning the others not to follow his example [which was specifically referred to in the published citation] is very commendable and I would gladly see him get the decoration'.[635]

Nor did this attitude disappear after the South African War. On 30 Sep 1914, Sir Douglas Haig noted, on the recommendation for the VC submitted in respect of L/Cpl Dobson [who was awarded it], 'I fully appreciate the bravery shown..... but I am not in favour of this coveted reward being granted for bringing in wounded officers or men in European Warfare'.[636] This view was presumably communicated to Sir John French, at this time Haig's immediate superior, and he gave his opinion on the general issue in some detail in a letter to the WO on 25 Nov 1914: 'I have the honour to inform you that I am in agreement with the view that the Victoria Cross should not be awarded for the rescue of wounded in the case of officers unless under very exceptional circumstances.

'As regards men, I think it should be awarded, but in making recommendations I have been guided by the facts of the case. For instance the rescue of a wounded man lying exposed to fire between two trenches, or in a retreat, where a rescue has been made on the sole initiative of the non-commissioned officer or private are cases in which recommendations would be given.

'I am, however, quite willing to be guided by any ruling which may

634   PRO, WO 32/7463
635   PRO, WO 32/7482
636   PRO, WO 32/4993

be given, as no doubt the present system tends to lack uniformity.'[637]

There is no evidence that any such ruling was given and, due to the virtually complete 'weeding' [i.e. destruction] of all War Office files on First World War VC awards from 1915 on, it is not possible to study the detailed development of opinion on this point. However, from a perusal of the VC citations published in the *London Gazette* for the remainder of the War it would seem that the line of thought indicated in this letter may well have been followed in practice.

A further criterion for evaluating recommendations for the VC appears to have been introduced in the early days of the Second World War by the then MS, Maj-Gen Floyer-Acland. When the recommendation in respect of Sgt N.G. Leakey came before him he did not consider this of the required standard and, as will be recalled,[638] his view at that time prevailed. However, he also made observations in more general terms, which are of interest, 'Although Sgt Leakey certainly displayed great gallantry I regard his action as of the spontaneous nature, lacking the elements of long sustained courage and endurance which tell of the highest form of self-sacrifice'.[639] In another case which arose at much the same time, that of Cpl J.H. Edmondson, he expressed similar reservations but also indicated what he might consider as countervailing grounds. 'In offering my opinion in connection with recommendations for the Victoria Cross I am guided to a great extent by the answer to the question of whether the act was of a spontaneous nature and of short duration or a long sustained effort of great courage and determination.

'In this case the act was evidently of the spontaneous character. On the other hand, it is fair to assume that Edmondson would have realised that, having been wounded in the stomach, his chances of survival were negligible unless he immediately refrained from further activity and received early medical attention. Not to mention the pain that he must have been suffering, there is a definite element of very courageous self-sacrifice in this case and, taking all circumstances into account, I am prepared to advise the award of the Victoria Cross.'[640] The recommendation for Edmondson's VC went before King George VI on 29 Jun 1941 and was gazetted on 4 July. Due to the scarcity of Second World War VC material that has become available, it is difficult

637   *ibid*
638   See p223
639   PRO, WO 32/9955
640   PRO, WO 32/9956

to assess how far Floyer-Acland's criteria were followed, but one's impression from reading Second World War citations is that his reluctance to accept the spontaneous act was not made a general principle. To some extent it represents a harking back to the reservations of Lord Elcho in respect of the ignorant bombardier over eighty years previously. But, whilst one can readily accept that the act of long sustained courage and devotion is of an even higher quality than what Gen Floyer-Acland described as 'the spontaneous act', there is nothing in the Warrants which would justify regarding the latter as of insufficient quality for the award of the Victoria Cross.

Chapter 21

The Honour of the Victoria Cross

THE VICTORIA CROSS, when instituted, was something very novel, an individual award which, not being an order of chivalry, conferred no personal precedence on its holders, nor, incidentally, did it incorporate any such feature of social distinction as has been the case in some foreign awards, such as entitling ranker recipients to receive a salute. However, Queen Victoria was evidently struck by the idea that its recipients should receive some honorific mark, for on 29 Jun 1857, three days after she had pinned the Crosses on the first batch of recipients in Hyde Park, she remarked, in the course of a letter to Lord Panmure, 'The Queen thinks the persons decorated with the Victoria Cross might very properly be allowed to bear some distinctive mark after their name. The Warrant instituting the decoration does not style it an order, but merely "a Naval and Military decoration", and a distinction; nor is it, properly speaking, an order, being not *constituted*. VC would not do. KG means a Knight of the Garter; CB, a Companion of the Bath; MP, a Member of Parliament; MD a Doctor of Medicine, etc, etc — in all cases denoting a person. No one could be called a Victoria Cross. VC, moreover, means Vice-Chancellor at present. DVC, decorated with the Victoria Cross, or BVC, bearer of the Victoria Cross, might do. The Queen thinks the last the best'.[641]

Lord Panmure replied to this letter on 2 Jul[642] but, curiously enough, made no reference to the subject of the VC, and in fact appears never to have discussed with the Queen this particular subject of the use of initials after their names by VC holders. Certainly, from 1858 on the Army List printed an Old English 'VC' *before* the names of all recipients, following the analogy of its treatment of Waterloo Medallists, who had always been indicated by an Old English 'W' in the same place. However, nothing seems to have been laid down officially regarding the

641　*Panmure Papers,* ii, pp398/9
642　Royal Archives, E9/68

use of initials after their names by recipients and, despite the very logical reasoning of the Queen's letter, it was the simple 'VC' which soon crept into popular usage.

One point on which the peculiar usage of the Army List gave no lead, however, was the position of these initials among others. A general principle often held was that the correct sequence was (1) orders (2) decorations (3) medals, so that a man who held both the CB, [which is an order] and the VC, [neither an order or a medal, so a decoration] — a not uncommon circumstance in the later 19th century, would on that basis style himself 'CB, VC'. But even at that time there was some notion of the primacy of the Cross and even in WO documents of the period one is as likely to find 'VC' preceding 'CB' as the reverse. Matters were even further confused by the institution in 1886 of the Distinguished Service Order which was in name an order, and so entitled to precedence, yet clearly an inferior in the standard of conduct required for its award.

It seems that it was at the time of the coronation of King George V, when a large number of formal documents were circulating, listing numerous dignitaries with all their awards after their names that the question became acute, the matter being raised as one for decision in November 1911. It then appeared that the Admiralty favoured adopting the practice of putting the VC after all orders, or else that the King's Pleasure should be taken; the WO practice at the time was to put the VC in front of all orders, whereas *Burke's Peerage* did the reverse.[643] The MS's view was that the King's Pleasure should be taken; the AG thought it seemed logical that the order of letters should accord with the precedence of the awards; the CGS asked why there was any need to consult the King further in view of what had been settled in the 1904 *Dress Regulations* [which related to the order in which decorations should be worn, a topic to be considered presently], the Quartermaster General echoed this in pointing out that the new dress regulations had just been settled by the King. Mr Brade, the Assistant Secretary, then went to discuss the matter with the College of Heralds. This was a source to which the WO had just previously turned for advice on the marshalling of honours in the order of the Coronation procession published in the *London Gazette*; but, unfortunately the instructions then issued had not been followed, so that the *Gazette* had printed such inconsistencies as The Earl of Dunmore, MVO, VC, and Earl Roberts VC, KG, KP, etc. There was, Brade found, no precedent in the VC

643   PRO, WO 32/7497, and for all this paragraph

Warrant, but the instruments of the orders did lay down precedence, so from this one could argue that they should take precedence. As he pointed out also, the *Dress Regulations* did not settle styling, only wearing.

It was hardly surprising that, in this welter of confusion, Mr Brade should do as suggested, and take the King's Pleasure. This he did on 27 Feb 1912. On the 28th, Sir Frederick Ponsonby, at this time Assistant Private Secretary to the King, replied: 'His Majesty says there can be no doubt that the Victoria Cross should go first of all orders and decorations. It is quite apart from any order of Chivalry, and although it carries no rank with it, hitherto the invariable custom has been to place it before all other decorations.

'The King therefore wishes that in all Alphabetical lists such as the *Army* and *Navy Lists* the VC should be put before the name in Old English letters, and further that in addresses or where its abbreviation is placed in juxtaposition with the abbreviations of Orders of Chivalry the VC should come first',[644] a ruling which Brade conveyed to the Admiralty and Norroy King of Arms on 7 Mar.[645] Thus the point was finally settled.

As will be seen from what has just been said, closely allied to the question of the order in which initials should be placed after a recipient's name was that of the order in which decorations should be worn. Early photographs of recipients wearing their Cross show that the situation was one of almost complete anarchy. Some men would wear all their decorations and medals in one line, with the VC in the centre, flanked on either side by lesser awards; others, with perhaps four awards, would wear these at the four points of a diamond formation or, if they possessed five awards, would use the same diamond formation and add the fifth at its centre. Often there seems to have been an attempt to wear the Cross as closely adjacent as possible to the campaign medal for the war in which it was won. The first attempt to regulate such matters seems to have been the *Army Dress Regulations* of 1891. These formed one of the rare pieces of official business dealt with by King Edward VII as Prince of Wales; they worked on the basis of the 'Orders, Decorations and Medals' principle, established the familiar style of all awards in a single line, and placed the Victoria Cross after the Royal Victorian Order [which was the junior order] and prior to the DSO [evidently here regarded as a decoration, despite its name].[646] Interestingly

644   VCR, iii p192
645   *ibid*
646   PRO, WO 32/7489

enough, in these regulations it was also laid down that the DCM was to be worn immediately after the campaign medal to which it related. These regulations did not remain in force very long, however, for in 1904 a new set was promulgated and it was in these that it was finally laid down that the VC should be worn first of all awards, which has been its position ever since.[647]

The wearing of a miniature bronze cross on the ribbon of the VC when the ribbon alone was worn arose out of the discussion as to how a man could indicate the possession of a bar to any award when the ribbon alone was worn.[648] The question had clearly originated in connection with the Military Cross, and in the concern of King George V that such second awards should be visibly indicated. His first thoughts seem to have run along the lines of a distinctive ribbon to indicate this but, in a letter to the Secretary at the War Office on 26 Jun 1916 Sir Frederick Ponsonby wrote, 'The King has spoken to Prince Louis of Battenburg on the matter, and he has suggested, in order to avoid the difficulty of making a special ribbon for every isolated case, that a white rose, the size of a threepenny bit, might be placed on the ribbon to denote the presence of a bar'. It was at this point that the War Office asked whether the matter was to be considered in relation to awards òther than the MC, and received a reply from Ponsonby on 13 Jul to say that the King most certainly did so wish. At this point the Quarter-master General's department prepared a card [which still exists in the PRO file] bearing the ribbons of the VC, MC, DCM and MM each adorned with the threepenny-bit sized rose [double the size that was finally adopted]. This card appears to have gone before the Army Council on 20 Jul, and it was evidently at this point that the idea arose of using a miniature bronze cross on the VC ribbon, for in the letter from the WO forwarding the card to Ponsonby for submission to the King, on 21 Jul, was the remark, 'As regards the Victoria Cross the Military Members of the Council think that a small Victoria Cross in bronze, the medal being in bronze, would be better than a silver rose. Perhaps you would ask His Majesty if this meets with his approval'. Ponsonby's letter of 22nd indicated that it did, and a new card which, as well as showing the other ribbons bearing silver roses of a reduced size bears the ribbon of the VC with a miniature Cross upon it, is also in the file, marked 'Approved by the King' and dated 16 Aug 1916.

647   *ibid*
648   PRO, WO 32/5394 for this and the following paragraph.

So far the discussion had only related to the display of a miniature Cross on the ribbon of the VC to denote possession of a bar. The further step, by which the miniature should be worn on the ribbon by all holders, followed on 17 Mar 1917, when Ponsonby wrote once more to the WO to say that the King had now definitely decided that in future a miniature bronze VC should be fixed to the VC ribbon when worn in khaki and in the event of a man receiving a bar to his VC he should wear two miniature VCs side by side on the ribbon, a decision which was published in Army Orders of 24 Mar 1917.

As has already been shown,[649] it was in the Warrant of 1920 that the formal change of the ribbon to red for all services took place. However, the occasion for action was the creation of an entirely new service, the Royal Air Force, on 1 Apr 1918, and for which the existing Warrant made no provision as to the colour of the ribbon. A decision was evidently taken by the King very shortly after this, and can presumably be linked very closely with the gazetting of the first two VCs to members of the new Air Force, Lts Jerrard and McLeod on 1 May 1918, for in a letter of 10 May [which does not seem to survive] the Admiralty were informed by the WO that 'the King had commanded that the colour of the riband of the Victoria Cross should be the same whether awarded for Services in the Navy, Army or Air Force, i.e. the red colour of the riband of the Victoria Cross awarded in the Army'.[650] This command said nothing about those naval Crosses that had already been issued and were being worn with a blue ribbon. The remaining detail was filled in on 10 Jul 1918, when a further letter went from the WO to the Admiralty which, after quoting the earlier letter, continued, 'I have now received The King's command that the above order is to be retrospective with regard to all Victoria Crosses which have been awarded to the Navy.

'Will you therefore be good enough to take the necessary steps to have the blue riband issued with all Victoria Crosses awarded in the Navy replaced by the red riband whether worn with the Decoration, either full-sized or miniature, or as a ribbon sewn on the coat.'[651]

From this point one can say that all what might be termed the 'incidentals' of the Cross – the use of initials, the place in which it is worn, the use of miniature Crosses on the ribbon, and the colour of the ribbon, had assumed the form which they now bear.

---

649   See p176
650   VCR, iv p42
651   *ibid*

One other matter may be regarded as falling within the province of this chapter, namely the bestowal of the VC on Unknown Warriors. It has sometimes been stated that such a presentation was made to the British Unknown Warrior, but this story appears to be without foundation. As can be seen by any visitor to Westminster Abbey, a Congressional Medal of Honor was bestowed by the United States Government, and this gesture was in fact reciprocated with the presentation of a Victoria Cross to the American Unknown Warrior at Arlington National Cemetry, which is the only case where this has been done.

So far as the WO papers show[652] the first recorded mention of the subject was an enquiry by Sir Alexander Godley, the MS, on 21 Oct 1921. He understood that Lord Cavan, the CIGS, had been deputed to lay the Cross on the tomb of the American Unknown Warrior and he wished to know what should be inscribed upon it. The reply he was given was that the matter would be discussed at the Cabinet meeting of 26th, at which it was decided that Lord Cavan should take the wreath inscribed from King George V and Earl Beatty the Cross; the inscription, he was told, would be, 'To the Unknown Warrior of the United States', though Sir Maurice Hankey subsequently telephoned to add the words, 'of America' to this. Hancocks were informed to this effect on 27th, and on 28th a letter went from the WO to the British Embassy in Washington to say, 'We have had the VC inscribed and it will be sent out today to the American Department of the Foreign Office for transmission by [diplomatic] bag to the Embassy..... After consideration here it is not thought necessary that Lord Cavan should take duplicate VC' − this last seeming to have been a suggestion by the Admiralty lest anything should miscarry. In fact, a receipt for 'One Victoria Cross, inscribed, "The Unknown Warrior of the United States of America" dated the 28th October, 1921', and preserved in the Victoria Cross Register[653] shows that the DMS did hand it over that day. It had also been decided at the Cabinet meeting that the King's wreath would suffice for the British Government − both the WO and the Admiralty had been considering laying ones of their own − and Lord Stamfordham was to telegraph the Embassy regarding this. In the event, though the Cross arrived in time for the ceremony − it had been forwarded in the diplomatic bag in HMS *Eurydice* on 31 Oct and its receipt was acknowledged from the Embassy on 11 Nov − Lord Cavan did not, and

652   All the papers on this episode are to be found in PRO, WO 32/4996
653   VCR, iii p344

both parts of the ceremony were in fact performed by Earl Beatty on 11 Nov 1921.

At the same time that the matter of this Cross was being discussed the question of a similar action in regard to the French Unknown Warrior was also raised. The decision reached on 26 Oct 1921, was that no official representation would be made, but that the PM or the Foreign Secretary would sound M. Briand as to its desirability.[654] Nothing more seems to have happened following this until the matter was reopened in 1924, by a letter from Mr Victor Fisher, the Honorary Director and founder of 'The Friends of France' to the S of S for War, then Mr Stephen Walsh.[655] Mr Fisher stated that he had recently returned from France, where a number of distinguished personages had indicated to him that such a conferment would be greatly appreciated. Quoting the analogy of the American case he thought it extraordinary that the same had not been done for the French, and suggested that it would be appropriate to act now, whilst the Inter-Allied Conference was sitting.

Mr Lyon, an Assistant Secretary, forwarded this letter to Sir H.J. Creedy, who was now the PUS, on 17 Jul, indicating that Mr Walsh would be glad of advice. Creedy, in referring the question to the CIGS and the AG, was somewhat unenthusiastic. He thought that in view of past history they would be well advised not to reopen the question of exchanging decorations for unknown warriors. They had, as he pointed out, already put the Italians off, and they could hardly deal with one without the others. The Earl of Cavan, the CIGS, agreed with this; Gen Whigham, the AG, referred back to the views of Sir Henry Wilson, who had formerly disliked the procedure, as leading to a situation in which a general interchange of decorations for unknown warriors took place between all allied nations. He was therefore equally against the proposal and thought the initiative should not be taken in the manner suggested. As a result of this unanimity of advice, Walsh endorsed the papers, 'We ought not to reopen this matter' on 28 Jul, and on 9 Aug a letter was sent from his PS to Fisher, to the effect that after careful consideration and reviewing all the circumstances the S of S found himself in agreement with the decision of his predecessors that it would be unwise to take the action suggested.

A further case of conferment of a VC on an unknown warrior looked likely to arise after the Second World War when there was a proposal

654   PRO, WO 32/4996
655   PRO, WO 32/5653

for a similar interment at Arlington. On 1 Jan 1951, a draft report on the subject was produced at the WO: 'The Victoria Cross was given to the United States Unknown Warrior of the First World War, and it may be considered that similar action should be taken now. It is the rule that the Victoria Cross is not given to foreign subjects, but no doubt an exception could be made again in this instance under the last Clause of the Warrant

'The Victoria Cross given in 1921 was inscribed on the reverse, "The Unknown Warrior of the United States of America" and it was presented on behalf of King George V by Admiral of the Fleet Lord Beatty.

'Presumably the inscription now would be "The World War II Unknown Serviceman of the United States of America".'[656]

However the United States finally abandoned the project of selecting an Unknown Serviceman for interment at Arlington, so the matter lapsed.

656   VCR, iv, insert at p43

APPENDIX I
'The Original VC Warrant'
Public Record Office WO 98/1

It has long been considered that there exists no means of adequately rewarding the individual gallant services of officers of the lower grades in the Military Service as well as Non-Comd. officers and soldiers in the Army and Warrant Officers and Seamen in the Navy.

The Cross of CB being bestowed only in very rare and exceptional cases, on any below the rank of Field Officer. The Medals, when granted in the Army are for long service or meritorious conduct rather than for bravery in the field, or distinction before an enemy, except in cases where a general Medal is granted for some particular Campaign or a Clasp for some special engagement, in which case all share equally in the boon, and those particularly distinguished by their valour remain unmarked.

For the purpose of filling the hiatus which exists in the honours at present at the disposal of the Sovereign, it is proposed to institute a new Military Order, the insignia of which, though trifling in intrinsic value, shall be highly prized and eagerly sought after by the Officers and Men of Her Majesty's Military Services −

1 The Order to be styled 'The Military Order of Victoria'.
   Motto 'Pro patria mori'
   or   'Mors aut Victoria'
   or   'God defend the right'.
2 The Queen constitutes herself Sovereign of the Order.
3 The Order shall consist of one degree.
4 The insignia to be a cross of Steel, or bronze, suspended from the breast by a red ribbon for army and blue for Navy.
5 The order shall only be awarded to those who have served Her Majesty in the presence of the Enemy, and there displayed some signal act of Valour or devotion to their country, or who, so serving, shall by personal bravery contribute to the success of a Military operation of decided advantage to the General objects of a Campaign.
6 With a view to place all persons in relation to eligibility for the Order, on a perfectly equal footing, it is hereby declared, that, neither rank nor long service, nor wounds nor any other quality whatsoever save the merit of conspicuous bravery shall be held as sufficient qualification for the Order.
7 If the act in question be performed under the eye of the Officer Commanding the forces in the Field, or of a General commanding a division or of a General commanding a brigade such General Officer shall have the power of conferring the decoration on the spot, subject to confirmation of the Sovereign.
8 Commanding Officers of a Corps on separate or wholly detached service having the rank of Field Officer, shall have like power, where circumstances justify its exercise.

9 Where the Act shall not have been performed in sight aforesaid then the Claimant for the honor shall prove the Act to the satisfaction of the Officer Commanding his regiment who shall report the same through the usual channels to the Officer Commanding the forces in the Field, who shall call for such description and attestation of the Act as he may think requisite and on approval recommend the concession of the decoration.

10 Every person selected for the order under rules 7 and 8 shall be publicly decorated before the army or body to which he belongs and with which the act of bravery for which he is rewarded, has been performed, and his name shall be recorded in a general order, together with the cause of his especial distinction.

11 Every person selected under rule 9 shall receive his decoration as soon as possible and his name shall likewise appear in a General Order as above required.

12 The G.O. above referred to shall from time to time be transmitted to the registrar of the Order and by him registered.

13 As cases may arise not falling within the rules specified above, or in which a claim, though covered, has not been established in the field Her Majesty may, on the joint submission of the Secretary of State for War and Her Commander in Chief of Her Army, or the First Lord of the Admiralty, in the case of the Navy; confer the decoration but never − Her Majesty being graciously pleased to bind herself herein − without conclusive proof of the act of bravery.

14 The Order will consist of
    1st The Sovereign
    2nd a Grand Master (hony)
    3rd a Grand Registrar (Sec of State for War for the time being)
    4 A Secretary Pd [Paid] ⎫ Appd by the Queen on recommend-
    5 A Registrar Pd [Paid] ⎭ ation of Secretary of State for War

15 Every Non-Comd Officer and Soldier or Warrant Officer or Seaman who shall become a Member of the Order, shall on his discharge be entitled to a pension of £20 a year.

16 Any member of the Order, convicted before a Court Martial of cowardice, mutiny or desertion shall be at once expelled from the Order, and cease to derive any prospective privileges from it.

17 Any member, who having retired from the active service of Her Majesty, shall be convicted of a felony shall in like manner be expelled from the order.

18 The number of Members shall be unlimited.

19 Any member of the order who, after having received the Cross of the Order shall again perform an act, which, if he had not received such cross would have entitled him to it, then such further Act of Bravery shall be recorded by a bar across the upper arm of the Cross, and for every additional act of bravery an additional bar may be added, and in the case of Non Comd Officers and Soldiers of the Army or Warrant Officers and

Seamen each additional bar shall carry with it an addition to the pension in Rule 15 of £5 a year.

APPENDIX II

Prince Albert's Memorandum

Nottingham University:
Newcastle Collection, Document Ne C 9701b

Memorandum

Windsor Castle,
January 22d, 1855.

The question of rewards for military service by Decoration is one of the most difficult.

The object to be attained is: to reward specific services and to encourage the Army generally by the notice taken of special cases of merit.

The difficulty which meets us, is: to establish, first a competent tribunal for ascertaining in what the services of 'A' differ from or are superior to the services of B; and secondly (if such a difference does exist) a sure mode of bringing them to the notice of Govt. with a certainty that a similar superiority on the part of C is not overlooked.

It is clear, that, if these considerations are not fulfilled, instead of encouraging you *disgust* the Army which you mean to reward, adding to the feelings of disappointment in those who receive no reward that of resentment at the injustice of seeing others rewarded, whom they think inferior to themselves.

The *Order of the Bath* was instituted for such reward for Officers of the Army and Navy. It was limited to those of a certain Rank to whose duties alone that degree of responsibility attends which allows you to distinguish between their merits. (For instance, if a Battn distinguish itself the mode in which it was led by its commanding officer is appreciated, whilst the Officers in the Ranks, having no choice of action must be supposed to have shown equal obedience and courage). It has been limited in number in order to preserve its value and make it a just object of ambition. The condition has been attached to its bestowal: that an officer's name must have been mentioned in a Public Dispatch, in order to give a security, that the service for which an officer is to be rewarded has been really marked and judged of by the only competent authority, his commander.

It has been found open to the following objections, service officers feel, that their services may have been equally meritorious under those of their commander, and yet are left unremarked. The limitation of numbers must leave many cases of necessity unrewarded. The difficulty of distinguishing between the merits of different officers in responsible situations and the unwillingness on the part of Commanders to incur the odium of making the distinction, have led them to mention nearly everybody in their Dispatches and the Govt is then left, either to do possible injustice or to allow the reward to become a mere appendage of a certain rank.

Another mode of Reward adopted for the Army has been that of giving *Medals for particular actions and campaigns.*

Here no attempt is made to distinguish between the services of individuals, Gels [sic], Officers and men are all treated alike, and supposed to have all done their best towards producing a result, which, as a whole, the Crown thinks worthy of reward. This mode is open to none of the former objections, but is exposed to some of its own:- It leaves individual merits unnoticed, and even here the necessity of distinguishing between actions becomes an embarrassment to the Govt. The Troops which fought at Balaclava [sic] cry out at this moment at not sharing in the honours bestowed upon Inkerman, to which, it is true, the Govt can reply, that it marked an important success in the one instance, while the other was (to use the D of Wellington's expression) an *'untoward event'.* It has no reply, however to the remonstrance of the Troops 'Why are we to be punished for the mistakes of our Commanders? Have we not done all that troops could do under such difficult circumstances?'

It is now proposed to establish a 3d mode of reward, neither reserved for the few nor bestowed upon all, which is to *distinguish on a liberal scale individual merit in the Officers of the Lower Ranks, in Sergeants and in Privates.*

I admit fully the want of such a reward, but it must practically have great difficulties as renouncing either of the above principles. How is a distinction to be made, for instance, between the individual services of the 200 survivors of Ld Cardigan's Charge? If you reward them all it becomes merely a Medal for Balaclava, to which the Heavy Brigade and the 93d have equal claims.

The only mode I see, in which the difficulty could be overcome seems to me to be something like the following:-

1 That a small cross of Merit for *personal deeds of valour* be established.
2 That it be open to all ranks.
3 That it be unlimited in number.
4 That an annuity (say of £5) be attached to each cross.
5 That it be *claimable* by an individual on establishing before a jury of his peers, subject to confirmation at home, his right to the distinction.
6 That in cases of general actions it be given in certain quantities to particular Regiments, so many to the Officers, so many to the sergeants, so many to the men (of the last say 1 per Company) and that their distribution be left to a jury of the same rank as the person to be rewarded. By this means alone could you ensure the perfect fairness of distribution and save the Officers in

command from the invidious task of making a selection from those under their orders, which they now shrink from in the case of the Bath. – The limitation of the Numbers to be given to a Regmt at one time enforces the *necessity* of a selection and diminishes the pain to those who cannot be included.

I would advise no reference to the Legion of Honour, the distribution of which is entirely arbitrary and guided by no principles, which is given indiscriminately to Soldiers and Civilians, and has long been made a tool for corruption in the hands of the French Govt the Number of whose members extends to 40,000 and which has almost become a necessary appendage to the French dress.

I would leave the Order of the Bath unmentioned, and let the system of conferring Medals for actions continue as heretofore.

A
[ALBERT]

APPENDIX III

'Copy Memorandum on Proposed Victoria Cross'
Royal Archives E6 69

Dec. [?] /55

It has long been considered that there exists no means of adequately rewarding the individual gallant services of officers of the lower grades in the Naval & Military services as well of warrant & petty officers, seamen and marines in the Navy & of non-commissioned officers and soldiers in the army, the cross of CB being confined, except in very rare and particular cases to the higher ranks in both services.

Medals, when granted both in the Navy & Army are given for long service or meritorious conduct rather than for bravery in action or distinction before an enemy, except in cases where a general medal is granted for some particular action or campaign, or a clasp added to these Medals for some special engagement, in which case all share equally in the boon, and those who have particularly signalized themselves by their valour, remain undistinguished from their comrades.

For the purpose of supplying the deficiency which exists in the honors at present at the disposal of The Sovereign, it is proposed to institute a new Naval and Military order; the insignia of which, though trifling in intrinsic value, shall be highly prized and eagerly sought after by the officers, and men of Her Majesty's Naval & Military services.

1 The order would be styled 'The Military Order of Victoria'
   Motto: 'God defend the Right' or 'For Queen & Country'.
2 The Queen constitutes Herself Sovereign of the Order.
3 The order to consist of one degree.
4 The number of members shall be unlimited.

5 The Insignia to be a Cross of Steel or Bronze suspended from the breast by a blue Ribbon for the Navy & a red Ribbon for the Army.

6 Any member of the order who after having received the cross of the order, shall again perform an act, which if he had not received such cross would have entitled him to it, then such further act of bravery shall be rewarded by a bar across the upper arm of the cross; & for every additional act of bravery, an additional bar may be added, & in the case of warrant & Petty officers, seamen & marines, or of non-comd. officers & soldiers each additional bar shall carry with it an addition to the Pension in Rule 16 of £5 a year.

7 The order shall only be awarded to those officers or men who have served Her Majesty in the presence of the Enemy; and shall have there performed some signal act of Valour or devotion to their country, or who so serving shall project, and by personal bravery contribute to the success, of a Naval or Military operation.

8 With a view to place all persons on a perfectly equal footing in relation to eligibility for the order it is hereby declared that neither rank, nor long service, nor wounds, nor any other circumstance or condition whatsoever save the merit of conspicuous bravery shall be held as sufficient qualification for the order.

9 If the qualifying act be performed under the eye of the Admiral in command of a Fleet, or of the officer commanding the Forces in the Field, or of an Admiral Commanding a Squadron, or of a General Commanding a Division; or of an Admiral or Commodore commanding a Naval force or of a General Commanding a Brigade, such Admiral, Commodore or General officer shall have the power of conferring the decoration on the spot, subject to confirmation by The Sovereign.

10 Where the act shall not have been performed in sight of a Commanding Officer as aforesaid, then the claimant for the honor shall prove the act to the satisfaction of the Captain commanding his Ship, or of the Officer commanding the Regiment, to which the Claimant belongs, & such captain or such Commanding officer shall report the same through the usual channel to the Admiral or Commodore Commanding the Force employed on the service, or to the officer commanding the forces in the field, who shall call for such description & attestation of the act as he may think requisite, & on approval, shall recommend the grant of the decoration.

11 Every person [sic] for the order under rule 9 shall be publicly decorated before the Naval, Marine, or Military force or body to which he belongs, and with which the act of bravery for which he is rewarded shall have been performed & his name shall be recorded in a general order together with the cause of his especial distinction.

12 Every person selected under rule 10 shall receive his decoration as soon as possible, & his name shall likewise appear in a general

order as above required, such general order to be issued by the Naval or Military Commander of the Forces employed on the service.

13 The General orders above referred to shall from time to time be transmitted to the Registrar of the Order, & be by him registered.

14 As cases may arise not falling within the Rules specified above, or in which a claim though well founded may not have been established on the spot, Her Majesty will on the joint submission of Her Secretary for War and of Her Commander in chief of Her army, or on that of the Lord High Admiral or Lords Commissioners of the Admiralty in the case of the navy, confer the decoration; but never (Her Majesty being graciously pleased to bind Herself herein) without conclusive proof of the performance of the act of bravery for which the claim is made.

15 The order will consist of,
    1st   The Sovereign
    2nd   A Grand Master (Honorary)
    3rd   A Grand Registrar. (Secretary of State for war − time being)
    4th   A Secretary (Paid) ⎱ Approved by the Queen on recom-
    5th   A Registrar (Paid) ⎰ mendation of Secty of State

16 Every warrant officer, Petty officer, seaman or marine, or Non Comd. officer or soldier who shall become a member of the order, shall on his discharge, be entitled to a pension of £15 a year, & each additional bar conferred under Rule 6 on each warrant or Petty officers or non-Comd officers or men, shall carry with it an additional pension of £5 per annum.

APPENDIX IV

The Warrant Instituting the Victoria Cross

Public Record Office WO 98/1

Appd. Victoria R

Victoria by the Grace of God of the United Kingdom of Great Britain and Ireland Queen Defender of the Faith &c. To all to whom these Presents shall come Greeting! Whereas We taking into Our Royal consideration that there exists no means of adequately rewarding the individual gallant services either of Officers of the lower grades in Our Naval and Military Service or of Warrant and Petty Officers Seamen and Marines in Our Navy and Non-commissioned Officers and Soldiers in Our Army. And Whereas the third Class of Our Most Honorable Order of the Bath is limited except in very rare cases to the higher ranks of both Services and the granting of Medals both in Our Navy and Army is only awarded for long service or meritorious conduct, rather than for bravery in Action or distinction before an enemy, such cases alone excepted while [sic] a general Medal is granted for a particular Action or Campaign or a Clasp added to the Medal for some special engagement, in both of which cases all share equally in the boon and those who by their valour have particularly signalized themselves remain undistinguished from their comrades. Now for the purpose of attaining an end so desirable as that of rewarding individual instances of merit and valour We have instituted and created and by these Presents for Us Our Heirs and Successors institute and create a new Naval and Military Decoration, which We are desirous should be highly prized and eagerly sought after by the Officers and Men of Our Naval and Military Services and are graciously pleased to make ordain and establish the following rules and ordinances for the government of the same which shall from henceforth be inviolably observed and kept.

Firstly It is ordained that the distinction shall be styled and designated the 'Victoria Cross' and shall consist of a Maltese Cross of Bronze with Our Royal Crest in the centre and underneath which an Escroll bearing this inscription 'For Valour'.

Secondly It is ordained that the Cross shall be suspended from the left breast by a Blue Riband for the Navy and by a Red Riband for the Army.

Thirdly It is ordained that the names of those upon whom We may be pleased to confer the decoration shall be published in the *London Gazette* and a registry thereof kept in the office of Our Secretary of State for War.

Fourthly It is ordained that anyone who, after having received the Cross, shall again perform an Act of bravery which, if he had not received such Cross would have entitled him to it, such further act shall be recorded by a Bar attached to the riband by which the Cross is suspended and for every additional act of bravery an additional Bar may be added.

Fifthly It is ordained that the Cross shall only be awarded to those Officers or Men who have served Us in the presence of the Enemy and shall then have performed some signal act of valour or devotion to their Country.

Sixthly It is ordained with a view to place all persons on a perfectly equal footing in relation to eligibility for the Decoration that neither rank nor long service nor wounds nor any other circumstance or condition whatsoever save the merit of conspicuous bravery shall be held to establish a sufficient claim to the honour.

Seventhly It is ordained that the Decoration may be conferred on the spot where the act to be rewarded by the grant of such Decoration has been performed under the following circumstances:

I. When the Fleet or Army in which such Act has been performed is under the eye and command of an Admiral or General Officer commanding the Forces.

II. Where the Naval or Military Force is under the eye and command of an Admiral or Commodore Commanding a Squadron or detached

Naval Force or of a General Commanding a Corps or Division or Brigade on a distinct and detached Service when such Admiral Commodore or General Officer shall have the power of conferring the Decoration on the spot subject to confirmation by Us.

Eighthly It is ordained where such act shall not have been performed in sight of a Commanding Officer as aforesaid then the claimant for the honour shall prove the act to the satisfaction of the Captain or Officer Commanding his Ship or to the Officer Commanding the Regiment to which the Claimant belongs and such Captain or such Commanding Officer shall report the same through the usual channel to the Admiral or Commodore Commanding the Force employed on the Service or to the Officer Commanding the Forces in the Field who shall call for such description and attestation of the act as he may think requisite and on approval shall recommend the grant of the Decoration.

Ninthly It is ordained that every person selected for the Cross under rule seven shall be publicly decorated before the Naval or Military Force or body to which he belongs and with which the act of bravery for which he is to be rewarded shall have been performed and his name shall be recorded in a General Order together with the cause of his especial distinction.

Tenthly It is ordained that every person selected under rule eight shall receive his Decoration as soon as possible and his name shall likewise appear in a General Order as above required, such General Order to be issued by the Naval or Military Commander of the Forces employed on the Service.

Eleventhly It is ordained that the General Orders above referred to shall from time to time be transmitted to our Secretary of State for War to be laid before Us and shall be by him registered.

Twelfthly It is ordained that as cases may arise not falling within the rules above specified or in which a claim though well founded may not have been established on the spot We will on the joint submission of Our Secretary of State for War and of Our Commander-in-Chief of Our army or on that of Our Lord High Admiral or Lords Commissioners of the Admiralty in the case of the Navy confer the Decoration but never without conclusive proof of the performance of the act of bravery for which the claim is made.

Thirteenthly It is ordained that in the event of a gallant and daring act having been performed by a Squadron Ship's Company a detached body of Seamen and Marines not under fifty in number or by a Brigade Regiment Troop or Company in which the Admiral General or other Officer Commanding such Forces may deem that all are equally brave and distinguished and that no special selection can be made by them, Then in such case the Admiral General or other Officer Commanding may direct that for any such body of Seamen and Marines or for every Troop or Company of Soldiers one Officer shall be selected by the Officers engaged for the Decoration; and in like manner one Petty Officer or Non-commissioned Officer shall be selected by the Petty Officers and Non-commissioned Officers engaged; and two Seamen or Private Soldiers or Marines shall be selected by the Seamen or Private

Soldiers or Marines engaged respectively for the Decoration; and the names of those selected shall be transmitted by the Senior Officer in Command of the Naval Force Brigade Regiment Troop or Company to the Admiral or General Officer Commanding who shall in due manner confer the Decoration as if the acts were done under his own eye.

Fourteenthly It is ordained that every Warrant Officer Petty Officer Seaman or Marine or Non-Commissioned Officer or Soldier who shall have received the Cross shall from the date of the act by which the Decoration has been gained be entitled to a Special Pension of Ten Pounds a year; and each additional bar conferred under rule four on such Warrant or Petty Officers or Non-Commissioned Officers or Men, shall carry with it an additional pension of Five Pounds per annum.

Fifteenthly In order to make such additional provision as shall effectually preserve pure this Most Honorable distinction it is ordained that if any person on whom such distinction shall be conferred be convicted of Treason, Cowardice, Felony or of any infamous Crime, or if he be accused of any such offence and doth not after a reasonable time surrender himself to be tried for the same his name shall forthwith be erased from the Registry of Individuals upon whom the said Decoration shall have been conferred by an especial Warrant under Our Royal Sign Manual, and the pension conferred under rule fourteen shall cease and determine from the date of such Warrant. It is hereby further declared that We Our Heirs and Successors shall be the sole judge of the circumstances demanding such expulsion; moreover We shall at all times have power to restore such persons as may at any time have been expelled, both to the enjoyment of the Decoration and Pension.

Given at Our Court at Buckingham Palace this twenty-ninth day of January in the Nineteenth Year of Our Reign and in the Year of Our Lord One Thousand Eight Hundred and Fifty Six

By Her Majesty's Command
Panmure

To Our Principal Secretary of State for War.

APPENDIX V

Warrant Extending Eligibility for the Victoria Cross to Military Forces of the Honourable East India Company

Victoria Cross Register, i, pp58-60

Victoria R.

Victoria by the Grace of God, of the United Kingdom of Great Britain & Ireland, Queen Defender of the Faith To all to whom these presents shall come, Greeting! Whereas We did, by a Warrant under Our Royal

Sign Manual, countersigned by one of Our Principal Secretaries of State, and bearing date at Our Court at Buckingham Palace, the twenty ninth day of January, 1856, in the Nineteenth year of Our Reign, constitute & create a new Naval & Military decoration, to be styled & designated the 'Victoria Cross', which decoration We expressed the desire should be highly prized & eagerly sought after by the Officers & Men of Our Naval & Military Services, & did also make, ordain & establish the rules & ordinances therein set forth for the Government of the same to be thenceforth inviolably observed & kept.

And whereas for divers reasons Us thereunto moving, We are desirous of rewarding the individual gallant services of Officers & Men of the Naval & Military Service of the East India Company, by the bestowal of the said decoration which We are desirous shall be highly prized & eagerly sought after by the Officers & Men of the said Service.

Now know Ye that We, of Our especial grace, certain knowledge, & mere motion have thought fit hereby to signify Our Royal Will & Pleasure that the said Decoration shall be conferred on the Officers & Men of the Naval & Military Service of the East India Company who may be qualified to receive the same in accordance with the rules & ordinances made, ordained, & established by Us for the Government thereof, by Our said recited Warrant, and We do by these Presents for Us, Our Heirs & Successors, ordain & appoint that it shall be competent for the Officers & Men of the said service to obtain the said decoration in the manner set forth in the rules & ordinances referred to, or in accordance with any further rules & ordinances which may hereafter be made & promulgated by Us, Our Heirs & Successors, for the Government of the said decoration.

Given at Our Court at Windsor, the Twenty ninth day of October 1857, in the Twenty first year of Our Reign.

By Her Majesty's Command,
                    Panmure

APPENDIX VI

Warrant Extending the Victoria Cross to Cases of Conspicuous Courage and Bravery Displayed under Circumstances of Danger but not before the Enemy.

Public Record Office, WO 32/7345

Victoria R.

Victoria, by the Grace of God, of the United Kingdom of Great Britain and Ireland, Queen, Defender of the Faith, To all to whom these Presents shall come, Greeting!

Whereas by a Warrant under Our Royal Sign Manual, countersigned by one of Our Principal Secretaries of State, and bearing date at Our Court at Buckingham Palace the Twenty-ninth day of January, 1856, in the nineteenth year of Our Reign, We did constitute and create a new Naval and Military Decoration, to be styled and designated the 'Victoria Cross', which decoration We expressed Our desire should be highly prized and eagerly sought after by the Officers and men of Our Naval and Military Services, and did also make, ordain, and establish the rules and ordinances therein set forth for the government of the same, to be thenceforth inviolably observed and kept,

And whereas by another Warrant, under Our Royal Sign Manual, countersigned by one of Our Principal Secretaries of State, and bearing date at Our Court at Windsor, the Twenty-ninth day of October 1857, in the Twenty first year of Our Reign, We thought fit to signify Our Royal Will and Pleasure that the said decoration shall be conferred on the Officers and men of the Naval and Military Services of the East India Company, who may be qualified to receive the same, in accordance with the rules and ordinances made, ordained, and established by Us for the government thereof by Our said first recited Warrant,

And Whereas by the rules and ordinances established by Our said Warrant, it is, amongst other things, ordained that the Victoria Cross shall only be awarded to those Officers or men who have served Us in the presence of the Enemy, and shall have then performed some signal act of valor or devotion to their country, and that with a view to place all persons on a perfectly equal footing in relation to eligibility for the decoration, neither rank, nor long service, nor wounds, nor any other circumstance or condition whatsoever, save the merit of conspicuous bravery shall be held to establish a sufficient claim to the honor,

And, Whereas, for divers reasons Us thereunto moving, We are desirous of rewarding individual instances of conspicuous courage and bravery which may be displayed by Officers and men in Our Naval and Military Services, and in the Naval and Military Services of the East India Company, under circumstances of extreme danger, such as the occurrence of a fire on board Ship, or of the foundering of a vessel at Sea, or under any other circumstances in which through the courage and devotion displayed, life or public property may be saved.

Now know Ye, that We, of Our especial Grace, certain knowledge, and mere motion, have thought fit hereby to signify Our Royal Will and Pleasure that the said decoration shall be conferred on the Officers and men in Our Naval and Military Services and in the Naval and Military Services of the East India Company, who may perform acts of conspicuous courage and bravery under the circumstances referred to in this Our Warrant.

Provided, nevertheless, and We do hereby, for Us, Our Heirs and Successors, declare, ordain, and appoint that nothing herein contained shall be deemed or construed to have the effect, of altering, abrogating, or dispensing with the rules and ordinances set forth in Our said just recited Warrant, or any of them, except so far as may be necessary for the purpose of enabling Us to confer the said decoration on the Officers and men of Our Naval and Military Services or of the Naval and Military Services of the East India Company in conformity with the provisions of this Our Warrant.

Given at Our Court at Buckingham Palace, this Tenth day of August, 1858 in the Twenty second year of Our Reign.

By Her Majesty's Command
J. Peel

APPENDIX VII

Warrant Extending Eligibility for the Victoria Cross to Non-Military Persons Bearing Arms as Volunteers

Victoria Cross Register, i, pp. 146-150

Victoria R.

Victoria, by the Grace of God of the United Kingdom of Great Britain and Ireland, Queen, Defender of the Faith, To all to whom these Presents shall come, Greeting! Whereas by a Warrant under Our Royal Sign Manual, countersigned by one of Our Principal Secretaries of State, and bearing date at Our Court at Buckingham Palace the 29th day of January 1856, in the nineteenth year of Our Reign, We did constitute and create a new naval and military decoration to be styled and designated the Victoria Cross, which decoration We expressed Our desire should be highly prized and eagerly sought after by the Officers and men of Our Naval and Military services and did also make ordain and establish the rules and ordinances therein set forth for the Government of the same, to be thenceforth inviolably observed and kept.

And Whereas by another Warrant under Our Royal Sign Manual countersigned by one of Our Principal Secretaries of State and bearing date at Our Court at Windsor, the 29th day of October 1857, in the Twenty first year of Our Reign, We thought fit to signify Our Royal Will and Pleasure, that the said decoration shall be conferred on the Officers and men of the Naval and Military Service of the East India Company — now Our Indian Naval and Military Forces — who may be qualified to receive the same in accordance with the rules and ordinances made ordained and established by Us for the Government thereof by Our first recited Warrant aforesaid.

And Whereas during the progress of the operations which We have undertaken against the Insurgent Mutineers in India, it has not infrequently happened that non military persons who have borne arms as volunteers against the mutineers both at Lucknow and elsewhere have performed deeds of gallantry in consideration of which they are not according to the strict provisions of Our first recited Warrant eligible for this high distinction.

Now know ye that We of Our especial grace, certain knowledge and mere motion, have thought fit hereby to signify Our Royal Will and Pleasure that the said decoration shall be conferred on such non military persons as aforesaid, who may be qualified to receive the same in accordance with the rules and ordinances made ordained and established by Us for the Government thereof by Our said first recited Warrant, and We do by these Presents for Us, Our Heirs, and Successors, ordain and appoint that it shall be competent for such non military persons as aforesaid to obtain the said decoration in the manner set forth in the rules and ordinances referred to, or in accordance with such further rules and ordinances as may hereafter be made and promulgated by Us, Our Heirs and Successors for the Government of the said decoration provided that it be established in any case that the person was serving under the orders of a General or other Officer in Command of Troops in the Field.

Given at Our Court at Osborne House Isle of Wight, the 13th day of Decr 1858, in the Twenty second year of Our Reign.

By Her Majesty's Command,
J. Peel

APPENDIX VIII

Warrant Extending the Victoria Cross to the Local Forces in New Zealand and in the Colonies and their Dependencies Generally

Public Record Office, WO 32/7370

Victoria R.

Victoria, by the Grace of God, of the United Kingdom of Great Britain and Ireland, Queen, Defender of the Faith. To all to whom these Presents shall come, Greeting!

Whereas, by a Warrant under Our Royal Sign Manual, counter-signed by one of Our Principal Secretaries of State, and bearing date at Our Court at Buckingham Palace, the 29th day of January, 1856, in the Nineteenth year of Our Reign, We did constitute and create a new Naval and Military decoration, to be styled and designated the Victoria Cross, which decoration We expressed Our desire should be highly prized and eagerly sought after by the Officers and men of Our Naval and Military Services, and did also make, ordain, and establish the rules and Ordinances therein set forth for the government of the same, to be thenceforth inviolably observed and kept.

And whereas, during the progress of the operations which We have undertaken against the Insurgent Native tribes in Our Colony of New Zealand, it has happened that persons serving in the local forces of Our said Colony, have performed deeds of gallantry in consideration of which they are not, according to the strict provisions of Our said recited Warrant, eligible for this high distinction, Now know ye, that

We, of Our especial grace, certain knowledge, and mere motion, have thought fit hereby to signify Our Royal Will and Pleasure that the said decoration may be conferred on such persons aforesaid, who may be qualified to receive the same in accordance with the rules and Ordinances made, ordained, and established by Us for the government thereof, by Our said recited Warrant, and We do by these Presents for Us, Our Heirs and Successors, ordain and appoint that it shall be competent for such persons aforesaid to obtain the said decoration in the manner set forth in the rules and Ordinances referred to, or in accordance with such further rules and Ordinances as may hereafter be made and promulgated by Us, Our Heirs and Successors, for the government of the said decoration, provided that it be established in any case that the person was serving with Our Troops, under the orders of a General or other Officer, under circumstances which would entitle an Officer or Soldier of Our Army to be recommended for the said decoration, in accordance with the rules and Ordinances prescribed in Our said recited Warrant, and provided also that such person shall be recommended for it by such General or other Officer.

And We do further, for Us, Our Heirs and Successors, ordain and appoint that the said decoration may also be conferred, in accordance with the rules and Ordinances prescibed in Our said recited Warrant, and subject to the provisoes [sic] aforesaid, on such persons who may be qualified to receive the same, in accordance with the said rules and Ordinances, as may hereafter be employed in the local Forces raised, or which may be raised in Our Colonies and their dependencies, who may be called upon to serve in co-operation with Our Troops, in military operations which it may be necessary to undertake for the suppression of Rebellion against Our authority, or for repelling invasion by a Foreign enemy.

Given at Our Court at Osborne House, Isle of Wight, this First day of January, 1867, in the Thirtieth year of Our Reign.

By Her Majesty's Command
J. Peel

APPENDIX IX

Warrant Redefining the Qualifications for the Victoria Cross and Extending Eligibility to Auxiliary and Reserve Forces

Public Record Office, WO 32/7397

Victoria R.

Whereas doubts have arisen as to the qualification required for the decoration of the Victoria Cross, and whereas the description of such qualification in Our Warrant of 29th January 1856 is not uniform,

Our Will and Pleasure is that the qualification shall be 'conspicuous bravery or devotion to the country in the presence of the enemy', and that Our Warrant of 29th January 1856 shall be read and interpreted accordingly.

It is Our further Will and Pleasure that Officers and men of Our Auxiliary and Reserve forces (Naval and Military) shall be eligible for the decoration of the Victoria Cross under the conditions of Our said Warrant, as amended by this Our Warrant.

Given at Our Court at Osborne this 23rd day of April 1881, in the forty fourth year of Our reign.

By Her Majesty's Command,

Hugh C.E. Childers

APPENDIX X

Warrant Extending Eligibility for the Victoria Cross to the Indian Ecclesiastical Establishments

Public Record Office WO 32/7399

Victoria R & I

Victoria by the Grace of God of the United Kingdom of Great Britain and Ireland Queen, Defender of the Faith, Empress of India, To all to whom these Presents shall come, Greeting!

Whereas by a Warrant under Our Royal Sign Manual countersigned by one of Our Principal Secretaries of State and bearing date at Our Court at Buckingham Palace the 29th day of January 1856 in the Nineteenth year of Our Reign, We did constitute and create a new Naval and Military decoration to be styled and designated the 'Victoria Cross', which decoration We expressed Our desire should be highly prized and eagerly sought after by the Officers and Men of Our Naval and Military services, and did also make, ordain, and establish the rules and ordinances therein set forth for the Government of the same to be thenceforth inviolably observed and kept;

And Whereas, by another Warrant under Our Royal Sign Manual, countersigned by one of Our Principal Secretaries of State and bearing date at Our Court at Windsor the Twenty-ninth day of October 1857 in the Twenty first year of Our Reign, We thought fit to signify Our Royal Will and Pleasure that the said decoration shall be conferred on the Officers and Men of the Naval and Military services of the East India Company who may be qualified to receive the same in accordance with the rules and ordinances made, ordained, and established by Us for the government thereof by Our first recited Warrant aforesaid,

And Whereas it has been represented to Us that the Members of the Indian Ecclesiastical Establishments, although not receiving Military Commissions, are liable to be attached to an Army in the field and are then required to perform the same duties as the Commissioned Chaplains of Our Army, who are eligible for this decoration,

Now Know ye that We of Our especial grace, certain knowledge, and mere motion have thought fit hereby to signify Our Royal Will and Pleasure that the said decoration shall be conferred on such persons as aforesaid who may be qualified to receive the same, in accordance with the rules and ordinances made, ordained, and established by Us for the Government thereof by Our said first recited Warrant and We do by these Presents for Us, Our Heirs and Successors, ordain and appoint that it shall be competent for such persons as aforesaid to obtain the said decoration in the manner set forth in the rules and ordinances referred to, or in accordance with such further rules and ordinances as may hereafter be made and promulgated by Us, Our Heirs and Successors, for the Government of the said decoration provided that it be established in any case that the person was serving for the time being under the orders of a General, or other Officer, in Command of Troops in the Field.

Given at Our Court at Osborne House, Isle of Wight, this Sixth day of August 1881, in the Forty fifth year of Our Reign.

By Her Majesty's Command.

Hugh C.E. Childers.

APPENDIX XI

Warrant Extending the Victoria Cross to the Native Officers, Non-Commissioned Officers and Men of the Indian Army

The Official Army List, Jan.1912, pp.2186a-2187

George R.I.

GEORGE, by the Grace of God, of the United Kingdom of Great Britain and Ireland, and of the British Dominions beyond the Seas, King, Defender of the Faith, Emperor of India, to all to whom these presents shall come, Greeting!

WHEREAS Her Majesty, Queen Victoria, by a Warrant under her Royal Sign Manual, countersigned by one of Her Principal Secretaries of State, and bearing date at Her Court at Buckingham Palace, the twenty-ninth day of January, one thousand eight hundred and fifty-six, in the nineteenth year of Her reign, did institute and create a new naval and military decoration, to be styled and designated the 'Victoria Cross', which decoration She expressed Her desire should be highly prized and eagerly sought after by the officers and men of Her Naval and Military Services, and did also make, ordain, and establish the rules and ordinances therein set forth for the government of the same, to be thenceforward inviolably observed and kept.

And whereas for divers reasons Us thereunto moving, We are desirous of rewarding the individual gallant services of native officers, non-commissioned officers and men of Our Indian Army by the bestowal of the said decoration, which We are desirous shall be highly prized and eagerly sought after by the said native officers, non-commissioned officers and men.

Now know ye that We, of Our especial grace, certain knowledge, and mere motion, have thought fit hereby to signify Our Royal Will and Pleasure that the said decoration shall be conferred on the native officers, non-commissioned officers and men of Our Indian army who may be qualified to receive the same in accordance with the rules and ordinances made, ordained and established for the government thereof by the said recited Warrant, and We do by these Presents, for Us, Our Heirs and Successors, ordain and appoint that it shall be competent for the native officers, non-commissioned officers and men of Our Indian Army to obtain the said decoration in the manner set forth in the rules and ordinances referred to, or in accordance with any further rules and ordinances which may hereafter be made and promulgated by Us, Our Heirs and Successors, for the government of the said decoration.

And We do further, for Us, Our Heirs and Successors, ordain and appoint that in place of the special pension conferred by the fourteenth rule of the said recited Warrant, every native officer who shall have received the Cross shall from the date of the act by which such decoration has been gained be entitled to a special pension of five hundred and twenty-five rupees a year, and each additional bar conferred under the fourth rule on such native officer shall carry with it an additional pension of one hundred and fifty rupees a year. In the case of a warrant or non-commissioned officer or soldier the special pension shall be one hundred and fifty rupees, with seventy-five rupees additional for each additional bar. On the death of a recipient of the Cross these pensions shall be continued to his widow until her death or remarriage.

Given at Our Court at St. James's this 21st day of October, in the second year of Our Reign, and in the year of Our Lord one thousand nine hundred and eleven.

By His Majesty's Command,
                    HALDANE OF CLOAN.

APPENDIX XII

Warrant Effecting a General Revision and Recodification of the Conditions of Award of the Victoria Cross.

Public Record Office, WO 32/3443

[Signed] George R.I. THE VICTORIA CROSS WARRANT

GEORGE R. AND I.

WHEREAS Her late Majesty Queen Victoria, by a Warrant under Her Royal Sign Manual dated 29th January, 1856, did create a Naval and Military Decoration to be styled and designated 'The Victoria Cross', and did express Her desire that this decoration should be highly prized and eagerly sought after by the Officers and Men of Her Naval and Military Services.

AND WHEREAS by divers subsequent Warrants other Officers and Men were admitted to and made eligible for the decoration, and certain amendments were made to the Rules and Ordinances attaching thereto.

AND WHEREAS We deem it expedient that the said Warrant and subsequent Warrants before referred to, as also the Rules and Ordinances affecting the same, shall be consolidated, varied and extended.

NOW, THEREFORE, We do hereby declare that the said Warrants, and the Rules and Ordinances heretofore in force for the Government of the said Decoration, shall for that purpose be amended, varied, modified and extended; and in substitution thereof We by these presents, for Us, Our Heirs and Successors, are graciously pleased to make, ordain and establish the following Rules and Ordinances for the Government of the same which shall from henceforth be inviolably observed and kept:-

Firstly, it is ordained that the distinction shall as heretofore be styled and designated 'The Victoria Cross', and shall consist of a Maltese Cross of bronze with our Royal Crest in the centre and underneath it an escroll bearing this inscription: 'For Valour'.

Secondly, it is ordained that the Cross shall be suspended from the left breast by a red riband, and on those occasions when only the riband is worn a replica of the Cross in miniature shall be affixed to the centre of the riband.

Thirdly, it is ordained that the Cross shall only be awarded for most conspicuous bravery or some daring or pre-eminent act of valour or self-sacrifice or extreme devotion to duty in the presence of the enemy.

Fourthly, it is ordained that the Cross may be awarded posthumously.

Fifthly, it is ordained that the names of all those persons upon or on account of whom We may be pleased to confer or present the decoration shall be published in the *London Gazette,* and a Registry thereof kept in the Office of Our Secretary of State for War.

Sixthly, it is ordained that:-
   (1)   Officers, Warrant Officers and subordinate Officers hereinafter referred to as Officers, Chief Petty Officers and Petty Officers hereinafter referred to as Petty Officers, men and boys herein-

after referred to as Seamen, serving in — *(a)* our Navy or in ships of any description for the time being under Naval Command; *(b)* our Indian Marine Services; *(c)* Navies or Marine Services of our Dominions, Colonies, Dependencies or Protectorates; and *(d)* our Mercantile Marine whilst serving under Naval or Military Authority, or who in the course of their duties may become subject to enemy action;

(2)   Officers, Warrant Officers, Non-Commissioned Officers, men and boys hereinafter referred to as Marines, serving in our Marines;

(3)   Officers, Warrant Officers (Classes I. and II.), Non-Commissioned Officers, men and boys hereinafter referred to as Privates, of all ranks serving in our Army, our Army Reserve, our Territorial or other forces, and the Forces of our Dominions, Colonies, Dependencies or Protectorates;

(4)   Officers, Warrant Officers, Non-Commissioned Officers, and Airmen in the ranks of Our Air Force, or the Air Forces of our Dominions, Colonies, Dependencies or Protectorates;

(5)   British and Indian Officers and men of all ranks of Our Indian Army, the Imperial Service Troops of Native States of India, or any other Forces there serving under the Command, guidance, or direction of any British or Indian Officer, or of a Political Officer attached to such Forces on Our behalf, and

(6)   Matrons, sisters, nurses and the staff of the Nursing Services and other Services pertaining to Hospitals and Nursing, and civilians of either sex serving regularly or temporarily under the Orders, direction or supervision of any of the above mentioned Forces

shall be eligible for the decoration of the Cross.

Seventhly, it is ordained that if any recipient of the Cross shall again perform such an act of bravery, as would have made him or her eligible to receive the Cross, such further act of bravery shall be recorded by a Bar to be attached to the Riband by which the Cross is suspended, and for every such additional act of bravery, an additional Bar shall be added, and any such Bar or Bars may be awarded posthumously. For every Bar awarded a replica of the Cross in miniature shall be added to the riband when worn alone.

Eighthly, it is ordained that every recommendation for the Award of the decoration of the Cross shall be made and reported through the usual channel to the Senior Naval, Military or Air Force Officer Commanding the Force, who shall call for such description, conclusive proof as far as the circumstances of the case will allow, and attestation of the act as he may think requisite, and if he approve he shall recommend the grant of the decoration to Our Lords Commissioners of the Admiralty, Our Secretary of State for War and the Royal Air Force as the case may be, who shall submit to Us the names of every one so recommended whom they shall consider worthy: in the case of there being no British or Indian Officer, then the Political Officer attached to the Force shall, after obtaining conclusive proof of the act of bravery as far as is possible, if he approve, submit the recommendation to Us through the proper channels.

Ninthly, it is ordained that in the event of any unit of our Naval, Military or Air Forces, consisting in the case of our Navy of a squadron, flotilla or ship's company, or of a detached body of seamen or marines; or in the case of our Army of a regiment, squadron, battery or company, or of a detached body of soldiers; or in the case of our Air Force of a squadron or other body of airmen, having distinguished itself collectively by the performance of an act of heroic gallantry or daring in the presence of the enemy in such a way that the Admiral, General or other Officer in Command of the Force to which such an unit belongs, is unable to single out any individual as specially pre-eminent in gallantry or daring, then one or more of the officers, warrant officers, petty officers, non-commissioned officers, seamen, marines, private soldiers or airmen in the ranks comprising the unit shall be selected to be recommended to Us for the award of the Victoria Cross in the following manner:-

(a) When the total personnel of the unit does not exceed 100, then one officer shall be selected for the decoration by the officers engaged; and in like manner one warrant officer or petty officer, or non-commissioned officer of the unit shall be selected by the warrant officers, petty officers or non-commissioned officers engaged, and one seaman, marine, private soldier, or airman in the ranks shall be selected by the seamen, marines, private soldiers or airmen in the ranks engaged.

(b) When the total personnel of the unit exceeds 100 but does not exceed 200, then the number of seamen, marines, private soldiers or airmen in the ranks to be selected in the manner described in *(a)* shall be increased to two.

(c) When the total personnel of the unit exceeds 200 in number, the number of Crosses to be awarded in accordance with these provisions shall be the subject of special consideration by Our Lords Commissioners of the Admiralty or by one of Our Secretaries of State for submission to Us.

(d) The selection to be by a secret ballot in such manner as shall be determined in accordance with the foregoing provisions by the Officer directing the selection to be made.

(e) The death of any person engaged shall not be a bar to his selection.

(f) The names of the persons recommended in accordance with these provisions shall be submitted to Us in the manner laid down in Rule 8.

Tenthly, it is ordained that every recipient of the Cross, not being nor ranking as a Commissioned Officer nor in the case of Our Navy, being or ranking with a warrant officer, nor coming within Rule 11, shall from the date of the act by which such decoration has been gained, be entitled to a special pension of Ten Pounds a year, and each additional Bar conferred under Rule 7 on such recipient shall carry with it an additional pension of Five Pounds per annum.

Eleventhly, every Indian Officer of Our Indian Army of rank junior to that of Second Lieutenant who shall have received the Cross shall, from the date of the act by which such decoration has been gained, be entitled to a special pension of Five hundred and twenty-five rupees a year, and each additional Bar conferred on such Indian Officer shall carry with it an additional pension of One hundred and fifty rupees a year. In the case of a Warrant or Non-Commissioned Officer or soldier of Our Indian Army aforesaid We ordain and award a special pension of One hundred and fifty rupees, with Seventy-five rupees additional for each additional Bar. On the death of these recipients of the Cross these pensions shall be continued to his widow until her death or remarriage.

Twelfthly, in order to make such additional provision as shall effectually maintain pure this most honourable distinction, it is ordained that if any person on whom such distinction shall be conferred be convicted of treason, cowardice, felony, or of any infamous crime, or if he or she be accused of any such offence and doth not after a reasonable time surrender himself or herself to be tried for the same, his or her name shall by an especial Warrant under Our Royal Sign Manual forthwith be erased from the registry of individuals upon whom the said decoration shall have been conferred and the pension conferred under Rules 10 and 11 shall cease and determine from the date of such Warrant. It is hereby further declared that We, Our Heirs and Successors, shall be the sole judges of the circumstance demanding such expulsion; moreover, We shall at all times have power to restore such persons as may at any time have been expelled, both to the enjoyment of the decoration and pension, and notice thereof of expulsion or restoration in every case shall be published in the *London Gazette*.

Given at Our Court at St. James's this *7th* day of *March, 1919* in the *Ninth* Year of Our Reign.

Winston S. Churchill,
    By His Majesty's Command.

[Note. In the original version of this Warrant, in PRO file WO 32/3443, the dating clause appears as above, the italicised portion being manuscript insertions in the blanks of a printed text. When the Warrant was finally published, the printed version became:

Given at Our Court at St. James's this 22nd day of May, in the eleventh Year of Our reign, and in the year of Our Lord one thousand nine hundred and twenty.

By His Majesty's Command,
    WINSTON S. CHURCHILL]

APPENDIX XIII

Warrant Effecting a Further General Revision of the Conditions of Award of the Victoria Cross

Public Record Office, WO 32/3442

GEORGE R.I.

GEORGE THE FIFTH, by the Grace of God, of Great Britain, Ireland and the British Dominions beyond the Seas, King, Defender of the Faith, Emperor of India; to all to whom these Presents shall come, Greeting!

WHEREAS Her late Majesty Queen Victoria, by a Warrant under Her Sign Manual dated the 29th day of January, 1856, did create a Naval and Military Decoration to be styled and designated 'The Victoria Cross', and did express Her desire that this Decoration should be highly prized and eagerly sought after by the Officers and Men of Her Naval and Military Services.

AND WHEREAS by divers subsequent Warrants other Officers and Men were admitted to and made eligible for the Decoration, and certain amendments were made to the rules and ordinances attaching thereto.

AND WHEREAS the said Warrant and subsequent Warrants before referred to, as also the rules and ordinances affecting the same, were consolidated, varied, and extended by a Warrant under Our Sign Manual dated the 22nd day of May 1920.

NOW, THEREFORE, We do hereby declare that the rules and ordinances contained in Our said Warrant heretofore in force for the governance of the said Decoration, shall be abrogated, cancelled and annulled; and in substitution thereof We by these Presents, for Us, Our Heirs and Successors, are graciously pleased to make, ordain and establish the following rules and ordinances for the governance of the same which shall from henceforth be inviolably observed and kept:-

Firstly: It is ordained that the distinction shall as heretofore be styled and designated 'The Victoria Cross', and shall consist of a Maltese Cross of bronze with Our Royal Crest in the centre and underneath it an escroll bearing this inscription: 'For Valour'.

Secondly: It is ordained that the Cross shall be suspended from the left breast by a red riband of one inch and a half in width, and on those occasions when only the riband is worn a replica of the Cross in miniature shall be affixed to the centre of the riband.

Thirdly: It is ordained that the Cross shall only be awarded for most conspicuous bravery or some daring or pre-eminent act of valour or self-sacrifice or extreme devotion to duty in the presence of the enemy.

Fourthly: It is ordained that the Cross may be awarded posthumously.

Fifthly: It is ordained that the names of all those persons upon or on account of whom We may be pleased to confer or present the Decoration shall be published in the *London Gazette,* and a Registry thereof kept in the Office of Our Principal Secretary of State for War.

Sixthly: It is ordained that:-

(1)   Officers, Warrant Officers and subordinate Officers hereinafter

referred to as Officers, Chief Petty Officers and Petty Officers hereinafter referred to as Petty Officers, men and boys hereinafter referred to as Seamen, serving in – *(a)* Our Navy or in ships of any description for the time being under Naval Command; *(b)* Our Indian Marine Service; *(c)* Navies or Marine Services of Our Dominions, Colonies, Dependencies or Protectorates; and *(d)* Our Mercantile Marine whilst serving under Naval, Military or Air Force Authority, or who in the course of their duties may become subject to enemy action;

(2) Officers, Warrant Officers, Non-Commissioned Officers, men and boys hereinafter referred to as Marines, serving in Our Marines;

(3) Officers, Warrant Officers Classes I and II, Non-Commissioned Officers, men and boys hereinafter referred to as Privates, of all ranks serving in Our Army, Our Army Reserve, Our Territorial or other Forces, and the Forces of Our Dominions, Colonies, Dependencies or Portectorates;

(4) Officers, Warrant Officers, Classes I and II, Non-Commissioned Officers, and other Airmen serving in Our Air Force, Our Air Force Reserve, Our Auxiliary Air Force, or the Air Forces of Our Dominions, Colonies, Dependencies or Protectorates;

(5) British and Indian Officers and men of all ranks of Our Indian Army, the Imperial Service Troops of Native States of India, or any other Forces there serving under the command, guidance, or direction of any British or Indian Officer, or of a Political Officer attached to such Forces on Our behalf, and

(6) Matrons, Sisters, Nurses and the Staff of the Nursing Services and other Services pertaining to Hospitals and Nursing, and Civilians of either sex serving regularly or temporarily under the orders, direction or supervision of any of the above mentioned Forces

shall be eligible for the Decoration of the Cross.

Seventhly: It is ordained that if any recipient of the Cross shall again perform such an act of bravery, as would have made him or her eligible to receive the Cross, such further act of bravery shall be recorded by a Bar to be attached to the riband by which the Cross is suspended, and for every such additional act of bravery, an additional Bar shall be added, and any such Bar or Bars may be awarded posthumously. For every Bar awarded a replica of the Cross in miniature shall be added to the riband when worn alone.

Eighthly: It is ordained that every recommendation for the award of the Decoration of the Cross shall be made and reported through the usual channel to the Senior Naval, Military or Air Force Officer Commanding the Force, who shall call for such description, conclusive proof as far as the circumstances of the case will allow, and attestation of the act as he may think requisite, and if he approve he shall recommend the grant of the Decoration to Our Lords Commissioners of the Admiralty, Our Principa¹ Secretary of State for War or Our Principal Secretary of State for Air as the case may be, who shall submit to Us the names of every one so recommended whom they shall consider worthy: in the case of there being no British or Indian Officer, then the Political Officer attached to the Force shall, after obtaining conclusive proof of the act of bravery as far as is possible, if he approve, submit the recommendation to Us through the proper channels.

Ninthly: It is ordained that in the event of any unit of Our Naval, Military or Air Forces, consisting in the case of Our Navy of a squadron, flotilla or ship's Company, or of a detached body of seamen or marines; or in the case of Our Army of a regiment, squadron, battery or company, or of a detached body of soldiers; or in the case of Our Air Forces of a squadron or other body of airmen, having distinguished itself collectively by the performance of an act of heroic gallantry or daring in the presence of the enemy in such a way that the Flag, General, Air or other Officer in Command of the Force to which such an unit belongs, is unable to single out any individual as specially pre-eminent in gallantry or daring, then one or more of the personnel comprising the unit shall be selected to be recommended to Us for the award of the Victoria Cross in the following manner:-

(a) When the total personnel of the unit does not exceed 100, then one officer shall be selected for the Decoration by the officers engaged; and in like manner one warrant officer or petty officer or non-commissioned officer of the unit shall be selected by the warrant officers, petty officers or non-commissioned officers engaged, and one seaman, marine, private soldier, or aircraftsman shall be selected by the seamen, marines, private soldiers or aircraftsmen engaged;

(b) When the total personnel of the unit exceeds 100 but does not exceed 200, then the number of seamen, marines, private soldiers or aircraftsmen to be selected in the manner described in *(a)* shall be increased to two;

(c) When the total personnel of the unit exceeds 200 in number, the number of Crosses to be awarded in accordance with these provisions shall be the subject of special consideration by Our Lords Commissioners of the Admiralty or by one of Our Principal Secretaries of State for submission to Us;

(d) The selection to be by a secret ballot in such manner as shall be determined in accordance with the foregoing provisions by the Officer directing the selection to be made;

(e) The death of any person engaged shall not be a bar to his selection;

(f) The names of the persons recommended in accordance with these provisions shall be submitted to Us in the manner laid down in the Eighth Clause of this Our Warrant.

Tenthly: It is ordained that every recipient of the Cross, not being or ranking as a Commissioned Officer and in the case of Our Navy and Our Marines, not being or ranking with a warrant officer, and not coming within the Eleventh Clause of this Our Warrant, shall from the date of the act by which theDecoration has been gained, be entitled to a special pension of ten pounds a year, and each additional Bar conferred under the Seventh Clause of this Our Warrant on such recipient shall carry with it an additional pension of five pounds a year.

Eleventhly: Every Indian Officer of Our Indian Army of rank junior to that of Second Lieutenant who shall have received the Cross shall, from the date of the act by which such Decoration has been gained, be entitled to a special pension of five hundred and twenty-five rupees a year, and each additional Bar conferred on such Indian Officer shall carry with it an additional pension of one hundred and fifty rupees a year. In the case of a Warrant or Non-Commissioned Officer or Soldier of Our Indian Army aforesaid We ordain and award a special pension of one hundred and fifty rupees a year with seventy-five rupees a year additional for each additional Bar. On the death of a recipient of the Cross to whom this clause applies the pension shall be continued to his widow until her death or remarriage.

Twelfthly: It is ordained that a reproduction of the Cross known as a Miniature Cross which may be worn on certain occasions by those to whom the Decoration is awarded shall be half the size of The Victoria Cross and that a Sealed Pattern of the said Miniature Cross shall be deposited and kept in the Central Chancery of Our Orders of Knighthood.

Thirteenthly: It is ordained that it shall be competent for Us, Our Heirs and Successors, by an Order under Our Sign Manual and on the recommendation to that effect by or through Our First Lord of the Admiralty or one of Our Principal Secretaries of State to cancel and annul the award of The Victoria Cross to any person, together with any pension appertaining thereto not already paid, and that thereupon his or her name in the Register shall be erased; but that it shall be competent for Us, Our Heirs and Successors, to restore the Decoration when such recommendation has been withdrawn and with it such pension as may have been forfeited.

Fourteenthly: It is ordained that notice of cancellation or restoration in every case shall be published in the *London Gazette.*

Lastly: We reserve to Ourselves, Our Heirs and Successors full power of annulling, altering, abrogating, interpreting or dispensing with these regulations, or any part thereof, by a notification under Our Sign Manual.

Given at Our Court at St. James's, this 5th day of February, in the 21st year of Our Reign, and in the Year of Our Lord one thousand nine hundred and thirty-one.

By His Majesty's Command,
                    T. SHAW

APPENDIX XIV
Warrant to Include Burmese Forces on the Separation of Burma from India
Victoria Cross Register, iii, p.355

GEORGE R.I.

GEORGE THE SIXTH by the Grace of God, of Great Britain, Ireland and the British Dominions beyond the Seas, King, Defender of the Faith, Emperor of India; to all to whom these Presents shall come, Greeting!

WHEREAS His late Majesty King George V, by a Warrant under His Royal Sign Manual dated the 5th day of February, one thousand nine hundred and thirty one, was pleased to make, ordain and establish rules and ordinances for the governance of the Decoration of the Victoria Cross reserving to Himself, His Heirs and Successors full power of annulling, altering, abrogating, augmenting, interpreting or dispensing with these rules and ordinances, or any part thereof, by a notification under Royal Sign Manual;

AND WHEREAS on 1st April, 1937, Burma ceased to be part of India, and We are desirous that Officers, Non Commissioned Officers and Men of Our Burma Army and other Military Forces in Burma shall be considered eligible for the award of the Decoration;

NOW THEREFORE WE do by these Presents for Us, Our Heirs and Successors ordain and appoint that the Fifth Paragraph of the Sixth Clause and the Eighth and Eleventh Clauses of the said Warrant shall be cancelled and annulled and the following substituted therefore:-

(5)   British, Indian or Burman officers and men of all ranks of Our Indian and Burma Armies, the Indian States' Forces of Indian States or any Forces serving in India or Burma under the command, guidance or direction of any British, Indian or Burman Officer, or of a Political Officer attached to such Forces on Our Behalf and

Eighthly: It is ordained that every recommendation for the award of the Decoration of the Cross shall be made and reported through the usual channels to the Senior Naval, Military or Air Force Officer Commanding the Force, who shall call for such description, conclusive proof, as far as the circumstances of the case will allow, and attestation of the act as he may think requisite, and, if he approve, he shall recommend the grant of the Decoration to Our Lords Commissioners of the Admiralty, Our Principal Secretary of State for War or Our Principal Secretary of State for Air, as the case may be, who shall submit to Us the names of every one so recommended whom they shall consider worthy; in the case of there being no British, Indian or Burman Officer, then the Political Officer attached to the Force shall, after obtaining conclusive proof of the act of bravery as far as is possible, if he approve, submit the recommendation to us through the proper channels.

Eleventhly: Every Indian Officer of Our Indian Army and Burman

Officer of Our Burma Army of rank junior to that of Second Lieutenant who shall have received the Cross shall, from the date of the Act by which such Decoration has been gained, be entitled to a special pension of five hundred and twenty five rupees a year, and each additional Bar conferred on such Indian Officer or Burman Officer shall carry with it an additional pension of one hundred and fifty rupees a year. In the case of a Warrant or Non-Commissioned Officer or soldier of Our Indian or Burma Armies aforesaid We ordain and appoint a special pension of one hundred and fifty rupees a year, with seventy-five rupees a year additional for each additional Bar. On the death of a recipient of the Cross to whom this clause applies, the pension shall be continued to his widow until her death or remarriage.

Given at Our Court of St. James's, this 9th day of May, 1938, in the Second Year of Our Reign, in the Year of Our Lord one thousand nine hundred and thirty-eight.

By His Majesty's Command,
LESLIE HORE–BELISHA

APPENDIX XV

Warrant to Include New Grade of Warrant Officers
Issued with Army Order 144 of 1939

GEORGE R.I.

GEORGE THE SIXTH by the Grace of God, of Great Britain, Ireland and the British Dominions beyond the Seas, King, Defender of the Faith, Emperor of India; to all to whom these Presents shall come, Greeting!

WHEREAS His late Majesty King George V, by a Warrant under His Royal Sign Manual dated the 5th February 1931, was pleased to make, ordain and establish rules and ordinances for the governance of the Decoration of the Victoria Cross reserving to Himself, His Heirs and Successors full power of annulling, altering, abrogating, augmenting, interpreting or dispensing with these rules and ordinances, or any part thereof, by a notification under Royal Sign Manual;

AND WHEREAS by a Warrant under Our Sign Manual dated the 9th day of May 1938, We did ordain that Officers, Non Commissioned Officers and Men of Our Burma Army and other Military Forces in Burma should be considered eligible for the award of the Decoration;

AND WHEREAS by a Warrant under Our Sign Manual dated the 14th day of September, 1938, We did deem it expedient to introduce into Our Regular Army a new class of Warrant Officer;

AND WHEREAS We deem it expedient that the said Warrant dated the 5th day of February, 1931, should be amended to provide for the award of the Decoration to all classes of Warrant Officers;

NOW THEREFORE WE do by these presents for Us, Our Heirs and Successors ordain and appoint that the Sixth Clause, sub-paragraphs (3) and (4) shall be altered by the deletion of the words 'Classes I and II', and that the said alterations shall have effect from the 14th day of September, 1938.

Given at Our Court of St. James's, this 21st day of August, in the 3rd year of Our Reign, and in the year of Our Lord one thousand nine hundred and thirty nine.

By His Majesty's Command,
KINGSLEY WOOD.

APPENDIX XVI

Warrant to Include the Indian Air Force on its Formation
Issued with Army Order 8 of 1941

GEORGE R.I.

GEORGE THE SIXTH by the Grace of God, of Great Britain, Ireland and the British Dominions beyond the Seas, King, Defender of the Faith, Emperor of India; to all to whom these Presents shall come, Greeting!

WHEREAS His late Majesty King George V, by a Warrant under His Royal Sign Manual dated the 5th February 1931, was pleased to make, ordain and establish rules and ordinances for the governance of the Decoration of the Victoria Cross reserving to Himself, His Heirs and Successors full power of annulling, altering, abrogating, augmenting, interpreting or dispensing with these rules and ordinances, or any part thereof, by a notification under Royal Sign Manual;

AND WHEREAS by a Warrant under Our Royal Sign Manual dated the 9th day of May 1938, We did ordain that Officers, Non Commissioned Officers and Men of Our Burma Army and other Military Forces in Burma should be considered eligible for the award of the Decoration;

AND WHEREAS by a Warrant under Our Sign Manual dated the 14th day of September, 1938, We did deem it expedient to introduce into Our Regular Army a new class of Warrant Officer;

AND WHEREAS by a Warrant under Our Sign Manual dated 21st August, 1939, We did ordain that all classes of Warrant Officers shall be eligible for the Decoration;

AND WHEREAS we are desirous that Officers, Warrant Officers, Non Commissioned Officers and Airmen of Our Indian Air Force shall be eligible for the award of the Decoration;

NOW THEREFORE We do by these Presents for Us, Our Heirs and Successors ordain and appoint that the Sixth Clause, sub paragraph (4) of the Warrant dated 5th February, 1931, as amended by the Warrant dated 21st August, 1939, shall be cancelled and annulled and the following substituted therefore:-

(4)   Officers, Warrant Officers, Non Commissioned Officers and other Airmen serving in Our Air Force, Our Air Force Reserve, Our Auxiliary Air Force, Our Indian Air Force, or the Air Forces of Our Dominions, Colonies, Dependencies or Protectorates;

AND WE DO FURTHER ordain and appoint that the Eleventh Clause as ordained in the Warrant dated 9th May, 1938, shall be cancelled and annulled, and the following substituted therefore:-

Eleventhly: Every Indian Officer of Our Indian Army and Burman Officer of Our Burma Army of rank junior to that of Second-Lieutenant and every Indian Officer of Our Indian Air Force of rank junior to that of Pilot Officer who shall have received the Cross shall, from the date of the act by which such Decoration has been gained, be entitled to a special pension of five hundred and twenty-five rupees a year, and each additional Bar conferred on such Indian Officer or Burman Officer shall carry with it an additional pension of one hundred and fifty rupees a year. In the case of a Warrant or Non-Commissioned Officer or soldier of Our Indian Army, Our Indian Air Force or Burma Army aforesaid We ordain and award a special pension of one hundred and fifty rupees a year, with seventy-five rupees additional for each additional bar. On the death of a recipient of the Cross to whom this clause applies the pension shall be continued to his widow until her death or remarriage.

Given at Our Court at St. James's this 25th day of January, 1941, in the 5th Year of Our Reign.

By His Majesty's Command,
DAVID MARGESSON.

APPENDIX XVII

Warrant to Include the Home Guard and Women's Services, to Allow Direct Submission by Dominions Governments, and to Extend the Financial Provisions for Indian and Burmese Forces

Public Record Office, WO 32/9954

GEORGE R.I.

GEORGE THE SIXTH, by the Grace of God, of Great Britain, Ireland, and the British Dominions beyond the Seas, King, Defender of the Faith, Emperor of India, to all to whom these Presents shall come, Greeting!

WHEREAS His late Majesty King George V, by a Warrant under his Sign Manual, dated 5th February, 1931, was pleased to make, ordain and establish rules and ordinances for the governance of the Decoration of the Victoria Cross, reserving to Himself, His Heirs and Successors full power of annulling, altering, abrogating, augmenting, interpreting or dispensing with those rules and ordinances, or any part thereof, by a notification under Royal Sign Manual;

AND WHEREAS WE are desirous that persons of any rank in Our Home Guard and any lawfully constituted force corresponding thereto shall be eligible for the award of the Decoration; that the position of Our Women's Auxiliary Services in the matter shall be regularised; that provision shall be made for direct submission to Us in the case of any of Our Dominions, the Government whereof shall so desire; and that eligibility for monetary awards shall be extended to all Our Indian and Burma Forces within the limits of rank to be laid down;

NOW THEREFORE WE do by these Presents for Us, Our Heirs and Successors ordain and appoint that the Sixth Clause of the said Warrant, as amended by Our Warrants dated 9th May, 1938, 21st August, 1939 and 25th January, 1941, the Eighth Clause as ordained in Our Warrant dated 25th January, 1941, shall be *cancelled* and *annulled* and the following *substituted* therefor:-

Sixthly: It is ordained that the persons eligible for the Decoration of following *substituted* therefor:-

(1) Persons of any rank in the Naval, Military and Air Forces of Our United Kingdom of Great Britain and Northern Ireland, of India, of Burma, of Our Colonies and of territories under Our suzerainty, protection or jurisdiction or under Our jurisdiction jointly with another power, or belonging to any other part of our Dominions, Our Government whereof has signified its desire that awards of the Cross shall be made under the provisions of this Our Warrant, or belonging to any Territory under Our protection administered by Us in such Government, including the Home Guard and any lawfully constituted force corresponding thereto, and, in India, members of the Frontier Corps and Military Police, and members of the Indian States' Forces, and, in Burma, members of the Burma Frontier Force and Military Police, and including also members of the Naval, Military and Air Force Nursing Services and of the Women's Auxiliary Services;

(2) Members of Our Merchant Navy;

(3) Our faithful subjects and persons under Our protection in civil life, male and female, serving regularly or temporarily under the orders, directions or supervision of any of the above-mentioned Forces or Services;

Eighthly: It is ordained that every recommendation for the award of the Decoration of the Cross shall be made or reported through the usual channel to the Senior Naval, Military or Air Force Officer Commanding the Force, who shall call for such description, conclusive proof as far as the circumstances of the case will allow, and attestation of the act as he may think requisite, and if he approve he shall recommend the grant of the Decoration to Our Lords Commissioners of the Admiralty, Our Secretary of State for War or Our Secretary of State for

Air as the case may be, or, in the case of any of Our Dominions, the Government whereof shall so desire, the appropriate Minister of State for the said Dominion, who shall submit to Us the names of every one so recommended whom they shall consider worthy;

Eleventhly: In the case of Our Indian and Burma Forces, a recipient of the Cross or bar, within the limits of rank to be laid down, and, on the death of such recipient, his widow, shall be entitled to receive under regulations to be issued by Our Governor-General of India and Our Governor of Burma such special pension or additional pension as may be provided out of the revenues of India or the revenues of Burma, as the case may be.

AND WE do ordain and appoint that the Ninth Clause of the Warrant dated 5th February, 1931, shall be amended by the relettering of sub-paragraph *'(f)'* as *'(g)'* and by the insertion of the following sub-paragraph:-

(f)   Reference in this Clause to male members of Our Forces shall be deemed to include the equivalent ranks of Our Women's Auxiliary Services.

AND WE do further ordain and appoint that sub-paragraph *(c)* of the Ninth Clause, and the Thirteenth Clause of the Warrant dated 5th February, 1931, shall be amended by the insertion after 'Secretaries of State' of the words 'or, in the case of any of Our Dominions, the Government whereof shall so desire, the appropriate Minister of State for the said Dominion', in each case.

Given at our Court at St. James's, this 31st day of December, 1942, in the 7th year of Our Reign.

By His Majesty's Command,
P.J. GRIGG.

APPENDIX XVIII

Warrant Recoding the Conditions of Award of the Victoria Cross, Incorporating the Increase of Pension and the Extension of this to Commissioned Officers

Special Army Order 65 of 1961

ELIZABETH R.

ELIZABETH THE SECOND, by the Grace of God, of the United Kingdom of Great Britain and Northern Ireland, and of Her other Realms and Territories Queen, Head of the Commonwealth, Defender of the Faith: to all to whom these Presents shall come, Greeting!

WHEREAS His late Majesty King George V, by a Warrant under His Royal Sign Manual dated the 5th day of February 1931, was pleased to make, ordain and establish rules and ordinances for the governance of the Decoration of The Victoria Cross reserving to Himself, His Heirs and Successors full powers of annulling, altering, abrogating, augmenting, interpreting or dispensing with those rules and ordinances or any part thereof, by a notification under Royal Sign Manual;

AND WHEREAS the provisions of the said Warrant were amended by Warrants under the Royal Sign Manual of His late Majesty King George VI, dated the 9th day of May 1938, the 21st day of August 1939, the 25th day of January 1941 and the 31st day of December 1942;

AND WHEREAS WE deem it expedient that the provisions of the said Warrant be further amended and augmented;

NOW, THEREFORE, WE do hereby declare that the rules and ordinances contained in the said Warrant heretofore in force for the governance of the said Decoration, shall be abrogated, cancelled and annulled; and in substitution thereof We by these Presents, for Us, Our Heirs and Successors, are graciously pleased to make, ordain and establish the following rules and ordinances for the governance of the same which shall from henceforth be inviolably observed and kept:-

Firstly: It is ordained that the distinction shall as heretofore be styled and designated 'The Victoria Cross', and shall consist of a Maltese Cross of bronze with Our Royal Crest in the centre and underneath it an escroll bearing this inscription: 'For Valour'.

Secondly: It is ordained that the Cross shall be worn on the left breast pendant from a red riband of one inch and a half in width, and on those occasions when only the riband is worn a replica of the Cross in miniature shall be affixed to the centre of the riband.

Thirdly: It is ordained that the Cross shall only be awarded for most conspicuous bravery, or some daring or pre-eminent act of valour or self-sacrifice or extreme devotion to duty in the presence of the enemy.

Fourthly: It is ordained that the Cross may be awarded posthumously.

Fifthly: It is ordained that the names of all those persons upon or on account of whom We may be pleased to confer or present the Decoration shall be published in the *London Gazette,* and a Register thereof kept in the office of Our Principal Secretary of State for War.

Sixthly: It is ordained that the persons eligible for the Decoration of the Cross shall be:-

(1) Persons of any rank in the Naval, Military and Air Forces of Our United Kingdom of Great Britain and Northern Ireland, of Member Countries of the Commonwealth overseas, the Governments whereof have signified their desire that awards of the Cross shall be made under the provisions of this Our Warrant, of Our Colonies or Our other Territories or of the Territories under Our Protection or Administration, (including members of the Home Guard and any lawfully constituted Force corresponding thereto), and including also members of the Naval, Military and Air Force Nursing Services and of the Women's Auxiliary Services;

(2) Members of Our Merchant Navy;

(3) Our faithful subjects and persons under Our protection in

civil life, male and female, serving regularly or temporarily under the orders, directions or supervision of any of the above-mentioned Forces or Services.

Seventhly: It is ordained that if any recipient of the Cross shall again perform such an act of bravery as would have made him or her eligible to receive the Cross, such further act of bravery shall be recorded by a Bar to be attached to the riband by which the Cross is suspended, and for every such additional act of bravery, an additional Bar shall be added, and any such Bar or Bars may be awarded posthumously. For every Bar awarded a replica of the Cross in miniature shall be added to the riband when worn alone.

Eighthly: It is ordained that every recommendation for the award of the Decoration of the Cross shall be made and reported through the usual channel to the Senior Naval, Military or Air Force Officer Commanding the Force, who shall call for such description, conclusive proof as far as the circumstances of the case will allow, and attestation of the act as he may think requisite, and if he approve he shall recommend the grant of the Decoration to Our Lords Commissioners of the Admiralty, Our Secretary of State for War or Our Secretary of State for Air as the case may be, or, in the case of any Member Country of the Commonwealth Overseas, the Government whereof shall so desire, the appropriate Minister of State for the said Member Country, who shall submit to Us the names of every one so recommended whom they shall consider worthy.

Ninthly: It is ordained that in the event of any unit of the Naval, Military or Air Forces mentioned in the Sixth Clause of this Our Warrant, consisting in the case of a unit of Naval Forces of a squadron, flotilla or ship's company, or of a detached body of seamen or marines; or in the case of a unit of Military Forces of a regiment, squadron, battery or company, or a detached body of soldiers; or in the case of a unit of Air Forces of a squadron or other body of airmen, having distinguished itself collectively by the performance of an act of heroic gallantry or daring in the presence of the enemy in such a way that the Flag, General, Air or other Officer in Command of the Force to which such a unit belongs, is unable to single out any individual as specially pre-eminent in gallantry or daring, then one or more of the personnel comprising the unit shall be selected to be recommended to Us for the award of the Victoria Cross in the following manner:-

(a) When the total personnel of the unit does not exceed 100, then one officer shall be selected for the Decoration by the officers engaged; and in like manner one warrant officer or petty officer or non-commissioned officer or leading rating of the unit shall be selected by the warrant officers, petty officers or non-commissioned officers or leading ratings engaged, and one seaman, marine, private soldier or aircraftman shall be selected by the seamen, marines, private soldiers or aircraft-men engaged;

(b) When the total personnel of the unit exceeds 100 but does not exceed 200 then the number of seamen, marines, private

soldiers or aircraftmen to be selected in the manner described in *(a)* shall be increased to two;

(c) When the total personnel of the unit exceeds 200 in number, the number of Crosses to be awarded in accordance with these provisions shall be the subject of special consideration by Our Lords Commissioners of the Admiralty or by one of Our Principal Secretaries of State or, in the case of any Member Country of the Commonwealth overseas, the appropriate Minister of State for the said Member Country, for submission to Us;

(d) The selection is to be by a secret ballot in such a manner as shall be determined in accordance with the foregoing provisions by the Officer directing the selection to be made;

(e) The death of any person engaged shall not be a bar to his selection;

(f) Reference in this Clause to male members of any Forces shall be deemed to include the equivalent ranks of the Women's Auxiliary Services of such Forces;

(g) The names of the persons recommended in accordance with these provisions shall be submitted to Us in the manner laid down in the Eighth Clause of this Our Warrant.

Tenthly: It is ordained that every recipient of the Cross, not coming within the provisions of the Eleventh Clause of this Our Warrant, to whom the Cross may be awarded after the 31st day of July 1959 shall from the date of the act by which the Decoration has been gained, be entitled to a special pension of one hundred pounds a year.

Eleventhly: It is ordained that, subject to such exceptions as We, Our Heirs and Successors may ordain, a member of the Forces of a Member Country of the Commonwealth Overseas to whom the Cross or bar may be awarded after the 31st day of July 1959, shall receive such special pension or pensions as may be provided from the revenues of that Country, under regulations made by the said Country.

Twelfthly: It is ordained that, as from the first day of August 1959, every recipient of the Decoration:-

(a) who was then receiving from moneys provided by Our Parliament of the United Kingdom of Great Britain and Northern Ireland a special pension awarded under the rules and ordinances relating to the Decoration in force from time to time, or

(b) who would then have been so receiving such a special pension if he had not been or ranked as a Commissioned Officer or in the case of Our Navy and Marines he had not been or ranked with a Warrant Officer, or

(c) in respect of whom such a special pension would have been currently in issue on the 31st day of March 1955, if he had not been or ranked as a Commissioned Officer and would, if it had been so in issue, have fallen within any of the descriptions of pensions in the annexe contained in the First Schedule to The Pensions (India, Pakistan and Burma) Act, 1955,

shall receive a special pension of one hundred pounds a year, which in cases coming within category *(a)* above shall be in substitution for any special pension in respect of the Decoration which was previously in issue to him.

Thirteenthly: It is ordained that where a recipient of the Decoration coming within the provision of *(a)* of the Twelfth Clause of this Our Warrant was a Gurkha Commissioned Officer or a soldier of Our Brigade of Gurkhas, his widow shall receive, with effect from the date of his death and until her re-marriage or death, a special pension equal to the special pension which was in payment to him immediately before the first day of August, 1959.

Fourteenthly: It is ordained that reproductions of the Cross known as a Miniature Cross which may be worn on certain occasions by those to whom the Decoration is awarded shall be half the size of The Victoria Cross and that a Sealed Pattern of the said Miniature Cross shall be deposited and kept in the Central Chancery of Our Orders of Knighthood.

Fifteenthly: It is ordained that it shall be competent for Us, Our Heirs and Successors, by an Order under Our Sign Manual and on the recommendation to that effect by or through our First Lord of the Admiralty or one of Our Principal Secretaries of State or, in the case of any Member Country of the Commonwealth Overseas, the Government whereof shall so desire, the appropriate Minister of State for the said Member Country, to cancel and annul the award of The Victoria Cross to any person, together with any pension appertaining thereto not already paid, and that thereupon his or her name in the Register shall be erased; but that it shall be competent for Us, Our Heirs and Successors, to restore the Decoration when such recommendation has been withdrawn and with it such pension as may have been forfeited.

Sixteenthly: It is ordained that notice of cancellation or restoration in every case shall be published in the *London Gazette.*

Lastly: We reserve to Ourself, Our Heirs and Successors full power of annulling, altering, abrogating, augmenting, interpreting or dispensing with these regulations, or any part thereof, by a notification under Our Sign Manual.

Given at Our Court at St. James's, this 30th day of September, in the 10th year of Our Reign and in the year of Our Lord One thousand nine hundred and sixty-one.

By Her Majesty's Command,

JOHN PROFUMO.

APPENDIX XIX

The Shape of the Victoria Cross

In the 1856 Warrant the Victoria Cross is described as a Maltese Cross. This description has been objected to, and with reason, for the distinctive feature of the Maltese Cross is that the end of each arm is indented; true Maltese Crosses are to be seen in the badge of the Royal Victorian Order and in the insignia of the Order of St. John of Jerusalem. As an alternative the description of Cross Pattée has been offered by Gordon,[1] Smyth[2] and Jocelyn.[3] Even though this is not a subject upon which Jocelyn can be regarded as speaking with authority, since he uses the same term to describe the Distinguished Service Order, whose cross is of quite different geometric construction,[4] this consensus does make it worth examining this proposed description.

The distinguishing adjectives, of which pattée (or paty) is one, which can be applied to the cross in heraldry are many and various, and it has been held that the adjective proposed is only correctly used to describe one whose ends split into three points, whilst the simple splay-armed and square-ended cross should be described as formée (or formy).[5] The evolution of these various forms and terminology has been discussed at length by the late H. Stanford London, in *The Coat of Arms*.[6] However, one point that emerges clearly is that, in the best heraldic usage, whether the cross is blazoned paty or formy, the arms swell from centre to extremity in a curve, and not in a straight line. The Iron Cross is therefore an example of a true cross paty, which is as it should be, as it is modelled on the cross of the Teutonic Order and that, when it appears in heraldry, is so blazoned.[7] 'The straight-sided form found in some modern manuals was never a separate and distinct pattern but is an ill-drawn formy cross dating from a time when heraldic art was near its nadir..... The sooner it is banished and forgotten the better'.[8] Its earliest occurence in this form seems to have been in Guillim's

1   Major L.L. Gordon, *British Orders and Awards*, p18
2   Brigadier J.G. Smyth, *The Story of the Victoria Cross*, p15, note 1
3   Captain Arthur Jocelyn, *Awards of Honour*, p40
4   Op. cit., p43. The geometry of its cross is in fact that of a circle, with four smaller circles inscribed in the angles. In the Warrant it is described simply as 'a cross' without further elaboration.
5   See e.g. W. St.John Hope, *A Grammar of English Heraldry*, revised ed. by A.R. Wagner, pp89-90
6   Vol.iv, 33, pp358-364 and Vol.v, 34, pp26-33
7   See e.g. *The Coat of Arms*, vi, 42, pp78-80
8   H. Stanford London, *The Coat of Arms*, iii, 23, p285

Display of Heraldry of 1660,[9] far too recent a date to confer heraldic respectability.

The awkward fact therefore emerges that, so far as English heraldry is concerned, there is no appropriate term which identifies unambiguously the shape of the Victoria Cross. Were the matter being discussed within a Scottish context, however, a specific term would be available, as Lord Lyon (the final authority for Scottish heraldry) has ruled 'That the heraldic adjective "formee", though sometimes erroneously used as, or stated to be synonymous with "Patee", which in British..... heraldry denotes an ordinary..... properly with concave outlines, is different from and may be supplemental to the adjective pattee..... That the adjective formee implies a straightedged broadening of the said ordinary from the centre to the edge of the shield'.[10] As a correspondent pointed out 'the Victoria Cross, in the Royal Warrant of its institution..... miscalled a Maltese Cross..... is clearly a paty with straight sided arms now called formy by the Lord Lyon'.[11] H. Stafford London, who was at the time he was writing Norfolk Herald Extraordinary and could therefore be regarded as representing the authoritative English view, commented 'If the Lord Lyon really said that..... it is much to be regretted. Heraldists have trouble enough to cope with the corruption and perversion of heraldic terms by the theorists and bookmakers of the 15th, 16th and 17th centuries, and it is really too much that they should in the 20th century have the added infliction of new meanings arbitrarily assigned to old terms without any justification, historical or etymological, and this is all the more regrettable when the new meanings are invented to describe an unreal and unnecessary distinction'.[12] If, therefore, a heraldic term has to be found to describe the shape of the Victoria Cross, some authority can be cited for using the adjective 'formy' but such use will certainly not be universally acceptable to heraldists. Those so using it should also be warned that the same description is applied by an equally distinguished heraldic authority, C.W. Scott-Giles, the present Fitzalan Pursuivant Extraordinary, to denote a cross whose arms are splayed only at the extremities,[13] a form which almost exactly reproduces the shape of the Military Cross!

---

9   *The Coat of Arms*, iv, 33, p359

10   *Lyon Register* xxxvi, 48, 5 May 1947. Quoted in full in *The Coat of Arms*, iii, 25, p42

11   *The Coat of Arms*, iii, 24, p332

12   *The Coat of Arms*, iii, 23, p285

13   e.g. in *Civic Heraldry* (1st Edition) the arms of Carlisle (pp110-111) and Wolverhampton (pp157-158).

BIBLIOGRAPHY

(1) Manuscript Sources

As will be apparent from the source references, the vast bulk of the material upon which this book is based is drawn from unpublished manuscripts. The following are the sources from which these have been obtained:

(i) *Department of Manuscripts, Nottingham University.*
Papers of the Fifth Duke of Newcastle.

(ii) *Messrs Hancocks & Co. (Jewellers) Ltd.*
Two albums of designs for works manufactured by them.

(iii)*Royal Archives, Windsor Castle.*
Queen Victoria's Journal.
Royal Archives E5, E6, E25 and G42.
Containing memoranda of Prince Albert and letters to Queen Victoria and her private secretary from the Duke of Newcastle, Lord Panmure and officials at the War Office.

(iv) *Ministry of Defence, Stanmore.*
The Victoria Cross Register, which at present comprises four volumes recording all awards of the Victoria Cross from its inception to the present. Up to 1914 a great many other letters being sent out from the War Office on the subject of the Victoria Cross, and other items which arose concerning it were also copied into the Register, but from the outbreak of the First World War most of such related material disappears and it thenceforth records little more than citations, presentation of Crosses, deaths of recipients and the terms of new warrants as issued.

(v) *Public Record Office*
Two War Office classes have provided nearly all the material used, WO98, The Victoria Cross, and WO32, Registered Papers. WO98 contains two pieces, 98/1, containing the 1856 Warrant and two copies of the so-called 'Original Warrant', a draft version that preceded it, and 98/2, which is a box of Horse Guards papers dealing with submissions for the award of the Cross from 1857 to 1864. Piece numbers 98/3 and 98/4 have in fact been allocated to the first two volumes of the Victoria Cross Register, although these are, of course, at Stanmore. WO32, a huge class, includes among its contents all surviving War Office files on the Victoria Cross. For the earlier period, from 1856 to about 1907, the proportion of material that has been preserved is high, and some two hundred files survive, covering a large majority of the recommendations and warrant revisions of those years. Thereafter the position changes radically. Of the recommendations of the First World War the only papers that have been retained are those of French's 1914 recommendations, that of Martin-Leake's bar, and those relating to the Gallipoli landings. Similarly in the case of the Second World War, papers have only been preserved in the case of some half dozen individual awards. When I undertook the bulk of my researches —mainly in 1967 and 1968 — no shelf list existed of virtually all the earlier files in this class, nor had they yet received their PRO piece numbers. I could therefore only then cite them by reference to box number and War Office file number. Since a Search Room list is now

available showing piece numbers for all these documents I have updated all references to these files in accordance with the piece numbers now allotted.

(2) Printed Sources

The Panmure Papers edited by Douglas and Ramsay, 2 volumes, London, 1909.

Hansard's Parliamentary Debates. Principally the Third Series, vols. cxxxvi to cli, but also a number of later volumes, when matters relating to the Victoria Cross were discussed, almost invariably as the result of parliamentary questions.

The Times. Chiefly of value as evidence of the state of public opinion regarding military reward at the time of the Crimean War and immediately after, but also for setting the context within which various later decisions relating to the Victoria Cross were taken. There is not usually any direct reference to the matters themselves.

(3) Books on the Victoria Cross

Of the very large number of books on this subject, virtually all confine their attention to how the decoration was won or who the recipient was. Of these probably still the best is Volume I, *The Victoria Cross,* of O'Moore Creagh and E. M. Humphris' three volume work, *The VC and DSO* (1924), which contains the citations for all recipients up to the end of 1920, together with photographs of many of them and as full biographical information on each as could then be obtained. On the biographical side it would be superseded should the so-far unpublished work of the late Mrs Margaret Pratt, to which she had given the title *Aristocracy of the Brave,* eventually appear. *The Victoria Cross,* by Lieutenant Colonel Rupert Stewart, who was himself the head of the War Office Section MS3, appeared in 1928 and reprints all VC citations from the *London Gazette* up to November, 1921. It is often more convenient to use than Creagh and Humphris if only the citation is required, since in the latter the citation often tends to be buried amidst the biographical information; Stewart has also a very useful chronological index of gazettings.

In all the other books the accounts given are told in the authors' words, rather than in those of the *London Gazette.* What may be regarded as the best continuation of Creagh and Humphris for the Second World War, and after, are the three companion works by John Frayn Turner, *VCs of the Royal Navy* (London 1956), *VCs of the Air* (London 1960) and *VCs of the Army, 1939-1951* (London 1962), all of which contain come biographical detail. The only book which has attempted to cover VC winners from the institution of the Cross up to the present day is J. G. Smyth's *The Story of the Victoria Cross,* but this suffers from the grave defect of being selective in the individuals it deals with. It is, however, the only book to give any account of the inter-war rallies of VCs.

Such earlier books as D. H. Parry's *The VC Its Heroes and their Valour* (New and enlarged edition, 1913) are of interest, as the accounts they give of the exploits are often fuller than those in the citation and help, by treating several winners at once, to bring out the character of what was in such instances, a single episode. Parry, though selective in the episodes he describes, appears to have been well-informed about matters relating to the Cross as an institution. P. A. Wilkins' *The History of the Victoria Cross*

(1904) is, despite its title, simply a series of accounts of the way in which the Cross was won, but it is complete for its period, and is still of value for the very fine series of photographs of the recipients, which often yield good contemporary evidence on the way in which medals were then worn. To some extent F. Gordon Roe's *The Bronze Cross* (1945) may be regarded in the same category as providing a similar photograph album for the recipients of the Second World War, though it was, unfortunately, produced a little too soon to acheive a completeness in this respect. However, the comparatively short historical introduction to the portrait section is one of the better pieces of work to appear on the subject, more of his remarks being authenticated by source material than is revealed by his footnotes.

(4) Other Secondary Sources
Volumes II and III of Creagh and Humphris' work (see above) are useful in providing comparable material on the DSO, as does Lieutenant Colonel Ian Bisset's *The George Cross* (London 1961) on that decoration. J. H. Mayo's *Medals and Decorations of the British Army and Navy* (Two volumes, London 1897) gives much documentation on all other medals and decorations.

For the political framework of this study I have relied mainly on volumes xiii and xiv in the *Oxfrod History of England*, E. L. Woodward, *The Age of Reform, 1815-70* (Oxford 1938), R. C. K. Ensor, *England, 1870-1914* (Oxford 1936), making particular use of the lists of cabinets in both volumes to keep track of the changing Secretaries of State for War, supplementing this for more recent years by *Whitaker's Almanack*, which has also been my source for identification of civil and military officials at the War Office.

A large number of other works have added details of fact, comment and opinion at various points in these pages. Since, however, reference has been made to the source of all such material at the point it has been used, and the works in question have been of use only at these specific points, I have not thought it necessary to list these in this bibliography.

EXPLANATION OF
ABBREVIATIONS USED IN THIS WORK

AAG	Assistant Adjutant General	KP	Knight of the Order of St Patrick
Acct-Gen	Accountant General	*L/Cpl	Lance-Corporal
AG	Adjutant General	*L/Sgt	Lance-Sergeant
AMS	Assistant Military Secretary	*Lt	Lieutenant
*Apr	April	*Lt-Col	Lieutenant-Colonel
ARA	Associate of the Royal Academy	*Lt-Gen	Lieutenant-General
*Aug	August	*Maj	Major
*Bn	Battalion	*Maj-Gen	Major-General
*Brig-Gen	Brigadier-General	*Mar	March
*Bt-Lt-Col	Brevet-Lieutenant-Colonel	MC	Military Cross
*Bt-Maj	Brevet-Major	MM	Military Medal
*Capt	Captain	MP	Member of Parliament
CB	Companion of the Bath	MS	Military Secretary
CGM	Conspicuous Gallantry Medal	MVO	Member of the Royal Victorian Order
CGS	Chief of the General Staff	NCO	Non-Commissioned Officer
CIGS	Chief of the Imperial General Staff	*Nov	November
CinC	Commander in Chief	OC	Officer Commanding
CMG	Companion of the Order of	*Oct	October
	St Michael and St George	PM	Prime Minister
CO	Commanding Officer	POW	Prisoner of War
*Col	Colonel	PRO	Public Record Office
*Cpl	Corporal	PS	Private Secretary
*CSM	Company Sergeant-Major	*Pte	Private
DAG	Deputy Adjutant General	PUS	Permanent-Under-Secretary
DCM	Distinguished Conduct Medal	*QMS	Quartermaster-Sergeant
DCIGS	Deputy CIGS	RAF	Royal Air Force
*Dec	December	RAMC	Royal Army Medical Corps
DMS	Deputy Military Secretary	RE	Royal Engineers
DSC	Distinguished Service Cross	*Regt	Regiment
DSM	Distinguished Service Medal	RIN	Royal Indian Navy
DSO	Distinguished Service Order	RINVR	Royal Indian Naval Volunteer Reserve
*Feb	February	*2nd/Lt	Second-Lieutenant
FO	Foreign Office	*Sep	September
*F/O	Flying Officer	*Sgt	Sergeant
GC	George Cross	*Sgt-Maj	Sergeant-Major
GCB	Knight Grand Cross of the Bath	SofS	Secretary of State
*Gen	General	*Tpr	Trooper
GM	George Medal	USofS	Under-Secretary of State
GOC	General Officer Commanding	VC	Victoria Cross
HM	His/Her Majesty	VCR	Victoria Cross Register
HMG	His/Her Majesty's Government	WAAC	Women's Auxiliary Army Corps
HQ	Headquarters	WO	War Office
HRH	His/Her Royal Highness		
ILN	Illustrated London News		
*Jan	January		
*Jul	July	NB – The abbreviations marked with an asterisk
*Jun	June	have only been used in conjunction with an actual
KCB	Knight Commander of the Bath	date, person or unit.
KG	Knight of the Order of the Garter		

INDEX

THE EVOLUTION OF THE VICTORIA CROSS

30th Ft: 224 (Walker)
East Lanc Regt: 147 (Smith)
32nd Ft: 227 (Browne); 228
33rd Ft: 46
34th Ft: 52
Border Regt: 236 (Mott)
Dorsetshire Regt: 234 (Vickery)
41st Ft: 52
Welch Regt: 217 (Fuller)
42nd Ft: 44; 88 (Spence)
43rd Ft: 219-220 (Smith)
44th Ft: 43
Essex Regt: 77-78 (Parsons and Stirling); 107
Derbyshire Regt: 236 (Bees)
47th Ft: 44; 52
49th Ft: 43-44; 52 (Walters)
R Berks Regt: 262 (House)
50th Ft: 44
52nd Ft: 208 (Hawthorne)
53rd Ft: 55 & 227 (Dynon); 101
54th Ft: 137-142; 155 (Walsh)
55th Ft: 44; 52
56th Ft: 44
57th: 43-45; 52; 224 (Gardiner); 255 (Down and
    Stagpoole)
59th Ft: 158-159, 166, 242 (all Sartorius)
60th Rifles: 101; 198 (Thompson); 235 (Sutton)
KRRC: 63; 217 (Dimmer)
61st Ft: 215 (Reade)
62nd Ft: 44; 55
Manchester Regt: 178 (Evans and Henderson);
    236 (Forshaw)
64th Ft: 208
North Staffordshire Regt: 147 (Carmichael)
65th Ft: 235 (McKenna); 254
67th Ft: 207 (Chaplin and Lane)
68th Ft: 44; 52; 219 (Murray)
DLI: 107
71st Ft: 44
HLI: 249
Seaforth Highlanders: 207 (Brownlow and Sellar)
75th Ft: 228 (Coghlan)
Gordon Highlanders: 77 (Gordon); 77 & 82
    (Younger); 95-97 (McKay); 158 (Dick-Cunyng-
    ham); 186-187, 189, 195, 234 (all Findlater);
    194 (Robertson); 259
77th Ft: 44; 92 (Park)
78th Ft: 103; 157 (Bogle); 205 (Crowe)
79th Ft: 44
80th Ft: 256 (Booth, Harward and Tucker)
R Irish Rifles: 147 (McFadzean)
84th Ft: 101-102; 103 (Willis and Holmes);
    193 (Boulger)
86th Ft: 216 (Pearson)
Connaught Rangers: 220-221 (Murray)
90th Ft: 52 & 69 (Alexander); 101
92nd Ft: 158
93rd Ft: 101; 105
94th Ft: 198 (Flawn); 220; 221 (O'Grady);
    236 (Fitzpatrick)
R Munster Fus: 106, 109-110 (all Cosgrove)
Rifle Bde: 51; 69-72 (Hawkes); 144-146, 198-199,
    216 (all O'Hea); 146-147 (Cates); 234 (Jones
    and Whirlpool); 258 (Congreve)
AMS: 120 (Lloyd)
AHC: 54, 238-239 (all Farmer)
RAMC: 91-92; 96 (Chavasse and Martin-Leake);
    168; 216 (Martin-Leake); 217 (Ranken)
Military Train: 215 (Morley); 234 (Symons)
AVC: 254
AAC: 148 (Duncan)
RAF: 148 (Pugh); 269 (Jerrard and McLeod)
Merchant Navy: 134
Home Guard: 147 (Foster)

Indian Service
Indian Navy: 53 & 227 (Mayo); 157 (Rennie); 209
Indian Naval Bde: 69, 128-129 (all Chicken)
Bengal Staff Corps: 2 (Scott); 54 & 213 (Ridgeway);
    73-74 (Hamilton); 74 (Cook); 212 (Channer,
    Cook, Hammond and Vousden)
Bombay Staff Corps: 211 (Chase)
Indian Staff Corps: 56; 74; 74, 76, 79, 88 & 133
    (all MacLean); 107-108 (Maxwell); 120;
    133 (Adams); 166-167 (Badcock and Boisragon)
Bombay Cavalry: 38 (Forbes)
2nd Bombay Light Cavalry: 227 (Blair)
6th Bengal Cavalry: 221, 242-244 (Sartorius)
18th Bengal Lancers: 107
Corps of Guides: 120
Royal Deccan Horse: 237-238
Bengal Art : 101; 228 (Bonham)
Bombay Art: 227 (Keatinge)
Bengal Engrs: 70-71, 83-84, 87 (all Home and
    Salkeld); 226-227 (Thackery)
Bengal Sappers and Miners: 208 (Smith)
QVO Madras Sappers and Miners: 148 (Subraman-
    ian)
Bengal NI: 53, 93 & 227 (Daunt); 128 (Cafe)
Bombay NI: 72-73 & 88 (Phillipps); 119 (Kerr)
1st European Bengal Fus: 128 (Brown)
1st Bengal Fus: 93 & 237 (McGovern)
1st Madras Fus: 69 (Ryan); 101
2nd Bengal European Fus: 226-227 (Cadell)
2nd Bengal NI: 226 (Travers)
8th Punjab Regt: 57 (Kamal Ram)
6/9th Raj Regt: 148 (Islam-ud-Din)
13th Bengal NI: 200-202, 235 (all Aitken)
15th Punjab Regt: 237 (Gian Singh)
19th Madras NI: 237 (Clogstoun)
25th Bombay LI: 227 (Waller)
28th Punjab Regt: 178 (Ishar Singh)
46th Bengal NI: 226 (Browne)
66th Bengal NI: 252 (Tytler)
Frontier Force Rifles: 148 (Kirpa Ram)
Gurkhas: 123; 125; 202
Ind Med Est: 69; 216 (Fitzgibbon)
Ind Med Service: 178 (Andrews)
Bengal Med Service: 228
Bombay Med Estab: 228
Bengal Ecclesiastical Dept: 129-131 (Adams)
Bengal Ordnance Dept: 227 (Miller)
Bengal Police Bn: 53 & 227 (Baker); 129

Overseas
KAR: 223; 263 (Leakey)
WIR: 68; 120; 125; 143 & 216 (Bourke); 209;
    236 (Gordon)
Cape Mtd Yeo: 155; 244-246 (McCrea)
CMR: 155; 167 (Scott)
ILH: 77 & 82 (Albrecht)
Landrey's Light Horse: 60
Nourse's Horse: 155; 220
Roberts' Horse: 107
Scottish Horse: 54, 238 & 259 (all English)
SA Constabulary: 216
Canadian Mtd Rifles: 236 (Holmes)
A & S Highlanders of Canada: 148 (Rennie)
Quebec Regt: 47 (Rutherford)
AIF: 189 (Keyzor)
AMF: 263 (Edmondson)
W Australian MI: 54 (Bell); 238; 259
NZMF: 210 & 222 (Hinton)
NZ Cont: 54, 238 & 259 (all Hardham)
Auckland Militia: 149-155, 243, 255 (all Heaphy)
RNZAF: 222 (Trigg)